10 Women of Mystery

10 Women
of
Mystery

Earl F. Bargainnier

Bowling Green State University Popular Press
Bowling Green, Ohio 43403

CONTENTS

Introduction

Ten Women of Mystery may give the immediate impression of *femmes fatales,* sirens, vamps, Mata Haris or whatever other term one wishes for exotic and dangerous females, but that is not the intent of this collection of essays. It is instead an attempt to present the achievements of ten women writers of mystery and detective fiction. Five of the writers are American, four are British and one is a New Zealander. Though some of them, notably Sayers, Marsh, Lathen and Cross, have been successful in other fields—and though whether married or not they have also had to fulfill the requirements of that ignored other career, homemaker—all have attained their greatest fame as writers in the genre of mystery fiction. Studies of their fiction is scant, and these essays provide an introduction to the body of their work and analysis and evaluation of specific elements within that work.

A large body of classic detective fiction has centered on the village or country house and involved a considerable emphasis on the social life of the participants in the fashion of a novel of manners. Of significance in such fiction is that women are *necessarily* present and involved in the happenings. Unlike the battlefield, the political or economic area, the wild west or the remote mountain or exotic wilderness of fiction, from which women have been historically excluded for reasons of plausibility, the world of the village, the country house and often the neutral place (train, ship, etc.) naturally contain women. In fact, it would be as difficult to exclude women from the one as to include them as basic participants in the other (except as a sort of consolation between scenes: the "romantic" rather than comic "relief" from the "high drama" of various kinds of adventure novel). Thus it can be said that there has been little plot-role potential for women in a wide range of popular fiction because of its concern with a world in which women had little direct role or effect. During the period in which classic detective fiction flourished, women were most often adjuncts in adventure fiction or primary images in romantic fiction written solely for, and usually but not always by, women.

It is often claimed, and supported with impressive evidence, that in the Golden Age (1920-1939), detective fiction was very

1

popular—one of every four books printed—and was the only popular fiction regularly read by "professional people": doctors, lawyers, presidents, etc. More importantly, it is fiction read equally and heavily by both men and women and perhaps the only one in which women have excelled as writers of a form *read regularly by men*. For centuries there have been women writers of all sorts whose writings have been almost totally read by other women, but mystery writing is a unique area of popular fiction in the widespread success of women writers, the widespread use of women as important characters and the widespread occurrence of *male* readers. Therefore a volume examining the special contributions of a number of women mystery writers may be expected to shed light on this significant example of common interests in recreative reading among men and women and on the reasons behind the early and uncharacteristic near-equality of women in this field.

The choice of writers for examination in this volume requires no justification. However, many other women mystery writers could have been chosen. Since Seeley Register's *The Dead Letter* of 1867, the work usually cited as the first mystery novel by a woman, many women have found the genre a congenial form on which to base a writing career. (One could go back even further, for Mary Shelley's *Frankenstein* and Charlotte Bronte's *Jane Eyre* have greatly influenced the course of popular fiction, including that of mystery and detection. Indeed, if *Rebecca* is the mother of the modern gothic romance, the most popular form of mystery today, then *Jane Eyre* is its great-grandmother.) Though most people disagree with Rex Stout's assertion that Dr. Watson was a woman, women have been narrating stories of murder and other assorted crimes and of the detectives who solve them for over a hundred years. Obviously ten essays hardly begin the task of explaining the role of the woman writer in the development of this major type of popular literature, but they are a beginning. All the writers chosen exhibit great skill of characterization, adroitness in creating various kinds of tension, and preference for complexity of plot and character relationships over wild action, such as chases and gun battles; at the same time, as a group they demonstrate a range and variety suggesting the scope of women writers of mystery fiction.

The intention has not been to enshrine these women as a pantheon of the "greatest" women mystery writers. Rather the editorial plan has been to apply serious literary criticism to their fiction in order to analyze the characteristic and distinctive qualities of each writer.In a sense, each essay can be considered an introduction to the writer's work, placing it in the context of the entire genre of mystery and detective fiction. Such a group of writers could easily have been grouped in various ways: as entertainers, novelists of manners, psychological novelists, feminists, literati, realists, etc. The present arrangement is chronological by birth of the author and divided by nationality—with the hope that Dame Ngaio will not object to inclusion with her British colleagues. This arrangement provides an opportunity to view the changing styles, structures and values within the genre, not so much as a progression as a necessary adaptability of any popular literary type.

. When Dr. Nancy C. Joyner showed the list of writers chosen to P.D. James, that novelist expressed no doubts as to the worthiness of those chosen (she happened to be reading Amanda Cross's *Poetic Justice* at the time), but she felt it "odd" that Marjorie Allingham and Patricia Highsmith were not included. Others will surely have similar feelings, but ten was the limit. The obvious omission of Agatha Christie is deliberate: the sheer amount of her fiction defies adequate treatment as a whole in a short essay. Aside from Christie, a number of collections of essays would be required to cover just the best-known women mystery writers, and though to suggest those who would be deserving of study is probably to offend by omission of someone's favorite, forty are presented here as likely candidates. Among British authors are Marjorie Allingham, Josephine Bell, Phyllis Bentley, Christianna Brand, Daphne du Maurier, Elizabeth X. Ferrars, Georgette Heyer, Patricia Highsmith, Elspeth Huxley, F. Tennyson Jesse, Marie Belloc Lowndes, Helen MacInnes, Gladys Mitchell, Patricia Moyes, Baroness Emmuska Orczy, Joyce Porter, Helen Simpson, Mary Stewart, Patricia Wentworth and Ethel Lina White. A similar list of American writers might include Charlotte Armstrong, Leigh Brackett, Vera Caspary, Elizabeth Daly, Dorothy Salisbury Davis, Miriam Allen deFord, Lillian de la Torre, Doris Miles Disney, Mignon G. Eberhart, Dorothy B. Hughes, Elizabeth Linington, Helen McCloy, Lillian O'Donnell, Lenore Offord, Helen Reilly, Mabel Seeley, Phoebe Atwood Taylor, Dorothy Uhnak, Carolyn Wells and Phyllis Whitney. Both lists could be lengthened considerably, but they are long enough to indicate the significant position women hold in the world of mystery and detective fiction.

In the last hundred years women have written all types of mystery and detective fiction. They dominated the classic British detective story of the between-the-wars period. In the United States they invented what Ogden Nash derisively called the Had-I-But-Known mystery, but though his verse is amusing, it too easily dismisses a very popular type of fiction, one which still flourishes. Women have written hard-boiled detective novels, gothics, spy novels, police procedurals and thrillers. In fact, there is no type of novel presenting a crime, its investigation and its solution that has not been written by women. Their detectives have included both policemen, whether sergeants and lieutenants in New York and Los

Angeles or inspectors from Scotland Yard and chief constables in Devon, and amateurs of all kinds: men and women, young and old, rich and poor, suave and clumsy, dignified and silly, ordinary and bizarre, brilliant and ineffectual. The variations are so numerous that it is impossible to generalize about a typical woman mystery writer or a "woman's school" of mystery writing. The only generalization that can be made is that women have contributed significantly to the development and the nature of mystery and detective fiction, and they have enjoyed great individual success in doing so. After all, Agatha Christie is the single most popular writer of the twentieth century.

In spite of their success in the genre, many women have followed, whether by choice, circumstance or pressure, the examples of the Brontes and George Eliot and used masculine pseudonyms of one kind or another for their fiction. Some have used initials as camouflage (I know of one fan of P.D. James who assumed for three years that she was a man): Elizabeth Thomasina Meade Smith appeared as L.T. Meade, Fryniwyd Tennyson Jesse as F. Tennyson Jesse, Mary Violet Heberdeen as M.V. Heberdeen and also as Charles L. Leonard, and Edith Caroline Rivett as E.C.R. Lorac. Others have used parts of their own names: Emma Redington Lee (Lee Thayer), Deloris Stanton Forbes (Stanton Forbes, as well as Tobias Wells, and with Helen Rydell, Forbes Rydell), and Dora Shattuck (Richard Shattuck). Still others have used masculine names with the first letters of their own, as Edith Pargeter (Ellis Peters) and Elizabeth Linington (Lesley Egan, as well as the better-known Dell Shannon). Finally, there are the masculine pseudonyms which seemingly have no relation to the writer's actual name: Winifred Ashton (Clemence Dane), Mrs. Zenith Jones Brown (Leslie Ford and David Frome), Norah Lofts (Peter Curtis), Lucy B. Malleson (Anthony Gilbert), Gladys Mitchell (Stephen Hockaby) and Georgiana Randolph (Craig Rice and Michael Venning). The whys and wherefores of pseudonyms are puzzling—and, therefore, appropriate among mystery writers—but the use of masculine pseudonyms indicates, if nothing else, that some, whether the authors employing them or others, have rightly or wrongly considered murder an unfeminine subject. The puzzling aspects of pseudonyms are complicated even more by the fact that some women mystery writers have chosen to use feminine pseudonyms, as evidenced in this volume by Tey, Lathen and Cross. Others include Harriet S. Adams (Carolyn Keene), Doris Bell Collier Ball (Josephine Bell), Mary Christianna Lewis (Christianna Brand), Morna Doris Brown (Elizabeth X. Ferrars), Gwendoline Butler (Jennie Melville), Heidi Huberta Freybe (Martha Albrand), and Dora Amy Ellis Dillon Turnbull (Patricia Wentworth). Whatever the reason for these women's use of male, female or neuter (i.e., initials) pseudonyms, men, except for a very few gothic novelists, use only male or neuter pseudonyms; this is especially surprising in view of women being among the most successful mystery writers, as Christie and Sayers demonstrate. The only conclusion is that it never hurts to be a man or to be perceived as a man even in a field where women are recognized as significant; the converse is practically never true. (A related issue is that until recently, e.g., Cross's Kate Fansler, principal detectives have been almost always male. This assumption of the male point of view by so many women mystery writers, nearly always without glaring errors or inconsistencies, is a matter which deserves serious study.)

A great many writers have been mentioned—and others could have been—but their names serve as evidence of the activity of women mystery writers in the more than a century from Anna Katharine Green to Ruth Rendell, the earliest and most recent writers examined in these essays. As stated earlier, this volume is considered just a beginning. The contributors have taken their task seriously, and though the critical approaches vary, all, I believe, provide information and interpretation which will lead to greater appreciation and understanding of the fiction created by these ten women of mystery and of their genre as popular art.

* * *

This introduction has been a collaborative effort, and I wish to express my thanks to Professors Jane S. Bakerman, Kathleen Gregory Klein and Nancy Ellen Talburt for their major contributions. However, since the responsibility of combining the thoughts of the four of us is mine, they are absolved of any factual errors, stylistic solecisms or fallacious opinions.

Earl F. Bargainnier

Contributors

Jane S. Bakerman is Associate Professor of English at Indiana State University. She has published numerous articles, interviews and reviews in such journals as *American Literature, The Armchair Detective, Critique, The Mystery Fancier,* and *Room of One's Own.* Recently she has served as advisor and contributor to *American Women Writers, I-IV* and *Twentieth Century Crime and Mystery Writers.*

Earl F. Bargainnier is Fuller E. Callaway Professor of English Language and Literature at Wesleyan College. A former president of the Popular Culture Association in the South, he now serves as editor of that association's journal, *Studies in Popular Culture.* He is the author of over three dozen articles on nineteenth and twentieth century literature and culture, as well as *The Gentle Art of Murder: The Detective Fiction of Agatha Christie* (Popular Press, 1981).

Jeanne F. Bedell is Assistant Professor of Humanities at the University of Missouri—Rolla. She has published articles on Conrad, Louisa Alcott, and composition, as well as on detective and espionage fiction. She has received a grant from the National Endowment for the Humanities to study female characterization in the fiction of Wilkie Collins and another from the Joint Center for Aging Studies to examine images of aging in detective fiction.

Steven R. Carter is Assistant Professor of English at the University of North Carolina at Wilmington. A former Fulbright scholar, he has published essays on detective fiction by Ross Macdonald, Julian Symons, Ishmael Reed, James Jones, John Fowles and others. He has also published articles on science fiction, black literature and contemporary literature. He is currently working on a book about Lorraine Hansberry.

Jan Cohn is Professor of English and Chairman of the Department of English at George Mason University. She has written on various subjects in English and especially American literature, as well as popular culture. Her books include *The Palace or the Poorhouse: The American House as a Cultural Symbol* and *Improbable Fiction: The Life of Mary Roberts Rinehart.*

Barrie Hayne is Associate Professor of English and Associate Chairman of the Department of English at the University of Toronto. He has published a number of articles on Cooper, Poe, Mrs.

Stowe and other writers of nineteenth-century America. He contributed several articles to *Twentieth Century Crime and Mystery Writers.*

Nancy C. Joyner is Professor of English at Western Carolina University. She has published numerous articles on modern poets and novelists and *E.A. Robinson: A Reference Guide* (G.K. Hall, 1978). She also wrote the article on Ngaio Marsh in *Great Writers of the English Language* and articles on Helen McCloy, Hugh Holman and Dorothy B. Hughes in *Twentieth Century Crime and Mystery Writers.*

Kathleen Gregory Klein is Associate Professor of English and Coordinator of Women's Studies at Indiana University, Indianapolis. She has presented numerous papers on women in detective fiction at the meetings of the Popular Culture Association, has published "Feminists as Detectives: Harriet Vane, Kate Fansler, Sarah Chayse" in *The Armchair Detective*, and is currently writing a book-length study of the professional female detective in British and American detective fiction, 1864-1980.

John M. Reilly is Associate Professor of English at the State University of New York at Albany. He has published articles and bibliographical essays in the field of Afro-American literature and serves on the boards of two journals—*Obsidian* and *MELUS*. His most recent publication is *Twentieth Century Crime and Mystery Writers*, a reference volume which he edited for St. Martin's Press in New York and Macmillan in London.

Nancy Ellen Talburt is Professor of English and Assistant Vice President of the University of Arkansas. Besides contributing articles to *Twentieth Century Crime and Mystery Writers*, she is co-editor with Lyna Lee Montgomery of *A Mystery Reader: Stories of Detection, Adventure, and Horror (Scribner's, 1975).*

Dorothy L. Sayers
(Courtesy of Popperfoto)

Dorothy Leigh Sayers

1893 Dorothy Leigh, born June 13, only child of Reverend Henry and Helen Leigh Sayers in Oxford
1909 Entered Godolphin School
1912 Entered Somerville College, Oxford University
1915 Achieved First Class Honors in Modern Languages
1920 Awarded Master of Arts degree by Oxford University when first women's degrees awarded
1922 Employed as copywriter by Benson's Advertising Agency, London
1923 *Whose Body?*, first novel, introduces Peter Lord Wimsey
1924 Son John Anthony born January 3, in Bournemouth
1926 Married Oswald Arthur Fleming, April 13, London
1929 Founding of the Detection Club
1936 Began to compose dramas: *Busman's Honeymoon* co-authored with Muriel St. Clare Byrne, and *He That Should Come,* Nativity play
1937 *Busman's Honeymoon,* final Lord Peter Wimsey novel; shifted to theological writing with *The Zeal of Thy House*
1949 *The Divine Comedy,* translations: *Hell,* 1949; *Purgatory,* 1955
1950 Received Honorary Doctorate of Letters, University of Durham
1957 Died suddenly, December 17 in Witham

by Kathleen Gregory Klein

"the purest literature we have"

The twelve novels and several volumes of short stories by Dorothy L. Sayers (beginning in 1923 and concluding publication in 1939)[1] span almost the complete two decade period of the Golden Age of detective fiction. Actually, it would be more accurate to state that they were a significant reason for the period's title; well-written, cleverly plotted and fascinatingly peopled, they are as popular fifty years later as when they were first published. They are excellent illustrations of the classic detective story as well as demonstrations of what else could be done with the form. Sayers' detective hero, Lord Peter Wimsey, second son of the 15th Duke of Denver, is really born of Poe's Auguste Dupin via Conan Doyle's Sherlock Holmes; the intelligent amateur, dedicated to his avocation, is ideally suited for the required ratiocinative detecting. Building his characterization with every novel, Sayers gradually develops Lord Peter's emotional portrait as well as his physical and mental ones. In being provided a background, family, "beloved," and personal life, he eventually outgrows the stereotype of the detective superhero as Sayers' novels keep pace, outgrowing the convention expected in the purest detective fiction. Gradually, themes, social issues and characters demand more space than the puzzle-oriented, more traditional form would have allowed; the later novels interweave these elements with the restitution of social order which tracing the criminal can provide.

A founding member of the Detection Club in 1927 with G.K. Chesterton, Ronald Knox and others, Sayers promised to obey the rules of fair play.[2] The classic detective story, at its peak in the years between the two world wars, has several distinct and unchallenged characteristics; most importantly, it is a puzzle or an intellectual game—with heavy emphasis laid on the idea of game where minimal attention is paid to the physical sufferings of the victim or even the probable fate of the murderer. Like all games, this one has rules; different critics have set forth personal lists with shibboleths according to their own inclinations; but, all agree on certain basics: all clues discovered by the detective should be shared with the reader; the crime must be significant and the detective must actually detect its solution ratiocinatively; suspects must be identified and include the murderer among them from an early point in the novel; motives should be personal and rational.[3] All these rules obviously aim at participation in the detection by the readers and establish certain parameters on which they could depend. Like cricket officials, critics and reviewers of the *genre* have been quick to call fouls against violators. And yet virtually every novelist in the Golden Age viewed these restrictions elastically; in fact, the very stereotyped expectations developed by these rules provided authors with legitimate tricks to play on their audiences. Agatha Christie's often challenged *Murder of Roger Ackroyd* was defended as fair play by Sayers, who suspected that its detractors were merely miffed at having been so cleverly mislead.

Novelists became stereotyped by their style of construction and methods of detection. As detective and detective-novelist, Peter Wimsey and Harriet Vane (eventually, Lady Peter) are familiar with the traditions of the *genre* and the contemporary practice of it. Harriet Vane's detective Robert Templeton (a name Peter had used as a cover in *Unnatural Death*) "was a gentleman of extraordinary scientific skill, combined with almost fabulous muscular development" (*Carcase*, Ch. 1). It is his personna into which she attempts to project herself when she discovers a corpse near Wilvercombe; naturally she is less knowledgeable and less successful than "the perfect archetypal Robert Templeton . . . [with] his shadowy and ideal brain" (*Carcase*, Ch. 1). Nevertheless, her cleverness often exceeds his, "[in] one book I wrote . . . I invented such a watertight crime that I couldn't devise any way for my detective to prove it, and had to fall back on the murderer's confession" (*Strong Poison*, Ch. 4). The novelist, of course, controls her material. But, when stumped by a real case in *Have His Carcase*, she and Wimsey even resort to considering solutions based on fictional detectives' favorite methods of discovery:

"There's the Roger Sheringham method, for instance. You prove elaborately and in detail that A did the murder; then you give the story one final shake, twist it round a freesh corner, and find that the real murderer is B—the person you suspected first and then lost sight of.

". . . well, there's the Philo Vance method. You shake your head and say: 'There's worse yet to come, and then the murderer kills five more people, and that thins the suspects out a bit and you spot who it is."

"Wasteful, wasteful," said Wimsey. "And too slow."

"True. There's the Inspector French method—you break the unbreakable alibi.

". . . There are plenty of methods left. There's the Thorndyke type of solution, which as Thorndyke himself says, can be put in a nut-shell. 'You have got the wrong man, you have got the wrong box, and you have got the wrong body.' . . ." (Ch. 33).

The ingenious puzzle solving approach works in a specific way in this novel as a cipher is finally untangled; but a more accurate reflection of Sayer's changing approach is mirrored in Harriet's difficulties with her novel *Death 'twixt Wind and Water* and Peter's suggestion solution [during their courtship at Oxford]: "abandon the jig-saw kind of story and write a book about human beings for a change" (*Gaudy*, Ch. 15).

Although Sayers eventually diminishes the puzzle solving focus in her works, the first four novels (*Whose Body?, Clouds of Witness, Unnatural Death, The Unpleasantness at the Bellona Club*), most of the short stories and *Five Red Herrings* conform most closely to the style favored by her contemporaries. The popular name applied to detective fiction—"whodunit"—describes the intentions of even the best of her contemporaries. Agatha Christie is perpetually concerned with the identity of the criminal; her three detectives—Hercule Poirot, Miss Jane Marple and Ariadne Oliver—trace the possible ways in which the crime might have been committed, but are finally concerned with the murderer. A famous example of using "how" to lead to "who" is found in *Murder On The Orient Express*, where Poirot's elaborate deductions lead him to accuse the group of passengers, no one of whom, he has ascertained, could have left all the clues. Josephine Tey, except in *Daughter of Time*, vacillates between "who" and "why," seldom blending the two in the same work, whereas Ngaio Marsh, whose novels frequently include a reconstruction of the crime by Roderick Alleyn, joins the question "who" with the challenge "how."

In the beginning Sayers is also concerned with these crucial matters almost exclusively. She claims to prefer novels where the methods of the criminal rather than his or her identity are the focus of the readers' and detectives' attention. What time General Fentiman died at the Bellona Club or who cleverly faked Sandy Campbell's accidental death beside the Scottish byrne (*Herrings*) are the challenges of Sayers' two dullest novels. The interminable chase after a non-existent person which apparently takes Wimsey and, later, the suspected Robert Fentiman all over Europe is described only in cryptic telegrams they send back to England; although the plan to keep the suspected murderer from cancelling his grandfather's exhumation is a plausible motive for his wild chase, no sensible rationale is provided for Wimsey's pointless trip. Even more thoroughly tedious are the train timetables and accounts of characters' movements in *Five Red Herrings*. Both painters and fishermen, all six suspects are virtually indistinguishable; the victim has been sufficiently unpleasant to be unmourned. Who committed the crime is a question which eventually becomes irrelevant; how it happened requires charts, lists and schedules to be made and frequently discarded as unworkable by the readers; why the death occurred is answered in one word—accident—so that the murder so painstakingly detected evaporates. Ironically, Sayers even uses the same trick in both novels: Peter questions the apparently natural deaths because he has noticed the absence of an expected item; retired General Fentiman did not wear a red poppy in his lapel on Armistice Day and Sandy Campbell's painting kit lacked a necessary tube of flake white paint. Since the narrator does not share this information with the readers until well after Wimsey has challenged the police to recognize what is missing, the sense of fair play expected from the novels is disrupted.

However, since the *genre*'s essential element is the detection of a serious crime (generally murder) and the withheld clues are not part of the actual solution to the crimes, the device is inoffensive although annoying. *Whose Body?* and *Unnatural Death* raise the more intriguing question of why the crime was committed. In the former, Wimsey is less concerned with why a man was killed than why his naked body, adorned with a pince-nez, should be left in a respectable, mild mannered architect's bathtub; to know why is, then, to recognize who was responsible. The novel is marred by the criminal's being a combination of two classic villains—the mad scientist and the trusted physician; and, in falling back on the criminal's confession rather than completely proving the case through investigation, the novel's somewhat gratuitous conclusion is not entirely satisfactory. Peter's habit of warning the "gentleman-murderer," so he may take the honorable course of suicide to avoid scandal, is begun here. Three criminals have the chance to evade hanging—two (Freke and Pemberthy) because of their social position in Wimsey's own world and the third (Tallboy) as a result of Peter's compassion. No such mercy is extended to Mary Whittaker, obviously responsible for her aunt's "unnatural death," and for the subsequent murder of two young girls and attempted murders of three other persons including Miss Climpson. Her responsibility is recognized early in the novel; Peter, Inspector Parker and Miss Climpson form a team to discover why she would have bothered to kill a dying woman. The picture of the disguised Mary Whittaker is a fairly unsuccessful attempt to portray her dual nature and, particularly, her lesbian tendencies. But, in a brilliant comic touch, Sayers appropriates the device of the long-lost heir from the colonies in creating Reverend Hallelujah Dawson, an illegitimate colored minister born in Trinidad, whose mistreatment by his distant cousin Mary Whittaker redefines him as a sympathetic character. A family tree identifying lines of descent plus several solicitors' cautions interpretations of a new inheritance law finally indicate the motive for the first murder; the subsequent ones, done to prevent information from being disclosed, misdirect and confuse the police—especially when the murderer is clever enough to leave *three* false sets of footprints.

However, Sayers came to demand more of her novels than the mere game playing which dominates the earliest works. She expresses this dissatisfaction with the idea of continuing in the same vein through her fictional counterpart, Harriet Vane:

> The rereading of one's own works is usually a dismal matter; and when she had completed her task she felt thoroughly jaded and displeased with herself. The books were all right, as far as they went; as intellectual exercises they were even brilliant. But there was something lacking about them; they read now to her as though they had been written with a mental reservation, a determination to keep her own opinions and personality out of view. She considered with distaste a clever and superficial discussion between two of her characters about married life (*Gaudy*, Ch. 4).

Deliberately, she begins to write novels with detection rather than detective novels; theme, characters, style and images are no longer subordinated to plot.

Although Sayers claims to have written *Strong Poison* to marry off and dispose of Peter Wimsey, she actually begins his re-creation there. The influence of Harriet Vane's established personality require changes in Peter before the two characters can successfully mesh. As this development comes to influence the novels' construction, the purely abstract and academic puzzle is balanced by personal changes and social concerns which affect Wimsey. His "hobby" of detecting crimes is continued with less flippancy and greater emotional investment in the victims and their killers. The crucial theme of the importance of work, which retrospectively can be seen in the first novel, begins more clearly to permeate the post 1930 works. Sayers' shifting focus can be easily identified by referring to two novels, called by different groups either tremendous or terrible detective stories—*The Nine Tailors* and *Gaudy Night*. An extended religious metaphor for Christian salvation parallels the detection in the former. The church in the Fens, where death occurs because of the New Year's bell ringing, is a symbolic Ark during the flood in which the inadvertent murderer is punished by divine justice; Wimsey's responsibility is to learn how and why but to leave human laws and retribution in the background. Oxford is also a refuge from the world and the site of possible death when Harriet Vane returns to investigate poison pen letters directed against members of her college; the solace here is academic and intellectual achievement, not religious involvement. Embodied in the mystery's solution is Harriet's fear about marriage—that passion will overcome reason. Oxford provides her an opportunity to re-examine herself and rediscover Peter; the mystery and the courtship are both resolved.

Some critics charge that the transition to the novel of manners and society in the vein of Wycherley and Shaw results in neither a good novel nor a good detective story.[4] They are entitled to their opinions; yet, a convincing case can be made for Sayers having accomplished exactly what she had intended. Writing first in the commercially popular style with wit and cleverness, she later blends the best-seller with her idea of the kind of fiction worth writing. Her career, she insisted, was all of a piece; certainly her detective fiction shows a unified but continually developing canon which still fascinates and challenges the most demanding reader.

Although best known for the Lord Peter Wimsey novels and short stories, Sayers created another series character, Montague Egg, and a single novel which includes neither of these detectives. The enterprising Mr. Egg, a travelling representative of Plummet & Rose, Wines and Spirits, Piccadilly, does not investigate murders by choice; detection is neither his vocation nor his avocation. Drawn into half-a-dozen cases haphazardly, Monty uses a good eye, an excellent nose and his rhyming advice from the Salesman's Handbook to uncover the criminal. "To serve the Public is the aim / Of every salesman worth the name," ("Maher-Shalal-Hashbaz") is a favorite aphorism which perfectly characterizes this middle class "commercial traveler" who solves crimes by knowing how to ride the trains without a ticket, or by recognizing a guilty change in a butler's supercilious tone, or by befriending a child and her favorite cat. Little detecting and less ratiocination are required for his conclusions; observation and parallel personal experiences provide the clues. The stories are lightweight by comparison with Sayers' only complete non-Wimsey novel, *Documents in the Case.*

Written in collaboration with Dr. Eustace R. Barton and published in the same year as *Strong Poison, Documents in the Case* includes only two minor characters from the Wimsey novels. However, written in epistolary form, the novel does reflect their typical theme—the importance of work and the worker's responsibility to the job. Several of the characters and their relationships reflect patterns Sayers was simultaneously working out in the Lord Peter series while here, as in the other mysteries, the same image which controls the novel's development provides the crucial clue for solving the mystery.

Returned from an engineering project in Central Africa after his father's death from mushroom poisoning, Paul Harrison compiles a file of letters and statements about household events in the year before the death. Suspicious of his young stepmother, Harrison investigates her former housekeeper-companion, a neurotic spinster, and the two young friends who had rented the upstairs maisonette at his father's address. The novelist John Munting and the artist Harwood Lathom are the focus of his suspicions. Retrieving the hospitalized Miss Milsom's letters to her sister, buying copies of Margaret Harrison's love letters to Harwood

Lathom, and receiving John Munting's letters to his fiancee, he re-examines his own mail from his father and discovers considerable discrepancies in the various accounts. Methodically he collects evidence, aided by the more imaginative Munting, who finally discovers the necessary proof.

The form of the novel—fifty-four letters, documents and statements plus a final newspaper clipping—quite carefully controls the unravelling of the mystery. Sayers has commented that the question of who committed the crime is not so interesting in a detective novel as how the crime was done.[5] The early sequence of letters reveal victim, murderer and motive while the entire impetus for the continuing search is to discover the method. Paul Harrison's introductory letter to Sir Gilbert Pugh, Director of Public Prosecutions, identifies the victim as his "late father" although the event is not reported until item 45, John Munting's statement, which is placed almost at the center of the novel. Freed from the need to speculate about which unattractive character might be killed, although George Harrison is really the only logical victim, the reader can begin the letters searching immediately for clues to the murder's identity. With the novel's limited roster of characters and the revelatory nature of the letters of the text, his identity and the motive are hardly in question after the first half-dozen chatty letters. With the only possible suspects being the two renters upstairs from the Harrisons, Sayers' use of John Munting, the articulate modern novelist and biographer, as one of the correspondents effectively eliminates him from suspicion. His early observations about his friend Harwood Lathom's attraction to Margaret Harrison and his patronizing of her husband identify the criminal and the cause of the crime. The novel includes only the letters by the inhabitants of Whittington Terrace in Bayswater and the addition of a statement by Paul Harrison. Ostensibly organized and presented according to their date of composition and also revealing the events in chronological order, the letters actually provide a steady but gradual release of information revealing the detection process.

Told exclusively from first person point of view, the narration lacks both the limited omniscience and clever evasion which would have resulted from a detached narrator. In exchange, it provides several different perspectives of the same event, each clearly told with bias and some degree of ignorance. Not even the combined views of the letter writers, contradicting one another as they do, can present the reader with a full and accurate description of events. Nevertheless, they are jointly revealing. Although events may be garbled and objective truth about them undiscovered, character and personality are continually revealed by both content and style of the letters. John Munting's respect and moderate affection for George Harrison despite his recognition of Harrison's limitations eliminate him as a serious suspect; this conclusion is reinforced in Munting's personal and critical stance about the distinctiveness of human life over laboratory compounds. Agatha Milsom's jealousies and pettiness are clear in her references to Harrison as the "Bear" and her simpering exaggerations about Lathom's attention to her. While Miss Milsom's letters are filled with underlinings and capitalization to impress the reader with her emotions, Paul Harrison's statements reflect the logical, orderly mind of an engineer weighing each point before it is stated. He deplores Munting's literary flair—"I regret that it [Munting's statement about Lathom] is so diffuse and adorned with so many unnecessary personal reflections and literary embellishments. It seems that this vanity of writers must be indulged at all costs, even where a straightforward summary of events would be more useful" (*Documents*, No. 49). Yet it is really Margaret Harrison's love letters which falsely appropriate the effusions of the romantic novel as she writes as Lolo [Laura] to her Petra [Petrarch] with the combination of hard calculation and exaggerated passion which demonstrates her shallow and self-protective instincts. Divided into two sections, the novel replaces Miss Milsom's sexual neuroses of the first part with Margaret Harrison's sexual promises in the second half. George Harrison's dry but affectionate letters to his son are replaced by Paul Harrison's statements, lists of suspects and opportunities, and investigations. Munting's letters to his fiancee give way to his statements, no less personal and creative. The balancing of one-way correspondences (no replies are ever printed) and statements or newspaper reports keep the tone of the novel from becoming tedious or lapsing into merely procedural matters. Revelation of characters or examination of social questions continues through the final entries.

Despite the absence of characters from the Wimsey novels, *Documents* strongly parallels the series in theme, use of images and character traits. The neurotic, sexually deprived spinster Agatha Milsom is a mirror image of Lord Peter Wimsey's Miss Climpson. Certainly their writing style is similar; the letters are filled with exclamation points and italicized words and phrases for emphasis as they relate, in detail, the domestic and personal aspects of other characters. But Miss Milsom is exactly what Katherine Alexandra Climpson escaped being. Miss Climpson is appropriately employed, using her talents to assist in the detection of crime; she is well paid, trusted and complimented by her employer, and secure in her own personality and social position. Agatha Milsom is a dissatisfied house-keeper and companion, an indifferent cook, a dilettante writer, an amateur artist whose calendar collages are made from candy wrappers, and a knitter with an eye for design but not much accuracy. She is dissatisfied with her position and her life; the opening letter identifies three different doctors she's consulted about her "problems." She is a frustrated spinster, fascinated by romantic novels and inclined to sexual fantasies. Even Margaret Harrison, the most tolerant character, ignores Miss Milsom's need for recognition and sacrifices the older woman's job and reputation to conceal her own love affair. Friendless, Agatha Milsom could be one of "thousands of old maids, simply bursting with useful energy, forced by our stupid social system into ... posts as companions, where their magnificent gossip-powers and units of inquisitiveness are allowed to dissipate themselves or even become harmful to the community ..." (*Unnatural Death*, Ch. 3), whom Peter Wimsey rescues by establishing the Cattery, typing bureau and undercover detective agency.

The correspondence from "modern" novelist John Munting to his "modern" novelist fiancee Elizabeth Drake echoes some elements of the Wimsey-Vane courtship which begins in *Strong Poison* (also written in 1930). In an early letter Munting insists, "...when I say I want you to keep your independence and exquisite detachment, I don't really mean it" (*Documents*, No. 13), even as Peter agrees with Harriet that his "instinct is to clap the women and children under hatches" (*Gaudy,* Ch. 16). But he shares Peter's view "...that love should be happy ... I don't want to feel that anybody's life and happiness is bound up with mine. What dignity is there in life if one is not free to take one's own risks?... people should set their own values on themselves and not 'live for others' ..." (*Documents*, No. 14); Peter encourages Harriet to reconsider marriage when he insists: "I know you don't want to give or to take ... you don't want ever again to have to depend for happiness on another person" (*Carcase*, Ch. 13). Although Peter and Harriet's courtship is more carefully worked out and the contradictions placed in perspective, Sayers experiments with some of the possibilities here. Each couple includes a nervy man with admitted public school notions of honorable behavior and a useful ability to laugh at his own shortcomings fortunately paired with a woman of talent and commonsense.

The recurrent image or motif which appears in the other novels and which provides Peter with the solution to the crime is embedded here both in descriptions of Margaret Harrison's relationships with men and in the scientific test which traps the criminal. Even as advertising, campanology, and scholarship provide the atmosphere and the solutions in later novels, the refraction of light through a prism defines this novel. Munting, the writer, establishes the image,

"Mrs. Harrson was the radiant prism for Lathom's brilliance," and later reinforces it by emphasizing the negative version, "I have not the superb and centralized self-confidence that could strike the colours from her prism" (*Documents*, No. 37). Nevertheless, Munting appreciates and recognizes her: "... I saw her in full prismatic loveliness, soaked and vibrated with color and light" (*Documents*, No. 37). Sayers comes back to that image to conclude the detection, even as Munting returns to it for "accurate" descriptions of Margaret Harrison. The absence of a beam of light shining through a polariscope when the fatal mushroom mixture is re-examined identifies the substance as artificially created. This darkness does not signal merely the absence of light but also the presence of murder. The brilliance of Margaret Harrison was not her own but a reflection of the company in which she found herself; artificially stimulated, it was also deadly as she persuaded Lathom to murder her husband. The inactive muscarine, its molecular structure the reverse of the natural form's, was as deadly a choice for Lathom as was Margaret; it proved the crime for which he was hanged.

The most significant connection between *Documents* and the Wimsey novels occurs in the importance they attach to the value of work and a worker true to his profession or craft. George Harrison's first letter to his son encourages him to "check *every* figure and test *everything*" (*Documents*, No. 15), while his second approves the younger man's dismissing an employee whose work was unsatisfactory in favor of "duty to the firm" (*Documents*, No. 20).

The senior Harrison's dedication to accuracy leads him to test innumerable recipes for wild living plants and animals before including them in his cookery book, to argue with the printers over errors in the three color process being used to reproduce his water color illustrations, and to challenge his publisher's "misuse" of grammar, punctuation and typography. The precision and care he has always taken in similar aspects of his hobby and job convince his son to investigate the coroner's verdict of accidental poisoning from deadly *Amanita muscario* mushrooms. George Harrison is as dogmatic about others' professional efforts as he is about his own. He finds Lathom's painting "in too much of a hurry, and his pictures have not the beautiful smooth finish ... but no doubt he will grow out of his slap-dash method when he is older"; Harrison is more favorable about the "kind thought which prompted the execution"than the painting itself which is "the kind of picture to attract a great deal of comment of one sort and another" (No. 20). While aware of Miss Milsom's loyalty to his wife, Harrison does not excuse her deficiencies: "she is very lazy and untidy, and instead of putting her mind to the housework, she litters the place with wool and bits of paper which she calls 'art materials' ... there is no harm, of course, in her doing needlework and making calendars, if it does not interfere with her duties" (No. 24); but he has earlier damned her abilities: "She has no real feeling for cookery" (No. 15).

The success of Harwood Lathom's portraits of a woman he loves and one he despises comes from his faithfulness to his talents. He sees through the veneers of conformity to paint a striking Margaret Harrison and a sarcastic treatment of Agatha Milsom. Another painter, Marlowe, characterizes the former as "none of your damned art—that's painting—a *painting*, I tell you" (No. 37), in which judgment Munting agrees. But he also recognizes how Lathom has used the women to serve his art and would take up and then discard all people as he casually had appropriated needed toasting forks from other boys at Eton. Lathom's dedication is only to his art.

The clearest evidence of Sayer's respect for work is found in John Munting's letters to his fiancee; working on the *Life and Letters* of an unnamed Victorian, he would like to "get rid of this damned Life and get back to my own stuff, but I'm being too well paid for it..." (No. 6). The tone and contents of subsequent letters make clear how conscientious he is to this commissioned writing; he studies the art of biography in *The Development of English Biography*, discusses Victorian materialism with the vicar who is more sensible and educated than expected, and he sticks "to the accursed *Life* like a leech" (No. 13). Munting also takes his fiancee's fiction seriously, envying her successful sales and encouraging her to "write your own stuff" (No. 6). Even the short-term job as detective which he unwillingly accepts is not abandoned despite nerves or school ties to the suspect. Even though he hopes to be left out of it, Munting does not bypass the opportunity to question the chemist Waters about polarization and synthetic poison; he persists—partially from a respect for the spark of life which cannot be recreated in a laboratory and partially because his intellectual curiosity will not let him leave the job unfinished. There may even be an ironic commentary on work in having the amateur detective a writer, working on both the *Life and Letters* and a novel, in a detective novel told through letters and written statements. Both writers, Munting and Sayers, bring the detection to a satisfactory conclusion.

At the opening of *Busman's Honeymoon*, letters and diary excerpts are used again to describe a single event from a variety of perspectives and to quickly characterize the writers, and Miss Climpson writes extensive missives full of facts and impressions to her employer; however, this novel's complete form is unique among Sayers' works. Although she wrote several short stories featuring wine and spirits salesman Montague Egg and contributed chapters to the Detection Club's collaborative efforts, no other full length works omit Lord Peter Wimsey. Keeping him (and Bunter, the family and friends) as a constant allows her to refine and improve the form from this base rather than to develop individual examples of the varying forms of the detective hero and his novel.

"I hold by my Whimsy"

Taking into account only his twelve novel length adventures, Lord Peter Wimsey solves nine murders, one suicide, two accidental deaths, one poisoned pen attack and numerous attempted murders and lesser crimes. The younger brother of the sixteenth Duke of Denver would seem an unlikely detective from his biography:

> He was a respectable scholar in five or six languages, a musician of some skill and more understanding, something of an expert in toxicology, a collector of rare editions, an entertaining man-about-town, and a common sensationalist. He has been seen at half-past twelve on a Sunday morning walking in Hyde Park in a top hat and a frock coat, reading the *News of the World*. His passion for the unexplored led him to hunt up obscure pamphlets in the British Museum, to unravel the emotional history of income-tax collectors, and to find out where his own drains led to *(Clouds,* Ch. 4).

The common sensationalist and drain investigator is the hero of the earlier novels; with no small measure of humor and irony, Sayers creates a personality as unlike Sherlock Holmes as possible. In *Clouds of Witness*, the narrator notes that "he [Wimsey] had taken to detecting as he might, with another conscience or constitution, have taken to Indian hemp—for its exhilarating properties—at a moment when life seemed dust and ashes, [but] he had not primarily the detective's temperament" (Ch. 4). Peter sees detection as an exciting distraction or diversion from remembering the horrors of the war and his former fiancee's marriage to another man. He takes it up as another person might have taken up crossword puzzles: "... a hobby. Harmless outlet for natural inquisitiveness, don't you see, which might otherwise strike inward and produce introspection an' suicide. Very natural, healthy pursuit—not too strenuous, not too sedentary; trains and invigorates the mind" *(Unnatural Death,* Ch. 4). This frivolous, flippant manner of speech extends to every possible topic of conversation; miscalled Lord Wimsey by an unknowing American railroad and shipping magnet, he intensifies the man's discomfort by a long history of his naming:

> "My name is Peter. It's a silly name, I always think, so old world and full of homely virtue and that sort of thing, but my godfathers and godmothers in my baptism are responsible for that, I suppose, officially—which is rather bad on them, you know, as they didn't actually choose it. But we always have a Peter, after the

third duke, who betrayed five kings somewhere about the War of the Roses, though
come to think of it, it ain't anything to be proud of. Still, one has to make the best of it"
(*Whose Body*, Ch. 4).

While this sort of improbable foolishness may have some benefit in
misleading a suspect, silly jingles sung in the House of Lords during
his brother's trial seem motivated purely by whimsicality. Whatever
his intentions, Peter succeeds in leaving even his friends with
George Fentiman's opinion, "... you have a kind of obvious
facetiousness which reminds me of the less exacting class of music-
hall" (*Bellona*, Ch. 1). However, appearances, like clues, can be
misleading: the monocle, which makes him "look like a bally fool all
the time" is a magnifying lens; his walking stick, marked off in
inches for measuring, has a sword inside and a compass in the head;
and his matchbox hides an electric torch (*Whose Body*, Ch. 2). While
being pumped about suspects in the Bellona Club case, one friend
comments on his similar duality in manner, "You sit there looking a
perfect well bred imbecile, and then in the most underhanded way
you twist people into doing things they ought to blush for" *(Bellona,*
Ch. 16). And, of course, he solves crimes through intelligence and
ratiocination, not merely bumbling and inadvertent stumbling onto
solutions.

Tiring of this high-bred, overstimulated, nervy aristocrat,
Sayers decided to marry him off and end his career (true to the rules
of the Detection Club which forbade a love interest).[6] For the wife,
she provided Harriet Vane, daughter of a country doctor, graduate
of Shrewsbury College (Oxford), detective-novelist, and, not
incidentally, accused of the murder of her lover because he had
offered to marry her. Peter's reaction is all that Sayers could hope
for; on first glance he falls in love, drags his mother to the trial to see
the "one and only," and agonizes over the jury's lengthy time in
deliberation. When a verdict is not reached, he enters the case,
smugly proposes marriage, and, unexpectedly, is faced with
emotional involvement unmatched even in the case which involved
his siblings.

"I do believe I'll pull it off ... I could work to make it up to her—... one wouldn't be
dull—one would wake up, and there'd be a whole day for jolly things to happen in—
and then one would come home and go to bed—that would be jolly, too—... Oh God!"
he said softly, sobered at once. "One month—four weeks—thirty-one days. There isn't
much time. And I don't know where to begin" (*Strong Poison*, Ch. 4).

Harriet refuses Peter's offer throughout the trial and during the
following five years; Sayers discovers that her puppet character
simply cannot be forced into the pattern she had chosen. Peter is too
much the conventional detective hero; he slides with ease from his
role as drawing room buffoon to master of clues; he hasn't the depth

or honest emotion which is immediately apparent in Harriet. She is rude, ungratefully grateful, badly dressed, and plain. While she might serve as Galatea to his Pygmalion or beggar maid to King Cophetua, she is not his equal—in wealth, rank or confidence. But neither is he her match in complexity. In the final five novels, Sayers fleshes out Peter's humanity, unwraps his weaknesses, and displays his uncertainty.[7] When his full personality is revealed and Harriet is reassured, they can marry, "two independent and equally irritable intelligences" (*Gaudy*, Ch. 22).

Although Harriet is frequently bitter and nasty to Peter in *Have His Carcase*, they do join forces in this rather padded novel to solve the unusual murder of Paul Alexis, a deluded gigolo who believed himself heir to the throne of Russia. Alone on a walking tour when she discovered the body, Harriet herself is suspected by the police and questioned by reporters. All of Peter's protective instincts and emotional impulses respond; this novel begins his metamorphosis. Most apparent is his jealousy; when another hotel dancer admires her step or one of the suspects begins a flirtation, Peter does not diplomatically control his emotions. He glares angrily at Harriet and loses his urbane veneer, possibly jeopardizing the case. He threatens one man: " 'Manners, please!' said Wimsey. You will kindly refer to Miss Vane in a proper way and spare me the boring nuisance of pushing your teeth out of the back of your neck' " (Ch. 11). The suave, imperturbable tone which should have joined these somewhat conventional terms is clearly lacking.

He is also unable to break through Harriet's defensiveness and even compounds his difficulties in reaching her when he's forced to admit he came to the seaside resort to rescue her again. Because she is reminded once more of her responsibility to be grateful to him and reinforced in her sense of inferiority, she rejects him again. His self-control snaps; his flippant manner is gone:

"Do you think it's pleasant for any man who feels about a woman as I do about you, to have to fight his way along under this detestable burden of gratitude? Damn it, do you think I don't know perfectly well that I'd have a better chance if I was deaf, blind, maimed, starving, drunken or dissolute, so that *you* could have the fun of being magnanimous? Why do you suppose I treat my own sincerest feelings like something out of a comic opera, if it isn't to save myself the bitter humiliation of seeing you trying not to be nauseated by them? Can't you understand that this dirty trick of fate has robbed me of the common man's right to be serious about his own passions?" (Ch. 13).

This self-revealing speech seems to come from an altogether different man from the one who had proposed to her in prison, offering "any minor alterations, like parting the old mane, or growing a tooth-brush, or cashiering the eyeglass" (*Strong Poison*,

Ch. 4).

Finally, the man's disappointment is matched by the detective's bitterness. When the mystery is solved and the strange plot of inheritance, Russian crowns and haemophilia unraveled, Peter's disgust for the whole episode is completely unlike his warnings to two earlier murderers, his rational arguing with Dr. Pemberthy to commit suicide, or his limited emotional response to the three actual and three attempted murders of Mary Whittaker: "He felt cold and sick" (*Unnatural Death*, Ch. 23). Here he rejects the people, the case, even the town: " 'Isn't that a damned awful, bitter, bloody farce? ... God! What a jape! King Death has asses' ears with a vengeance.... Let's clear out of this.... I'm fed to the back teeth. ... Damn it,' said Wimsey, savagely, 'I always did hate watering places' " (*Carcase*, Ch. 23). Detection becomes less a hobby and more a sickening, unpalatable business he'd prefer to avoid.

Peter's disgust for the criminals reaches its peak in *Murder Must Advertise* where the criminal world is filled with drug dealing, blackmail and murder. The organized criminals here contrast sharply with the greedy or mad villains of the other novels. However, several times the serious tone of the novel's social message combined with the sometimes still piffling Peter Wimsey clashes and grates. A forty year old man in a black-and-white harlequin suit diving off a fountain into a shallow pool and leading a woman on a wild chase by whistling "tom, tom the piper's son" might possibly be believable. The same man dangerously caught in a disguise, who pleads with the policeman, his brother-in-law, "disguised as a policeman? Oh, Charles do let me be a policeman! I should adore it," cannot, at that moment, be taken seriously (Ch. 19).

In the two false worlds, Pym's Publicity Agency and Dian de Momerie's drug crowd, Peter is always in disguise. Yet in these, and in his real world, a similar tone often breaks through. He questions the manipulation of other people for financial gain. A wealthy man, he begins to consider the effect of advertising on those who cannot really afford the items described. "He had never realized the enormous commercial importance of the comparatively poor ... those who, aching for a luxury beyond their reach and for a leisure forever denied them, [who] could be bullied or wheedled into spending their few hardly won shillings on whatever might give them, if only for a moment, a leisured and luxurious illusion. Phantasmagoria—" (Ch. 11). The essence of advertising he tells his sister and brother-in-law "is to tell plausible lies for money" (Ch. 5). This kind of business hypocrisy would be familiar to Major Tod Milligan who distributes large quantities of drugs although he does not use them himself; he does not intend to become addicted like those to whom he sells. Several violent murders occur in the novel as the drug ring tries to protect itself, but murder, Parker insists, is a lesser crime than drug selling since the latter causes physical and spiritual death as well as instigating other crimes. Peter agrees; his disgust for Milligan and Dian de Momerie is total. His only sympathy is reserved for Dean's murderer and blackmail victim, Tallboy, whom he helps to commit suicide.

Solving this crime brings him little satisfaction or self-congratulation; as Tallboy walks toward his death, Peter murmers from the Book of Common Prayer, " '. and from thence to the place of execution . . . and may the Lord have mercy upon your soul'," unable to celebrate the capture of the drug crew later that evening with Parker (Ch. 20). The diffidence with which he proposes this suicide and his uncharacteristic withdrawal from the final events demonstrate how changed the formerly detached detective hero is becoming. No longer amusing himself by intellectual puzzles or distracting his emotions from a lost fiancee, he is emerging as a three-dimensional human being with limitations to balance his strengths.

Peter's contradictory identification with both the killers and the victim in *The Nine Tailors* further removes him from the detached perspective of a conventional detective. Arriving accidentally and providentially at Fenchurch St. Paul, replacing an ill ringer during the New Year's bell ringing celebration, Peter joins with twelve others, including the Rector, to kill unknowingly a thieving, blackmailing murderer tied up in the bell tower. Although the body, stolen jewels and blackmailing demands are eventually detected, the method of death and the proof of the murderer's identity remain unknown. Climbing to the top of the tower during the ringing of a death knell, ironically rung for the man who had left the victim in the belfry, Peter is assailed by the "demoniac clamour," temporarily unable to move, and suddenly aware that loud and prolonged sound in a confined space can kill. In sharing some of what the dead man suffered, Peter pities him. Not simple compassion but shared experience of the two facets of crime he had only observed before alters Peter's perception of himself, as the pose of the clever, objective super-sleuth falls away completely.

Changed from cardboard to flesh, Peter Wimsey is reintroduced through *Gaudy Night* to Harriet Vane, as complex and real a person as she is herself. Here his unknown weaknesses are revealed finally to complete his portrait. Peter is childishly vain about his long slender hands; he's feeling middle-aged and tired; his role as "patter comedian" for the Foreign Office leaves him bitter and disillusioned. He is jealous of his nephew's ease with Harriet and of Reggie Pomfret's size, youth and attraction to her. To assuage his bruised ego he boasts about the three duels he'd been challenged to fight. He is exhausted by his travel yet dissatisfied with the results of his work. He is concerned about his spendthrift nephew, the future of the family estate at Duke's Denver ("I was born there and I shall be sorry if I live to see the land sold for ribbon-building and the Hall turned over to a Hollywood Colour-Talkie king" (Ch. 14), and bitter when he thinks Harriet has shared her problems with St. George whom she's known for only a few weeks while telling him nothing. Critical of himself—"the usual middle-aged prig" (Ch. 14)—his greatest bitterness is reserved for one of his regular proposals of marriage; he is confident of rejection:

Dear Harriet,
    I send in my demand notes with the brutal regularity of the income tax commissioners; and probably you say when you see the envelope 'Oh God! I know what this is!' The only difference is that, some time or other, one *has* to take notice of the income tax.
    Will you marry me?—It's beginning to look like one of those lines in a farce—merely boring til it's said often enough; and after that, you get a bigger laugh every time it comes (Ch. 11).

    Of course Peter is still intelligent, well-read, suave and he does solve the crime. However, seen through other eyes—Harriet's, Paul Delgardie's and his mother's—his humanity is as remarkable here as his strength. Clues about Peter's behavior from former novels are woven into the fabric of this changed character. His foolishness is given a new perspective when Harriet explains, "he was either frightfully bored or detecting something . . . . I know that frivolous mood and it's mostly camouflage—" (Ch. 2). The go-to-blazes arrogance of Wimsey of Balliol, "planted in the centre of the quad and laying down the law with exquisite insolence to somebody," here provokes his apology to Harriet whose novel he's been criticizing (Ch. 14). At dinner, before they've come to Oxford, he talks about the case described in *Murder Must Advertise*, showing compassion and regret, "the thing had come to a strange and painful conclusion" (Ch. 4); his nerves and headaches in reaction to the end of a case make him too ill to eat or talk; his sense of responsibility is shown to outweigh his gamesmanship. Honestly, he admits to Harriet, "I have been running away from myself for twenty years, and it doesn't work, " (Ch. 18). Because of these revealing episodes, Sayers can say that "even in the five years or so that she had known him, Harriet had seen him strip off his protections, layer by layer, till there was uncommonly little left but the naked truth," and make the reader share the feeling that Peter's emotions have been revealed rather than created in this book (Ch. 18).
    Paul Delgardie, Peter's maternal uncle, writes a postscript to

Gaudy Night which fills out more of the details: his sensitive childhood, difficulties both with father and at school, social and sexual initiation later rejected for pure love, betrayal and his withdrawal behind the detached mask of detection. This short biographical sketch also justifies Peter's apparent shallowness in the early novels and gives the impression that his complex personality has been revealed as the demands of the case (or the novel) required.

The third contributor to the redefining is Peter's mother, the Dowager Duchess of Denver. After his marriage and interrupted honeymoon, she describes her son's nervous shock after the war to Harriet, "I don't mean he went out of his mind or anything, and he was always perfectly sweet about it, only he was so dreadfully afraid to go to sleep ... and he couldn't given an order. ... I suppose if you've been giving orders for nearly four years to people to go and get blown to pieces it gives you ... an inhibition" (*Honeymoon*, "Epithalamion," Ch. 2). This not only clarifies Peter's brief attacks of nerves in earlier novels but also relates them to his sense of responsibility and compassion; he is shown to be not self-centered but concerned for others.

Nothing shows better the final, clever sign of Peter's rehabilitation than the contrast between his first and last recorded words. *Whose Body?* opens with, "Oh, damn!"—he has forgotten the catalogue for a book sale. Returning to collect it at home he is easily diverted by a phone call from his mother about a dead body in a bathtub. His tone is characteristically frivolous: "Exit the amateur of first editions; new motive introduced by solo bassoon; enter Sherlock Holmes disguised as a walking gentleman."

Shortly after, he even sings to Inspector Parker:

> "We both have got a body in a bath,
> We both have got a body in a bath—
>   For in spite of all temptations,
>   We both have got a body in a bath—
> We insist upon a body in a bath—" (Ch. 1)

Nothing of this attitude remains in the final "Oh, damn!" of *Busman's Honeymoon* as he waits for the eight a.m. execution of a murderer he has caught: "Quite suddenly, he said, 'Oh, damn!' and began to cry—in an awkward unpracticed way at first, and then more easily. So she [Harriet] held him, crouched at her knees, against her breast, huddling his head in her arms that he might not hear eight o'clock strike!" (*Honeymoon*, "Epithalamion," Ch. 3).

However, when the whole series, novels and short stories, is considered, Sayers' accomplishment can clearly be seen. She has created a detective whose competence matches any of his rivals'. His cases are intricate and clever; his methods are imaginative and perceptive; his solutions are inevitable and accurate. In addition, he is more than his fellow sleuths; he develops beyond their two-dimensional, puzzle solving characteristics to be also a complex, responsible and compassionate man. He is not so much a character as a person.

Responsible, in Sayers' mind, for the necessary development of Lord Peter Wimsey is his accused client Harriet Vane. One of the first, and few, liberated women of detective fiction, Harriet is university educated, with a profession which enables her to support herself adequately, if not, at the outset, comfortably. In her work, she is always competent and reliable; however, she questions her emotional judgment. This conflict between intellect and feeling characterizes her immediately. Having struggled with her basic principles and, finally, agreed to live with Philip Boyes, she, nevertheless, refuses to marry him, having been "put on probation, like an office boy, to see if I was good enough to be condescended to.... I didn't like having matrimony offered as a bad-conduct prize" (*Strong Poison*, Ch. 4). She is naturally accused of murder, having had opportunity and no proper womanly feelings. While on vacation after her acquittal, numerous rejections of Peter, and some financial success, Harriet discovers a corpse about to be washed away by the tide. Calmly, she empties his pockets, checks his fingerprints, notes his blood coagulation, and takes pictures of him and the site. Although Peter drives from London immediately to protect her from the press and to investigate the case, she is an able partner, on equal footing with him. Still satisfied with her intellectual decisions and dissatisfied with her emotional ones, Harriet argues with Peter and rejects his proposals throughout *Have His Carcase* and all but the last page of *Gaudy Night*. At Oxford, she hopes to find intellectual solace but her investigation of a poisoned pen attack at her old college confronts her squarely with her old problem of balancing passion and reason. Desperately determined not to make the same kind of mistake twice, she clings to "the only side of life I haven't betrayed and made a mess of" (*Gaudy*, Ch. 15). Even when she begins to see herself and Peter more clearly, when she finally admits to herself that she loves him, Harriet's perception of the case leaves her still mistrusting "people and feelings" (*Gaudy*, Ch. 15). Only when she discovers that Peter's view of marriage does not include possessiveness and the precedence of personal responsibilities over professional ones, as revealed in the solution of the case, can she agree, finally, to his Latin proposal ("*Placetne, magistra?*") (*Gaudy*, Ch. 23), when he addresses her by her university title. With marriage, despite a corpse in the honeymoon house, she is able to tell Peter, "All my life I have been wandering in the dark—but now I have found your heart—and am satisfied" (*Honeymoon*, "Prothalamion", Ch. 16). In the end, she and Peter provide—he, the perilously spinning top and she, the balanced center—the counterpoint to each other.

The most important subject which Sayers chooses to consider in the detective stories is not, surprisingly, good vs. evil, or even the illumination of crime; rather, she is concerned with work. In her collected essays, *The Mind of the Maker*, she addresses the subject in a chapter entitled "The Worth of the Work," developing her ideas of the Christian and his work. Work, she insists, must be considered "in terms of the work's worth and the love of the work, as being in itself a sacrament and manifestation of man's creative energy."[8] The attitude of the artist whose work and leisure time are similarly occupied is her example of the best approach: "his holidays are all busman's holidays."[9] She urges political parties and social institutions to reorient their platforms to value "the integrity of the work—the stipulation that it shall be both worth doing and well done."[10] She extends this charge in the essay's conclusion, writing, "That the eyes of all workers should behold the integrity of the work is the sole means to make that work good in itself and so good for mankind."[11]

Throughout the detective novels, Sayers develops the significance of work, often letting minor figures or episodes reveal the importance characters attach to their professions or crafts. Although Harry Gotobed serves as a bellringer at Fenchurch St. Paul in *The Nine Tailors*, he is also the church sexton and, thereby, responsible for preparing graves for parishioners. When the local squire died,

Mr. Gotobed, the sexton, was concerned with the grave—so much concerned that he preferred to give his whole mind to the graveside ceremonies, although his son, Dick, who assisted him with the spadework, considered himself quite capable of carrying on on his own. There was not, indeed, very much to do in the way of digging. Rather to Mr. Gotobed's disappointment, Sir Henry had expressed a wish to be buried in the same grave with his wife, so that there was little opportunity for any fine work in the way of shaping, measuring, and smoothing the sides of the grave. They had only to cast over the earth—scarcely firm after three rainy months—to make all neat and tidy and line the grave with fresh greenery. Nevertheless, liking to be well beforehand with his work, Mr. Gotebed took measures to carry this out on the Thursday afternoon (*Nine Tailors*, "A Full Peal," Holt's Ten Part Peal, The First Peal).

Gotobed's function in this scene, for the detective story, is to deliver the second corpse buried in the grave with Sir Henry's wife, beginning the investigation by Peter and the police. But while the episode meets this need, as well as providing both local color and characterization, it primarily emphasizes the respect and responsibility the sexton feels for his work. In this, he is matched by others in his community, especially the aged Hezekiah Lavender, former sexton and lead change ringer, whose responsibility is to toll the death bell for parisioners. When the unidentified body is discovered, he consults with the rector and the doctor, then rings his knell. " 'We've got to ring her [the bell] for every Christian soul dyin' in the parish,' persisted Mr. Lavender, 'That's set down for us' " (*Nine Tailors,* "A Full Peal," Holt's Ten Part Peal, The First Part).

Like these country men, Tom Puffett, who is a builder by trade but had been raised as a chimney sweep, articulates this respect for the work, the tools and his own part in the job. He assures Harriet, " 'I'm allus willin' to oblige. Not but what you'll allow us a chimney wot's choked like this chimney is ain't fair to a man nor yet to 'is rods. But I will make bold to say that if any man can get the corroded sut out of this 'ere chimney-pot, I'm the man to do it. It's experience, you see, that's what it is, and the power I puts be'ind it' " (*Honeymoon,* "Prothalamion," Ch. 4). The whole chimney sweeping incident is connected to both the love story and the detection of this novel. Inconveniences plague Harriet and Peter in their honeymoon house, only to convince them, on their wedding night that "such a series of domestic accidents could only happen to married people" (*Honeymoon,* "Prothalamion," Ch. 3). In a bride-groom's foolish outburst, Peter rejoices, "It is so long since I was taken into anybody's confidence about a sweep.... Only a wife would treat me with the disrespect I deserve and summon me to look upon the—[sweep]" (*Honeymoon,* "Prothalamion," Ch. 4). Later, uncovering the crime, Peter recognizes that the chain removed from the hanging cactus (whose weight, swinging like a pendulum, had killed the victim) had been hidden inside the chimney and was only dislodged in their efforts to have the chimney cleaned. Nevertheless, Puffett's repeated defense of the chimney's construction, his own equipment, and his disparagement of the former owner's refusal to pay for having the chimneys swept emphasize beyond all reference to the rest of the story the need to respect one's own and another's work, to give it its due recognition.

Sayers' opinion extends from manual labor to the arts, seeing each worker needing to be true to his craft. Two artists, each with an argument to win, demonstrate the same point by opposite means. In "The Unsolved Puzzle of the Man With No Face," Peter theorizes that a young artist, convinced to paint the portrait of a man he hated for a niggardly fee, could not do the job poorly, despite his inclination to repay a shabby offer with a bad painting. On the night of his first son's birth, Peter discovers a young modern painter challenged by his uncle's jeer that the nephew chose his style because he didn't know how to draw; the younger man's response, an example of false perspective, is designed to force the uncle "to confess that your draughtsmanship was a triumph of academic accuracy" ("The Haunted Policeman"). Both men, jealous of their talent, are unable to see it betrayed.

In her own way, Harriet Vane would recognize this attitude. While on trial for murder, she corrects the proofs of her latest detective novel. Recognizing her professional dedication, Peter, upon first seeing their son, questions her, "Do you feel it's up to standard?... Of course, *your* workmanship's always sound—but you never know with these collaborate efforts" ("The Haunted Policeman"). This humorous remark extends responsibility for the job beyond simple craft or profession to parenting or, even, to living in a way one can respect.

The most important work discussed in the series of novels is Peter's self-assumed job of detection. He is not always comfortable with the serious implications of criminal investigation; in the early novels he sees the process as part of an intellectual exercise from which he can withdraw when the fun is gone; Charles Parker forces him to see otherwise.

"It's a hobby to me, you see. I took it up when the bottom of things was rather knocked out for me, because it was so damned exciting, and the worst of it is, I enjoy it—up to a point.... It *is* a game to me, to begin with, and I go on cheerfully, and then I suddenly see that somebody is going to be hurt,and I want to get out of it."
"That's because you're thinking about your attitude. But that's childish. If you've any duty to society in the way of finding out the truth about murderers, you must do it in any attitude that comes handy.... Life's not a football match.... You can't be a sportsman. You're a responsible person" (*Whose Body?* Ch. 7).

Several cases later, Peter finds himself not only feeling responsible but also being troubled about his participation. He questions the local vicar, "Ought I to have left it alone?... Nothing really to do with me. Started in like a fool to help somebody who'd got into trouble about the thing.... And my beastly interference started the crimes all over again" (*Unnatural Death*, Ch. 19). When challenged by the dons at Shrewsbury College about the private citizen's participation in tracking criminals, Peter raises this case again, accusing himself of being responsible for two additional deaths and three unsuccessful attempts. But Harriet Vane has already defended his preoccupation with detecting, "Catching murderers isn't a soft job, or a sheltered job. It takes a lot of time and energy, and you may very easily get injured or killed. I dare say he does it for fun, but at least at any rate, he does do it. Scores of people must have as much reason to thank him as I have" (*Gaudy*, Ch. 2). By the time they're honeymooning, finding a corpse in the basement, Harriet's protective impulse would like to spare Peter the anxiety of another investigation; he is forced to remind her, "I can't wash my hands of a thing, merely because it's inconvenient to my lordship, as Bunter says of the sweep. I hate violence! I loathe war and slaughter, and men quarreling and fighting like beasts. Don't say it isn't my business. It's everybody's business" (*Honeymoon*, "Prothalamion," Ch. 7). Through this challenging and reconsideration of Peter's attitude toward detection, criminals and victims, Sayers integrates his activities into the fabric of society. Because he respects the work he does, he is not the eccentric detective of dime novels nor the super-sleuth of mystery serials; he is very much like Charles Parker, policeman, or Gerald Wimsey, Duke, or his own manservant, Mervyn Bunter. In another context, Harriet once thinks of him as representing England; because Peter cares about the job he has decided to take on, he does symbolize what Sayers hopes is society's view of its values.

Of the seven Peter Wimsey novels where the crime is murder, only one, *Have His Carcase*, does not show the murder committed in a manner which betrays the murderer's profession or craft. The characters who kill are thus doubly condemned by Sayers' standards: first, for not respecting life, and second, for not respecting their work. Even in more minor characters and crimes, lack of responsibility for one's job is a suspicious circumstance.

In the first three novels, Sayers conveniently chooses a medical murderer. Her motive is obvious; medical personnel are familiar with and unfrightened by death, while they have access to the knowledge and equipment or drugs with which to cause death. These people normally have the trust of those whom they treat, so the opportunity to murder is easily available. Finally, until the deadly doctor became a stereotype in detective fiction, the reader was usually as unwary and trusting as the victim. The great advantage of choosing a medical murder is the fear and horror inspired in readers by the irony that the one charged with preserving life is busy ending it.

The first two murderers are obviously suspicious characters; the third is more subtly contrived. Dr. Julian Freke, whose surname is too good a clue, abuses his position as head of the dissecting laboratory to exchange an impoverished cadaver for the body of his patient Sir Ruben Levy whom he murders during an official visit. The abuse is two-fold: the trust of both the hospital and his individual private patient, as well as apparent friend, is casually and callously disregarded. Even more reprehensible is Mary Whittaker's murder of her elderly aunt who is also her patient. Family ties as well as the nursing profession are irrelevant in Whittaker's determination to secure an inheritance. To cover up this crime, she methodically murders several other women—a former servant and a close friend—without hesitation. Like Sir Julian, she plots carefully, covering her steps at every point. Like him, she is calculating and coldblooded, unhesitating in her attempts to murder three more people. Unlike Sir Julian's motive which is revenge veneered with scientific curiosity, hers is simply greed. The same greed also motivates retired Army physician Dr.Pemberthy, newly specializing in "glands" and eager to open his own clinic. But he is more than a murderer; he is also a cad. Having encouraged Ann Dorland when he could hope to share her inheritance, he discards her when the complications of the will and two deaths threaten her portion. He betrays love, his profession and trust; General Fentiman, over eighty and retired, shares information about his family's wills which challenge Pemberthy's hopes of the clinic. So, to frustrate the intentions of the documents, he substitutes digitalis for the prescription Fentiman expected from him. He is allowed one moment of saving grace by Peter who suggests a confession exonerating Ann Dorland and "the honorable way out"—suicide. This redemptive gesture is, however, an ironic perversion of his oath to preserve life. Each of the three murderers plans suicide; one is frustrated, whereas two succeed. But all have destroyed the professional part of themselves.

Sayers shows little respect for lawyers in the novels, although only one is actually a murderer. Sir Impey Biggs, the famous counsel who defends the Duke of Denver, Harriet Vane and Frank Crutchley openly acknowledges that his only responsibility is to his client and to winning the case. If the truth is prejudicial to his client, Biggs prefers unsolved mysteries and unanswered questions. He is eloquent during the trial, even in defense of acknowledged murderer Frank Crutchley. The dishonest, embezzling solicitor Norman Urquhart, who kills Harriet Vane's former lover, Phillip Boyes, is neither flamboyant nor successful. Having mismanaged his elderly great aunt's estate, he must murder her heir to safeguard his first crime. He, then, substitutes a false will leaving himself the estate. Both by misuse of his power of attorney and by presentation of a phoney document, he violates his professional trust and abrogates his responsibilities, considering only his own financial need. Because both the aunt he deceives and the cousin he murders are his relations, the personal disrespect is added to professional.

Advertising is not so much a profession as a craft—a kind of creativity to order. However, blackmail victim Tallboy uses his position at Pym's Publicity to circulate distribution information to London's drug dealers. Despite his unwilling participation, he takes the money he's offered and kills his threatening blackmailer to avert discovery. Weekly the Nutrox Nerve Food large advertisement aids a large and profitable drug ring. The drugs, Peter and Charles Parker agree, are more deadly than a single murderer; Tallboy, by his participation, is a mass murderer. Needing to supplement his income, he misuses advertising, ironically promoting physical and spiritual death.

Unlike the weak and pitiable Tallboy, Frank Crutchley is a thoroughly nasty murderer. For a forty pound loan and a possible inheritance, he kills his part-time employer and would have married the man's middle-aged niece, had there been any money left to her. A man of two crafts, he betrays both in this crime. Hoping to buy a garage, he is obviously mechanical; he rigs a very cleverly weighted pendulum to be set off when the radio lid is lifted and the restraining strings loosened. A respected gardener, he later overwaters the prized hanging cactus which he'd used as the pendulum head in order to justify wiping the pot's outside where fingerprints, blood, skin or hair might have adhered. Of course he jilts the spinster, rejects the village girl he's gotten pregnant, and feels justified in having killed the old man. Neither his personal nor his professional reputation is admirable.

Even where no murder occurs, Sayers demonstrates a connection between disrespect for one's work and disrespect for the social order. Annie Wilson, the Shrewsbury College poisoned pen, was hired as a scout or college servant whose job is to facilitate the smooth domestic operation of the college. Instead, she disrupts it. The dons at the college, professionally dedicated to facts, evidence and proof in academic matters, begin to suspect each other of being the poltergeist, although the only possible evidence comes from unreliable personal inter-relationships and over-extended imaginations. Perhaps, in this light, even the suspicions against Harriet Vane in Phillip Boyes' murder are not unreasonable. Through her professional investigation into the availability of arsenic, she uncovers enough information to enable her to kill Boyes; only instinct—Peter's and Miss Climpson's—saves her from being seen as part of this group of betrayers of their professions.

Given Sayers' personal attitude about respect and love for work, it is inevitable that her villains should be identified with dishonoring their work in the context of murder. However, she also redresses the disrespect by making the solutions to the crimes come as a result of her detective's regard for the betrayed professions. In three of the later novels, it is not simply the infallible detective's careful investigation of physical evidence or even his esoteric and improbable knowledge about the murderer's work which makes him successful. His resolutions of the crime and the resumption of social order are a direct result of Wimsey's working knowledge of and real respect for the killer's craft.

Although he mocks the advertiser's attitude toward the carefully legal use of language, Peter does not stand off arrogantly from his work or colleagues at Pym's Publicity. He confides to his sister, "Every week when I get my pay-envelope, I glow with honest pride" (*Advertise*, Ch. 5). While he solves the puzzle of Victor Dean's murder and the drug trade's distribution, he also writes slogans for Dairyfield's Margerine and Twenty man's Tea. However, his great coup is the scheme for promoting Whifflets cigarettes with a campaign of coupons redeemable for everything from a holiday to diaper service (only funeral arrangements excluded). Peter's interest is not artificially contrived to help him fit in unobtrusively at Pyms, nor is it superficial. The ad campaign is, of course, a great success; all England begins to "whiffle." More important to Peter and Parker, his knowledge of the agency, the scheduling, the need to correlate copy and illustrations, and the company's penchant for literary slogans make solving the crime possible. Had Peter not entered fully into the business world at Pym's, becoming a sincere participant rather than an uninterested or disgusted observer, he still could have captured the criminal. But, Sayers chooses to integrate two themes—concerns for life and for work—in both the crime and the solution.

Although no real murder occurs in *The Nine Tailors*, blackmail, stolen jewels and accidental death do. The bell ringers at Fenchurch St. Paul share only their place of residence and this craft of change ringing. One is a sexton, another a publican, a third a laborer; each has his own different job but all are needed to ring the changes. When Peter replaces an ill man for a long New Year's peal, he becomes exhausted; however, he has taken his place with these more experienced and practiced ringers without making a mistake. They welcome his participation and admire his part in the group's success. Nothing could indicate more clearly Peter's regard for their work than his colleagues' acceptance of him. Later he employs his knowledge of the pattern of changes to break a cipher and discover previously stolen jewelry. Months later, entering the bell chamber during a ring (a privilege he assumes because of his earlier participation), he discovers how the death occurred. Although his solutions do not come entirely as a result of Peter's knowledge of ringing, this information provides the most vital clues which justify his more typical detective activities.

Because both require proven facts to substantiate a conclusion and both reject results marked by personal bias, detection and scholarship are often very similar. As an M.A. with a first in Modern History from Balliol, Peter has learned scientific method and logical analysis he uses in his professional detecting. When he returns to Oxford, over twenty years after coming down, to help Harriet Vane solve a case, his absolute respect for scholarly activity and his own understanding of the detached, inquiring mind lead him to

professional and personal satisfaction. Because he is able to set
aside emotional issues in order to consider the case dispassionately,
Peter avoids some of Harriet's misinterpretations about possible
suspects. Determined to prove to her that truth, no matter what it
may be, and work, no matter how it may hurt, are the most
dependable and valuable constants in her life, Peter meets the
academic community on its terms and in its setting. In presenting
evidence he is as much a scholar as a detective:

"I will first set out the salient points as they presented themselves to me when I came
to Oxford last Sunday week, so as to show you the bases upon which I founded my
working theory. I will then formulate that theory, and adduce the supporting
evidence which I hope and think you will consider conclusive. I may say that
practically all the data necessary to the formulation of the theory are contained in the
very valuable digest of events prepared for me by Miss Vane and handed to me on my
arrival" (*Gaudy*, Ch. 22).

Peter is not simply adopting a jargon here to make his remarks more
palatable to his audience of dons. He is demonstrating how he
values their work which had been so crudely challenged by the
letters and by their suspicions of one another. He and they are a
community in Oxford where "it's extremely difficult to be cheap"
(*Gaudy,* Ch. 14).

This pattern of the social order being broken by one person's
disrespect for life and work only to be restored by an equal respect
for both redirects the emphasis from detection for its own curiosity
to the place of detective investigation within modern society. The
restitution of an idealized *status quo* is, perhaps, more hopeful and
Christian than realistic.

The fame and popularity of Sayers' detective fiction are
incontrovertible; in the Golden Age of the genre, her works provide
perfect examples of what this kind of story ought to be. Well plotted
and well written, they satisfy both the imaginative and the
ratiocinative impulses of their readers; never merely novels of
detection, they also respond to literary and moral expectations.

In style, the series and the individual books are considerably
diverse, showing a pattern of change and development. Sayers tries
intellectual games, timetable puzzles, epistolary form and the
interweaving of detection with serious material or a love interest.
The thirteen novels and several dozen short stories do not fall
predictably into the same pattern in each case. However, they are
dependable for a careful, almost scholarly concern for language;
word choice and sentence patterns in both narration and dialogue
are believable and entertaining (if not altogether realistic). The
stories' most witty passages arise not from Peter's idle and piffling
remarks but through the author's aware use of language.

The novels, in particular, could be read by someone uninterested in detection simply for the rich and full description of the period. The atmosphere of privilege and wealth is luxuriously drawn; Peter's flat, his stuffy gentleman's club, and his sequence of elegant cars are carefully detailed, then contrasted with Charles Parker's middle-class upbringing or Mr. Rumm's fireside revival meeting. A Scottish village with its eccentric collection of painters and fishermen, an advertising agency with its witty writers, a woman's college with its two hundred students, dons, and staff can be visualized through Sayers' explicit descriptions, even if change-ringing never really is comprehended. Never satisfied with the staple country house or body in the library, Sayers fits her murders to each new setting, building a complete world for the investigation.

The characters who people these worlds may sometimes be stereotyped: the predictable servants, the slow-thinking locals, the flighty and the tedious duchesses with the beefy duke, or the absent-minded vicar. Nevertheless there are individually developed minor characters and some memorable episodes involving the stereotypes in unexpected behavior. A gleefully drunk Inspector Parker, the Dowager Duchess at an exhumation, or Marjorie Phelps declining cocoa and fizzy lemonade on Peter's behalf expand their personalities beyond conventional limitations. Peter is never bound by traditional expectations in his roles either as wealthy aristocrat or talented detective; new facets of his character are regularly developed throughout the series. He grows from a conventional puzzle solver into a feeling, responsible human being.

Clearly then, Sayers is not just writing detective fiction; she presents more than the usual respect for the value of life and the return of society to its ordered ways. Instead she chooses also to define social order and society's future in terms of work. Neither individuals nor segments of society which disdain or betray work are respected in the fiction. Through successful completion of his own work, the detective restores respect to the criminal's dishonored profession or craft; this, in turn, keeps the social order functioning. In meshing these two distinct elements, Sayers leaves her own unique stamp on the *genre* she helped create.

Notes

[1]The editions of Sayers' novels used for this study are listed below, preceeded by the original date of publication. All references will be included in the text by chapter number or short story title using, where necessary, the abbreviation given after each entry.

1923 *Whose Body?* (New York: Avon, 1961).
1926 *Clouds of Witness* (New York: Avon, 1966). (*Clouds*)
1927 *Unnatural Death* (New York: Avon, 1964).

1928 *Lord Peter Views the Body* (New York: Avon, 1969).   "The Abominable History of the Man with Copper Fingers," "The Bibulous Business of a Matter of Taste," "The Entertaining Episode of the Article in Question," "The Fantastic Horror of the Cat in the Bag," "The Fascinating Problem of Uncle Meleager's Will," "The Learned Adventure of the Dragon's Head," "The Piscatorial Farce of the Stolen Stomach," "The Adventurous Exploits of the Cave of Ali Baba," "The Undignified Melodrama of the Bone of Contention," "The Unprincipled Affair of the Practical Joker," "The Unsolved Puzzle of the Man with No Face," "The Vindictive Story of the Footsteps that Ran."

1928 *The Unpleasantness at the Bellona Club* (New York: Avon, 1963). (*Bellona*)
1930 with Robert Eustace, *Documents in the Case* (New York: Avon, 1968). (*Documents*)
1930 *Strong Poison* (New York: Avon, 1967).
1931 *Five Red Herrings* (New York: Avon, 1968). (*Herrings*)
1932 *Have His Carcase* (New York: Avon, 1968). (*Carcase*)
1933 *Hangman's Holiday* (New York: Avon, 1969).
"The Image in the Mirror," "The Incredible Elopement of Lord Peter Wimsey," "The Queen's Square," "The Necklace of Pearls," "The Poisoned Dow '08," "Sleuths on the Scent," "Murder in the Morning," "One Too Many," "Murder at Penticost," "Maher-Shalal-Hashbaz," "The Man Who Knew How," "The Fountain Plays."
1933 *Murder Must Advertise* (New York: Avon, 1967). (*Advertise*)
1934 *The Nine Tailors* (New York: Harbrace Paperbound Library, 1966).
1935 *Gaudy Night* (New York: Avon, 1968). (*Gaudy*)
1937 *Busman's Honeymoon* (New York: Avon, 1968). (*Honeymoon*)
1939 *In the Teeth of the Evidence* (New York: Avon, 1952).
"In the Teeth of the Evidence," "Absolutely Elsewhere," "A Shot at Goal," "Dirt Cheap," "Better Almonds," "False Weight," "The Professor's Manuscript," "The Milk Bottles," "Dilemma," "An Arrow O'er the House," "Scrawns," "Nebuchadnezzar," "The Inspiration of Mr. Budd," "Blood Sacrifice," "Suspicion," "The Leopard Lady," "The Cyprian Cat."
1972 *Lord Peter* (New York: Avon, 1972).
"The Abominable History of the Man with Copper Fingers," "The Entertaining Episode of the Article in Question," "The Fascinating Problem of Uncle Meleager's Will," "The Fantastic Horror of the Cat in the Bag," "The Unprincipled Affair of the Practical Joker," "The Undignified Melodrama of the Bone of Contention," "The Vindictive Story of the Footsteps that Ran," "The Bibulous Business of a Matter of Taste," "The Learned Adventure of the Dragon's Head," "The Piscatorial Farce of the Stolen Stomach," "The Unsolved Puzzle of the Man with No Face," "The Adventurous Exploit of the Cave of Ali Baba," "The Image in the Mirror," "The Incredible Elopement of Lord Peter Wimsey," "The Queen's Square," "The Necklace of Pearls," "In The Teeth of the Evidence," "Absolutely Elsewhere," "Striding Folly," "The Haunted Policeman," "Tallboys."

[2]Members of the Detective Club swore an oath:
President: Do you promise that your detectives shall well and truly detect the crimes presented to them, using those wits it shall please you to bestow upon them and not placing reliance upon, nor making use of, divine revelation, feminine intuition, mumbo jumbo, jiggery-pokery, coincidence or the act of God?
Candidate: I do.
In Dorothy L. Sayers, "Problem Picture," in *The Whimsical Christian* (New York: Macmillan, 1978), 139.
    [3]Julian Symons, *Mortal Consequences* (New York: Schocken Books, 1973), 101-3.
    [4]See, among others, D.Q. Leavis, "The Case of Miss Dorothy Sayers," *Scrutiny*, 63 (December, 1937), 334-5.
        [5]Such critics as Howard Haycraft have insisted that the well constructed

detective story must combine the questions of who and how so that the answers are simultaneously discovered; see Haycraft, *Murder for Pleasure* (New York: Appleton Century, 1941).

[6]Sayers announces her intention retrospectively in "Gaudy Night" in Howard Haycraft, *The Art of the Mystery Story* (New York: Simon & Schuster, 1946), 208-21.

[7]In "Gaudy Night," Sayers discusses the need and ways to change Peter; some are more successfully handled than others.

[8]Dorothy L. Sayers, *The Mind of the Maker* (Westport, Conn.: Greenwood Press, 1970), 218.

[9]Sayers, *The Mind of the Maker*, 219.

[10]Sayers, *The Mind of the Maker*, 223.

[11]Sayers, *The Mind of the Maker*, 225.

Angus McBean

Josephine Tey

Josephine Tey, Gordon Daviot

1896   Born in Inverness, Scotland
Studied at Anstey Physical Training College, Birmingham, England; then taught near Liverpool and in Tunbridge Wells

1923   Returned to Inverness to keep house for her father

1929   *Kif* (Gordon Daviot). *The Man in the Queue* (Gordon Daviot), first mystery novel

1931   *A Tarnished Halo* (Gordon Daviot)

1933   *Richard of Bordeaux* (Gordon Daviot) produced at New Theatre, London

1934   *Queen of Scots* (Gordon Daviot) produced at New Theatre, London. *The Laughing Woman* (Gordon Daviot) produced at New Theatre, London

1936   *A Shilling for Candles,* first mystery novel as Josephine Tey

1937   *Claverhouse* (Gordon Daviot)

1939   *The Stars Bow Down* (Gordon Daviot)

1946   *Leith Sands and other Short Plays* (Gordon Daviot). *The Little Dry Thorn* (Gordon Daviot) produced in Glasgow. *Miss Pym Disposes*

1948   *The Franchise Affair*

1949   *Brat Farrar*

1950   Death of Colin Mackinstosh, her father
To Love and Be Wise

1952   *The Privateer* (Gordon Daviot). Death on 13 February in Streatham, London. *The Singing Sands,* final mystery novel

1953-54 *Plays by Gordon Daviot* in three volumes

by Nancy Ellen Talburt

Josephine Tey is justly remembered for *The Daughter of Time*,[1] for her subject in it is the most famous murder in English history—that of the princes in the Tower—and her treatment makes use of the most popular fictional form of her day, that of the detective novel.

Although the novel is unrivaled in its pioneering adaptation of detecting to history, and splendidly audacious in its least-likely-suspect as villain, Henry VII of England, evaluations of Tey's success in writing a novel to match her ingenious subject have varied. Dilys Winn picks it as one of the five best detective novels, and for Anthony Boucher it was "one of the permanent Classics." James Sandoe calls it "the most astonishing detective story of them all," and Erik Routley feels that it is "uniquely memorable." On the other hand, Michele Slung is not sure it is a "masterpiece" but calls it a "provocative *tour de force*," and Julian Symons finds the book "really rather dull."[2]

Tey is the product of a vintage decade during which were also born in Great Britain (or the Empire) Agatha Christie, Dorothy Sayers and Ngaio Marsh. This is a distinguished company in which to earn recognition, numbering as it does premiere authors of classic detective fiction, a Dante scholar, the author of the world's longest running play, a founder of the British Commonwealth Theatre Company and assorted Dames and Commanders of the British Empire. Even apart from general acceptance of *The Daughter of Time* as a classic of mystery fiction, Tey's claim to recognition in such a group is not slight. Her first play to be produced, *Richard of Bordeaux* (written as Gordon Daviot), was the smash hit of the season on the London stage in 1933 and ran for over a year. As Sir John Gielgud, who directed and starred in it, recalls, "It was to the brilliant inspiration and sympathy of Gordon Daviot that I owed the biggest personal success of my career."[3]

Despite her versatility and her reputation as the author of one of the classics of detective fiction, Josephine Tey and her eight diverse and meticulously-written mysteries remain less known than the lives and works of her most famous contemporaries. The reason for this state of things seems clear. There is no great detective in Tey's novels, and there is no series of dazzling and intricate plots. Her use of the traditions of detective fiction is discriminating, informed and effective, but while in many particulars her novels are typical of this tradition, in other ways, such as in her consistent and perceptive exploration of the theme of imperiled innocence, they achieve a unique statement which transcends, and sometimes obscures, their nominal adherence to rule and formula. Furthermore, to her adaptations of the mystery she brings three other dimensions which, on occasion, compete with the detection aspect: an intimate view of life in the theatre with an extension of acting and impersonation into the "real" world; a singular use of history; and the creation of a number of Not-Married women whose vitality stops just short of a feminist statement. In short, her achievement lies as much in her departures from the genre's limits as in her successful utilization of its conventions.

How she developed and refined her talent and came to her special vision seems a question closely related to the two careers, as dramatist and as writer of mystery fiction, she successfully pursued from the distance of Scotland. A brief examination of the main events of her life and career and a review of her mystery novels is an instructive way to begin an assessment of her accomplishment.

*   *   *

"Josephine Tey" is a pen name, the second of two used by Elizabeth Mackintosh (1896-1952). Her unusual education began at the Royal Academy at Inverness, Scotland, and concluded at the Anstey School of Physical Training in Birmingham, England. Physical training as a discipline enjoyed a vogue in the early part of the century, and a number of young women from Inverness of Tey's generation studied at a school in Scotland (in Dunfermline) or at Anstey, rather than attending a university. The demanding curriculum seems to have combined elements of medical, chiropractic, physical theory, gymnastics and dance training. Upon graduation, Tey taught for some years at schools near Liverpool and in Tunbridge Wells in England before returning to keep house for her father in Inverness where she lived for the remaining twenty-nine years of her life.

Little else is known of her personal life, although Gielgud speculates: "She spoke very bitterly of the first World War in which I fancy she must have suffered some bereavement."[4] Former neighbors who now live at Crown Cottage (which was her home) report that "Beth" was very reclusive and did most of her writing in a tiny summerhouse. Gielgud's recollections include the information that she attended the movies twice a week and that she shunned photographers and publicity of all kinds and gave no interviews to the Press. According to his account, she referred to her novels published under the name of Josephine Tey (her mystery novels) as her "yearly knitting," as if they were of little account to her.[5] Her neighbors describe her interest in reading as being so extreme that she would emerge from her home to enter the taxi—which each Sunday took her and her father to visit her mother's grave—reading a book. The account of her death in the *Inverness Courier* has the comment: "While living in Inverness, Gordon Daviot took little or no part or interest in the life of the town, her spare time from the household duties being taken up by her writing, and she spent a good deal of each year in the South. Her trenchant wit, ready tongue and inquiring mind made her an interesting companion, and those who enjoyed her friendship will miss her stimulating personality."[6]

Tey began her career with the publication of poems and short pieces, of which two, a ghost story and an account of a violent murder by a woman, suggest an early interest in the mystery. The second contains a comment on the most-used theme in her mysteries: "If we were to count so little, it was surely unfair that we should suffer so much."[7] Four other sketches, of Highland life, are used again as incidents in Tey's last novel, posthumously published.

Until the second mystery, *A Shilling for Candles* in 1936, Tey published under the name of "Gordon Daviot" (Daviot is a picturesque district near Inverness where her family spent holidays). Thereafter, she used "Tey" for her mysteries and reissued the first one under that name. Her mystery writing was essentially concentrated in the last six years of her life when she published the best, and six out of a total of eight, of her mystery novels. The two earlier novels are competently done, and the first achieves a surprising, though non-detected, climax. *The Man in the Queue*, which introduces Detective Inspector Alan Grant of Scotland Yard, explores the favored conventions of contemporary detective novels and ends on a note which brings into question the entire process of "detection." Her second, published at the end of a period of great success as a dramatist, makes a second attempt to illustrate detection but comes instead to focus on the character and relationships of the dead girl. It concludes with a solution confirmed by physical evidence (a button torn from a coat) but arrived at by a chance occurrence and the drawing of a very uncertain inference. Alfred Hitchcock's favorite among his British films, *Young and Innocent* (1937), was based on this novel.

Of the six novels published at the end of her life, the most inspired may be *The Daughter of Time*, but the best executed of her novels, and the richest in general interest, is *The Franchise Affair*. In it, the eighteenth-century disappearance of Elizabeth Canning is represented in contemporary terms in a novel whose serious theme, the vulnerablilty of the innocent, is perfectly complemented by the surface lightness of its treatment. This surface is achieved by the skillful combining of an amateur detective (a country solicitor), a cool courtship and the devastating but comic tongue of old Mrs. Sharpe. There is a touch of parody in the treatment of the "artists" among whom the crime in *To Love and Be Wise* occurs, and the basic plot stratagem is quite bold. Deduction, reader involvement, fairly-shared clues, and the stunning climax make this novel remarkable. *Brat Farrar* is a mystery without significant emphasis on detection, an adventure and suspense story which makes good use of Tey's feeling for horses, countryside and English family life. The central figure, a sympathetic "criminal," is a very unusual achievement for Tey. *Miss Pym Disposes* is set in a closed society of women and girls at a school. In this novel the focus is on the personalities of the students, and the crime, which does not occur until the last quarter of the novel, begins as a rebellion against an unfair decision made by the headmistress. The amateur detective is a woman, an amateur psychologist, whose possession of key information comes to her largely by chance. The conclusion of the novel, as she agonizes over what to do with the evidence, is its outstanding feature. It is meant to disturb, if not surprise, and does.

The last novel, *The Singing Sands*, extends the suffering of the innocents, which has been a prominent feature of her fiction from the beginning of her career, to the detective himself. His healing occurs during a literal and symbolic return to boyhood and family in Scotland. He rejects the notion of retirement (and marriage) and personally pays his debt to B Seven who was instrumental in his recovery. The sympathetic identification of Grant with the dead man in B Seven is expressed in resentment at the callous behavior of the sleeping car attendant: "Someone had taken leave of life, had gone out from warmth and feeling and perception to nothingness, and all it meant to Damn His Eyes Gallacher was that he would be late in getting off duty" (9). It is impossible not to read into this novel further evidence for Gielgud's assertion that Tey had "known herself to be mortally ill for nearly a year, and had resolutely avoided seeing anyone she knew."[8]

Concurrent with her early career as a writer of fiction, Tey was writing plays. The great success of her first production was not repeated, but six of her plays were produced on the London stage during her lifetime. After their initial venture, Gielgud brought her *Queen of Scots* to the stage in 1934, with Laurence Olivier as Bothwell. The play had over a hundred performances, a very moderate success. Even less successful was *The Laughing Woman*, based on the life of Henri Gautier. It was over a decade before another play was staged in London, and *The Little Dry Thorn, Valerius*, and *The Stars Bow Down* all failed to find enthusiastic audience during the last years of Tey's life. Two and possibly all three had been written many years earlier. A number of plays were published, following her death, in a three-volume collection, most being one-act plays.

Three novels and a biography complete the canon of Tey's writings. One further contribution produced by her writings is the large number of adaptations for radio, film and television of her detective fiction. In addition to the two films made during her lifetime, at least five television productions have since been based on her novels. Many plays have also been done at drama festivals and for radio and television.

Her career was impressively varied. The two major professional interests, drama and detective fiction, can be seen to share some concerns, and, more surprisingly, to omit other correspondences. The most obvious sharing can be seen in her best non-mystery novel, *The Privateer*, her greatest dramatic success, *Richard of Bordeaux*, and her most famous mystery, *The Daughter of Time*, all of which are based on history. Moreover, all the plays performed in London were based on historical or biblical characters except *Valerius* which is historical in another sense. It is set in Roman Britain. Her interest in each work is the reinterpretation of historical characters to make them ordinary human beings, a process of de-mythologizing. Both "Richards" are presented more favorably than history has usually depicted them, Richard II being given a sense of humor and civility, Richard III being made fair, honorable and capable. Mary is neither the martyr nor the heroine that countless other interpreters of English and Scottish history have made of her. Reviews of the plays suggest that a lack of contrast results from the ordinariness of Tey's versions of such characters, which may account for their relative lack of theatrical success.

The sequence of her detective stories has more range than her plays, and the best of the novels are produced at the end of her life, not the beginning. Either she came to find her interest in the drama inseparable from her interest in history, or she became, like Madeleine March in *The Daughter of Time*, more interested in writing a detective novel "while it was fresh" than in creating a play, which, in one sense at least, could never be so. It is a little surprising that Daviot made so little use of Tey's accomplishments. No mystery finds its way into a play, and no contemporary crime is the subject of a serious drama. Whatever the intentions and whatever the effect of her early career, it appears that Elizabeth Mackintosh finally became Josephine Tey, not Gordon Daviot.

The absorbing interest in history which inspired the best of her writings had one further effect. In her will she left the proceeds from her writing to the National Trust for Places of Historic Interest or Natural Beauty, and the income, which still amounts to something like five thousand pounds per year, has resulted in the enrichment of the National Trust, over the years, by something in the neighborhood of half a million dollars.

It may be that the chief effect of Tey's success in the theatre and her steady and productive prosecution of a writing career was to provide her with the skill for presenting a scene dramatically, the perception to observe and analyze human behavior sensitively, and a gentle but ironic sense of humor. These talents, combined with the author's genuine interest in the characters and circumstances of her novels, even during the quieter moments of an adventure, make her novels thoroughly and consistently readable.

* * *

The most specific features of Josephine Tey's mystery novels can be determined by an analysis which reveals three things: her use of basic elements of detective fiction; her use of other conventions of mystery fiction; and the success of the inclusion in her mysteries of highly individualized subjects or views.

Mystery fiction is so broad in its subjects, scope and treatments that clear-cut, distinct categories within its bounds are difficult to establish. To make matters worse, terms such as the thriller, crime fiction and the detective story are often used to refer to overlapping sections of the same literary terrain. One example of a tentative taxonomy, as the authors call it, is that in *A Catalogue of Crime*[9] which attempts to interrelate different kinds of mystery. Tey's eight mysteries defy absolute placement in this listing, but its categories can be used to identify important correspondences between her novels and specific types in the mystery tradition. For example, five of the novels are "detection, official and a Yard wide," featuring as they do Detective Inspector Alan Grant of Scotland Yard. "Amateurs," on the other hand, make their appearance as principal character in two other novels, and a "private eye" plays a minor role in one of these. The remaining novel is non-detection, though some detecting occurs, and it can be classified as a "suspense" mystery, though it also contains elements of the neo-"gothic" novel combined with some from a type not included in this taxonomy, the crime or rogue novel. The "habitat" shifts from the "big city" to "open country, moor preferred" (Scottish highlands and the Hebrides) and from the suburbs of Larborough (Birmingham) to the shores of the channel near Westover and Whitecliffe (Dover?), including action in a country house in a "village," Salcott St. Mary. One novel is set in an "institution," a school of physical training. "Police routine" is employed and is the focus of attention in sections of some novels in which other police professionals support the efforts of the main detective, mainly by collecting and analyzing physical evidence. Although this particular taxonomy does not make use of them, the popular terms of "classic" and "golden age" detective story apply to Tey's works, especially in settings, style and cast of characters.

In addition to a taxonomy, a "poetics" of the detective story exists in the form of several quite different analyses and discussions, including among them the well-known essays by Chesterton, Knox, Van Dine, Sayers, Auden and Chandler, and several chapters in his study of formula fiction by John Cawelti. From these and similar treatments and from an examination of the practices of authors, a list of basic or staple elements of such fiction can be drawn up. The basic elements are: 1) a detective, 2) a plot which involves reconstruction, "deduction," the use of clues, and a satisfying (to the reader) concluding of the action, 3) a crime and a criminal, 4) a victim, and 5) suspects.

Similarly, a list of often-observed conventions or less intrinsically necessary but still popular and widely-used topics, motifs and approaches can be made. Although such a list would be quite long, if reasonably complete, some of the most often employed are *armchair detection, fair play,* the *locked-room* convention, the detailing of *police procedures*, and the often debated but regularly practiced inclusion of a *love interest.*

All mystery novelists use many of the elements and conventions which have been made popular by regular use and development. Most attempt to achieve a recognizable approach and product by their focus on a few. Before proceeding to a point-by-point comparison of Tey's practice with established custom in the use of the major and minor features, it is important to recognize that she, too, in a less obvious way, employed a consistent usage for favored elements. Instead of developing the individuality of a central figure (as did Doyle and Stout), writing variations on one kind of plot (as did John Dickson Carr), or organizing her novels to challenge the reader to a puzzle-solving duel (as did Ellery Queen), Tey arranged the materials of much of her writing to emphasize the trials of the innocent.

Standard mystery fiction does exist to produce suspense, to display suspicion of the innocent and the apparent innocence of the guilty until the conclusion, and to depict ill-treated victim and suspects. Tey's practice, on the other hand, is to extend the number of the sufferers, to extend the range of sufferings, and, more important, to reveal the character of her detectives by their participation in the sufferings of others, some of which they cause. Most important, these trials of the innocent raise questions concerning the nature of the world where the innocent suffer so regularly, and so much, and in many novels, no resolution is possible of the sort which regularly dispenses happiness to the innocent and punishment to the guilty at the conclusion of the classic detective novel.

The sufferings of Tey's characters go much beyond the social discomfort of being avoided by one's suspicious acquaintances or having to answer the sharply put questions of the Yard. Innocent sufferers represent every class of character: victim, suspect, criminal and detective. Some victims are wholly innocent (Patrick in *Brat,* the princes in *Time,* Christine Clay in *Shilling*). This is often not the case in detective fiction, where the sorrow for the death of the victim must not be allowed to detract from the interest in the investigation of the murder. Thus Roger Ackroyd is stingy, Philip Boyes is self-centered, and the King of Bohemia is a fool, though neither of the two former deserve being murdered. Even when innocent, the victim suffers off-stage, and death is instantaneous in most classic mysteries.

Tey employs two imaginative suffering-but-innocent criminals. Mrs. Wallis (*Queue*) is the technical criminal, but the prey of her "innocent" daughter. Brat Farrar is a criminal imposter but suffers three murderous attacks. An innocent suspect is hounded into a fall which results in a severe head injury. Another faints, suffers from exhaustion, and develops near pneumonia as a result of attempting to evade wrongful arrest. The detective suffers in conscience and in reputation for his persecution of a wrong suspect, and, later, spends a week in a hospital bed, and finally develops acute claustrophobia as a result of overwork. In Tey's third novel the treatment of innocent sufferer achieves a high point. No one who reads the novel will be likely to forget the sufferings of Mary Innes (*Pym*), whom the detective sentences to an extra-legal lifetime of restitution. Mary is first denied her deserved professional appointment by a prejudiced head mistress. Then she discovers that her best friend has committed murder on her behalf. The resolution of this novel is far from the return to innocence and order of the typical detective novel. The resolution of the fourth novel (*Franchise*), though less harsh, is similar. The innocent women lose their peaceful life and the means, their house and possessions, to an independence which they had only lately received and had much prized. The lightness of treatment and their strength and ability to cope do not detract from the resolution of this novel in which the regaining of their good name cannot begin to compensate them for their wholly undeserved losses. As Marion Sharpe says: "I suppose tomorrow life will begin again and be just the usual mixture of good and bad. But tonight it is just a place where dreadful things can happen to one" (*Franchise*, 233). In *The Daughter of Time* this theme reaches a climax. Richard III, though innocent as presented by Tey, suffers the loss of life, kingdom and future reputation, becoming the very type of the monstrous villain. The chief clue in the novel is a portrait which all viewers recognize as the face of someone who has felt, and suffered, a great deal. In this novel Tey charges historians with making apparent martyrs (suffering innocents) of actual criminals, as well as condemning the innocent Richard to undeserved calumny.

There are other uses of the suffering of the innocent in Tey, and it becomes one of her most consistent motifs, even when it is not the central theme of a novel. The regular appearance of this situation lessens the distance usually maintained between reader and what are often rather two-dimensional characters in much of detective fiction, and it is their ability to feel and their vulnerability to suffering which distinguish Tey's detectives.

Beyond her emphasis on the trials of the innocent, Tey's uses of the basic elements of detective fiction are less consistently unusual although all of her novels possess some important singularity.

The Detective, The Series Figure

The key element in detective fiction is, not surprisingly, the detective. Many series of works depend for their appeal on the strength and eccentricity of the central figure. While it is not necessary that he appear in numerous works (Sam Spade appears in only one novel), most great detectives do. Tey's primary difference from the pattern established by her famous peers is easy to spot. There is no great detective in her works. No one asks for an "Alan Grant" novel, or ever did. No "biography" of his life appears in any of the standard lists (*The Book of Sleuths, The Great Detectives*).

Detective Inspector Alan Grant does share the basic qualities of the gentlemen detectives of the twenties and thirties: financial and domestic independence, sartorial elegance, educated palate, ease in most surroundings and appearance: "If Grant had an asset beyond the usual ones of devotion to duty and a good supply of brains and courage, it was that the last thing he looked like was a police officer" (*Queue*, 11). His distinguishing feature is a Scottish ancestry. Like his peers he also has a special detecting technique (comparable to Poirot's "little grey cells") called "flair." Unlike Poirot, Grant is often taxed concerning his "flair," especially by his superiors: "Now, look here, Grant. Flair's flair. And you're entitled to your whack of it. But when you take to throwing it about in chunks it becomes too much of a good thing. Have a little moderation, for

Pete's sake" (*Love*, 220). The flair consists of an ability to read faces, an approach to apparent dead ends consisting of leaving them alone and returning later (mentally), and an ability which is never described but which consists of his quick perception of the essence of what is going on, whether or not, at the time, he understands what he sees. A part of his technique is illustrated in the following exchange with a suspect:

'The handle is a little silver saint with blue-and-red enamel decoration.'
'What?' she said involuntarily.
He was about to say, 'You've seen one like it?' but changed his mind.
He knew on the instant that she would say no, and that he would have given away the fact that he was aware that there was anything to be aware of (*Queue*, 24).

As a matter of fact the scene illustrates, in its context in the novel, one reason why Grant remains less than a great detective. He never finds out *why* that involuntary *what* is uttered. In the first novel in which he appears, Grant chases the wrong man across most of Britain to a confrontation in the Highlands in which the innocent man nearly dies. At the end of the novel, Grant thinks: "It had been so clear a case where evidence was concerned . . . he had been saved by the skin of his teeth and a woman's fair dealing . . . his thought went back over the trail that had led them so far wrong" (*Queue*, 222). Grant's case is perfect, but wrong. If not for a totally unexpected confession from a completely unsuspected person, Grant's evidence would have hanged an innocent man. Similarly, in the second novel, Grant corners a suspect in his hotel room, and, while Grant watches, the suspect escapes. It is the carefully-sought evidence provided by a girl which demolishes Grant's case against this suspect. In a very minor role, he prepares the Yard's case against the two innocent women in *The Franchise Affair*, a case which is demolished in court. Of the last three novels in which he appears, one is spent entirely in a hospital bed (alone), and one is spent on sick leave as Grant struggles with claustrophobia brought on by overwork. As early as the second novel he is reported wishing that "he was one of these marvelous creatures of super-instinct and infallible judgment who adorned the pages of detective stories, and not just a hard-working, well-meaning, ordinarily intelligent Detective Inspector" (*Candles*, 117).

Despite this somewhat overstated catalogue of Grant's shortcomings, it appears that divinity was intended to enter in at the nativity of the character, but that a writer of Tey's particular interests and talent ultimately found more appealing the vicissitudes of a more nearly mortal character. He is plainly intended to represent a superior (both logical and imaginative rather than plodding) approach to detection, contrasting with his associates and superiors as Dupin contrasts with Monsieur G., the Prefect of Police. His official "Watson" is described: "Williams was his opposite and his complement.... But he had terrier qualities that were invaluable in a hunt.... To Williams, Grant was everything that was brilliant and spontaneous" (*Love*, 88). Grant has a different "Watson" in each of the last two novels; in each case a young American is cast in the role and is duly impressed by the chance to sit at the feet of Scotland Yard. Each has a personal interest in the hunt and both are amateurs (any "Watson" might be considered, by definition, to be an "amateur," of course).

In the first novel Tey adapts characteristics of the great detective to other purposes, with a gentle ribbing of Holmesian leaps of inference as Grant dines at his favorite restaurant and converses with the maitre d', Marcel:

'...Ah, but Inspector Grant was a marvel. To have built a whole man out of a little dagger!... It was a thing *a faire peur*. If he, Marcel, was to bring him a fish fork with the entree, it might be made to prove that he had a corn on the left little toe.'
Grant disclaimed any such Holmesian qualities. 'The usual explanation advanced for such little mistakes is that the guilty one is in love' (*Queue*, 57-8).

Not the least of the irony of this scene is the fact that the "sinister Levantine" who stabbed a friend in the back with an Italian dagger, the man built by Grant, turns out to be a cockney charwoman.

While Grant has none of the eccentricities of the early detective titans and little of their genius, he does develop a Holmesian terseness and singlemindedness:

'Have you any hobbies?' the doctor asked ...
'No,' Grant said shortly.
'What do you do when you go on holiday?'
'I fish.'
'You fish?' ...And you don't consider that a hobby?'
'Certainly not.'
'What is it, then, would you say?'
'Something between a sport and a religion' (*Sands*, 7-8).

Grant's reappearance in 1949, after a virtual absence of 13 years, reveals him to be, as was Holmes after the Reichenbach Falls, a different man. Earlier interest in women had been confined to an unauthorized movement of the heart over Ray Marcable and a very casual friendship wiith Marta Hallard. In the last three novels, he and Marta are very good friends (*Love* and *Time*), he is fascinated by Lee Searle (*Love*), and he nearly succumbs to the attractions of a beautiful Scottish widow and retires (in *Sands*). But he is saved in time by that which is his first love, fresh evidence. He is at his most brilliant in *To Love and Be Wise* in which his much admired and admiring antagonist asks, "Are you the star turn at Scotland Yard?" and he replies, "Oh, no, I come in bundles" (241).

Tey is ahead of her time in recognizing while writing her first novel the limitations of the fiction in which the great detective is the center. Later, when her best works were written following the second World War, the frame and shape of things seemed so badly torn that not even a great detective could put them right. The great detective's lack of personal and even sexual relationships was no longer quite plausible, and the grotesquely distinguishing eccentricities of many series figures was an embarrassment. Though he remains an understatement, Grant's capacity for indignation and suffering make him sufficiently human to support his function as Tey's detective.

The Detective, The Amateurs

Tey's amateur detectives are more colorful than Alan Grant, although each appears in only one novel. Two function as the main detective and one is the central figure in a mystery in which he solves an old crime and is nearly killed by the murderer.

Miss Lucy Pym, comfort-loving author of a best seller, shrinks from the role of Providence which her fortuitous possession of otherwise unknown facts assigns to her. She is inquisitive and observant despite a natural indolence and the philosophy that one of the compensations of middle age is not having to do anything uncomfortable. A former schoolmistress and a temporary lecturer in a girls' school, she detects a furtiveness in the behavior of a student during an exam. She prevents the girl's cheating and later discovers the notes that were to have been used. When she discards the evidence of this crime, she sets in motion events which are widely destructive. The girl is given undeserved preferment by the headmistress who identifies with her as a less attractive and harder-working student than her fellows. The student dies in a deliberately-planned "accident," and the girl she supplanted gives up her future because of a friend's crime. By using her detecting abilities and deciding upon extra-legal justice of her own devising rather than the punishments of the law, Lucy Pym precipitates tragedy. The apparent wisdom of providing for mitigating circumstances rather than accepting the even-handed and blind justice of the law turns to folly. The results are a stark statement on the very popular tradition in detective fiction of "playing god." Grant is wrong when he sticks to the evidence and denies his knowledge of faces. Lucy Pym is wrong when she dispenses her own justice, giving more weight to psychology than to physical evidence. Josephine Tey does not give the reader an easy task. Unlike Grant, Pym must live with the knowledge that her wrong case against Mary Innes has resulted in a permanent punishment of the innocent. But what other solution existed? The conclusion of this novel is especially provocative when compared with the resolution of the typical detective novel. And it is not altogether surprising that this is Miss Pym's only venture into detection.

The second of Tey's amateurs finds himself at a low point in his quiet and pleasant but uneventful life when his phone rings. The call takes him away from his alien thought, "This is all you are ever going to have" (*Franchise*, 9), and its moment of subsequent panic is replaced by the twin delights of detection and romance. "To that douce country lawyer and gentleman, Robert Blair, Scotland Yard was as exotic as Xanadu, Hollywood, or parachuting," Tey tell us (12), and the best of her novels has begun.

At first Blair wishes strange females would not be inclined to throw themselves upon his protection. In looking at one of his new clients, he thinks: "For this money, Old Mrs. Sharpe was quite capable of beating seven different people between breakfast and lunch, any day of the week" (27). The following exchange between them is characteristic:

> 'You have my sympathy, Mr. Blair,' she said unsympathetically.
> 'Why, Mrs. Sharpe?'
> 'I take it that Broadmoor is a little out of your line.'
> 'Broadmoor!'
> 'Criminal lunacy.'
> 'I find it extraordinarily stimulating,' Robert said, refusing to be bullied by her (28).

Blair, though spirited, is entertainingly transparent, but he is indignant at the injustice he sees being perpetrated and his resolve and ingenuity at conducting an investigation upon which to build a defense in a criminal case are sufficient to win the reader and to hold one's interest.

Robert Blair is the only one of Tey's detectives to be given the dual roles of investigator and suitor. In both *The Franchise Affair* and Sayers' *Strong Poison*, the detective defends a woman accused of a crime, falls in love with her, and is rejected by her when the reader has been thinking (as Blair does, deep inside) that she would be doing pretty well to accept. Similarly, the ironic mockery that Marion directs toward Blair is very much like that which Harriet uses as a barrier between herself and Lord Peter. Blair is drawn with little subtlety, but his greatest virtue is his enjoyment of, and recognition of the justice of, Marion's mockery of his easeful life. Despite his successes, he too must accept providential help (as Grant does) in achieving a case which will not only free the innocent but also convict the guilty.

In *Brat Farrar* the detecting is the work of the central character, an impersonator who becomes the target of attacks by the man who killed the person being impersonated. Criminal and avenger, Brat accomplishes the unlikely feat of taking vengeance for a boy not known to have been murdered and earning his place in a family to which he does not know he belongs. Like Miss Pym, he must decide whether justice to the long-dead Patrick is worth the destruction of the Ashby family by the revelations of Simon's guilt.

Brat has more than a little in common with the heroines of the neo-gothic thriller like *Jane Eyre* or *Rebecca*. He is crippled, grows up in an orphanage, and is invited to accept an unholy bargain (by the murderer who knows that to reveal that murder was done he must also reveal that he is an imposter). He develops an "incestuous" love for his "sister," Nell, has his life threatened twice by riding accidents (once by a rogue horse), and, finally, in search of a literal family skeleton, drops from the end of a rope into a stone quarry on a rainy midnight. And like those heroines, he is ultimately rewarded with a real place in the family he has come to love and whose love and respect he has earned.

The plot sounds like a thriller, but the tone of the story is infused with tributes to the way of life at Latchetts, an English stud farm. There is no little irony in the coming to Latchetts of an illegitimate boy whose horsemanship was learned in America to set things right in an unmistakably English way.

The Plots

The plots of Tey's novels do not confer upon them that sort of indelible stamp which would cause readers to enter a bookstore and ask for "another Tey" as they do for another Christie. One perfect subject, *The Daughter of Time*, and one perfect and Ackroydal deceit, *To Love and Be Wise*, notwithstanding, Tey's plots are not generally what make her novels memorable.

Plot in the detective novel is not just a matter of how the final piece of a puzzle fits into the previously gathered ones to form a complete picture; it is also how the piece of information comes to the hands of the detective and whether the structure finally revealed unites all the facts and occurrences into a coherence.

Historically, chance or accident and suicide have been frowned upon as agents of discovery. The appearance is preserved that the intelligence of the detective is responsible for linking otherwise disparate elements of a case, or for providing the imaginative hypothesis whose testing will elicit the necessary information, or for escaping the confines of a limited view to see things in a new, true perspective and so solve the crime.

In Tey's novels, vital information often comes into the novel through the agency of Providence, the Press or the Public. The Press may be used by the police to circulate information and ask for public assistance, and the detective may then be given credit if such information is forthcoming. On the other hand, if an undesired newspaper story, like that pillorying the Sharpes, turns out to have positive effects, then Providence, or the Public, must be credited with the development, rather than the police. Providence may also be given credit for the solution to a murder which results from confession—Mrs. Wallis' confession, Simon's confession (once Brat has accused him), Beau's claiming of the shoe ornament, Heron Lloyd's confession. In five of her eight novels, Tey makes use of at least one confession. Two of these simply tidy things up: Frankie Chadwick's confession explains Betty Kane's fresh bruises, and Heron Lloyd's confession arrives with details just before Grant learns from his own discoveries that Lloyd's fingerprints were on the books of the murdered man. However, Mrs. Wallis' confession and Beau's are vital to the conclusions of the novels in which they occur. Without them, both novels would end with the reader as well as the detective left in the dark. The confirmation of Blair's theory concerning the whereabouts of Betty Kane rests upon the chance appearance before the eyes of a Copenhagen hotelier of an English gossip rag, the *Ack-Emma*, and upon his public spiritedness. Thus Providence assumes the shape of a Dane. In like manner, a man comes forward in the first novel to give evidence. This information, though misleading, is important to the action. False confessions are the policeman's horror, and there is a tacit confession by Mary Innes whose silence allows Miss Pym to continue thinking she created the accident which led to Barbara Rouse's death. This reliance upon Providence lessens as the series of novels continues, and Grant has a significant responsibility for plot resolution in the last three novels.

Several of the novels make use of an inversion of the normal sequence of events in detective fiction. In *The Franchise Affair* we assume the innocence of the accused and must proceed from the related hypothesis that the victim is really a criminal. This is a kind of inversion, though not the usual kind where the criminal is revealed and the reader's interest centers upon reconstruction, alone. A similar kind of inversion actually occurs, and is suggested by a barrage of clues, in *To Love and Be Wise*. Here, the ambiguity of the character of Leslie Searle may seem partly to account for his murder but actually provides numerous clues as to what really happened. In *Brat Farrar* the reader participates from the beginning in the scheme to defraud the Ashbys. Indeed, so involved does Tey make the reader that the chief interest in this adventure novel is not in what happened to Patrick, but in what will happen to the deserving, though criminal, Brat, when his imposture is, as it must be, discovered.

Clues mislead the reader and the detective. That is what they are put in detective fiction to do. The real clues should not appear to be clues at all—until the conclusion, that is. The best use of clues in Tey occurs in *To Love and Be Wise*, where they bombard the reader. Physical clues confirm the guilt of the killer in *A Shilling for Candles*. The clue which leads to her identity is a newspaper columnist's comment. Physical clues such as the blood on the dagger from the killer's hand play a large part in an era just before blood typing would have prevented the misuse of such information. A new lipstick and fresh bruises provide good clues to the questionable nature of Betty Kane's story. A wrong initial inference from clues (B Seven's poem) provides Grant a return of his health and the reader with a tour of the Hebrides, before the sands in the poem are equated with the Arabian desert rather than the Hebrides. The novel is much lengthened by this false trail.

In *The Daughter of Time* the nature of the subject produces an unusual plot. This novel is an excellent example of the difference between subject (story) and plot. The clues have been gone for hundred of years. No one can be interrogated. Everyone involved is already dead. A portrait gives impetus to Grant's flair and an American Watson appears and serves Grant, rather as Archie Goodwin does Nero Wolfe, as his legs. Grant asks the standard questions: what circumstances surrounded the death, what motives existed, what corroborating facts can be ascertained, and who benefitted. Here the focus must be on the investigation. An idea more potentially fascinating than the innocence of Richard III is emphasized. History is not fixed or set. It is not always true. It is, in fact, filled (American, Scottish and English history) with misinterpretations, half-truths and venerated scoundrels. The theme of the novel is its most important element, and the theme is *The Prevalence of Tonypandy*. Grant's painstaking reconstruction begins with an inversion, his doubt of Richard's guilt, and concludes with a comment on the origins of some kinds of "history."

Whatever the final disposition of clues, turns, surprises, climaxes and denouements, the satisfying conclusion to an engaging work is what counts with most readers. The early days of detective fiction saw the unnatural elevation of plot to the end which justified the novel. Tey's novels, flawed as the plots seem to be from this perspective, satisfy interests other than that for puzzle, although they do contain sufficient suspense and staggered and staggering developments to sustain the interest of any but the complete puzzle addict. And if Tey employs the *deus ex machina* consistently, at least the shape in which he appears varies significantly.

The Criminals and Their Crimes

The exotic and flamboyant master criminal, the Moriarty or Fu Manchu, would be as much out of place in Tey's fictions as his counterpart, the Great Detective. As Grant tells his young American colleague: "I know it's an awful come-down from the popular conception of the criminal as a dashing and cute character—but the criminal mind is an essentially silly one" (*Time*, 152). Likewise, the most bizarre crime is the stabbing in the back with an Italian dagger of a man in a theatre queue. In treating criminals and in devising crimes, Tey's methods are as restrained and her materials as realistic and lacking in melodrama as is her delineation of her detectives and her developing of plot. When Grant informs a highlander that he is after a murderer, he is told: "Why, drunk and incapable is the most horrible crime that this neighborhood has known since the flood" (*Queue*, 133). There are, on the other hand, a number of surprises in her novels in which the original crime turns out not to be a crime, and another crime is discovered. In two of the best novels, this development reverses the roles of criminal and victim.

Nothing else in Tey equals her audacity in bringing to the bar of accusation Henry VII of England, whom Grant accuses of complicity in the murder of the princes in the tower. Any discussion of her criminals must begin with him. Henry has, if guilty, cold-bloodedly eliminated two nearer claimants to the throne, claimants who happened to be his wife's brothers. The only justice which could reach him now is the justice of truth in the historical accounts of his life, and it is that which is proposed, though not yet achieved, by Brent Carradine through his book.

The first rule for criminals in detective fiction is that they must be amateurs. Professional criminals (guns-for-hire), cult members who kill for the sake of religion and madmen are all barred from participation because an individual motive, whether personal or professional (like Henry VII's), is one of the bases of detection. Not only are there clear motives in Tey, but there are some which are quite extraordinary. Of the criminals, three of the eight commit benevolent or altruistic crimes, acts committed entirely on behalf of someone else, and, while two deaths result from these crimes, none of the three criminals is punished (beyond a possible fine and a trial ending in acquittal) by law. Grant waxes eloquent on the un-

Englishness of the crime committed by the "Levantine," but the person who committed that stabbing (a man, the police surgeon had said) is a very English cockney woman whose years as a charwoman must have strengthened both her arms and her resolve. Mrs. Wallis protected her daughter from the man who had in his pocket a gun with which to shoot her before turning it on himself. She merely anticipated his suicide. The law cannot touch the actress, the villain of the novel, for whose sake the deed was done.

The other two altruistic criminals are very different. One (Beau Nash) kills as a result of an accident which was designed to injure. The object of her altruism bears the blame, instead of being the recipient of the largesse intended. But the perpetrator of the deed is not revealed or punished. The third altruistic criminal (Lee Searle) plans murder to revenge the death by suicide of her only relative, but abandons her plan, leaving the intended victim to be blamed for murder in her own disappearance. Not only does she escape with the threat of only a fine, but she earns Grant's admiration.

Two other adolescents commit crimes and pay for them. Betty Kane's crime was to lodge a false complaint of kidnapping and assault against two women chosen at random because their house seemed a good prop for her story. Her motive was to hide her own runaway trip with a married salesman. Her punishment is to be exposed in court as an immoral liar. In addition, the reader discovers that it is the salesman's wife, Frankie, who beat her. It is of Betty Kane that Tey's detective makes a statement that sums up his view that criminal tendencies are born in people as monstrous vanity and colossal selfishness. Such individuals cannot be changed: "You might as well talk of 'reforming' the colour of one's eyes" (*Franchise*, 176). It is not reform but retribution that Robert Blair wants: "He might not go all the way with Moses ... but he certainly agreed with Gilbert: the punishment should fit the crime" (*Franchise*, 176).

Simon Ashby is another cold-blooded adolescent, and he kills his twin at the age of thirteen to inherit the family estate. He fulfills all the promise of his youth in his maturity by making three attempts on the life of the man who impersonates the dead twin. In the third attempt he dies himself.

Two professionally-motivated crimes round out the list. An American woman seer kills a famous actress to make her professional fortune by having her prediction come true, and a professional archaeologist kills to steal the secret of a famous lost city stumbled upon by the young flier he murders.

The major crimes are set against a background in which the habitual or professional criminal makes a regular appearance, but never at the center of the action. Hamburg Willie's impersonation is detected through his love of cherry brandy, and Benny Skoll's unfortunate tendency to hang the loot from his most recent burglary upon his current companion leads to his arrest. Grant is aided in the first novel by a highly successful racketeer imported from America who, though cold and ruthless, is a sporting man and helps Grant to discover the identity of the murdered man. Grant concludes, looking at his get-well cards in a novel published twenty years later, that "the really likeable old lags were an out-moded type, growing fewer and fewer daily. Their place had been taken by brash young thugs with not a spark of humanity in their egocentric souls, as illiterate as puppies and as pitiless as a circular saw" (*Time*, 87).

Women and children are first in Tey; she uses a woman or an adolescent as the criminal in the first six of her eight novels. She is more consistent with tradition in having her criminals most often find their just deserts outside the punishment of the law, through accident, suicide or through having committed a justifiable crime from which they will somehow be spared the consequences. The use of the motivation of friendship or love—the altruistic motive—and her use of the adolescent as a morally responsible agent of death or malice are her best achievements in treating the criminal. Beau Nash and Betty Kane are particularly chilling beings.

The Victims

A victim, like a proper Victorian child, should be seen but not heard. Slight acquaintance on the part of the reader prevents messy sympathy from intruding.

A prominent feature of the detective fiction of Josephine Tey is an indentification of victim and suspect. Victims turn out to be suspect, as victims, and suspects are threatened, victimized and imperiled, becoming VICTIMS. Official victims have the traditional minor role, except as a reconstructed personality. Nevertheless, the VICTIMS (persecuted innocents who are not the apparent victims of the central or main crime with which the plot is concerned) are found in every category of character, from detective to such minor characters as Mrs. Wynn (Betty Kane's foster mother) and Zoe Kentallen (victim of high taxes, small inheritance, and widowhood—as well as an abruptly curtailed romance with Grant).

There is a natural correspondence of victim and suspect when suicide or careless accident is believed to be the cause of death, as in the deaths of Patrick Ashby and Bill Kenrick. But a cardinal rule of detective fiction is that suicide and accident are not allowed as causes of the chief death. Victims in the Tey novels are not always easily identifiable. The apparent victim in the first novel (*Queue*) is the murdered man. But since he is intent upon killing someone else, and is forestalled by his own death, he cannot be classified unequivocally as victim. On the other hand the woman who actually stabs him to death is herself the VICTIM of a maternally blind view of her actress daughter. In a real sense, Bert Sorrell is a VICTIM of the actress.

The victim in the second novel is unmourned by professional associates, but she is actually a sympathetic and kind person, though distrustful of people. The basis of the mistrust is clear when a mob of "admirers" trample her cottage and make a circus of her funeral.

The victim in the third novel (*Pym*) is a cheat and shamelessly curries favor with the headmistress of the school she attends. She cheats for "firsts," not simply to pass. In addition, she accepts a post she does not deserve. The injury which causes her death was not intended to be fatal, but Barbara Rouse is quite typical of the unattractive victims in classic fiction whose deaths leave few mourners.

In two novels (*Franchise* and *Love*) Tey makes the supposed victim the perpetrator of a hoax, and thus the criminal, instead. Both these situations are interesting, although only one involves a surprise. The real victims in each book are the accused criminals, in fact, so that the reversal is complete. The Sharpes are plainly VICTIMS, losing their home and possessions after being subjected to abuse and mob violence. Walter Whitmore is the only VICTIM who might be said to have benefitted (or perhaps it is only his fiance who benefits) from his VICTIMization.

Blameless children are the victims in two novels, and the specific details of the crimes are left somewhat hazy. In both cases the children must be killed so that they will not inherit (an estate in *Brat*, a kingdom in *Time*). Two victims are highly independent and reserved, a fact which makes the identification of their bodies at first a matter of some doubt. Both Chris Clay and Bill Kenrick are killed by individuals whose motives are to improve their professional reputations. The impersonality of the motive for these four crimes and five deaths makes each death seem more wasteful, especially as the reconstruction of the victim's characters after their deaths (for Patrick Ashby, Clay, and Kenrick) reveals them to have been admirable individuals. In contrast, one apparent VICTIM, Marguerite Merriam (*Love*) a suicide, is revealed as utterly selfish and unworthy of her cousin's admiration.

There are second VICTIMS in two novels (*Pym* and *Franchise*). Mary Innes is first devastated by not receiving the appointment she deserves for her exceptionally fine record in school, and then by an accusation and punishment for a crime she did not commit. This particular inversion of roles is among Tey's best achievements. The other VICTIM is Mrs. Wynn, whose experience during the trial of her foster daughter is described as a "crucifixion."

The Suspects

In Tey's world, the suspect's lot is not a happy one. And for Inspector Grant, the wrongly-accused person is a recurring nightmare. Whether for readers of detective fiction the criminal serves as a scapegoat for the punishment of a common sin, the suspects in a murder novel are often far from innocent. Still, it is usually true that their guilts do not include involvement in the primary crime.

Two suspects are really victims, the Sharpes and Walter Whitmore. Two others, suspected of suicide, are actually victims of murder, instead of the suicide and accident to which their deaths are at first attributed. They cannot suffer as a result of being suspected, except by reputation (in memory). Those wrongly suspected are Lamont (who is hounded from his London home, nearly dies in a fall while attempting to evade arrest, is charged with murder in front of his sweetheart, and is tried for murder), Tisdall (who is hounded into flight and illness and of whom Grant thinks: "From now on Robert Tisdall would be no more to him than the bluebottle he swatted on the windowpane, a nuisance to be exterminated as quickly and with as little fuss as possible" (*Candles*, 69), Innes (who is given a "life sentence" by Miss Pym), the Sharpes (who lose their home and most of their possessions), Walter Whitmore (who only experiences the minor discomfort of being suspected by everyone), and Richard III (who has been wrongly suspected and "convicted" by historians for over 500 years).

Just as King Henry VII is an exceptionally bold stroke as villain, so Richard III is a particularly long-suffering suspect, and a very good example of the damage that occurs when a crime is not solved and the innocent remain under suspicion. In Tey, it is never general suspicion that hangs over one's head, it is the obvious, direct, and announced suspicion that falls upon the person against whom a case is being assembled by the police who confidently expect to come up with enough evidence for a warrant in the immediate future.

Grant's flair operates to give him a just assessment of all those he suspects. But he can never disregard the physical evidence that the detective novel of Tey's time seems to be all about. He is a sensitive and reasonable man, caught as detective in a world where figures are supposed to be two-dimensional ciphers, constantly finding his judgment of faces, personalities and other reflections of character refuted by some bit of button, or scar, or left-handedness, or shoe in the river, or suitcase, or legacy. The tension between Grant's judgment and the physical evidence which he collects is one of the graces of Tey's fiction. Her substitution of a detailed and sympathetic presentation of the trials of one suspect for the interrogation and investigation of several red herrings is a major departure from detective tradition and the basis for her favorite theme, the trials of the innocent. Her discerning exploration of the suspect as victim, and her extension of peril to detectives and supposed criminals, provides a new dimension to the arrangement of the basic elements of detective fiction which essentially retain their traditional forms in her novels but which are combined to make new statements and raise new questions.

*   *   *

If the bare bones of the detective story consist of its detective, plot, criminal, victim and suspects, few authors and readers find the skeletal structure sufficient. Among the less vital but equally distinctive elements used to add substance (or padding, in some cases) to the structure, there are some of which Tey makes noteworthy use. These include three conventions, those of *armchair detection, fair play,* and the *locked room*, and a focus on *police procedures* and the use of a *love interest*, along with some others more incidentally introduced, all of which attest to her mastery of the major and minor aspects of mystery fiction.

To Love and Be Wise is a *fair play* novel. There is no point where the narrator comes forward to say that the reader has all the clues, but clues are plentiful and significant throughout the novel. Leslie Searle receives no mail. Everyone who meets Searle observes that there is something unreal, demonic or otherworldly about him. Lavinia Fitch describes it as a feeling of wrongness. His beauty seems to Liz as some morning of the world inhumanness. His charm is all powerful, and he is reported to have talked with Miss Easton-Dixon "like a couple of housewives swapping recipes" (77). Most important, the passage that sets off a warning buzz in Grant's head is provided for the reader, as well as the reason for its doing so, the report from the States and the theatre *Who's Who* passage. In this novel, even the display of shoes which triggers the final association in Grant's mind with the missing parcel or object from the space in Leslie Searle's bag is described. And to make the clues for the reader even better, and in the most approved tradition, the missing parcel is "suspected" early of being shoes and then this solution is dismissed because it is men's shoes that Grant is looking for, then. No other Tey novel plot is used to involve the reader in the precise sense in which *fair play* is customarily used.

In her last novel Tey sets the scene in circumstances which meet the requirements for a *locked room* crime, a sleeping compartment on ·a train. But the crime is at first thought to be an accident, and there is no reason to investigate the fellow inhabitants of the train. A narrowed circle of suspects also seems to exist in the first novel, until it becomes apparent that almost any number of people could have joined and exited from the queue without their comings and goings being remarked. However, in *Miss Pym Disposes* there is a *locked-room* crime. During an early morning practice in a gymnasium, a student is injured when a boom falls on her head. Only the visiting lecturer is about that morning and she sees wet footprints coming from the gym. She later finds a shoe ornament on the gym floor. "Nature's abhorrence," the school vacuum, has cleaned just before the practice so these circumstances isolate the scene of the crime, and the detective and the reader both know the circumstances. While the amateur detective's attention is drawn to the vital clues whose meaning is conferred by means of the locked-room situation, it is a long time before the final piece of evidence comes into her hand.

The *armchair detection* in Tey is done from the even more restricted confines of a hospital bed. Grant's recovery from injuries sustained while chasing a suspect is aided by amusements brought him by Marta Hallard. Normal reading materials fail, but a pile of portrait reproductions appeals to his consistent interest in faces. Drawn to the sensitive face of one of the figures, he discovers it to be a portrait of Richard III. His interest in the possessor of this face is aroused, and he arranges with Marta for a researcher. To the purists, any armchair detective who can have evidence brought to him is beyond the most strict boundaries of the form. But the evidence brought in this case is available to everyone, not something that visiting the scene of the crime would have put before the detective. The investigation gives Grant a chance to be a policeman in a new context, and the success of the investigation proves the validity of the policeman's approach to truth. As in the original instance of armchair detection, the purpose of the activity is not only to find the answer, but also to provide an alternative solution to the official version of what happened.

As the plausibility of the amateur detective being called in to discover secrets that have eluded the police becomes more and more strained, and the typical detective figure dwindles toward normality, officialdom looms larger. *Police procedures*—and the routine by means of which teams of investigators, following in the steps of Prefect G., comb available territories for information and subject what is found to minute scientific analysis—become increasingly prominent in detective fiction. Few have Holmes' resources in their sitting rooms. The *police procedural* novel has come to mean something fairly specific in the 1970s, but the scientific and technical aspects of investigative work, especially as applied by extensive institutional resources, have always had a share in the interest of a fictional form in which the investigation, and the scientific principles of cause and effect—and evidence-required-for-proof—were key distinguishing features from the beginning.

In Tey, Grant is the central figure, but he participates in an organization in which many individuals contribute to the investigative process. For example, subordinates question suspects, disguise themselves to learn neighborhood or church or household gossip, comb mountains of public responses to Press requests for help, and perform laboratory tests. Less common is the practice of Grant's superior (Barker, then Bryce) deciding when he has spent enough time upon a case, when to prosecute, when the case is to be dropped. In several novels, Grant points out that the conduct of the case is not in his hands alone, that he will have to travel up to London to lay matters before his chief before the next step will be decided upon. Another aspect of the police procedure element in the novels is the fact that more than one crime is being investigated at one time. Grant incidentally "nails" Wee Archie, by picking his pocket, while looking for clues to B Seven in the Hebrides. Herbert, though not guilty of the death of his sister, is found to be wanted in a number of other countries. Grant discovers a plot which has succeeded in smuggling an alien (patriot) into the country while looking for the murderer of Christine Clay. There is very little of the tone and atmosphere of the contemporary police procedural in Tey, but there is far more of the apparatus, from the laboratory reports to the discussions with the superior, of police work in her fiction than in that of most of her contemporaries.

The *love interest* is the most common non-vital element in mystery fiction. Described by Dorothy Sayers as a "fettering convention," it is found in mysteries as diverse as *The Moonstone* and *The Black Marble* and is staple in the Had-I-But-Known and the neo-gothic sort. Generally speaking, Tey avoids the temptation to fill in pages with the doings of individuals otherwise unrelated to the plot who can be happily united at the conclusion of the novel. Instead, she employs the love interest to reveal information important to the central situation in the novel, rather than as a diversionary device or as a sort of "love" rather than "comic" relief.

None of Tey's love attachments occupies much narrative space (except for the instance involving the lawyer-detective) but, in the first novel, two love interests shed light on the murder investigation. Grant wonders that his suspect, Lamont, can be so cold-blooded as to take time (as an escaping murderer) for love-making. His certainty of Lamont's guilt is also undermined by his admiration for Lamont's young woman, Miss Dinmont. This love affair provides counter evidence to that overwhelming physical evidence which points to Lamont's guilt. Grant's "flair" must not seem to be intuitive, or the detection aspect of the novel will fail, and the love affair supports his impression that Lamont is innocent. Grant's attraction to the actress, Ray Marcable, suggests the beginning of a love interest, but then Grant subjects her performance in a hit play to close scrutiny. Her character as revealed by her merciless upstaging of all her fellow actors cures Grant of an affection unbecoming a detective, but it is also a factor crucial to the murder.

The most serious love affair is the respectable Robert Blair's pursuit of the prickly Marion Sharpe. It provides impetus for his investigation and becomes a means of contrasting the two worlds they represent. Grant's friendship with Marta Hallard never approaches an affair, and he is in a weakened state when he nearly succumbs to Lady Zoe Kentallen. Even here (*Sands*), however, the attraction of what Zoe represents makes possible Grant's reaffirmed choice of the life of the detective, rather than that of a domestically-settled retirement.

A more original love interest provides the motivation for two crimes. The special love, or bonding, which the biblical David had for Jonathan exists between two friends and between two cousins. And in each case, when one is injured, the other takes revenge. Beau Nash arranges an accident for the girl who takes the job Mary Innes should have had. And Lee Searle plans the murder of the man she believes caused her cousin's suicide. The interest in these two situations is that in each the special friendship exists between two women. And in each the vengeance is cleverly plotted and perfectly executed. In her treatment of the relationships of Beau Nash with Mary Innes and Lee Searle with Marguerite Merriam, Tey makes her most uncommon use of the common motif of the love interest.

Of the many other favorite minor devices of the mystery author to be found in Tey, several deserve brief mention. One is the detective's tendency to take the law into his own hands. The most conspicuous example is Miss Pym's decision to secure an *illegal justice* and punish the guilty herself so as to spare the innocent families and the reputation of the school. The result of her decision is a strong argument against this tendency in detectives. On the other hand, less serious instances of the tendency occur. Grant desires entrance into the flat of a murdered man and secures the assistance of a fellow tenant, a painter:

'Give me a leg up,' said Grant.... As he drew his foot from the painty clasp of his

assistant, he said, 'I might tell you that you are conniving at a felony. This is housebreaking and entirely illegal.'
'It is the happiest moment of my life,' the artist said. 'I have always wanted to break the law ... and now to do it in the company of a policeman is joy that I did not anticipate my life would ever provide' (*Queue*, 76).

Two rituals common in detective fiction are *the hunt* and *the testing*. Tey's main use of the hunt is in her first novel where Grant comments: "There was a distinctive thrill in hunting your man in open country. It was more primitive and more human, less mechanized than the soulless machinery that stretched and relaxed noiseless steel tentacles on Thames bank. It was man against man" (*Queue*, 125). The hunt ritual in the final novel is transformed into a quest across similar territory in Scotland through which Grant searches for the "singing sands", and, incidentally, his health.

The theme of testing is more pervasive: all Tey's detectives are tested. Brat's is the most severe. As a criminal and imposter, he must be rigorously tested, morally, socially and physically, before he can be admitted to the rewards of the situation into which he comes as an interloper. He declines the first offer to become a criminal, and, when he finally accepts, his failure to find work, his love of horses, and his lonely life play a crucial role in his decision. The ultimate test is Simon's offer to keep silent (about Brat's imposture) if Brat will keep silent (about Patrick's murder).

Grant's testing in the last novel is by means of the shameful effects of claustrophobia, and its effects are realistically described. Detectives suffer all kinds of difficulties and are tested in countless ways, especially in novels of the hard-boiled variety, but it is rare to see respectable detectives suffer mental stress of this kind, which carries with it the disdain of Grant's chief and the pity of his subordinate, Williams.

The deep conservatism toward law and order coupled with the desire to see real justice done characteristic of the genre is consistent throughout Tey. Grant's attitude is summed up in an unusual statement to his adversary, Lee Searle, to whom he admits that he understands perfectly how one might want to commit murder as she had planned:

There are quite a few people I would willingly have killed in my time. Indeed, with prison no more pentitential than a not very good public school, and with the death sentence on the point of being abolished, I think I'll make a little list, *a la* Gilbert, then when I grow a little aged I shall make a total sweep—ten or so for the price of one—and retire comfortably to be well cared-for for the rest of my life" (*Love*, 250).

There is also in Tey the less attractive but characteristic ethnocentrism of the classic detective novel: Grant is casually chauvinistic toward foreigners (his attitude toward Americans is somewhat ambivalent, though negative). Scottish nationalism is treated with the same disdain as Irish rebellion. Class stereotyping is as common as that by nationality. Tey's and Grant's basic acceptance of the social order is occasionally contradicted by the novels, especially in such characters as Marion Sharpe and Lee Searle, whose behavior is unconventional if certain of their attitudes are not.

In her utilization of these minor conventions and motifs, most particularly in her adaptation of the love interest, Tey displays the same mastery of the form that is evident in her handling of the more basic ingredients of the detective novel.

* * *

Apart from her utilization and adaptation of major and minor elements of the mystery novel, Tey adds to her novels the richness of an individual vision and the not inconsiderable narrative and stylistic strengths of a professional dramatist. There are three areas in which her achievement involves the employment of characters or themes of a particularly individual sort. Specifically, she incorporates with great success the results of her own experience and expertise in the theatre, she uses her interest in history to provide unusual subjects for detection, and she creates a set of formidable women characters (her Not-Married women) whose vitality threatens to break the confines of the form in which they are placed.

The most pervasive in her fiction of these individual topics is the Theatre. Much of the reflection of the theatre in Tey's novels results from a subject matter which consistently includes actors, actresses, theatres and events connected directly with the world of the theatre. The striking setting of the first crime is a theatre queue. The dagger which is used in the crime was earlier used in a school production of *Macbeth*, and the character of Lady Macbeth is a false clue. The most important continuing character other than Grant is a leading actress, Marta Hallard, who is Grant's window on the theatre. A famous film star is the victim in the second novel (*Shilling*), and a famous stage star is the "villain," although not the criminal, in the first novel (*Queue*). A leading radio personality is the suspect in the sixth novel (*Love*) and the character of the dead actress, Marguerite Merriam, an important factor in the plot. Grant's major clue in this novel comes from his browsing in a copy of *Who's Who in the Theatre*. Grant discusses this case with Marta and is convinced that actors have a perception of human motive that other people do not have.

A second aspect of the theatre in her novels is impersonation and imposture, "acting" in real life. Her most famous imposter is Brat Farrar, who assumes the identity of the vanished Patrick Ashby. The exhilirating experience of this kind of acting is given in Brat's reaction:

> He had expected to be nervous and a little ashamed. And it had not been in the least like that. It had been one of the most exciting things he had ever done. A wonderful tight-rope sort of thing. He had sat there and lied and not even been conscious that he was lying, it had been so thrilling. It was like riding a rogue; you had the same wary, strung up feeling....
> So this, he thought, was what sent criminals back to their old ways when there was no material need. This breathless, step-picking achievement, this subsequent intoxication of achievement (*Brat*, 41-42).

The thrill described results partly from acting before an audience who do not realize they are watching a performance, but whose unfavorable reaction would spell disaster to the star.

Another major acting performance occurs in *To Love and Be Wise*. Lee Searle is first mistaken for a man. Then she recognizes the freedom of movement possible to a man but not to a woman and assumes a second identity as a man. This second identity suggests a way of carrying out a desired revenge upon the man who jilted and caused the suicide of her only relative.

A different kind of act is put on in *The Franchise Affair*. Betty Kane's demure, innocent school-girl manner is totally at odds with the chocolate-eating vamp Frankie Chadwick discovers in bed at her husband's cottage and with the young "wife" who laps up cream while on a business trip to Copenhagen with her "husband." The most tantalizing thing about Betty Kane, like her original, Elizabeth Canning, is that the reader is not sure her hidden self is ever revealed. Like other characters in Tey whose crimes are not justified, she is depicted as elementally vicious. The role of injured innocence she assumes may actually be consistent with her experience in a world that is not inclined to give her instantly every thing she desires. Her acting in accusing the Sharpes of abducting and beating her is faultless.

Personal references to the theatre and imagery drawn from it reinforce the connection between Josephine Tey and Gordon Daviot. Marta asks Grant for his views on the investigation being conducted more or less before her eyes in Salcott St. Mary:

> 'Tell me, Alan, it wouldn't be indiscreet or unprofessional, would it, to tell me who is your own favourite for the part?'
> 'The part?'
> 'The killer.'
> 'It would be both unprofessional and indiscreet. But I don't think there is any

wild indiscretion in telling you that I don't think there is one' (*Love*, 171).

Grant goes on to describe his feeling about the case as one of having an orchestra pit between him and reality.

Tey's typically ironic view (and the detective fiction author's love of "in" references) appears as Grant enters a theatre to confer with Marta:

'Perhaps they think I look like an author, he thought, and wondered who had written *Faint Heart*. No one ever did know who had written a play. Playwrights must lead blighted lives. Fifty to one, on an actuary's reckoning against their play running more than three weeks; and then no one even noticed their name on the programme.

And something like a thousand to one against any play ever getting as far as rehearsals even' (*Love*, 229).

An additional personal reference is Marta's attempts to talk a playwright into writing a play for her, and when success seems in sight, being told that the woman is going to write another of her "awful little detective stories" instead (*Time*, 90). Grant sympathizes with Marta's vexation because "good plays were the scarcest commodity in the world and good playwrights worth their weight in platinum" (90). As he pursues the character of Richard III, Grant is described as knowing all about the breaking of the direct line of the throne of England because he had in his youth seen *Richard of Bordeaux* at the New Theatre four times (Daviot's hit play of 1933).

The world of illusion and artifice in the theatre gives it a basic kinship with detective fiction, since in the latter the primary need for deception means that much appearance will be contrary to reality. Tey's knowledge of the theatre extends the potential of her detective fiction and underscores this kinship.

The unusual subjects provided by history to *The Daughter of Time* and *The Franchise Affair* are well known. Less often discussed is Tey's focus on history-making in the former novel.

The use of historical research as the basis for a detective story plot succeeds for readers to the extent that their knowledge of British history is sufficient for their interest to be aroused but insufficient for them to know beforehand the details which Grant and Carradine's researches reveal—or, to the extent that the spirit of the chase can be said to be possible within the limits of Grant's hospital room. *The Daughter of Time* has been sharply criticized by historians for its failure to be good history, for lack of attribution of sources, for attacks upon professional historians, and, especially, for not agreeing with the received view of Richard III.

Examined as detective fiction, rather than history, the novel illustrates the techniques of detection used in the examination of materials unlike the customary evidence uncovered during an investigation. Historical documents, books, journals and even novels become the repositories of clues and the only source for "statements" of suspects. Brent Carradine's familiarity with the British Museum library coupled with Grant's C.I.D. experience forms an effective means of bringing history to life and light. One of the book's strengths is an assumption that the historical figures can be analyzed as though they were contemporaries, motivated by like concerns and subject to the same laws of human behavior.

The novel contains a second use of history, its examination of the process of history-making. By considering Scottish martyrs, the Boston Massacre, and the invasion of Tonypandy, Wales, by British troops, Tey organizes support for her central idea, the innocence of Richard III. As she illustrates, there is a human tendency in the collecting and preserving of information to create heroes, martyrs and villains in the historical accounts so that the truth of an occurrence is altered to fit a mythic theory. Those who know the truth do not speak up, and fiction prevails as history. Grant's cousin observes that people do not like to have their views of history changed. Historians have been proving her point ever since the publication of the book. Tey's complaint is that much of history is fiction; historians complain that her fiction is not history, but the debate is intriguing.

An old mystery is the basis for *The Franchise Affair*. Elizabeth Canning disappeared on her way home in 1753. Upon reappearing some weeks later, she claimed to have been kidnapped, held prisoner and starved by women in an old house which she described. One of the accused women was actually convicted before evidence was produced to give her an alibi. Elizabeth Canning was eventually convicted of perjury and transported to the United States where she lived out her life in apparent married respectability. Tey uses this mystery and hypothesizes a solution, that Elizabeth was with a lover (a solution suggested by earlier retellings of the tale). The unique aspect of Tey's treatment is that she views the events from the perspective of the accused women and makes the theme of her novel their public pillorying. The addition of a love affair heightens the effect of the women's plight by reflecting it in the eyes of a sympathetic witness.

There is, after all, a natural correspondence between the work of the historian and that of the detective. Both attempt to arrive at the truth by means of reconstruction in which each bit of information has its place in the final picture. Minutia become significant—bits of fabric, an entry in a household accounts book—and a successful theory must account for all the facts. What really happened is the question each seeks to answer. Tey's novels make less consistent use of history than her plays, but the use in one instance is remarkable, and the language is richer for "Tonypandy," too.

Tey was not an avowed feminist, but the lives of her main female characters are a feminist statement. They are all happily Not Married. The one-act play, *Clarion Call*, contains an observation that the demise (or disgraced survival) of marriage began with a working woman because the first person who did not want a husband was "the first girl that found a whole week's wages in her hand on Friday night instead of what was left over after the pub and the 'dogs' and the 'pools,' and she started a new fashion. A hundred years from now it'll be a disgrace to have a husband. They'll have to be hidden in back rooms out of sight, like keeping pet rabbits in a tenement," (in *Leith Sands and other Short Plays*). Tey's women characters are seldom married, and they fall into three categories: those who are not married yet, those who are widows, and those who are not married, by their own choice, and do not intend to become so, even though they are not yet past everything but tea and quadrille. It is those in the last group whose characteristics contribute most to Tey's novels.

Four women in Tey's mystery fiction represent a balanced range of reactions to the non-married state, and many minor characters buttress the positions taken by the primary four.

The reasons of each of the four for not being married indicate this range. Marta Hallard has no room in her life for Alan Grant—she plans to become a "Dame," not a "Mrs." Lucy Pym thinks wistfully of being cherished for a change, but is brought up short at the thought that the cherishing would have to be mutual, "she would inevitably have to mend socks, for instance. She didn't like feet" (*Pym*, 51). There are several reasons why Marion Sharpe refuses the proposal of Robert Blair: "For one, if a man is not married by the time he is forty, then marriage is not one of the things he wants out of life. Just something that has overtaken him; like flu and rheumatism and income-tax demands. I don't want to be just something that has overtaken you" (*Franchise*, 234). She goes on to tell Blair: "You, on the other hand, are used to being spoiled by Aunt Lin—Oh, yes, you are!—and would miss far more than you know all the creature comforts and the cosseting that I wouldn't know how to give you—and wouldn't give you if I knew how" (235), that she would not be an asset to his law practice, that he has his aunt and she, her mother, with whom they are accustomed to living. But her last reason is the most revealing: "You see, I am *not* a marrying woman. I don't want to have to put up with someone else's crotchets, someone else's demands.... There are a hundred thousand women just panting to look after some man's cold, why pick on me?" (235). Lee Searle makes no comment on the subject, possibly because she has the most original and compelling reason of the four—it would surely be inconvenient to someone habituated to spending half the year as a man (a photographer) and half as a woman (a painter) to be encumbered with a husband.

Beyond their preference for the not-married state, the four have little in common. The most unconventional, Lee Searle, is also the most shadowy because until the end of the novel she is seen only as her alter ego, Leslie Searle. Yet her literary kinship with Irene Adler is unmistakable. She dresses in men's clothing because of the freedom it provides, as Irene did. She is American, as Irene was. She is successful at her career (in fact, two), as Irene was. She makes up her mind not to commit the crime she had in mind, the murder of Walter Whitmore to avenge his treatment of Marguerite Merriam, because she is fair. Irene decides not to mail the compromising photograph because she no longer wishes to take revenge. Both are daring and extremely attractive. Grant's attitude toward Lee is very similar to Holmes' toward Irene:

> . . .he had thought for only one woman. That woman in Hampstead.
> Never, even at his most callow, had he gone to see any woman with eagerness as great as the one that was taking him to Holly Pavement this morning. . . .
> Damn the woman, he was beginning to admire her. As a colleague she would be wonderful (*Love,* 237).

Marta Hallard's career is her single concern. In one novel, she reveals every ability to minister to the comfort of Alan Grant, and he is suitably impressed:

> What a woman . . . . He had always thought that the first requisite in a wife was intelligence, and now he was sure of it. There was no room in his life for Marta, and none in her life for him; but it was a pity, all the same. A woman who could announce a surprising development in a homicide case without babbling on the telephone was a prize, but one who could in the same breath ask if he had had breakfast and arrange to supply him with the one he had not had was above rubies (*Love,* 177).

Still, just when a routine seems established, she decides that she has had enough of Salcott St. Mary and returns to London to await the rehearsal of her next play. Grant's view of her is consistent: "No questions, no hints, no little feminine probings. In her acceptance of a situation she was extraordinarily masculine. Perhaps it was this lack of dependence that men found intimidating" (200).

Like Marta and Lee, Lucy Pym has a career. She is different in having arrived in it by accident. Having read a number of psychology books to see if any made sense, she then wrote one herself which became a best seller. "Little Miss Pym" with her button nose and stuborn timidity is afraid to go to the inquest lest she stand and blurt out all she intends to conceal. Despite her life in London as a successful author, Lucy's girlishness offers the greatest possible contrast to Lee and Marta. Yet she, too, for all her difference, is a keen observer of her surroundings and is as firm as they in enjoying the life she has, free from domestic ties.

Unlike the other three, Marion Sharpe has no career. Perhaps she is the only one with the leisure for romance. Marion can hardly be considered modern and is far from being a superwoman. Her "shapes" don't stand up, and she has no career. Nevertheless, she is sensible, perceptive and strong. Unconcerned about housework and cooking, she still has the necessary taste and tact to provide appropriately when necessary for guests. She drives a golfball like a man. To Robert Blair, she looks the sort of woman who would have a stake as her natural prop, if stakes were not out of fashion. When she is told she should have been a nurse, she says: "Not me. I have no patience with people's fads. But I might have been a surgeon" (*Franchise*, 139). Her gentle mocking of Blair's easy life and formal manner make their "courtship" an entertaining spectacle. When he asks her to marry him (on the ninth green—his plan to ask her in the club house over tea is spoiling his game), and she declines what might be thought a handsome offer, it is perfectly clear that the territory of this novel is not that of ordinary popular fiction.

In less important roles, other Non-Married women appear. Bea Ashby (*Brat*) takes over the care of five orphaned nieces and nephews and continues her profession of horse trainer so successfully that she preserves the children's estate intact. Once they are settled she continues her career on a stud farm in Ireland. Lavinia Fitch and Miss Easton-Dixon (*Love*) pursue writing careers and have no room in their domestic establishments for a man. Lydia Keats (*Shilling*), lecturer and seer, so determinedly pursues her career that she commits murder to further it. Henrietta Hodge (*Pym*) draws from her life as Headmistress at Leys the satisfactions other women find in domestic or romantic relationships.

The Not-Married woman adds a quality to Tey's fiction which takes it beyond the normal boundaries of its kind and time. She is not to be confused with the bright and forthright girl, heir of Beatrice and Rosaline, who appears rather more often in detective fiction (and elsewhere in Tey). She is older (in her thirties and forties) and wiser, and she does not use her wits and energy to attract the right man—she uses them to make and enjoy her own way in the world.

The most important qualities any writer can bring to the production of formula fiction are a personal view—a philosophy— and a fund of special experience or interest. The "lore," often derided by theorists of the form, to which the reader of detective fiction is introduced may be one of the chief delights new versions of old formulas offer, whether it consists of campanology, or a tour of Greece, or the world of horse racing. Josephine Tey's utilization of the "lore" of the theatre and the matter of history, combined with a felicitous realization of a set of Non-Married women, supplies in her works a final, necessary ingredient.

The world of Josephine Tey's mysteries is shaped by a special vision. It also obeys most of the rules which were never written down for members of its exclusive club. Proper language and dress are mandatory. Corrupt police and detectives are not allowed. There is a proper place for everyone, and the social order must not be overturned. Force will not prevail over reason. The *Id* will not triumph over the *Super-ego*. Progress and the superiority of western culture over primitive or eastern cultures are assumed. These rules are seldom questioned in the classic detective novel, and the possibility of alternate views seldom intrudes. But in the works of Tey, some innocent people do suffer, some of the guilty do escape justice, and Robert Blair may not live happily ever after. There is a network of fine cracks in the restored world to which the characters are returned at the end of her novels.

She is most heterodox in her ambiguous conclusions to *Miss Pym Disposes* (where justice does not prevail), *The Man in the Queue* (where the case perfectly constructed by the typical detective method is wrong), and *The Franchise Affair* (where the beam that falls into the lives of the Sharpes in the person of Betty Kane narrowly misses them but leaves them with an altered view of the ultimate triumph of good). Grant's attitudes toward women are perfectly orthodox, but characters like Marion Sharpe, Lee Searle and Marta Hallard provide for a different perception.

While the readability of Tey's novels derives partly from her improvisations on the standard traditions of mystery fiction, it is primarily her exploration of the sufferings of the innocent and the reflections of her personal experience and views of the theatre, history and women which raise her works well above the level of the average detective novel. She produces a sense of quiet drama in her novels, in splendidly realized scene after scene. The characters come alive, not as deep and complex creations or always as very clever figures in drawing room comedy, but as human figures observantly drawn, caught momentarily up in a small crisis. There are many slight turns in Tey's best novels, and she has an ability to maintain pace and momentum without the more artificial aids such as a body to end each chapter. Moreover, throughout every work is the humorously ironic observation of all that occurs. There is, in fact, more variety and originality in her eight novels than in many longer shelves of her contemporaries' works, and her place in detective fiction is secure.

Notes

[1]References to all of Tey's novels will be cited in the text, using, where necessary, the abbreviation given after each entry.

1929   *The Man in the Queue* (New York: Berkley, 1970) (*Queue*)
1936   *A Shilling for Candles* (New York: Macmillan, 1954) (*Shilling*)
1946   *Miss Pym Disposes* (New York: Macmillan, 1968) (*Pym*)
1948   *The Franchise Affair* (New York: Pocket Books, 1977) (*Franchise*)
1949   *Brat Farrar* (New York: Dell, 1966) (*Brat*)
1950   *To Love and Be Wise* (New York: Berkley, 1970) (*Love*)
1951   *The Daughter of Time* (New York: Berkley, 1970) (*Time*)
1952   *The Singing Sands* (New York: Berkley, 1971) (*Sands*)

[2]Dilys Winn, "From Poe to the Present," in Dilys Winn, ed., *Murder Ink* (New York: Workman Publishing, 1977), p. 6; Anthony Boucher, "Reports on Criminals at Large," *New York Times Book Review*, 24 February 1952, p. 31; James Sandoe, "Introduction," in *Three by Tey* (New York: Macmillan, 1968), p. ix; Eric Routley, *The Puritan Pleasures of the Detective Story* (London: Gollancz, 1972), p. 180; Michele Slung, "Women in Detective Fiction," in John Ball, ed., *The Mystery Fiction Story* (San Diego: Univ. Extension, University of California, San Diego, 1976), p. 131; Julian Symons, *Mortal Consequences* (New York: Schocken, 1973), p. 159.

[3]John Gielgud, *Early Stages* (London: Heinemann, 1974), p. 143.

[4]John Gielgud, "Foreword," in *Plays by Gordon Daviot* (London: Peter Davies, 1952), p. x.

[5]Ibid.

[6]"Miss Elizabeth Macintosh," *The Inverness Courier*, 15 February 1952, p. 4.

[7]Gordon Daviot, "Madame Ville D'Aubier," *The English Review*, February 1930, p. 234.

[8]Gielgud, "Foreword," p. x.

[9]Jacques Barzun and Wendell Hertig Taylor, *A Catalogue of Crime* (New York: Harper and Row, 1971), end-papers.

Dame Ngaio Marsh
Photo by Angus McBean

Ngaio Marsh

1899   Edith Ngaio Marsh born on 23 April in Christchurch, New Zealand, daughter of Henry Edmund and Rose Elizabeth Seager Marsh. (*Ngaio* is Maori for "a flowering tree" or "light on the water.")

1905-10   Attended Miss Ross's School, Christchurch

1906   Family moved from suburb of Fendalton to the Port Hills district now called Cashmere, overlooking Christchurch, which has remained her New Zealand home

1910-14   Attended St. Margaret's College, Christchurch

1915-20   Attended Canterbury University College School of Art, Christchurch

1920   First appearance on stage, touring New Zealand with the Allan Wilkie Shakespeare Company

1923   First direction of plays for amateur societies in New Zealand

1928-32   Co-owner of interior decorating shop in London

1932   Death of mother; return to New Zealand

1934   *A Man Lay Dead*, first detective novel, written while in England, published; since, her time has been spent variously in New Zealand and England

1942   *New Zealand* (with Randal M. Burdon) published

1943   Began directing Shakespeare at Canterbury University

1944-52   Producer-director for D.D. O'Connor Theatre Management in New Zealand, Australia, and England.

1946   Director, Canterbury University College Student Players, first all New Zealand Shakespeare company; *A Play Toward: A Note on Play Production* published

1948   Officer, Order of the British Empire

1950   *Surfeit of Lampreys,* play adapted from *Death of a Peer,* produced in London

1950-51   Producer-director, British Commonwealth Theatre Company

1960   *Perspectives: The New Zealander and the Visual Arts* and *Play Production* published

1961   *False Scent,* play adapted with Eileen MacKay from her novel, produced in Worthing

1963   Doctor of Literature, Canterbury University

1964   *New Zealand,* for juveniles, published

1965   *Black Beech and Honeydew,* autobiography, published

1966   Dame Commander, Order of the British Empire

1972   *Murder Sails at Midnight,* play adapted from *Singing in the Shrouds,* produced in Bournemouth
1978   Grand Master Award of the Mystery Writers of America
1980   *Photo Finish,* her thirty-first novel published

by Earl F. Bargainnier

Ngaio Marsh's detective novels have made her New Zealand's most famous author.[1] However, in spite of her popularity, she has always been reticent about her fiction, saying that there is only so much that can be said on the subject.[2] She has much preferred to discuss her work in the theatre, as is evident in her autobiography, *Black Beech and Honeydew*. Her success as a director, especially of Shakespeare, was rewarded by her becoming Dame Ngaio in 1966 (she refers to the title as her "damery"), but her international fame is the result of Roderick Alleyn and the novels in which he has solved murders since 1934. Beginning in the Golden Age of British detective fiction, Marsh has generally been considered one of the four most significant women writers of what has come to be known as the classic British detective story, the others being Sayers, Christie and Allingham. She is the only one of the four surviving, and in 1980, in her eighty-first year, has published Alleyn's thirty-first case.

Any study of Marsh's work must begin with Roderick Alleyn. As her sole detective and the protagonist of all her fiction, no aspect of that fiction can be examined without in some way including him. He has been described by Erik Routley as "the last romantic hero of detective fiction...[who] makes Lord Peter Wimsey look like a frivolous neurotic" and as "a very satisfying and amiable kind of superman."[3] Allen is the epitome of the British sleuth, who surprises everyone by not being a bit like a detective. He hates murders, yet his career is spent in solving them. He is a man who an actress decides has star-quality and about whom a journalist can wonder if he has "it." That same journalist, who becomes Alleyn's "Watson," can say on first meeting him that "he doesn't conform to my mental pictures of a sleuth-hound" (*Man*, 140). Yet Alleyn is a Chief Detective-Inspector, then a Superintendent, and finally a Chief-Superintendent of Scotland Yard. He exemplifies the later development of the Golden Age British detective. As one of the most significant of the gentlemen-policemen, he prepares the way for the police procedural novel so prevalent today. Though Alleyn has the handsome appearance, the aristocratic background—with all its attendant qualities, the charm, the bookishness, and the witty facetiousness—of some other gentlemen-detectives, his attitudes toward others, his authority, and his methods of detection make him something other than the conventional Golden Age British detective.

According to Marsh, Alleyn's name is the result of her family ties, but certainly her involvement in the theatre influenced the choice of his last name, that of Edward Alleyn, Elizabethan tragedian, founder of Dulwich College, and husband of John Donne's daughter. After giving him his name, Marsh endowed him with a striking physical appearance. Known in the newspapers as "Handsome Alleyn" and "The Handsome Super," he is "a monkish-looking person with a fastidious mouth and well-shaped head" (*Wreath*, 86). This image is developed by a character's thinking that he looks like a "grandee turned monk, but retaining some amusing memories" (*Overture*, 151). This same character thinks of Alleyn as a drawing by Durer, and that idea is repeated by Marsh: "There was a certain austerity in the chilly blue of his eyes and in the sharp blackness of his hair. Albrecht Durer would have made a magnificent drawing of him" (*Tie,* 125). His London flat reflects his appearance, for it has "a contradictory air of monastic comfort that was, if he had realized it, a direct expression of himself"—and it contains a Durer drawing (*Tie*, 265). On his first appearance, Alleyn is specifically described in the following manner: "he was very tall, and lean, his hair was dark, and his eyes grey with corners that turned down. They looked as if they could smile easily but his mouth didn't" (*Man*, 45). Since he ages only from forty-one to forty-seven in the course of the novels, his appearance does not change; rather this basic presentation is expanded upon. For example, in *The Nursing Home Murder*, he has "a clear-cut and singularly handsome profile ... an intelligent and well-bred face, with a straight nose, firm mouth and dark eyes" (11-12), and Nigel Bathgate, Alleyn's "Watson," thinks of him as follows: "He isn't in the least like a detective.... He looks like an athletic don with a hint of the army somewhere. No, that's not right: it's too commonplace. He's faunish. And yet he's got all the right things for 'teckery. Dark, thin, long. Deep-set eyes—" (*Ecstasy*, 152).

His handsomeness is enhanced by his "general air of uncontrived elegance" (*Black*, 121). When he is dressed for a reception in white tie and tails, and wearing all his orders and decorations, his wife says, "You look as if you did it as a matter of course every night" (*Black*, 69), and he is always presented as being impeccably dressed. He can even be facetious about his sartorial elegance: " 'Am I tidy?' he asked, 'It looks so bad not to be tidy at an arrest' " (*Enter*, 194). Adding to his handsomeness and his dress in creating his personal image is his voice, which is described variously as "the inspector's markedly Oxonian voice" (*Man*, 48), "a bloody posh accent" (*Shrouds,* 39) and a voice of "a royal blue of the clearest sort" (*Vulcan*, 148).

In *A Man Lay Dead*, Rosamund Grant observes, "This man Alleyn, with his distinguished presence and his cultured voice and what-not, is in the Edwardian manner" (106), and she is not far off the mark. Alleyn was born in 1896 into the British aristocracy, being the younger son of a baronet. He received his M.A. from Oxford in 1915 and served for a short time in the diplomatic service before becoming a police constable at twenty-two. His reason for such a change of careers is never explained, but is described as "a remarkable story." His upper-class background is, of course, a significant element in both his image and his work. A few details of his personality can illustrate. He set the tone at his Oxford college, but when reminded of that he is horrified. He speaks Latin, French, German and Italian. He seems to be continually and always politely refusing drinks pressed upon him, for he does not drink on duty, yet he is a wine expert, shuddering at the Invalid Port used in the ceremonies of a pseudo-religious cult. Rather surprisingly, Alleyn is not Church of England; he is a non-believer, who feels "his own lack of acceptance to be tinged with a faint regret" (*Shrouds*, 144). Finally, as a true gentleman, he limits his swearing to *damn, hell* and *bloody*.

More important than such personal characteristics is the effect of his background on his career as a detective. In case after case, he encounters people who have known his father, mother, brother or cousins; or he meets relatives of former classmates or classmates themselves, for Alleyn's social world is the small one of the British Establishment. When Inspector Fox, his aide, asks him if the Prime Minister is a friend, Alleyn casually replies, "I know the old creature, yes" (*Nursing*, 61). Members of the upper-class request Alleyn from the Yard when murder occurs in their circles, for he is one of them, a gentleman. At the same time, he has a marked effect on the servants of the rich and well-born. In *Hand in Glove*, Alfred the butler says to the cook that "class is class and to be treated as such. *In* the Force he may be, and with distinction. *Of* it, he is not" (111). A somewhat similar reaction is that of the butler in *The Nursing Home Murder*: "Nash, who carried in his head a sort of social ladder, had quietly decided that police officers of all ranks were to be graded with piano-tuners. Chief Detective-Inspector Alleyn did not conform, in appearance or manner, to this classification. Nash performed a reluctant mental somersault" (64). In fact, Alleyn's "class" puts servants in such awe that he generally has Inspector Fox, whose "technique on the working side of the green baize doors was legendary at the Yard," question them.

(*Wreath*, 204).

However, it should not be thought that because of his background and connections Alleyn is a snob. He inwardly writhes "under his blatant recognition of his snob-value" (*Tie*, 225-26). Whenever his brother, Sir George Alleyn, is mentioned, his usual reaction is one of "falling over backwards rather than profit by their relationship" (*Rome*, 129). Nor will Alleyn allow aristocratic suspects to take advantage of his own position: he refuses to "respond to this appeal from blue blood to blue blood" (*Curtain*, 223). This refusal is an example of one of the principal elements of Alleyn's character: his personal and professional fastidiousness. In his dealing with others, he is nearly always ultra-polite; the only exceptions are when being facetious with friends and when forced to exert his official authority. He is always free with compliments to assisting officers, and he is more than willing to stay off a case not under his jurisdiction unless asked or ordered to take it over. The result is that he is highly admired by his colleagues. Mr. Fox says, "Six years, I think it is now, and never a moment's unpleasantness, thanks to your tact and consideration" (*Bar*, 303). Alleyn dislikes asking directly for people's fingerprints because it makes him feel so selfconscious. (Strangely, he *is* willing to eavesdrop during a case.) His fastidiousness forbids him from using with full force one of his powers: "He knew very well that with such women he carried a weapon that he was loath to use, but which nevertheless fought for him. This was the weapon of his sex. He saw with violent distaste that some taint of pleasure threaded her fear of him" (*Tie*, 229). He is even so fastidious that he finds motorcycle police to have a "peculiar air of menacing vulgarity" (*Black*, 35).

A significant aspect of Alleyn's fastidiousness is his attitude toward his job. He is continually introspective about his work, calling it "indecently preposterous." He considers murder "a crime in bad taste," and when forced to attend a sex show in *When in Rome*, his only comment is "infamous." On one occasion he is called squeamish by another character, and his mother says that she can always tell by his manner "when he is going to make an arrest. He gets a pinched look" (*Artists*, 315). The reason for such statements is that Alleyn is opposed to capital punishment; he says, "As the law stands, its method of dealing with homicides is, as I think, open to the gravest criticism. But for all that, the destruction of a human being remains what it is: the last outrage" (*Water*, 152). Yet in *When in Rome* he allows a murderer to excape punishment. Such a view for a fictional detective is unusual. At the end of one case, Fox says, "It's the kind of case he doesn't fancy. Capital charge and a woman. Gets to thinking about what he calls first causes.... Society. Civilization. Or something" (*Scales*, 315). It is at such moments that Alleyn suffers *angst*; the end of the case in *Overture to Death* provides an explicit example: "The arrest came like a wall of glass between himself and the little group.... He knew that most of his colleagues accepted these moments of isolation....But, for himself, he always felt a little like Mephistopheles, who looked on his own handiwork. He didn't enjoy the sensation. It was the one moment when his sense of detachment deserted him" (311). Thus, at times the gentleman is at war with the detective.

Part of his charm is the result of his fastidiousness. His wife Troy has more experience of that charm than anyone else: "the charm to which his wife never alluded without using the word indecent" (*Shrouds*, 79). His charm causes people to confide in him, trust him, and allow him to maneuver them. When questioning suspects, he suits his manner to whatever the particular person expects of or wants from him, and, as a result, he gets what he wants from them. Both fastidiousness and charm are inherent in Alleyn's personality, but he uses these qualities to be the successful detective he is.

Another element of his personality is his bookishness. Alleyn alludes to or quotes from writers as diverse as Poe, Doestoevski, Horace Walpole, Lewis Carroll, Rabindranath Tagore, A.A. Milne, George Moore, Pinero, Pirandello, Marlowe, "Baron Corvo," Dickens and Dr. Johnson. However, references to authors are not the only indication of his bookishness; his knowledge is encyclopaedic. A miscellany of his learning would comprise, among many other items, Greek mythology; musical terminology, piano-playing, and seventh century plainsong; gardening, including pests and sprays for them; painting, from the *Hours* of the Duc de Berry to Gustave Dore; poetry, of the writing of which he describes himself as "an undistinguished amateur" (*Spinsters*, 91); magic, esoteric ritual, and fertility rites; the effects of color-blindness and the purpose of a relief outfall sewer; and Madame Vestris, Rasputin's death, and Tom Taylor's Hawkshaw. He can refer to dactylography, to pipkins, cruses, and pottles, and to his subordinates as "my myrmidons" and "a perambulation of police." He is an expert at crossword puzzles and has "the knack" of being able to fill in missing words and letters in blotting-paper impressions. He is an inveterate punster and a user of allusions for teasing, as when he tells Fox that he has "the wit of a Tyburn broadsheet" (*Overture*, 232).

Over and over, Alleyn's extensive knowledge, vast reading and catholicity of taste are emphasized. He admires the Sherlock Holmes stories: "Holmes wasn't such a boob when all's said. Personally I think those yarns are jolly clever"(*Man*, 117). One of his favorite quotations, and an indication of his own method of detection, is from E.M. Forster's *Howard's End*: "Only connect. Only connect" (*Tinsel*, 119). He is also fond of the Gilbert and Sullivan operas; he quotes from them in nine of the novels. By far his favorite subject is William Shakespeare; there are allusions to or quotations from his works in all thirty-one novels. In *Killer Dolphin*, Peregrine Jay, a writer and director, thinks that "Alleyn knew as much as he did about Shakespearean scholarship and was as familiar with the plays as he was himself" (135). Alleyn can trade appropriate quotations with scholars and members of the theatre, whistle Ophelia's song and even determine the amount of time a killer has to commit murder during a recital of Shakespearean speeches in *Colour Scheme* by his knowledge of their lengths. On one occasion, he reminds himself "of a mature Hamlet," and his cases do not obliterate his preoccupation with the Bard. When he is "keeping obbo" (observation), he passes the time by quoting to himself appropriate passages, and in *The Nursing Home Murder*, after a day at Scotland Yard, "he went to his flat near Coventry Street, bathed, changed into a dinner-jacket, dined, and read the first scene in *Hamlet*, to which he was partial" (63). Alleyn's Shakespeareanism is obviously the result of Marsh's career as a director of ten of Shakespeare's plays, but, though at times the quoting may seem excessive, it is largely justified by his Oxford education and his general intellectuality.

Related to the bookishness are his theatricality and facetiousness. His flair for the dramatic is evident in such entrances as the following from *Night at the Vulcan*: "It was upon this line that Alleyn, as if he had mastered one of the major points of stage technique, made his entrance upstage and centre" (164). Alleyn admits to Nigel Bathgate that he enjoys "a dramatic close to a big case," for "It casts a spurious but acceptable glamour over the more squalid aspect of my profession" (*Ecstasy*, 305). Similar to his theatricality is what Alleyn himself calls "my professional facetiousness" (*Enter*, 173). Nigel Bathgate and Inspector Fox are the usual recipients of Alleyn's sallies. When Fox calls him "chief," Alleyn says that it makes him "feel like a cross between an Indian brave and one of those men with jaws and cigars in gangster films" (*Nursing*, 74). Of Bathgate's analysis of a case, Alleyn says, "I shall be able to cast a superior eye over it and then shatter it with a few facetiae" (*Ecstasy*, 168). Toward Bathgate, Alleyn says that he "feels like a form master who goes in for favorites" (*Ecstasy*, 150). Alleyn calls Fox "Brer Fox," "Foxkin," and even "my old foxglove, my noxious weed" (*Ecstasy*, 233). When Bathgate asks, "Isn't it true that when there's a cast-iron alibi the police always prick up their ears?" Alleyn replies, "Personally, I let mine flop with a thankful purr" (*Nursing*, 146). Dozens of other examples could be listed, for

Alleyn is a firm believer in irony, and he makes such use of it that it is not surprising that Bathgate can explode with "Facetious ass!" (*Ecstasy*, 111) or that Fox occasionally casts "his eyes towards heaven" (*Enter*, 82) or says, "Come off it, sir" (*Ecstasy*, 233).

Another aspect of this facetiousness is Alleyn's mock modesty. He proclaims that he is "invariably gulled by detective novels" (*Ecstasy*, 172) and that he does not understand the law (*Enter*, 50), neither statement being accepted. The major examples of this trait are his continual statements about his "filthy memory." He says that he must have his Woolworth note-book to write down details; Bathgate's comment is "Don't be affected" (*Man*, 120). The true situation is presented in *Hand in Glove*: "At the Yard, Alleyn was often heard to lament the inadequacy of his memory, an affectation which was tolerantly indulged by his colleagues. His memory was in fact like any other senior detective officer's, very highly trained...." (117), as his habit of quoting proves.

Alleyn's facetiousness could easily become a weakness in his presentation, but Marsh makes sure that the reader knows he is not malicious: "Alleyn ... never made too much fun of anybody" (*Nursing,* 63). Since the "fun" is almost always with his two closest friends, it is presented as being harmless. In fact, whenever Alleyn feels that he has wounded, he apologizes. In *Death in Ecstasy* the following illustrative conversation among the three friends occurs:

[Alleyn:] "Please forgive me if I am odiously facetious sometimes. It's a bad habit I've got. I assure you that if I really thought you slow in the uptake I should never dream of ragging you. You're kind enough to let me show off and I take advantage of it. Do forgive me."

He looked so distressed and spoke with such charming formality that Nigel was both embarrassed and delighted.

"Chief Detective-Inspector," he said, "I am your Watson, and your worm. You may both sit and trample on me. I shall continue to offer you the fruits of my inexperience."

"Very nicely put, Mr. Bathgate," said Fox.

Alleyn and Nigel stared at him, but he was perfectly serious. (141)

And so there is charm and fastidiousness even in his facetiousness.

Nigel Bathgate and Inspector Edward Walter (Teddy) Fox are Alleyn's closest friends, but they are not the only recurrent characters in the novels. Others among the staff of Scotland Yard are Detective-Sergeants Thompson and Bailey, Alleyn's "flash and dabs" men; Detective-Sergeant Gibson, who eventually becomes a Superintendent; and Sir James Curtis, the Home Office Pathologist, called by Alleyn, "the great man." Outside of the Yard, there are Mr. Rattisbon, a stereotypical lawyer, who appears in five of the novels, and Alleyn's family. That family consists of Agatha Troy Alleyn, his wife; Ricky Alleyn, his son; Lady Helena Alleyn, his mother; and

Sir George Alleyn, "the blasted Baronet," his ambassadorial brother. This company of people is presented as being very important to Alleyn, and at least some of them appear in all of the novels set in England. Alleyn is alone in the three early New Zealand novels—*Vintage Murder, Colour Scheme* and *Died in the Wool*—and then he becomes homesick for them: "he was caught up in a wave of nostalgia: for Troy, his wife, for London; for Inspector Fox with whom he was accustomed to work; for his own country and his own people" (*Wool*, 213).

Bathgate unofficially and Thompson, Bailey and Fox officially make up Alleyn's working team. Bathgate is introduced in *A Man Lay Dead*, in which he meets Angela North, whom he marries in 1937. He is a twenty-five year old reporter for the *London Clarion*. He appears in eight of the first fifteen novels and then disappears; in these novels he is used by Alleyn to ward off other journalists, to question suspects in an informal manner, and to serve as Alleyn's sounding board. In the first novel, Alleyn says, "Every sleuth ought to have a tame half-wit, to make him feel clever. I offer you the job, Mr. Bathgate—no salary, but a percentage of the honour and glory" (*Man*, 112-13), and so Bathgate becomes his Watson, if not the narrator of his cases. Such facetious put-downs are, as already indicated, numerous, but the relationship is one of friendship; for example, Alleyn is the godfather of Bathgate's first child. Thompson, Alleyn's photographer, rarely speaks and is hardly developed; rather he is simply a dedicated and expert police officer, whose attitude toward Alleyn is expressed in one of his longest speeches: "We'd both go back on P.C. nightduty before we'd let you down, if you know what I mean, sir" (*Enter*, 228). Bailey, the fingerprint expert, is characterized by the word *mulish*, as in "a man of few words, great devotion and mulish disposition" (*Glove*, 111). His idiosyncrasy is to look more morose whenever he discovers something important. As stated earlier, Alleyn's attitude toward these two men is one of compliments and consideration

Much more developed is Inspector Fox, Alleyn's chief assistant. Fox is described by Alleyn as "sane," "nice-minded," "a concealed classicist," "a wise old bird," and "the perfect embodiment, the last loveliest expression, of horse sense" (*Enter*, 139). He is a bachelor of about fifty; his only romance occurs in *Scales of Justice*, but it is half-hearted and ends quietly. However, he does have his successes with female servants:

> "No doubt they respond more readily to your unbridled body-urge," said Alleyn.
> "That's one way of putting it, Mr. Alleyn," Fox primly conceded. (*Scent*, 155)

Troy Alleyn thinks of him as "a cross between a bear and a baby who exhibits the most pleasing traits of both creatures" (*Vulcan,* 185). Fox is "an innocent snob," particularly in his relations with Alleyn. Though he may at times tease Alleyn in a bland and gentle manner, he is proud of Alleyn's education, elegance, and detective methods: "Mr. Fox, as was his custom, glanced compacently at his subordinates. He had the air of drawing their attention to their chief's virtuosity" (*Fool,* 229). His protectiveness towards Alleyn is compared to that of a nurse towards her charge, as when he presides over Alleyn's lunch "with all the tranquil superiority of a Nannie" (*Tie,* 155). When Fox is poisoned in *Death at the Bar,* Alleyn shows that Fox's devotion is deserved, for Alleyn is frantic and furious at the possibility of his friend's dying; Fox's only comment is "Very incovenient." Such laconic statements are typical of him. When he says that a suspect is "very quiet but you can see he's put out," the authorial comment is "This, in Fox's language, could mean anything from being irritated to going berserk or suicidal" (*Black,* 206). Throughout the novels, there is a running joke about Fox's attempts to learn French from records, and since Alleyn's French is perfect, it is a good illustration of Marsh's technique of contrast between the two. Fox is definitely lower-middle class; he looks like a policeman in his bowler hat; his language is simple, without literary allusions; and he is slow and sure rather than brilliant. Therefore, he is an excellent complement to the aristocratic Alleyn. Marsh never lets Fox take center-stage from Alleyn, but in him she creates a "loveable" and contrasting second-lead to her star.

Of the recurrent characters not actively engaged in crime-solving, the most important is Agatha Troy Alleyn, called Troy by her husband. Marsh has stated that both her agent and publisher were opposed to her introducing Troy to the series of novels; however, she insisted. From the landed gentry, Troy "is a reticent character and as sensitive as a sea-urchin, but she learns to assume and even feel a certain detachment," and she becomes a very famous artist, her painting being "far from academic but not alway non-figurative."[4] From the time she appears in *Artists in Crime,* the sixth novel, Alleyn is deeply in love with her. Troy resists Alleyn's attraction for a time, for she is repulsed by his profession, but after an acquaintance of about two years, they are married. Knowing her feeling, Alleyn wishes to keep his life with her and later their son separate from the "squalor, boredom, horror, and cynicism of a policeman's lot" (*Ditch,* 112). Troy realizes his attitude: "Alleyn's refusal to allow his work a place in their relationship...was founded, she knew, in her own attitude during their earliest encounters which had taken place against a terrible background; in her shrinking from the part he played at that time and in her expressed horror of capital punishment" (*Curtain,* 285). Ironically,

Troy's interest in her husband's work grows, while he still wishes her to be out of it; he tells her that "we'd better observe the usual rule of airy tact on your part and phony inscrutability on mine" (*Spinsters, 12*). In a lecture at a police academy, he tells the men, "In the Force our wives are not called upon to serve in female James-Bondage...any notion of their involvement in our work would be outlandish, ludicrous and extremely unpalatable" (*Constables, 80*). He even goes as far as to say he would quit his job before allowing it to interfere with Troy's painting, which he considers far more important. However, Troy does become involved inadvertantly in cases, e.g., *Final Curtain, Spinsters in Jeopardy,* and *Clutch of Constables*. When she does, Alleyn agonizes: "I'm up against a silly complexity in my own attitude toward my job...I've adopted...an unrealistic approach; Troy in one compartment, the detection of crime in another" (*Curtain, 180*). In spite of this one discordant element—which Troy takes much more in stride than Alleyn—their marriage is a very happy one, for they are two intelligent people, each prominent in his and her careers, and neither dominating the other.

Among the other members of his family, his son Ricky appears in *Spinsters in Jeopardy* and *Last Ditch*. In the first he is six and is described by his father as "pedantically mannered" and as "a precocious little perisher." In *Last Ditch* he is a novel-writing don in his early twenties, who calls his father "Cid," after the Criminal Investigation Division, falls in love, and wonders how so fastidious a man as his father could have chosen police work. Alleyn's mother appears in *Artists in Crime* and *Death in a White Tie*, and his knightly brother finally appears in *Black As He's Painted*. Lady Helena Alleyn is a grand dame of sixty-five, who resides in the country, has extensive social connections, raises Alsatians, and indulges in various handicrafts. She and Alleyn are close, and she is anxious for him to marry and happy when he does. The best word to describe her is *sensible*, and Alleyn obviously inherits that quality from her. Of Alleyn's older brother, their mother says, "It's a pity he hasn't got your brains" (*Artists, 30*). Yet George is very high in the diplomatic service, at one point being Ambassador to Italy, and when he appears, he is "Sir George Alleyn, K. C. M. G., etc., etc.," but on that appearance he fulfills Alleyn's previous comments about his being an ass, with such statements as "My brother, the bobby...Ridiculous, what?" (*Black, 113*). Sir George is simply the traditional bumbling aristocrat, and a foil for his brother.

For Roderick Alleyn is anything but a comic aristocrat. He is "possessed of an effortless authority" (*Scent, 207*), and he is aware of it: "Quite deliberately he used the whole force of that thing people call personality and of which he knew—how could he not know?—he had his share. He imposed his will on hers as surely as if it was a tangible instrument" (*Tie,* 306). This personal authority is one of the effects of his background and one of the elements of his success as a detective, but there are others.

Alleyn's methods of detection are a combination of those of the master detective in the Holmes and Poirot tradition and of those of normal police routine, making him a transitional figure between Golden Age detective fiction and the modern police procedural. As a master-detective, he has abilities the normal policeman does not; "in her consideration of the genus of C. I. D. Troy was invariably brought up short by the reflection that her husband fitted into none of the categories" (*Constables,* 107). His aides are aware of and accept his superiority. When Alleyn finds an important piece of string after a room has been thoroughly searched, Thompson says, "You've got to have the eyes for it" (*Glove,* 185). Again and again, his powers of observation are stressed, as in *Death at the Bar*: "Alleyn might have been a guest in the house, and with no more interest than politeness might allow his gaze shifted casually from one dust-covered surface to another. After a few minutes, however, he could have given a neat drawing, and nice attention to detail, of the private tap-room" (150-51). His relationship with Troy is given part of the credit for such ability; he has a double vision: "As a stringently trained policeman, he watched automatically for idiosyncrasies. As a man very sensitively tuned to his wife's way of seeing, he searched for consonancies" (*Black,* 35).

Another element of the master-detective in Alleyn, which has already been discussed, is his ability to provide the image people want or expect. By fitting his approach to the individual in his interviews, he wins their confidence. "Mr. Fox once said of his superior that he would be able to get himself worked up over the life-story of a mollusc, provided the narrative was obtained first-hand" (*Vulcan,* 212). This apparent intense interest in the concerns of those involved in a case of murder is one of his most successful methods of gaining information. Another method is reconstruction of the murder. In *Enter a Murderer, Death and the Dancing Footman,* and *Death of a Fool,* as well as others, Alleyn restages the events of the murder in order to trap the killer. Although he says that he does not do it "out of any desire to figure as the mysteriously omnipotent detective" (*Man,* 174), which would be "impossibly vulgar," the effect *is* of an omnipotent detective stage-managing others. Of course, as a master detective, Alleyn generally knows quite early the identity of the murderer. Troy asks, "Rory—when did you first—?" "Oh—that. Almost from the beginning, I think,' said he with a callow smirk" (*Tinsel,* 279). His usual problem is to find evidence to justify his theory: "The case was developing along lines with which Alleyn was all too familiar. He had now very little doubt as to the identity of William Compline's murderer and also very little substantial proof to support his theory or to warrant an arrest" (*Footman*, 353). One method of finding that needed evidence is what he calls a "hag," which is "the ruthless taking-to-pieces of the case and a fresh attempt to put the bits together in their true pattern" (*Wreath*, 240). Such a recapitulation of everything known also allows the reader to see how brilliant a detective he is, in putting those pieces together.

Other items contributing to the master-detective image are the admiration of other policemen, one of whom describes his textbook on methods as "the Scourge of the Service"; his success in disguise, whether as a communist or a bookish health-seeker; his ability to do without sleep or to tell himself to wake at a certain time and do it; his willingness to use tricks, and his intuition of evil. Also, though Alleyn is aristocratic and elegant, he is not afraid of dirt and is willing to engage in physical activity most men in their middle-forties would avoid. He crawls through harbor water under a jetty, descends into a sewer ditch and into an ancient Roman well, climbs a tree during a storm to fetch a sliver of tinsel, and in another storm chases an escaping murderer, receiving a concussion. In the first novel, he even hides inside a chimney to spring out at the last moment and arrest a gang, with "Put 'em up, my poppets" (163). Such is Alleyn the master-detective.

In *Vintage Murder*, Alleyn says, "I'm an incurable nosey parker. Detect I must, if I can" (60), and detect he does. Though there are the grand touches of the master-detective, Alleyn believes in routine police procedure and in distrust of conjecture. He defines his professionalism "as an infinite capacity to notice less and less with more and more accuracy" (*Dolphin*, 178-79). In his comments on detective fiction, he insists that "real" police activity is different and uninteresting. For example, in *The Nursing Home Murder*, he says, "any faithful account of police investiagation, in even the most spectacular homicide case, would be abysmally dull. . . . The files are a plethora of drab details, most of them entirely irrelevant. Your crime novelist gets over all that by writing grandly about routine work and selecting the essentials. Quite rightly. He'd be the world's worst bore if he did otherwise" (140). Similar comments are made by him in *Death of a Peer* (137) and in *Death at the Bar* (186), in the latter case adding, "Routine is the very fibre of police investigation." His course of action is to find the answers to a series of basic questions—which he thinks of in Latin: "The old tag jog-trotted through his mind: *Quis? Quid? Ubi? Quibus? auxilis? [sic] Cur? Quomodo? Quando?* Which might be rendered: 'Who did the deed? What was it? Where was it done? With what? Why was it done? And how done? When was it done?"'(*Water, 194*). When these are answered, by slow accumulation of facts, the case is solved. In *Colour Scheme*, Alleyn states most fully his attitude toward the nature of the detective process:

Police investigation, we protest, is not a matter of equally balanced motives, tortuous elaborations, and a final revelation in the course of which the investigator's threat hangs like an *ignis fatuus* over first one and then another of the artificially assembled suspects. It is rather the slow amassment of facts sufficient to justify the arrest of someone who has been more or less suspect from the moment the crime was discovered. (330)

Such a process does not allow for what Alleyn calls "the hateful realms of surmise and conjecture" (*Glove*, 191). He says that "when you find a cop guessing, you kick him in the pants" (*Fool*, 131). However, he occasionally transgresses his own rule, but is aware of it: "I'm doing what I always say you shouldn't do. I'm speculating" *(Scales, 162).*

Along with conjecture, Alleyn distrusts motive in determining who is a murderer. He says, "I *despise* motive...I *despise* it...We can't ignore it, of course...[but] Opportunity's the word, my boy. Opportunity" *(Fool,* 198). In another novel, he says that "motive is one of the secondary elements in police investigation" (*Water*, 194). The stress on opportunity rather than motive is a principal factor in his method, and it is matched by his belief in a reliance on pattern, the fitting-in of each little piece of evidence to determine what is the odd—and conclusive—piece. This belief leads him to say, "'Beware of fancy-touches' should be neatly printed and hung above every would-be murderer's cot" (*Vintage,* 115). The fancy touches lead to bungling and make the pattern easier to see, just as the determination of opportunity eliminates others and points to the probable murderer. Opportunity and pattern are the keynotes of Alleyn's methods of detection.

Alleyn's introspection toward his profession has already been discussed, but some additions and qualifications need to be made. At one point, he indicates to Bathgate that nothing must interfere with his professional duties, but on another occasion he says, "What rot they talk when they teach us we should never get involved. Of course we get involved: we merely learn not to show it" (*Black,* 144). Involvement is human, and when lecturing to a police class, Alleyn warns the students not to lose their humanity: "If you lose it altogether you'll be, in my opinion, better out of the force, because with it you'll have lost your sense of values and that's a dire thing to befall any policeman" (*Constables,* 180). His concern for the human element is the cause of such remarks as "Fox, in many ways ours is a degrading job-of-work" (*Ecstasy,* 234) and "Our job, God save the mark, is first to protect society and then as a corollary to catch the criminal" (*Shrouds,* 131). At the same time that Alleyn is required to do things that offend his sensibilities, he has to accept these as part of the nature of being a policeman. His defense is that he is a piece of state machinery, which anyone can start but only the state can switch off: "once you have set in motion the chariot wheels of Justice, you can do nothing at all to arrest or deflect their progress....you switched on a piece of complicated and automatic machinery which, once started, you cannot switch off. As the police officer in charge of this case I am simply a wheel in the machine. I must complete my revolutions" (*Nursing,* 200). Therefore, whatever he is required to do, he does—no matter what his own likes or dislikes may be, while trying to retain the humanity which he so highly values.

By now it should be evident that Alleyn is a mass of disparate elements. The reason is that Marsh unconsciously created a transitional figure. He has the aristocratic background; the personal charm, fastidousness, and handsomeness; and the bookish facetiousness of the gentleman-detective of the "between-the-wars" school of British detective fiction. But he is also a policeman, using a team of subordinates in "routine" police investigation, and in this respect he looks forward to the later procedural novels, for there is more police routine in the early novels than in any other group of British detective novels of the 1930s. Marsh is generally effective in creating a seamless character out of these two quite different strains of detective fiction. When there are inconsistencies or contradictions, they are the result of the forty-six year time-span of the novels, rather than of a lack of focus on her part. Indeed, much of the success of Marsh's detective fiction is due to her ability to adapt within Alleyn the many different elements of both types and still make him a character whom the reader both admires and cares about.

The settings in which Alleyn moves and the people whom he encounters are other elements of Marsh's success. She has stated, "I have always tried to keep the settings of my books as far as possible within the confines of my own experience."[5] Since her experience has included being a painter, an actress, and a director, as well as a New Zealander, she has naturally incorporated her other careers into her fiction. Troy Alleyn's profession is the most obvious example of Marsh's use of her painting in the novels. Marsh's theatrical career has contributed to the scenic effect, which is characteristic of her novelistic technique; her fiction is largely dialogue presented in a series of drama-like scenes. In choosing specific settings, she follows the Golden Age closed circle, or isolated, convention. Within that convention, she manipulates a relatively small number of place-types with great ingenuity of detail.

Though some belong to more than one, most of her settings fall into one of five categories. The largest number are the nine which take place in English country houses. Whether the situation is a snowed-in houseparty (*Death and the Dancing Footman, Tied Up in Tinsel*), a weekend murder game (*A Man Lay Dead*), a treasure-hunt party (*Hand in Glove*), Troy's presence to paint the master of the house's portrait *(Final Curtain, Tied Up in Tinsel)*, the planning of an amateur play *(Overture to Death)*, or just life in the big houses around an idyllic village (*Scales of Justice, Grave Mistake*), these novels are typical of Golden Age detective fiction and are among the best of their kind. Next are the seven which either occur in the theatre or involve theatrical families. No writer has used the theatrical scene for murder as often as Marsh—though if he continues, Simon Brett may surpass her—and her love and knowledge of the theatre is the obvious reason for this predilection. Her experience has enabled her to employ the theatre as an integral element of her detective fiction, involving plot, characterization, and atmosphere, as well as setting. Seven novels are set outside England, four in New Zealand. Why Marsh has not more frequently used her native country cannot be answered. Its combination of the exotic and the British would seem to offer many opportunities for her descriptive skill and for all sorts of misdirection. Certainly, the four set there *(Vintage Murder, Colour Scheme, Died in the Wool Photo Finish)* are not only excellent examples of Marsh's detective fiction, but attractive introductions to her antipodean homeland. The fourth group is another particular specialty of Marsh; five novels are concerned with some form of cult (*Death in Ecstasy, Spinsters in Jeopardy, Death of a Fool, Dead Water,* and *Last Ditch*). A cult, whether sexual, religious, or folk-mythic and whether bogus or sincere, provides a colorful background, a cast of eccentric characters, and numerous, and often strange, red herrings to complicate murder, and Marsh has been highly and rightly praised for her ability to manipulate these elements. The last group consists of four novels which take place in London high society. Three are essentially comic novels of manners: *Death of a Peer, A Wreath for Rivera,* and *Black As He's Painted.* The fourth, *Death in a White Tie,* which Marsh has said could be called *Seige of Troy,* recounts Alleyn's seemingly unsuccessful courtship of his future wife. The four works which do not exactly fit these categories are *The Nursing Home Murder, Death at the Bar,* and the two "in transit" novels, *Singing in the Shrouds* and *Clutch of Constables.*

Populating these settings with Alleyn, his aides and his family are the victims, murderers and suspects whom he confronts in his investigations. Again, the most obvious statement to be made about her characters is that they are typical of the Golden Age. Her victims are either unlikeable—philanderers, rich and disagreeable elderly people, bitchy or neurotic women, blackmailers, etc.—or unknown, so that the reader feels nothing when they die, the major exceptions being *Death in a White Tie* and *Death at the Bar*. They are always much less interesting than her murderers or, even more, her suspects, who may vary from the comic through the romantic to the eccentric, unpleasant, or nasty. Examples of the purposefully comic are the frenetic Lord Pastern and Bagott of *A Wreath for Rivera*, Mrs. Bunz, the amateur folklorist of *Death of a Fool,* Percival Pyke Period, the obsessed genealogist of *Hand in Glove*, and Samuel Whipplestone and his delightful cat Lucy Lockett of *Black As He's Painted*. Twenty-four of Marsh's novels contain a young romantic couple in some way involved in the investigation of murder: as witnesses, suspects, or aides to Alleyn. Neither the young man nor the young woman is ever the guilty person; rather their relationship is used to complicate the case. A few of these couples verge on the silly, but most are attractive types, such as Edward Manx and Carlisle Wayne of *A Wreath for Rivera* and Peregrine Jay and Emily Dunne of *Killer Dolphin*. Setting aside the murderers, other unpleasant characters abound. Whether engaged in non-murderous criminal activity or just possessing grating defects of personality, they scatter suspicion and make Alleyn's job more difficult. They range from Captain Maurice Withers of *Death in a White Tie*, who is "the sort of man who breathes vulgarity into good clothes" (125) through Master Trevor Vere, the obnoxious child-actor of *Killer Dolphin,* and the many effeminate homosexuals to the aging sybaritic Lady Sonia Braceley of *When in Rome*. All in all, Marsh exhibits virtuosity in the creation of varied minor characters, while staying within her own experience. As with her settings, the large number of painters and actors and actresses reflect her other professional interests, as the similar number of New Zealanders and Australians reflects her antipodean origin.

Marsh's murderers are also a varied lot. There are six female murderers and two murderous duos; the rest are men. Four of the women are middle-aged and "country," wishing to preserve their status, while the other two are beautiful young women who wish to marry wealth and position, one even killing her father to enable her to do so. With the exception of two spies and six crooks, three of whom have "respectable" covers, Marsh's murderers are amateurs. Their motives are most often greed or the desire to protect themselves from ruin. However, three are insane, and there are single examples of murder as the result of sudden anger, of religious mania, and even of a perverted kind of pity. The most murderous profession in Marsh's fiction is medicine. Five murders are committed by doctors; no other profession comes close—only two are committed by actors. Marsh is expert in using the least-likely suspect ploy, but she is perhaps even better with its opposite, the most-obvious suspect. Quite often her murderers are not only the most obvious suspects, but also the most unpleasant, yet she is still able to create that essential doubt as to guilt in the mind of the reader. Examples include *Overture to Death, Death at the Bar, Death and the Dancing Footman, A Wreath for Rivera* and *Singing in the Shrouds*. The fact that so few generalizations can be made about her murderers is a compliment to Marsh's versatility in finding opponents for Alleyn.

However, one generalization that can be made is that her murderers employ some of the most bizarre methods ever devised to dispatch their victims. (Perhaps the nature of these methods explains why in twenty-one of the novels only one murder occurs. The most murders occur in *Black As He's Painted*, where there are three.) Even when the actual method is not bizarre, it is accompanied by some form of fancy or grotesque embellishment, as the singing of the strangler in *Singing in the Shrouds*, the victim's defenestration after being hit with an iron poker in *Tied Up in Tinsel*, or the sleeping pills forced into the suffocated victim's mouth in *Grave Mistake*. Ten novels contain public murders, that is murders committed in the presence of many people; it is Marsh's favorite type. The murder in *Enter a Murderer* takes place during the performance of a play, and that in *Overture to Death* just before a play begins when a gun concealed in a piano ends the performance—as well as the pianist. A model is killed by a dagger jutting upward from her posing stand in front of art students in *Artists in Crime*; a jeroboam of champagne spoils a birthday party and the head of the host when it falls from the flies of a theatre in *Vintage Murder*; a man is poisoned while being operated on in *The Nursing Home Murder;* another is killed during a game of darts in *Death at the Bar*; and Rivera of *A Wreath for Rivera* is stabbed with a petit-point needle inserted into an umbrella handle while playing the accordion in a nightclub filled with people, including Alleyn and Troy. Strange as they may be, these public murders by no means exhaust Marsh's ingenuity. In *Final Curtain* she cleverly used thallium and the symptoms it produces long before Agatha Christie made that poison and those symptoms famous in *The Pale Horse*. Victims are stabbed by a murderer sliding down the bannister of a flight of stairs, skewered through the eye while sitting in an elevator, tricked into walking into a pit of boiling mud, hacked with a sheep hook and then baled in wool, given an analgesic drug in face powder and pesticide in a perfume atomizer, coshed with pottery pigs and bronze dolphins, decapitated, and crushed by a six-hundred pound drain pipe. The most bizarre murder of all is that of Colonel Cartarette in *Scales of Justice*. Kneeling by a stream he is first hit by a golf club swung from a floating punt and then, to add injury to injury, is stabbed with a shooting stick, by the murderer's inserting it into the Colonel's skull and sitting on it.

Marsh's penchant for such bizarre, even outlandish, methods of murder contrasts with her usual moderation in presenting the action of her novels. She apparently believes that the single act of violence which is the impetus of the remaining action must be striking and original. Though that act is more talked about than seen—as is the case with most writers of classic British detective fiction—she always makes sure that it is so striking that her characters will be shocked, frightened, puzzled and utterly unable to stop talking about it until Alleyn provides the final explanation.

It has already been noted that much of Marsh's fiction is dialogue. Her novels move at a leisurely pace, and most are longer than the average detective novel. She has not escaped criticism for the structure of her novels. Jean M. White has said, "In her fondness for background and character, Dame Ngaio sometimes does neglect to get on with the main business of detection. Then, particularly in the earlier books, she hastens to retrieve with post-murder interrogations and perhaps a reprise of suspects, motives, and movements. It is as if she suddenly has remembered that she really set out to write a detective story and not a novel of manners."[6] White is correct in her assessment of the early novels, and even though Marsh bcomes more assured in her narration of the central investigation in later ones, she still spends many pages on matters other than detection. The already mentioned romance in most novels is one instance. The course of Alleyn's courtship of Troy in *Artists in Crime* and *Death in a White Tie,* Inspector Fox's interest in Nurse Kettle of *Scales of Justice,* Ricky Alleyn's infatuation with Julia Pharamond in *Last Ditch*, and the pairings of other lesser characters permit Marsh to explore character and character relationships. Similarly the theatrical world and the various cults provide other opportunities for her to indulge "her fondness for background and character."

There is also the element of comedy, perhaps most evident in the presentation of the Lamprey family of *Death of a Peer*, a family based upon one whom Marsh knew well, as evidenced by their large role in her autobiography. (Roberta Grey of the same novel is obviously Marsh's view of herself on her arrival in England in the late 1920s.) Other comic elements, from among many, are the hiring of only murderers as servants in *Tied Up With Tinsel,* the activities of Lord Pastern and Bagott in *A Wreath for Rivera*, and the satirical treatment of overly dramatic actors and actresses in so many novels. Some readers may prefer "straight detection," with nothing except a crime and its solution. Marsh will not satisfy them; rather she appeals to the reader who enjoys meeting interesting people involved in a crime within a detailed setting and seeing their relationships and reactions and who is not overly anxious to discover whodunit.

On another level, much of the structure of Marsh's novels is naturally determined by the conventions of classic detective fiction. When she began to write, she modeled her novels on those prevalent in the 1930s. Therefore, her early works reflect the devices and techniques already used by Sayers, Christie and others, and many of these continue into the later novels: maps, connected chapter titles, repeated characters, mention of previous cases, the mid-novel recapitulation, the lists of various sorts (clues, questions, suspects), the detective's laying traps for the murderer, the action stopping with the arrest of the murderer, the final summation by the detective, and on and on. The rule of fairness to the reader was made much of in the Golden Age, and Marsh has been scrupulous in laying out all of the necessary information. A re-check of any novel after the final summation demonstrates that. Her fairness may be clearly seen in her habit of presenting the murderer's thoughts shortly after the crime. Whether the murderer is frightened, remorseful, jubilant or contemplating his next move, that he is the murderer can be deduced—with a correct reading; *Death in a White Tie* providing probably the best illustration. In a number of her later novels Marsh uses a device which some may think unfair, but is actually not. Again and again, Alleyn will tell Fox or other characters some discovery or conclusion, but the reader is not privileged to know what is said. From dozens of instances, here are two:

As they left Alleyn took from his desk the second volume of a work on medical jurisprudence. It dealt principally with poisons. In the train he commended certain passages to Fox's notice. He watched his old friend put on his spectacles, raise his eyebrows and develop the slightly catarrhal breathing that invariably accompanied his reading.

"Yes," said Fox, removing his spectacles as the train drew into Ancreton Halt, "that's different of course." (*Curtain*, 198-99)

[Alleyn:] "Now, let me explain."

He did so at some length and they listened to him with the raised eyebrows of assailable incredulity.

"Well," they said, "I suppose it's possible." And, "It might be, but how'll you prove it?" And, "Even so, it doesn't get us all that much further, does it?" And, "How are you to find out?" (*Fool*, 170-71)

Irritating as such omissions may be, they are not unfair, for Alleyn has simply made a deduction which, on the evidence *already* given, *could* have been made by the reader.

The structural feature of Marsh's novels most often criticized is the amount of time Alleyn spends interrogating one witness or suspect after another. The early novels especially are characterized by a long parade of interviews, sometimes repetitious, with chapter titles giving the names of the persons questioned. It can be argued that,though weak from a narrative standpoint, such a series of interviews is a prime illustration of Alleyn's continual insistence that most police work is routine and even tedious. Also, they indicate Marsh's interest in character, since they emphasize the reactions of those involved, and the influence of her theatrical work, for each is a dramatic scene, practically all dialogue.

From these interviews, Alleyn not only pieces together the sequence of the crime, discerns motives and eliminates some suspects, but also obtains verbal clues by his questioning, whether lies or truth. What is surprising, however, is that most of the cases hinge not on verbal clues, but on physical ones. (In this respect, Marsh differs considerably from Agatha Christie, to whom she is so often compared.) Half an onion, a notched stethoscope, trout scales, a dead cat, color blindness, a glove, an angled mirror, a lost diamond clip, a druidic costume, a fishing line, a new flashbulb for a camera, a damp sheet of music—these are just a few of the physical clues which lead Alleyn to solutions.

Before he reaches them, Marsh makes his job more difficult by throwing all sorts of red herrings in his path. She is fond of including another crime which complicates the investigation of the murder. Most often that crime is drug-dealing. It appears in seven novels, from the early *Enter a Murderer* to the late *Last Ditch.* Blackmail, theft and illegal gambling are other "extra" crimes present, as well as communist plots in *A Man Lay Dead* and *The Nursing Home Murder.* She also includes the mysterious or sinister figure, whose background is unknown, dubious or suspicious, such as "G.P.F." of *A Wreath for Rivera,* Vassily Conducis of *Killer Dolphin,* and Nikolas Markos and Doctor Basil Schramm of *Grave Mistake.* Another type of red herring appears in the novels in which murder occurs within a large family; this is the Golden Age convention of the members being either at cross purposes, as in *Final Curtain,* or attempting to shield each other, as in *Death of a Peer.* It is enough to say that Marsh is never at a loss to find ways of impeding Alleyn's process of discovery, which only makes his ultimate success even more brilliant.

After his interrogations and the collection of clues, Alleyn knows the murderer, but on five occasions he employs a reconstruction of the crime with all principal suspects present in order to trap that murderer. The usual explanation is that there is not enough evidence to justify an arrest otherwise. After using this device in her first three novels, Marsh returned to it only twice, in *Death of a Fool* and *Death and the Dancing Footman*; in the latter Alleyn says to Fox, "I hate the semipublic reconstruction stunt—it's theatrical and it upsets all sort of harmless people. Still it has its uses. We've known it to come off, haven't we?" (374), and Fox agrees. But though a reconstruction may produce a murderer's confession or total collapse and certainly provides a dramatic arrest, Marsh apparently realized that continuous reconstructions to provide final solutions would not only be boringly predictable, but would hardly indicate Alleyn's powers of deduction. Those critics who have accused her of overusing reconstructions have obviously not made an accurate count.

Though Roderick Alleyn appears in all the novels, they are not of the same pattern. He solves twenty-one cases in three days or less, *Death and the Dancing Footman* in approximately six hours. (*The Nursing Home Murder* requires nine days, and that is the maximum.) However, the placement of the murder in a novel and Alleyn's first appearance vary widely. The earliest murder— excluding those that have occurred before a novel opens, e.g., *Died in the Wool* and *Singing in the Shrouds*—occurs on page 19 of *Spinsters in Jeopardy*; the latest on page 195 of *Colour Scheme*. Between these two extremes, most occur somewhere between pages 50 and 105 in novels of 230 to 330 pages, allowing plenty of time for the reader to meet the principal suspects, her usual, but not invariable, method. One would assume that Alleyn would appear shortly after the murder, and that is generally true, but in five novels he is introduced on the first page, and in five others he also appears before murder happens. In eight he does not appear until after page 100, and in *Colour Scheme*, where he is in disguise—admittedly rather obvious—his actual identity is not revealed until the very last line.

As noted, most of the novels follow the classical formulas— many with individualized distinctiveness—but others do not. *Spinsters in Jeopardy* is Hitchcockian with the Alleyn family accidentally witnessing a murder from a train, the six-year-old Ricky being kidnapped in the Maritime Alps and a subsequent chase to rescue him, and an orgiastic cult in a cliff-hanging castle as a cover for drug-dealing, whose meeting is invaded by Alleyn and the young Raoul Milano in disguise. *Colour Scheme* offers a World War II spy story blended with theatrical satire, a Cinderella-type romance, and the exotic Maori culture and the landscape of New Zealand's North Island. Troy's dominance of the action in *Clutch of*

Constables and Ricky's in *Last Ditch* are not typical roles for family members of a fictional British detective. The hysteria and commercialism surrounding the spring of the Green Lady in *Dead Water* is an effective and unusual backdrop for murder. Even more is the Marsh-invented folk-myth of the Mardian Morris of the Five Sons and Betty, Crack and Fool, which is the structural framework of *Death of a Fool*—and nothing less than a fictional *tour de force*. The differences between the absurdly comic antics of the Lamprey family in *Death of a Peer* and the tense four-suspect puzzle of *Died in the Wool* are other indications of Marsh's range, and examples could be multiplied. The point that the past few pages have attempted to make clear is that, in spite of Roderick Alleyn's always being present, there is *variety of structure*, as well as detail, in Marsh's fiction, a fact that some critics have failed to acknowledge.

The values present in Marsh's novels are those of the upper-middle class, tempered by her career in the theatre. Like most of her Golden Age colleagues, Marsh is a detached observer of the foibles and frailties of her characters. Though they may be treated romantically, there is always distance between them and their creator. This is true even of Alleyn; no one can say that Marsh fell in love with her detective. Her basic view of her characters is one of amusement, especially evident in the numerous satiric portraits scattered throughout the novels. Though conservative in her view of society's need for stability and of the necessity of protecting property, she is liberal, again in comparison with most Golden Age writers, in matters of morals. There are few authorial comments on moral, as opposed to criminal, lapses in the novels, the major exception being the taking of drugs, about which she obviously feels strongly, nor does religious belief play a significant part. However, she does present the police as a moral force. Never is there a doubt that Alleyn, Fox and their aides are on the side of justice; rather they are the exceptional upholders and preservers of what is best in their society. Her presentation of Troy Alleyn's career—and Alleyn's considering it more important than his own—provides an added dimension to her works, one unusual enough in the 1930s to cause opposition to Troy's introduction. In summary, Marsh follows the conventions of Golden Age detective fiction, but her own acutely clear-eyed and sensitive nature have enabled her to incorporate elements of the novel of manners, of romance, of satire, of character and of her personal interests to create a distinctly individual body of work.

When one considers that Marsh has been writing detective fiction for forty-six years, with little sign of diminished power, one can only be surprised by the consistently high level of her accomplishment. Though she has not written as much in that long period as others in her field, she has brought a style to her work which those more prolific must envy. Readers have come to expect and to delight in the distinguishing characteristics of her fiction, including her leisurely plots, with little physical action; her bizarre murders, sometimes more zany than horrible; her clever dialogue which rarely becomes silly; her skill at description which never becomes padding or clutter; her exploration of character and character-types; and her creation of one of the most famous of gentlemen-policemen, Roderick Alleyn. She has accepted the formulas and conventions of the Golden Age, but, while remaining within their boundaries, has adapted them in her own way through five decades into the 1980s, and that is no mean achievement.[7]

Notes

[1]The editions of Marsh's novels used for this study are listed below, preceded by the original date of publication. All quotations will be cited in the text using, where necessary, the abbreviations given after an entry:

1934 *A Man Lay Dead*, New York: Pyramid, 1973. (*Man*)
1935 *Enter a Murderer*, New York: Berkley, 1963 (*Enter*)
1936 *The Nursing Home Murder*, New York: Pyramid, 1973 (*Nursing*)
1936 *Death in Ecstasy*, New York: Berkley, 1974 (*Ecstasy*)
1937 *Vintage Murder*, New York: Pyramid, 1973 (*Vintage*)
1938 *Artists in Crime*, New York: Berkley, 1963 (*Artists*)
1938 *Death in a White Tie*, New York: Pyramid, 1974 (*Tie*)
1939 *Overture to Death*, New York: Pyramid, 1974 (*Overture*)
1940 *Death at the Bar*, New York: Berkley, 1962 (*Bar*)
1940 *Death of a Peer*, New York: Berkley, 1961 (*Peer*)
1941 *Death and the Dancing Footman*, New York: Berkley, 1961 (*Footman*)
1943 *Colour Scheme*, New York: Berkley, 1961 (*Scheme*)
1945 *Died in the Wool*, New York: Berkley, 1978 (*Wool*)
1947 *Final Curtain*, New York: Berkley, 1961 (*Curtain*)
1949 *A Wreath for Rivera*, New York: Berkley, 1962 (*Wreath*)
1951 *Night at the Vulcan*, New York: Pyramid, 1974 (*Vulcan*)
1953 *Spinsters in Jeopardy*, New York: Berkley, 1961 (*Spinsters*)
1955 *Scales of Justice*, New York: Berkley, 1960 (*Scales*)
1956 *Death of a Fool*, New York: Pyramid, 1973 (*Fool*)
1958 *Singing in the Shrouds*, New York: Pyramid, 1974 (*Shrouds*)
1958 *False Scent*, New York: Berkley, 1967 (*Scent*)
1962 *Hand in Glove*, New York: Pyramid, 1973 (*Glove*)
1963 *Dead Water*, New York: Berkley, 1970 (*Water*)
1966 *Killer Dolphin*, New York: Berkley, 1967 (*Dolphin*)
1969 *Clutch of Constables*, New York: Berkley, 1978 (*Constables*)
1971 *When in Rome*, New York: Berkley, 1972 (*Rome*)
1972 *Tied Up in Tinsel*, New York: Pyramid, 1973 (*Tinsel*)
1973 *Black As He's Painted*, New York: Pyramid, 1976 (*Black*)
1977 *Last Ditch*, Boston: Little, Brown, 1977 (*Ditch*)
1978 *Grave Mistake*, Boston: Little, Brown, 1978 (*Grave*)
1000 *Photo Finish*, Boston: Little, Brown, 1980

Marsh has written only three short stories. All involve Roderick Alleyn, and all were originally published in *Ellery Queen's Mystery Magazine*: "I Can Find My Way Out" (1946), "Death on the Air" (1948), and "Chapter and Verse: The Little Copplestone Mystery" (1973).

[2]Marsh's few major comments on her work may be found in *Black Beech and Honeydew*, Boston, 1965—but 220 of the 287 pages are concerned with her life before she wrote her first detective novel; "Roderick Alleyn," *The Great Detectives,* ed. Otto Penzler, Boston, 1978, pp. 3-8; "Portrait of Troy," *Murderess Ink,* ed. Dilys Winn, New York, 1979, pp. 142-43; and a 1972 statement quoted in *Contemporary Novelists,* ed. James Binson, New York & London, 1976, p. 908, part of which says: "The earliest books were written in the style of the time—post-Dorothy Sayers—and had perhaps some affinity with Marjorie Allingham rather than with Agatha Christie. They have developed, I hope, into stories of crime and its detection in which the emphasis is on style and character rather than on mechanics."

[3]*The Puritan Pleasures of the Detective Story*, London, 1972, p. 147. Nicholas Blake comments that one line of development in detective fiction is a "toning down from the Sherlock Holmes to the Roderick Alleyn type" ("The Detective Story—Why?" *The Art of the Mystery Story,* ed. Howard Haycraft, New York, 1976, p. 404). The present discussion of Alleyn is largely based upon my article "Roderick Alleyn: Ngaio Marsh's Oxonian Superintendent," *The Armchair Detective,* 11 (January 1978), 63-71.

[4]"Portrait of Troy," pp. 142 & 143.

[5]"Portrait of Troy," p. 142. For a discussion of Marsh's use of the theatre as setting (and more) for detective fiction, see my article "Ngaio Marsh's 'Theatrical' Murders," *The Armchair Detective,* 10 (April 1977), 175-181.

[6]"Murder Most Tidy: Ngaio Marsh," *The New Republic,* 30 July 1977, p. 36. LeRoy Panek says that the inevitable formula in Marsh's pre-World War II novels is "introduction, murder, interviews, recapitulation, action, reenactment, and summary. It always happens this way" (*Watteau's Shepherds: The Detective Novel in Britain 1914-1940,* Bowling Green, Ohio, 1979, p. 196). This statement is a demonstrable over-simplification.

[7]Several months after this essay was completed, I learned from Little, Brown and Company that *Photo Finish*, Marsh's thirty-first novel, would be published in late 1980. Ms. Elaine Isherwood of Little, Brown arranged for an advance copy to be sent to me so that I might include the following comments, and she has my sincere appreciation.

Photo Finish is typical of Marsh's work, and, in spite of an unexplained three-year wait by the murderer to effect his crime, it is evidence that age has not weakened her ability to charm and mystify. It shows her roots in the Golden Age more clearly than her other recent novels. The victim is an internationally famous soprano, who is killed after the performance of a new opera. The murder occurs at a luxurious island lodge in the middle of a lake in the Westland of South Island, New Zealand, during a raging storm: in other words, the Golden Age closed circle. As characters say, they are "cut off" and the murderer is "one of us."

Troy and Alleyn are present, for Troy has been commissioned to paint the soprano's portrait. When murder occurs, Alleyn must again reluctantly take charge; his reactions are that he is "poking about without authority" (211) and is "expected to behave like everybody's idea of an infallible sleuth" (219). Of course he is and solves the case in less than twenty-four hours. He is somewhat more philosophical than usual, but otherwise is unchanged. His knowledge of Italian provides a major clue; he quotes from or alludes to Shakespeare, Congreve, Gilbert, Shaw, Strindberg and Stoppard; he suffers because of Troy's involvement; and on five occasions he gives his conclusions to other characters without the reader's being allowed to know them. (Alleyn and Troy's dizzying trip over the pass from Canterbury Plain to Westland offers Marsh the opportunity to describe again the thrill of her first such trip, which she earlier presented in *Black Beech and Honeydew*.)

Other elements that are repetitions or variations of earlier novels include the operatic world, so closely related to the theatrical; the emphasis upon physical clues; drug dealing as a red herring (as well as two new ones: a malicious *paparazzo* and hints of *mafiosi*); a very bizarre death; and various distinctive suspects and witnesses: a homosexual secretary, an unflappable housekeeper, a voluble Italian singing teacher, a reserved financier, a doctor as Alleyn's aide, a handsome young composer, and a hysterical Italian maid—not all of whom are what they seem.

All in all, *Photo Finish* is an excellent example of Golden Age detective fiction as written in the 1980s. Like Dame Ngaio, the formulas and conventions endure.

P. D. James
Photo by Jerry Bauer

P.D. James

1920	Phyllis Dorothy James born on August 3 in Oxford, England
1931-37	Educated at Cambridge Girls' High School
1941	Married C.B. White
1942	Daughter, Clare, born
1944	Daughter, Jane, born
1949-68	Administrative assistant, North West Regional Hospital Board, London
1962	First novel, *Cover Her Face,* published
1964	Husband died
1968	Short story, "Moment of Power," won first prize in *Ellery Queen's Mystery Magazine*
1968-79	Senior civil servant, Criminal Department of Home Office London
1971	*Shroud for a Nightingale* won Edgar from Mystery Writers of America and Silver Dagger from British Crime Writers Association
1972	*An Unsuitable Job for a Woman* won award from Mystery Writers of America
1975	*The Black Tower* won Silver Dagger
1980	*Innocent Blood* published, a Book-of-the Month Club selection and prospective film

by Nancy Carol Joyner

P.D. James' writing career formally commenced in 1962, when, at age forty-two and an administrator for the National Health Service, she published her first novel, *Cover Her Face*. Faber and Faber, the first publishing house to which the manuscript was sent, accepted it and has continued to be her British publisher for the ensuing seven novels. Just as she has never had a manuscript rejected, she has never produced a book that did not receive critical approval, and each publication has brought her a wider audience and more enthusiastic critical attention. Other successful writers have begun their publishing careers when they were past forty—Sherwood Anderson is an example— and other writers of detective fiction have held demanding non-literary jobs while writing prolifically—Josephine Bell and Joseph Wambaugh come to mind; nevertheless, such careers are exceptions that prove the rule. P.D. James' career, and her writing, are exceptional.

She is, in several interpretations of the phrase, a serious writer. Like her frequently solemn detective, Adam Dalgliesh, the style of her books is serious, the novels themselves invite serious analysis, and James is thoroughly serious about her career. This singularity of purpose has contributed to the increasing complexity and sophistication of her work. This study will focus on her developing achievement and those elements of content and style that make her writing distinctive.

I. Background and Influences

In an omnibus edition of three previously published novels, *Crime Times Three*, James concludes her graceful introduction with this paragraph:

One of the most common questions any crime writer is asked is why did you choose to write mystery fiction? In my case it was because I had always enjoyed reading mysteries (Dorothy L. Sayers was a potent early influence); I thought I might be able to write a mystery rather well; I reasoned that such a popular genre might have the best chance of acceptance by a publisher; and I saw the writing of detective fiction with its challenging disciplines, its inner tensions between plot, character, and atmosphere, and its necessary reliance on structure and form as the best possible apprenticeship for a serious novelist. Perhaps the chief reason why I am glad to have

108

these three early books reissued in hardcover is that each was a landmark in my gradual realization that, despite the constraints of this fascinating genre, a mystery writer can hope to call herself a serious novelist (ix).

Such a straightforward delineation of motives not only provides a key to James' style but also indicates the order of her priorities: the bottom line for her is the serious pursuit of her craft. She does not write "for fun," as is the claim of some mystery writers, nor does she seek a therapeutic outlet for the tensions created in her other responsibilities as homemaker and civil servant, nor does she set out primarily to find an easy way to supplement her income. The most important thing about the writing to her is the writing itself.

She has said that she always wanted to be a writer, but that the agitation of her life during World War II, her early marriage to a man who returned from that war an invalid, and the demands of raising her children had seemed to preclude her attempting to do so earlier. In a recent interview she talked about the difficulties of getting started:

I was nineteen when the war broke out and was living in London.... You don't start a novel when you don't know if you're going to see the morning.... And then my husband went away to war; he was a doctor. He came back ill; I had to look after him and two children and find a good safe job that would really bring in a wage check. In my mid-thirties I realized these were excuses because there is never an absolutely propitious time to starting down to write.[2]

When she did "start down to write," she did so in the early morning before she went to her job—between 6:00 and 8:00 a.m. Having established that work pattern, she has thrived on it, producing not only eight novels but also a book of non-fiction, *The Maul and the Pear Tree* (with Thomas A. Critchley, 1971), some six short stories, and several articles dealing with crime fiction. She has become a regular reviewer for the *Times Literary Supplement* and is in increasing demand from editors soliciting theoretical articles on mystery fiction. In fact, the demands (as well as the rewards) of her writing are now such that in December 1979 she resigned her position in the Criminal Department of the British Home Office.

When James' books first appeared in paperback in the United States, in a uniform edition of Popular Library books, there was emblazoned on the front cover, "Agatha Christie's Crown Princess," a phrase taken from Antonia Fraser's review of *An Unsuitable Job for a Woman*. No mystery accrues to the publicists' choice of gimmick—it was, after all, the year of Christie's demise— but certainly to crown James as Christie's successor is an unsuitable attribution. Recently she told an interviewer that the only legitimate comparisons between her and Christie are that they are both female, British and middle class. The principal difference between them, she has pointed out, is that Christie is more "psychologically reassuring," and she suggests that a potential reader might think, " 'Perhaps I won't read another P.D. James—I need something lighter.' By lighter, they may mean something like a Christie, not so involved in the actual pain of people." Although the two writers do have in common a facility for domestic detail, their methods and presumably their purposes are sharply distinct. The difference is seen most obviously, perhaps, in a consideration of the reader's reaction to Christie's Poirot and James' principal detective, Adam Dalgliesh: while Poirot is seen as basically a risible character, Dalgliesh is presented in such a way as to elicit the reader's empathy.

The two mystery writers whom James has often cited as influences are Dorothy L. Sayers and Margery Allingham. Reading Sayers was an early enthusiasm and of her she has recently written, "To her admirers she is the writer who did more than any other to make the detective story intellectually respectable and to change it from an ingenious but lifeless sub-literary puzzle into a specialized branch of fiction with serious claims to be judged as a novel."[3] In the same article she observes that Margery Allingham and Ngaio Marsh are the two most noteworthy followers of Sayers. In response to a television interviewer's question, "Who is your very, very favorite mystery writer—male or female?" she answered, "Margery Allingham," pointing out her attention to character and sense of place. While Sayers' hero, Lord Peter Wimsey, and Allingham's principal character, Albert Campion, are both among the British nobility and differ from Dalgliesh in that respect, there is nevertheless a similarity in presentation of the three detectives. James may be considered a literary descendent of Sayers and Allingham in many other ways, particularly in the care in which a variety of backgrounds are depicted and in the examination of the characters' motivations. For instance, James' creation of life in a school of nursing in *Shroud For a Nightingale* is quite as memorable as the advertising firm in Sayers' *Murder Must Advertise* or Allingham's dressmaking establishment in *The Fashion in Shrouds*. The permutations of attitude of James' Cordelia Gray in *An Unsuitable Job for a Woman* are as carefully recorded as those of Harriet Vane in Sayers' *Gaudy Night* and Gina Brande in Allingham's *Flowers for the Judge*.

Although James' formal education ended upon the completion of her work at the secondary school level, she is extraordinarily well read and incorporates in her novels frequent erudite allusions. Evelyn Waugh, Hardy and Trollope are among her favorite British writers, but the novelist whom she most admires is Jane Austen, and she has reported that among Austen novels she considers *Emma* the best. James' most recent novel, *Innocent Blood*, which represents her first departure from the classic detective formula, has been compared by at least one reviewer with the work of Austen.

To place James in the tradition of Sayers and Allingham, as well as Austen, is by no means to suggest that she is merely derivative. Her detectives, her settings, and, most distinctively, her style, are unquestionably her own. To her credit, a steady progression can be seen in her twenty year career; significant differences in idea and execution are obvious in a consideration of her first novel and her most recent one. Many readers agree with Carolyn Heilbrun that in the last two decades James has established herself as the best practitioner of the classic mystery novel.[4]

II. The Murder Sites

The first novel, *Cover Her Face*, is James' most conventional one in setting, dealing as it does with a murder in the Maxie's country house, Martingale, with the chief suspects the family members, houseguests and household servants. The first scene, an unsuccessful dinner party, introduces most of these suspects as well as the victim, Sally Jupp, a refugee from St. Mary's Refuge for Girls, who has been hired by Eleanor Maxie to work as a house-parlour maid. Sally has managed her job very well despite the demands of her young baby and the disapproving eye of Martha Bultitaft, the old family retainer. On the morning following the annual church fete, however, Sally is discovered in her locked bedroom dead. Detective Chief-Inspector Adam Dalgliesh is called in, and after he interviews all the suspects at Martingale and makes some excursions back to London, he calls the principals together for a final interview where the murderer confesses. It is a classic, locked-room story, distinguished by a remarkable fluency of language, incisive, brief descriptions, such as that of the family doctor, who "loved small fast cars from which he could only extricate himself with difficulty, and in which he looked like a wicked old bear out on a spree" (15), and an extraordinary portrait of the victim.

Quickly following her first novel came *A Mind to Murder,* in which most of the action occurs in London in the Steen Clinic, an exclusive establishment for the treatment of psychiatric disorders. Enid Bolam, the murder victim, had been the thoroughly unpopular administrative officer for the clinic. Dalgliesh, promoted to the rank of Superintendent here, acquaints himself with the medical and domestic staffs of the Steen and proceeds to unravel the mystery by discovering the complicated interrelationships among the employees. Professional as well as personal animosities are explored, including arguments over the best methods of treatment for the patients and bureaucratic jugglings for position. A particularly clever kind of blackmail provides a complication to the plot, and one of the significant figures involved in the solution of the mystery is Miss Bolam's cat, Tigger. Again there is a locked-room formula at work, but this story is more complex than the preceding one and concludes with the excitement of an imminent second murder. In this novel James brings to bear her specialized knowledge of the British hospital system and pokes genial fun at the medical establishment, such as the administrator's telling Dalgliesh that psychiatrists are easier to deal with than surgeons, "the real *prima donnas*" (43), or a secretary's offering her own psychoanalysis of the victim (91). Using as a background a medical institution has become James' most successful pattern.

The next novel, *Unnatural Causes*, however, shifts the scene from a medical establishment to a writers' colony, where Dalgliesh finds himself inadvertently and uncomfortably involved in the investigation of a murder while on a holiday visit to his aunt. Here the murder is introduced in the eye-catching first words of the book:

The corpse without hands lay in the bottom of a small sailing dinghy drifting just within sight of the Suffolk coast. It was the body of a middle-aged man, a dapper little cadaver, its shroud a dark pin-striped suit which fitted the narrow body as elegantly in death as it had in life. (7)

This "dapper little cadaver" is Maurice Seton, writer of second-rate mysteries and neighbor to a motley group of literary sorts—a critic, an editor, a writer of romantic novels, and a luminary whose last book had been published thirty years earlier. The official investigator in the case is the self-effacing little detective with the inspired name of Reckless. The investigation is conducted through the houses of Monksmere Head and along the coast, with occasional forays into London. This is the first novel in which there are multiple murders; it ends melodramatically with Dalgliesh himself an intended victim. Because many of the suspects are caricatures of literary types, this novel comes closest to having a comic tone of any James has written.

Shroud for a Nightingale, which won awards from the British Crime Writers Association and the Mystery Writers of America, takes as its colorful setting the Nurse Training School at Nightingale House, where two student nurses and one instructor are poisoned before the mystery is solved. The first murder is unquestionably the most spectacularly dramatic in all of James' novels, for Nurse Pearce meets her fate during a student demonstration of intra-gastric feeding when lysol is mixed with the warm milk poured into the oesophageal tube. When Dalgliesh is called in, he encounters a world depressing because of "the stultifying lack of privacy, and ... the small pettinesses and subterfuges with which people living in unwelcome proximity try to preserve their own privacy or invade that of others" (122). In this novel the investigation extends beyond the closed society of the dormitory, touching as it does upon the private lives of some of the doctors and patients and even extending to a bit of international intrigue. One of the most memorable interludes involves a dance competition in London, where Masterson, Dalgliesh's assistant, gleans an important clue. Again the novel ends melodramatically, with Dalgliesh being physically attacked and a midnight fire set with the intention of obscuring evidence. It is altogether James' most elaborately plotted novel to date, indicating her increasing aptitude in handling a large number of characters and locales.

James' fifth novel, *An Unsuitable Job for a Woman*, is a radical departure from her pattern, not only because Dalgliesh has only a minor role but also because she has abandoned the closed circle of the classic mystery novel. Cordelia Gray is commissioned to investigate the circumstances surrounding the suicide of the son of a prominent Cambridge scientist. Having moved into the cottage where Mark Callender was found hanged, she traces clues that involve Mark's tutor, several student friends, his family, his nurse, his mother's doctor and so forth. Conversations with this large group of people and research in the university library convince Cordelia that Mark was in fact murdered. She is hampered both by her inexperience and the active efforts of several different people to obfuscate the facts. These efforts lead to two of the more notable scenes in the novel: once she comes home late at night to find an effigy hanging in her living room, and shortly thereafter she is attacked, loses consciousness, and when she comes to finds herself down a well with the cover closed. The plot culminates with Cordelia going to the murderer's residence, where, almost immediately after the confrontation and accusation, she witnesses the fatal shooting of the murderer. It concludes with Cordelia being questioned in Dalgleish's office, steadfastly recalcitrant about revealing the name of the second murderer.

The Black Tower, winner of a Silver Dagger Award, marks a return to James' earlier pattern in that Dalgliesh investigates a variety of maleficent acts at Toynton Grange, "a private home for the young disabled" (9). He goes there at the behest of Father Baddeley, a saintly old family friend, but arrives days after the priest's death. He stays in the priest's lodgings, Hope Cottage, on the pretext of sorting out the library he has inherited, and encounters blackmail, poison pen letters, sexual perversions and perversities, a drug smuggling ring, as well as the largest number of murders and attempted murders in any of the novels to this point. These bizarre activities are made to appear plausible because of the unusual setting, a convalescent home, owned and operated by the unspecifically religious Wilfred Anstay, where a motley group of patients who are debilitated by vague but sinister diseases find refuge. Part of the evil doings take place on the rocky Dorset coast and in the black tower, a folly that had been built to serve as a tomb for Wilfred's grandfather. When Dalgliesh first inspects it, two of the ambulatory inhabitants explain it to him. One says,

> I like the black tower.... It's a symbol really, isn't it? It looks magical, unreal, a folly built to amuse a child. And underneath there's horror, pain, madness and death. (111)

At the risk of his own death Dalgliesh manages to unravel the tangled skein of clues that explain the plethora of crimes. It is James' most complex book so far, and, because of the unifying influence of the black tower and Dalgliesh's personal interest in solving the crime, it is, I feel, her most successful work.

Death of an Expert Witness has been criticized in some quarters because of the confusing of characters and subplots. While it may be true that stories of individual characters give the book an air of digressiveness, it is nevertheless also true that the settings for the murders are very clearly presented. The main story is framed by investigations in the clunch field, "the local name for the soft chalk they mined here from the middle ages onward" (27). Like the eponymous black tower of the preceding novel, this part of the landscape is described in symbolic terms, this time a "wasteland" (1). The principal setting, however, is Hoggart's laboratory, a fictional forensic science establishment in East Anglia. Found murdererd in his lab is the Principal Scientific Officer in charge of the Biology Department, Dr. Edwin Lorrimer, a man as thoroughly competent as he is thoroughly disliked, so mean that he tells the truth to his insufficient assistant and shouts at children. Dalgliesh, unusually aloof, is called in to untangle the complicated strands of this mystery, sorting out a confusing array of personal and professional motives for this crime which entirely too many people had the opportunity to commit. Like three previous novels, this book deals with a medical, bureaucratic establishment, with the setting most closely resembling *A Mind to Murder*. Unlike *A Mind to Murder,* however, a second murder is not averted, and the person who has knowledge potentially dangerous to the murderer is found hanging in the unused seventeenth century chapel close to the lab.

Literally the longest of James' crime novels, *Death of an Expert*

Witness is also the largest in scope insofar as the scene, as well as the characters, is concerned. The town of Chevisham, the locale, becomes important to the plot, with relatively minor excursions to local entertainments, such as a performance featuring Morris dancers, and a careful description of the Moonraker, an establishment run by the Gotobeds where Dalgliesh and his lieutenant find accommodations during their stay. Dalgliesh first sees Chevisham from a helicopter as he is being conveyed to his case, and the description of his view from above the sprawling area is particularly appropriate to this sprawling and complex novel.

As reviewers have clamorously noted, James' most recent novel, *Innocent Blood,* is not bound by the constraints of the classic mystery. So many elements of the traditional form are included, however, that it merits attention here. Two violent deaths are meticulously described, one in an Essex village and one in London. Two amateur detectives appear: Philippa Palfrey, the protagonist who is searching for her roots by seeking out her natural mother, and Norman Scase, father of the twelve-year-old murder victim, who seeks revenge by also searching for Philippa's natural mother. From the first chapter, clues are carefully planted that lead up to the climactic revelation. The primary setting of this book is London, James' home throughout her adult life, and she describes the streets and parks of that great city with meticulous care. Although she used a London setting in *A Mind to Murder,* she is able in *Innocent Blood* to treat more neighborhoods and to do so more expansively. The flat where Philippa and her mother live temporarily is called Mell Street in the book but is clearly modelled on London's Bell Street. Most often, however, James describes actual places without bothering to disguise names. On more than one occasion James has said that setting is of primary importance to a novel. The more she writes, the larger and more vivid her settings become. This use of setting is one of her strongest areas of development.

III. The Murder Sights

James is a firm believer in realistic detail. Not only is she able to paint her backgrounds for the action so clearly that the reader has no trouble seeing them with the mind's eye, but also she demonstrates this same aptitude in her descriptions of individuals and actions. This predilection is observed nowhere more forcefully than in her description of the corpses that inevitably appear in her novels. They are painstakingly treated, as a few examples will indicate:

Here was chaos. The chair was overturned. The floor was littered with records. . . .

And in the middle of this confusion, like a plump and incongruous Ophelia afloat on a tide of paper, was the body of Enid Bolam. On her chest rested a heavy and grotesque image carved in wood, her hands folded about its base so that she looked, horribly, like a parody of motherhood with her creature ritually laid to her breast *(Mind,* 17).

or this:

The neck was elongated so that her bare feet, their toes pointed like a dancer's, hung less than a foot from the floor. The stomach muscles were taut. Above them the high rib cage looked as brittle as a bird's. The head lolled grotesquely on the right shoulder like a horrible caricature of a disjointed puppet. The eyes had rolled upwards under half-open lids. The swollen tongue had forced itself between the lips *(Woman,* 92).

James frequently embellishes the descriptions of her bodies with metaphor—a face that has "the vacuous look of an adult clown" (*Witness,* 20-21) for instance. She also brings into play her inordinately fine command of the language in these descriptions, as in "the wound was a neat grumous slit in the heavey forehead" *(Tower,* 258).

The preceding descriptions are certainly more vivid than one usually finds in mysteries of this sort. But these descriptions are of the already dead and therefore necessarily stationary. Far more vivid are her rather rare descriptions of the dying. In *Shroud For a Nightingale,* the first death takes place during a classroom demonstration, and with it James surpasses herself:

One second she was lying, immobile, propped against her mound of pillows, the next she was out of bed, teetering forward on arched feet in a parody of a ballet dancer.... And all the time she screamed, perpetually screamed, like a stuck whistle. Miss Beale aghast, had hardly time to register the contorted face, the foaming lips, doubled like a hoop, her forehead touching the ground, her whole body twitching in agony.... The screaming had stopped now. It was succeeded by a piteous moaning and a dreadful staccato drumming of heels on the wooden floor (25-26).

James once remarked that Christie's victims are so politely described that the reader sometimes expects them to get up off the floor and take a bow. James does not have that worry with her own corpses; they are unequivocally dead.

James' descriptive powers are not limited, of course, to the dead people in her books. The novels are filled with precise details of every sort. Ordinarily the houses in which the crimes have been committed are presented in Dalgliesh's view and the reader's simultaneously. Restaurants, churches and law offices are also carefully noticed. But it is in particular, small details that James is at her best. The interior of one of the cottages in *The Black Tower* is partially described in this way:

There was a square table set in the middle of the room bearing what looked like the remains of a late lunch; a torn packet of water biscuits spilling crumbs; a lump of cheese on a chipped plate; butter oozing from its greasy wrapping; a topless bottle of tomato ketchup with the sauce congealed around the lip. Two bloated flies buzzed their intricate convolutions above the debris (164).

While James uses a respectable amount of dialogue and sometimes uses dialect creditably, she is better at conveying emotional states through physical description. Notable, for instance, is Brenda Pridmore's reaction to discovering one of the bodies in *Death of an Expert Witness:*

She had no memory of closing the lab door or coming down the stairs. Inspector Blakelock was still behind the counter, rigid as a statue, the telephone receiver in his hand. She wanted to laugh at the sight of his face, he looked so funny. She tried to speak to him, but the words wouldn't come. Her jaw jabbered uncontrollably and her teeth chattered together (82-83).

The following two pages describe the flurry of activity from the heightened point of view of Brenda in shock: the lights seem brighter, the voices are higher, the faces more grotesque; it is as though Brenda were watching a play from the stalls. Finally she notices Mrs. Bidwell, the cleaning woman, who speaks directly to her, " 'Did you find him then? You poor little bugger!' " (83). It is only then that the scene regains some normality for her: "She felt Mrs. Bidwell's arms go around her shoulders. The smell of the mackintosh was pressed into her face. The fur was as soft as her kitten's paw. And, blessedly, Brenda began to cry" (83). This careful delineation of an hysterical reaction is remarkable in its vividness. The choice of detail gives the description an extraordinary verisimilitude.

Such scenes in which an individual's heightened emotional state is described are not common in James' work, but they appear with increasing frequency in her late novels. Brenda Pridmore's subsequent discovery of a second body is similarly skillfully written (*Witness*, 290-93). Ursula Hollis manages to negotiate a set of stairs although she is unable to walk in the *Black Tower*. In the same novel, James also demonstrates his skill when Grace Willison does not die "ungently" through suffocation. *Innocent Blood* includes numerous descriptions of this sort, notably Philippa's reaction when she discovers her real mother is alive and a convicted murderer (20), and Mary Ducton's description of her murder of the child (154-65). As her writing develops, James' powers of description markedly increase.

IV. The Principals

James' featured detective is Adam Dalgliesh, a police inspector who has published at least two volumes of poetry and whose misgivings about his profession are matched only by his conviction that he is good at what he does. He is introduced in *Cover Her Face,* when he first goes to view the body of Sally Jupp:

> He stood very still looking down at her. He was never conscious of pity at moments like this and not even of anger, although that might come later and would have to be resisted. He liked to fix the sight of the murdered body firmly in his mind. This had been a habit since his first big case seven years ago when he had looked down at the battered corpse of a Soho prostitute in silent resolution and had thought, "This is it. This is my job." (63).

Aside from learning something of his methodology in this initial scene, the reader discovers that the Detective Chief-Inspector is an experienced officer, having been on the police force at least seven years. James has said that she decided against making her detective hero an amateur in the interest of realism. She calls him "above all, a professional detective" (*Crime, viii*). In the course of the six novels in which he appears, he has been awarded two promotions—first to superintendent and then to commander.

Dalgliesh's manner and methods are presented as being entirely professional. For one thing, "he had never been known to lose his temper with a witness" (*Cover, 108*). The adverb "gravely" is frequently used to describe how he responds to outrageously irrelevant or illogical statements from witnesses. Free of affectation and eccentricity, Dalgliesh is generally accorded a rather unenthusiastic respect by the people whom he interrogates. For instance, one of the nurses sees him coming through the lunch line in the hospital dining hall in *Shroud For a Nightingale* and thinks:

> He seemed utterly at ease and almost oblivious of the alien world around him. She thought that he was probably a man who could never imagine himself at a disadvantage in any company since he was secure in his private world, possessed of that core of inner self-esteem which is the basis of happiness. . . . Probably he would be thought handsome by most women, with that lean bony face, at once arrogant and sensitive. It was probably one of his professional assets (139-40).

While Dalgliesh presents to the world an almost unassailable composure, the reader is privy to his vicissitudes of mood and to the introspection that is his single most marked characteristic. *Unnatural Causes* and *The Black Tower* are the two novels most revealing about his private attitudes and are the two novels, incidentally, that allude to his childhood as a parson's son. In *Unnatural Causes* his predominant mood seems to be one of irrascibility as he becomes embroiled in a murder investigation while on holiday. *The Black Tower* delineates his recuperation from an illness he had feared was mortal and his resultant despondency:

More than his job now seemed to him trivial and unsatisfactory. Lying sleepless as so many patient must have done before him in that bleak impersonal room, watching the headlamps of passing cars sweep across the ceiling, listening to the secretive and muted noises of the hopital's nocturnal life, he took the dispiriting inventory of his life (8).

Relatively little is known about Dalgliesh's private life. That he is a widower and a poet is mentioned regularly but briefly in the novels. His natural reserve would naturally prohibit his alluding to his personal life while on the job. In the first novel, when a mother asks him a rhetorical question about his son, he responds this way:

He wondered what she would say if he replied, "I have no son. My only child and his mother died three hours after he was born."... He could imagine her frown of well-bred distaste that he should embarrass her at such a time with a private grief at once so old, so intimate, so unrelated to the matter at hand (*Cover, 96*).

Dalgliesh does, however, become personally involved with one of the murder suspects in this case, Deborah Riscoe, and the first novel ends with his unsuccessful struggle to think of something to say to her that is neither maudlin nor insincere. He sees her briefly in the next novel, *A Mind to Murder*, when she attends the "ritual autumn sherry party given by his publishers" (21). At the sight of her he is reminded that he is "on the brink of love" and is disconcerted by the possiblity of a strong commitment. This consideration serves as a frame for the third novel, *Unnatural Causes*, which begins and ends with his thinking about Deborah: at the beginning he is wondering whether or not to propose to her and at the end he writes a literarily respectable amorous sonnet to her, which he does not mail before he receives her letter telling him that she "could no longer bear to loiter about on the periphery of his life waiting for him to make up his mind" (256). Dalgliesh finds the murderess herself extremely attractive in the next novel, *Shroud For a Nightingale*, although there is no suggestion of a liaison there. In *The Black Tower* an allusion is made to several women friends, with James' other detective, Cordelia Gray, in prominence, but it is made clear that all of these relationships are casual at best.

James has said that her readers have frequently asked her about Dalgliesh's private life and wonder if he will re-marry. She claims ignorance on the point herself, but says that it is "highly doubtful" that he should do so (*Crime, vi*). Because readers do become interested in the personal lives of the detective hero, it is important that the romantic adventures of Dalgliesh be mentioned, but, in keeping with the tradition, it is equally important that those concerns be only briefly mentioned. To focus on romance would make the novels subscribe to an entirely different genre.

An Unsuitable Job for a Woman has been the one novel so far devoted to the adventures of Cordelia Gray, a detective heroine who has received considerable critical attention because of her sex.[5] Gray may be considered a professional detective, although in this novel she is hardly more than an apprentice, having become the inadvertent sole owner of a detective agency when her ineffective partner commits suicide. She is a sturdy twenty-two year old who has grown up in a series of foster homes because her "itinerant" father had no time for her. She is young, resilient, intelligent, and inexperienced.

Her first case, a presumed suicide that she discovers is really murder, concludes with her complicity in the death of the murderer and her refusal to tell the truth to Scotland Yard, represented by Adam Dalgliesh. The solution of the case includes a quotation from Blake and involves her in the life of a group of Cambridge University students. She is able to solve the case through her own powers of deduction and because she remembers numerous bits of advice her former partner had given her. When she lies on the witness stand and to Dalgliesh, she does so to protect the murderer of the murderer, thus achieving a higher justice than she believes would have been possible in a court of law. This idealism and refusal to accede to the system are appropriate to her youth and sharply distinguish her from Dalgliesh, who scrupulously follows the rules.

Although the protagonist of James' most recent novel, *Innocent Blood*, is not in the strict sense a detective, she nevertheless bears a strong resemblance to Cordelia Gray. Rather than attempting to solve a murder mystery in *Innocent Blood*, the adopted Philippa Rose Palfrey sets out to discover her identity through the search for her real parents. Like Cordelia she is inexperienced, intelligent and independent. Unlike Cordelia she has been given an upper middle class upbringing with a strong emphasis on culture and aesthetic considerations.

In James' full canvas there are of course many notable characters other than the protagonists of the novels. For one thing, Adam invariably has assistants of one sort or another as he investigates the murders. Sometimes the assistant is someone with whom Dalgliesh is uncomfortable, as in the case of Detective Inspector Reckless in *Unnatural Causes*: "He couldn't guess what Reckless was feeling, he could only recognize with a kind of hopeless irritation his own awkwardness and dislike" (205). Usually, however, Dalgliesh and his assistants get along very well. Two of the principal assistants are Sergeant Charles Masterson of *Shroud For a Nightingale*, a large man "generally considered handsome, particularly by himself" (58) who extracts important evidence during a bizarre tango contest (225-40), and the honorable John

Massigham of *Death of an Expert Witness*, the eldest son of a peer who does well in "this far from orthodox job" (102). Because "Honjohn," as the police call him behind his back, does so well, and because James is following her mentors, Sayers and Allingham, in picking a detective from the nobility, it is possible that he will appear in a second novel. However, thus far James has not reintroduced assistant detectives in later novels.

James does not limit her considerable abilities at charaterization to the detectives, of course. In the eight novels numerous victims, villains, red herrings, and characters who are redundant to the plot line are vividly drawn. Sally Jupp, the charming conniver of *Cover Her Face*, Mary Taylor, the elegantly sophisicated matron of the John Carpendar School of Nursing (*Shroud*), Henry Carwardine, the patient presented with dignified pathos in *The Black Tower*, and Maxim Howarth, the palely passionate director of Hoggatt's Lab *(Witness)* are all notable for their strongly individualistic portrayals.

Although James occasionally entertains the reader with pleasantly eccentric, two-dimensional characters, she has deservedly been singled out as a mystery writer who is adept at dealing with complex personalities who often are driven by some psychological aberration. The exploration of these subterranean complexities of the characters contributes to the seriousness of tone of the James canon.

V. The Principles

That element of good writing variously called the author's philisophical stance, world view, or general attitude, is best discerned in parts of the novel that do not pertain directly to plot, setting, or characterization. It appears in expository embellishments to the main story or in apparently incidental observations of characters or author. Such material in James' novels may be divided thematically into three areas: aesthetic, intellectual, and ecclesiastical. An examination of themes from these perspectives indicates an emerging pattern: characters most sophisticated about art and scholarly pursuits often are deficient in moral perceptions, and vice versa. With the striking exception of the chapel murder scene in *Death of an Expert Witness*, however, the church is consistently a symbol for order and altruism.

To support this thesis it need only be pointed out that among James' murderers are a scholar, an artist and an art connoisseur. But James' references to art do not stop there. When Adam is called to the murder case at the Steen Clinic, for instance, he recalls that that is the place with an original Modigliani (*Mind*, 26). In the course of Cordelia Gray's investigation, she notices that what she has thought is a print is an original Renoir (*Women, 124*). The single painting in Maxim Howarth's sitting room is "a Sidney Nolan oil of Ned Kelly" (*Witness, 207*). These details are almost always used in conjunction with an unsavory group or individual. In James' world evidence of aesthetic acuity is an implicit indictment of, if not sheer villainy, at least an unsympathetic attitude toward other members of one's society.

People associated with intellectual pursuits represent a more eclectic attitude on the part of James: some are reprehensible, but some, on the contrary, are to be admired. Edwin Lorrimer in *Death of an Expert Witness* and Sir Ronald Callender of *An Unsuitable Job for a Woman* seem as accomplished as they are unpleasant. On the other hand, Henry Carwardine of *The Black Tower* and Dalgliesh himself are both sympathetic and erudite characters. Often Dalgliesh demonstrates his ability at philosophical colloquy (*Shroud*, 87 and *Witness*, 186). Usually, however, this kind of activity is in reference to one of the more sinister characters in the novels.

Religion is treated quite differently from philosophy and art. Two clergymen, Father Baddeley in *The Black Tower* and Canon Hubert Boxdale in the short story, "Great Aunt Allie's Flypapers," are thoroughly good men.[6] Religious ceremonies and church buildings themselves are frequently mentioned and usually emphasize moral responsibility (*Mind*, 160-62, *Blood*, 170-71, 305-11). Some characters, to be sure, suffer from an excess of religious fervor, as is the case of Enid Bolam in *A Mind to Murder* and Nurse Pearce in *Shroud for a Nightingale*. Significantly, each of these characters tries to impose her religious practice upon her colleagues and each is a murder victim. Most of the references to ecclesiastical habits or theology, however, indicate that James sees religion as a positive force in society.

Finally, P.D. James is distinguished not only because of her deftness in creating plot, setting and character, but also because of her demonstration of moral sensitivity and humanistic concerns. These attitudes permeate the novels, manifesting themselves in her awareness of societal reform and her acceptance of physically and psychologically maimed human beings as being worthy subjects. In "The Art of Fiction" Henry James deals with the moral sense of the novel and makes as a final point "the very obvious truth that the deepest quality of a work of art will always be the quality of the mind of the producer." It only belabors the obvious to aver the high quality of P.D. James' art.

Notes

[1]James' eight novels are listed below. All quotations will be cited in the text using, where necessary, the abbreviation given after an entry.

1962   *Cover Her Face*, New York: Scribner's, 1966 (*Cover*)
1963   *A Mind to Murder*, New York: Scribner's, 1967 (*Mind*)
1967   *Unnatural Causes*, New York: Popular Library (*Causes*)
1971   *Shroud for a Nightingale*, New York: Scribner's (*Shroud*)
1972   *An Unsuitable Job for a Woman*, New York: Popular Library (*Woman*)
1975   *The Black Tower*, New York: Popular Library (*Tower*)
1977   *Death of an Expert Witness*, New York: Popular Library (*Witness*)
1980   *Innocent Blood*, New York: Scribner's (*Blood*)
Also two omnibus editions have appeared, each with an introduction:
1979   *Crime Times Three*, New York: Scribner's (*Cover, Mind, Shroud*)
1980   *Murder in Triplicate*, New York: Scribner's (*Causes, Woman, Tower*)

[2]Interviews with James used in this section include one with the author in New York, June 3, 1980; one on a Washington, D.C. talk show, *Panorama*, June 4, 1980; and one published by Jane S. Bakerman in *The Armchair Detective* 10 (January, 1977), 55-57, 92.

[3]"Dorothy L. Sayers; From Puzzle to Novel," in *Crime Writers,* ed. H.R.F. Keating (London: British Broadcasting Corporation, 1978), p. 64.

[4]"James P.D.," in *Twentieth Century Crime and Mystery Writers*, ed. John M. Reilly (New York: St. Martin's Press, 1980), 857.

[5]See Lillian de la Torre, "Cordelia Gray: The Thinking Man's Heroine," in *Murderess Ink*, ed. Dilys Winn (New York: Workman, 1979), pp. 111-112; and Carolyn G. Heilbrun, "A Feminist Looks at Women in Detective Novels," *Graduate Woman*, July/August 1980, 15-21.

[6]*Verdict of Thirteen: A Detection Club Anthology* (New York: Harper & Row, 1978), pp. 1-24.

Ruth Rendell
(Courtesy of Hutchinson Publishing Group, Ltd)

Ruth Rendell

1930	Born 17 February to Arthur and Ebba Elise (Kruse) Grasemann in London
1948-52	Reporter and sub-editor, *Essex Express and Independent*
1950	Married Donald (Don) John Rendell
1964	First novel published, *From Doon with Death*
1974	Edgar award of Mystery Writers of America for *The Fallen Curtain*
1975	Silver Cup award from Current Crime for *Shake Hands Forever*. Divorced from Don Rendell
1976	Gold Dagger award from Crime Writers' Association for *A Demon in My view*
1977	Remarried Don Rendell
1980	Twenty-first book published, *The Lake of Darkness*

by Jane S. Bakerman

I

Fans of good mystery and suspense writing give high marks to Ruth Rendell who generally produces one solid, enjoyable book each year, alternating non series novels with tales about her continuing character, Reg Wexford.[1] The Wexford books are straight detective fiction, but the other books are usually suspense stories, often inverted mysteries, in which the criminal and his crime are identified early; the suspense arises from the readers' knowledge of the horrors to come and from tensions within and between characters.

Quickly recognized for her skill, Rendell has progressed from the fairly simple *From Doon with Death* to complex plots employing sensitively delineated characters. In doing so, she has steadily reaffirmed the accuracy of an early review:

> It is Miss Rendell's treatment which gives the story its special quality.... Doon's character is ... subtly revealed from the beginning, not by unconscious authorial telegraphy but purposefully.... There have never been enough mysteries of this high order.[2]

Correctly identified as "an outstanding realist of the genre,"[3] Rendell earns that title by creating sound dialogue, vivid glimpses of life in London and the English countryside, and unobtrusive but extremely careful plotting.[4] Her plots are enlivened by skillful use of detail—of dress, of lawns and gardens, of shop windows, of street scenes—and none is extraneous; "Items which appear earlier and are seemingly unrelated suddenly achieve significance."[5] But perhaps Rendell's sharpest tool is irony; every plot is informed by ironic contrast, and that fact may contribute to the sense one reviewer has that some of her novels are "ice-cold studies."[6] Usually, however, the device lends depth and meaning to the work.

Sometimes, the irony is fairly standard material, for instance, the presence of evil and corruption in seemingly decent, middle-class suburbanites *(Doon, Painted)*, or the slow revelation of the potential home-wrecker hidden beneath Nesta Drage's demure widowhood *(Sickness)*. At other times, it points up the fallibilities of likeable people such as Anthony Johnson, a psychologist who interacts for several months with a psychopath without noticing a single symptom (*Demon*). Very usefully, it can underscore theme as in Ambrose Engstrand's denunciations of fiction. Ambrose believes that fiction undercuts readers' awareness of reality, and his dicta contrast painfully with protagonist Alan Groombridge's realization of his fantasies (*Make*). In an inversion of *Macbeth*, irony is the source of the entire plot, for "A Bad Heart" curtain reveals the attitudes and feelings of a latter day Duncan, a man so guilt ridden that all his perceptions are twisted.

The union of irony and theme is especially important in *The Lake of Darkness*, a novel dominated by theme, which depicts the efforts of three very different men to control the destinies of other human beings. The men vary greatly in the worthiness of their motives, but they are alike in the intensity of their purposes. Each formulates a carefully wrought scheme and sets it in motion, and as each presses toward his goal, the tension is great, the dramatic irony high, for the reader knows parts of the truth still hidden from each of the plotters. In every instance, coincidence intervenes; each scheme goes wrong, building toward a vastly ironic triple surprise ending.

The three men represent the Fates, spinning, measuring, snipping, and their maneuvers, of course, comprise the complex but very clearly drawn plot, the first level of action. Underlying their machinations, however, is a second level of examination and meaning, for it is *true* fate, in the shape of coincidence, which steps in and ultimately controls each situation. Rendell, in this way, affirms Burns' truism about the "best laid schemes," and also suggests that it is folly for human beings to meddle in matters beyond their understanding or scope. To play God is to invite disaster.

Because the men inhabit the same general area of London and because they know each other slightly, each is, to some degree, informed of the activity of the others, but none fully understands the others' aims or intentions. This overlapping awareness is necessary for the development of the plot, of course, vital to the dramatic irony. But on the second level of meaning, the characters' dim awareness is also important. What does it mean, Rendell inquires, if the Fates are aware of one another only casually, know one another's intentions only imperfectly—if at all? It means, it seems, that Fate is fully as arbitrary, fully as capricious as our most despairing moments suggest that it is, that life is never really under our control, and that violent death is a good paradigm for the uncertainties of our existence.

Though the questions Rendell poses and the answers she suggests in *The Lake of Darkness* are not new, they are handled in a skillful and individualistic fashion. As is typical of Rendell's work, *Lake* treats well-known human problems and reexamines established responses to them in fresh ways, neither echoing the professional habits of other authors nor repeating herself, for there is only one unchanging element in her fiction, an element shared, indeed, with all of mystery-suspense fiction, the basis of every plot: the greatest irony of life—the constant threat and sudden presence of death.

Death by violent crime almost always lies at the heart of Rendell's fiction, but because she adheres to no formula, those crimes occur in a wide variety of situations. *Some Lie and Some Die* depicts a gigantic rock festival during which Dawn Stoner is bludgeoned to death. The grisly details of Wexford's investigation unfold starkly against the joy and exuberance of the festival goers. When Angela Hathall is found strangled, Wexford soon identifies the murderer; the difficulty lies in acquiring effective evidence, and the tension of *Shake Hands Forever* arises from an open, determined battle between policeman and killer. In the first chapter of *A Demon in My View*, Arthur Johnson strangles the shop window mannequin which has for years borne the brunt of his homicidal impulses. When the mannequin disappears, Arthur is forced onto the streets of London, and readers watch the Kenbourne Killer stalk human prey. Eunice Parchman, on the other hand, finds her victims at home; they are the family who employ her in *A Judgement in Stone*. The readers' growing attachments to George and Jacqueline Coverdale; Melinda, George's daughter; and Giles Mont, Jackie's son, make their awareness of the coming murders almost unbearable.

Though her plots stem from violence, Rendell never substitutes blood or sensationalism for development. Instead, she "uses crime as conveniently as Victorian novelists used to, as a tensing part of stories about people,"[7] for characterization is Rendell's chief concern, as she, herself, points out:

> The development of a human personality is what I'm really interested in. I like to work on characters. I want to know what will become of them...I think people can be driven to commit murder, and I'm very interested in the pressures that are put on people and the stresses that they suffer from other people.[8]

Her efforts are successful, as noted by fans and critics.

> Her characterization is outstanding—her people act and react believably, no matter how bizarre the situation....They are all memorable, if not always likeable. Her insights into human behavior and psychology bring a degree of depth to her characters which is all too rare in mystery fiction....They come alive when one opens the covers of Rendell's books, live a portion of their lives as one turns the pages,

and...live on after...the book is again closed.[9]

II

In the nonseries novels, characterization is the dominant element, and one good test of an author's skill is her ability to control the minor characters. They must come to life vividly but not overshadow the major characters or the plot line. Rendell fully commands this technique.

Creating a useful victim is one of the first problems facing the author. In order for the story to be intellectually and emotionally satisfying, the victim usually must be disliked, envied, or dangerous enough to be murderable without becoming merely a stereotyped character who fails to excite reader interest or concern. Rendell briskly reveals the sources of her victims' unattractiveness, and these sources are generally their attitudes toward others (they tend to be narrow and disapproving people) and their own comments, for frequently she wisely allows them to condemn themselves from their own mouths. So before they are victims, many are antagonists, people who seek to control or to damage others. Their validity as victims arises from their coldness and, often, their money.

Victim Maud Kinway of *One Across, Two Down* is a major motivational force. Wealthy Maud makes her home with her impecunious daughter and son-in-law, and she's a very instrusive member of the family, constantly deriding her son-in-law who is a failure by almost any standard but who, naturally, dislikes being reminded of it. Actually bold and arrogant, Maud claims she is afraid of Stanley and takes measures to protect herself against him, using her high blood pressure as an odd but effective weapon, "If I die of a stroke you get the lot but if I die of anything else it all goes to Ethel Carpenter" (31).

Maud also diminishes her decent, struggling daughter by exacerbating the very real difficulties of Vera's life, and she treats Vera like a child, offering outright bribes:

Just think what a life we could have together, Vee, you and me. I've got money enough for both of us. I'm telling you in confidence, I'm a wealthy woman by anyone's standards. You wouldn't have to go to work, you wouldn't have to lift a finger. We'd have a nice new house.... I could buy one of them bungalows outright (19).

Eventually, Maud's ploys become self-fulfilling prophecies, and her scheming and nagging are the primary outside forces which motivate Stanley's deadly behavior.

Like Maud, Patrick Selby is a victim, but because *To Fear a Painted Devil* (unlike *One Across, Two Down*) is not an inverted mystery, Patrick's personality must be antipathetic to a *number* of people. It is, and all those people become suspects.

'it's funny, nobody loved him. His wife was bored with him, he got in the way of his wife's lover...his girl friend's brother was afraid of him. Even I was annoyed with him because he cut down my father's trees. Edith disliked him because he played God with her children and.... Do you suppose he had his cold fishy eye on Smith King's little lot?' (129-30)

Handsome, successful, demanding, Patrick is hard on others, frequently treating his self-absorbed, scatty wife, Tamsin, like a foolish servant; "In the faint bloom on the dressing-table Patrick had written with a precise finger: Dust this" (32). Even when he seems to fall truly in love, Patrick merely serves his own ends, seeking to substitute a woman those chief goal is to be a perfect homemaker for careless Tamsin, who is terrified of divorce. It is of no consequence to Patrick that he will upset five lives to gain his ends.

Thus, Patrick and Maud generate motives for murder at every turn, and though they are not among Rendell's most subtle characterizations, they are very effective ones, neatly serving the purposes of the books in which they appear. somewhat more complex are Max Greenleaf (*Painted*) and Giles Mont (*Stone*), each of whom serves his book in a variety of ways.

Like the other characters in *To Fear a Painted Devil*, Greenleaf is a resident of a small, plush, recently developed suburb, but Greenleaf is an outsider to the community because he is foreign born; he never fully understands or accepts his neighbors, yet as a physician, he does have access to their homes and often to their thoughts. Because Max is an outsider like the reader, readers identify with him and explore the community via Max's point of view. Max Greenleaf is one of Rendell's few portraits of the amateur detective, and, though he dislikes the role, he discharges it effectively.

As an amateur detective, Greenleaf is not infallible. Though he hits upon part of the truth, his suspicions are misdirected; this ploy complicates the plot, sustains tension and suspense, and contributes to the realism of the story. This device is not unique to Rendell; the technique is used frequently in the detective story, but the author controls it beautifully, revealing her dexterity and her insight into character. The doctor's professional expertise makes him the logical character to discover key facts; his limited understanding of his neighbors keeps him from grasping the whole truth until the final explication, a beautiful wedding of characterization and plot development.

Greenleaf is a wise, experienced, mature man; Giles Mont is a seventeen-year-old who, "like all true eccentrics...thought other people very odd" (*Stone*, 25). Yet, this characterization also is deft and penetrating, and Giles is vital to the unity of *A Judgement in Stone*. He functions in four ways: his personal development forms a subplot; his inherent studiousness and his passion for reading contrast vividly with the illiteracy of the deadly central character, Eunice Parchman; his quest for faith points up the shallowness and horror of the maniacal religious fervor of Joan Smith, Eunice Parchman's co-murderer; and Giles' idiosyncracies offset the grueling tension of this inverted mystery. Because he is a loner, preferring books to people, Giles' mother and stepfather strive to integrate him more fully into the family and community. They fear that he will isolate himself so deeply in his studies that he will lose touch with people. His parents' gratification as Giles moves gradually into a fuller awareness of his family and their needs is enormously ironic to the reader, for he knows that the boy will never be given a chance to integrate fully; he is doomed.

Giles' contrast with illiterate Eunice Parchman works on two levels. On the one hand, it is obviously ironic that his passion for books threatens to isolate Giles from other people in a manner parallel to the way Eunice's desire to hide her illiteracy cuts off her relationships with others. But an even more terrible irony threatens. Eunice, Rendell argues, cannot emphathize with others because she has not learned to do so through reading. If Giles loses his ability to empathize because he substitutes reading for real life, the results would be identical.

One of Giles' absorbing interest is religion; he is seeking a faith which will serve him and which he can serve. Because he is immature, this search is hectic and the source of some of the humor in the novel:

Now he was on his way to Sudbury to buy a packet of orange dye. He was going to dye all his jeans and T-shirts orange in pursuance of his religion, which was, roughly, Buddhism. When he had saved up enough money he meant to go to India on a bus....That is, if he didn't become a Catholic instead. He had just finished reading *Brideshead Revisited* and had begun to wonder whether being a Catholic at Oxford and burning incense on one's staircase might not be better than India. But he'd dye the jeans and T-shirts just in case. (23).

Catholicism seems to "take," and Giles begins instruction with a local priest; Rendell suggests that when his death comes, the boy may be in a state of grace, and so suggesting she validates the seriousness of his quest and its redemptive flavor.

This tone is in sharp disparity with the treatment of the religious mania of Joan Smith, the second murderer. Joan is a late convert to the Epiphany People, a small sect which specializes in public confession and conversion of outsiders. She exploits her beliefs to gain attention (through lurid and frequent cataloging of her sins), to castigate others (by denouncing their sinfulness—as defined by Joan), and to control others' lives (by her missionary work). At no times does Joan's faith inform her life with gentleness or compassion, traits Giles is learning to display; instead, it exacerbates her incipient madness and thus helps to incite murder. The contrast is powerfully effective, reenforcing Giles' function as the unifying element in the novel.

The range, then, of Rendell's minor characters is great, and she is adroit at creating both unsympathetic and sympathetic personalities. That she has grown in her ability to handle minor characters is evident when the fairly simple treatments of Patrick Selby and Max Greenleaf are compared with the complex development of Giles Mont. Always in command of her minor figures, she has undertaken more and more intricate portaits of them, and the progression is very successful.

Though her ability to create strong minor characters is one good test of an author's skill, it is, or course, vital that major characters also be drawn so clearly that they assume true viability without standing in the way of quick, absorbing action. As would be expected of an author who does so well with minor characters, Rendell is very competent with major figures, the generating forces of her non series books, and she has discharged this task, also, with growing skill.

In her non-series novels, Rendell generally examines a central character who is in a state of crisis. The tension arises partly because of the circumstances of the moment—the character's life is being altered by a crime which he has perpetrated or in which he is in some other way entangled—and partly because of some inner weakness or desire. The main plot of each book revolves around the crime and the protagonist's involvement in it; the subplot of the novel reveals the protagonist's character. Two of these novels describe characters who are more acted upon than acting. Graham Lanceton of the *Face of Trespass* and Susan Townseld of the *Secret House of Death* are both victims of failed love, and they are both unwillingly dragged into murder cases.

Gray Lanceton is introduced during a stagnant period in his life; he is grubbily camping out in a friend's cottage in Waltham Forest, living meagerly on the slim proceeds from his first book, seeing almost no one, and allowing himself to drift helplessly. He's degenerated physically, and he's losing his grip on reality; "His memory had got very bad since the winter....he forgot the date and the things he had to do. Not that there were many of those. He did almost nothing" (*Face,* 7). During the last few months, he's considered suicide, and worst of all, he is the victim of a massive writer's block:

He had been ruined. The ream had been started on but only about a hundred of the sheets used up. How can you complete a novel whose purpose is to explore the intricacies of love...when halfway through you find your whole conception has been wrong? When you find that the idea of love on which you based it is vapid and false because you've discovered the true meaning? (35)

The truth he's discovered is unsavory. Bewitched by his love for Drusilla Janus, a married woman, Gray has begged her to leave her husband and come away with him. But Drusilla has an alternate plan; she wants both Gray and riches, and so "It seemed to him...that all his troubles had come upon him because he hadn't done what she'd asked conspired with her to kill her [wealthy] husband" (75).

In moments of self-awareness, Gray understands his situation, "For more than half his life he'd fended for himself; he'd got a good degree, written a successful book, been Drusilla's lover, but he was still a child" (169), and not the least symptom of his immaturity is his continuing lovesickness for Drusilla.

Memories of her were still in the forefront of his mind, lying down with him at night, meeting him when he first woke, clinging to him through the long empty days. He drugged them down with cups of tea and library books but they were a long way from being exorcised. (6)

There is another element to Gray's melancholy. He feels abandoned by his mother. A widow, she has remarried and gone to live in France. Gray reacts very much like a young child, hating and fearing his stepfather and allowing his relationship to his mother, whose health is very poor, to be totally disrupted.

In his mind he had two mothers, two separate and distinct women, the woman who had rejected her son, her country, and her friends for an ugly little French waiter, and the woman who, since her first husband's death, had kept a home for her son, loving him, welcoming his friends. (78)

As in the case of his relationship with Drusilla, Gray's feelings toward his mother are complicated by his extreme poverty, and when he allows himself to think about her money, he hates himself and takes refuge in day dreams. "She wasn't going to die for years and when she did, he'd have a flat of his own in London and a string of successful novels behind him" (43).

The general crisis of Gray's life deepens when he is called to France; his mother is really dying. This period of desperate unhappiness is complicated by a broken promise and by his one step toward maturity when he makes a major discovery; "Gray saw that he'd been wrong. The love hadn't been all on his mother's side but had been reciprocated to the full.... He felt a great surge of guilt for misunderstanding, for laughing and despising"(125).

For the first time since he's met her, Gray is honestly responsive to someone other than Drusilla; he even grasps that her deadly concept of love is not its full definition. This new awareness is all but useless, however, for when Gray returns to England, he is arrested for the murder of Drusilla's husband. He is inert, yielding to fate,

He felt too weak, too unarmed, to argue and he knew he never would. He must accept...he must always have hoped for an outcome of this kind; only his higher consciousness had struggled, deceiving him. He'd hoped for Tiny's death....Who spun, who held the scissors, and who cut the thread? (178)

Early in *The Face of Trespass*, Jeff Denman, one of Gray's friends, characterizes him accurately, " 'In a way, he's one of those people you've committed yourself to help, the misfits, you know, the lost' " (2), and in her novel, Rendell has examined the results of weakness, asking how much responsibility the passive Graham Lanceton must bear for the disasters that befall him. Certainly, for the estrangement with his mother, he must bear a good deal, for it was his narrowness which prevented a healthy love between them. But is he also partly responsible for Drusilla's wickedness? Was withdrawing overtly, though not covertly, from the relationship not enough? Should he have taken further steps? What, then, should they have been? Reader and protagonist alike are left to ponder these questions, and the careful examination of Gray's personality conveys the novel's theme.

Susan Townsend, like Graham Lanceton, tends to be controlled by the people around her, her state of mind largely the result of the attention or inattention of her former husband and of her two suitors, but Susan is a somewhat stronger person, capable of productive introspection and mercilessly honest with herself. In *The Secret House of Death*, Rendell portrays a woman slowly healing from deep emotional wounds; the realism of that portrait enriches the book.

Susan is recently divorced, trying to earn her living and start a new life, but a neighborhood scandal deters her:

She sat typing each afternoon in her window and wondered about the man's visits [to the woman next-door, Louise North], but unlike her neighbors, she felt no lubricious curiosity. Her own husband had walked out on her just a year ago and the man's visits to Louise North touched chords of pain she hoped had begun to atrophy. Adultery, which excites and titillates the innocent, had brought her at twenty-six into a dismal abyss of loneliness. Let her neighbours speculate as to why the man came, what Louise wanted, what Bob [North] thought, what would come of it all. From personal experience she knew the answers and all she wanted was to get on with her work, bring up her son and not get herself involved.[2]

Susan *is* involved, of course, for when Louise North and the stranger are murdered, it is she who discovers the bodies. The investigation of these killings is the main plot of the story; Susan's emotional progress is the equally gripping subplot.

Though she fully recognizes her former husband's faults and no longer loves him, Susan still misses the stability he represents, and, fighting the impulse steadily, she still expects a certain amount of comfort from him:

When life went smoothly, she preferred not to be reminded of Julian's existence and his telephone calls—incongruously more frequent at such times—were an uncomfortable disruption of peace. But when she was unhappy or nervous she expected him to know it and to a certain degree to be a husband to her again....
    She knew this was an impossible hope, totally unreasonable. (68)

Her loneliness is often exacerbated because of the behavior of acquaintances, for, like many divorced women, she's been dropped by the Townsends' circle of friends. Though she still remains determined to keep up her basic routine, the Susan of the early pages of the novel is fearful that one day she will surrender; she grasps the fact that "You went to bed early because there was nothing to stay up for. You lay in bed late because getting up meant facing life" (72). The depths of her loneliness and her tension over the murders is symbolized by a bad case of the flu, and her recovery is a sign of renewed interest in living:

Her ability to concentrate and reason normally, rediscovered in the past two days, brought her intense pleasure. It seemed to her that her illness had marked the end of a black period in her life and during that illness she had found fresh resources,... and made a friend of Bob North [widower of the murdered woman]. (97-98)

Susan doubts the validity of her growing intimacy with Bob North because she wonders if two wounded people really make one whole; the reader, however, fears for Susan's safety, for he knows that Bob is not only passionately in love with another woman but also that he is a murderer. He is pursuing Susan to control her, possibly to kill her, and so her progress toward emotional recovery is perhaps false and certainly dangerous. This dramatic irony unites the main plot, the murder plot, with the Susan subplot and creates great tension.

While Susan moves from the unfaithful hands of Julian into the bloody hands of Bob North, and while she is preoccupied with her recovery from the divorce, the main plot is taken over by a man who wishes to become the third influence in her life. David Chadwick, a friend of the murdered man, suspects Bob North's guilt and sets about trying to prove it. This investigation introduces him to Susan, and he is determined to save her from Bob North and from herself. Though the reader may regret Susan's failure to take full charge of her own life, he accepts David Chadwick as a symbol of her possible true regeneration and happiness.

Anthony Johnson of *A Demon in My View* once claims that " 'No one is responsible for another adult person' "(121); in *The Face of Trespass* and *The Secret House of Death,* Rendell explores some consequences of yielding oneself into the hands of others. Both novels are greatly strengthened by their author's ability to depict her passive central characters positively enough to sustain sympathy and interest but forthrightly enough to avoid sentimentality.

In contrast to Susan Townsend's attempted reintegration, Rendell provides in *One Across, Two Down* a study of the disintegration of a personality, that of the central character, Stanley Manning. Stanley is introduced as a rather weak man, prisoner of his own lack of drive and of an overwhelming compulsion to acquire his mother-in-law's funds:

he realised amid the turmoil of his thoughts that for almost the whole of his adult life the acquiring of that money had been his goal,. . . always it had been there, a half-concealed, yet shimmering crock at the end of a rainbow. To possess it he had stayed with Vera [his wife] and put up with Maud [his mother-in-law], and, he told himself, never bothered to carve out a career. He had wasted his life (164-65).

This moment of insight is rare for Stanley; most of his life, he's avoided introspection. One of his methods of dodging reality is his indulgence in shallow boasting, a habit which has begun early:

Seventeen he'd been when he'd run away from them all, his parents, his brothers.. . . Off to make his fortune, he'd told them, sick with envy and resentment of his two brothers, one halfway through a good apprenticeship, the other off to college. I'll be back, he'd said, and I'll be worth more than the lot of you. But he never had gone back.. . . (67)

Instead, he's embarked on a career of botched jobs, all the while yearning for Maud's money, his desired means of affirming his manhood and talent.

Stanley also consoles himself with his hobby, crossword puzzles.

He would sit down with the paper—he never bothered to read the news—and generally every clue had been solved twenty minutes later. Then an immense satisfaction bathed Stanley. Self-esteem washed away his pressing problems, every worry was buried, sublimated in those interlocking words.... (44-45)

These salves to his battered pride work reasonably well until Stanley takes determined but foolish steps to improve his personal and financial situations. He embarks on two ventures—murder and a fraudulent-antiques shop. He's capable of managing neither.

Riddled with fear at home because of the murder and dominated by a crooked, defrauding partner at the shop, Stanley begins to deteriorate. His disintegration is symbolized physically by the uncontrollable twitching of an eyelid; at first he uses his old panacea, the puzzles, to get relief.

When that therapy begins to fail (he can worry and work the puzzles simultaneously), he switches to creating crosswords, finally getting so adroit that he can invent a complete grid in his head. But, because Stanley has no inner stability at all, because he has no true strength of his own and has failed to establish any relationship which can now sustain him, his stopgap is bound to fail; the puzzles themselves become an obsession:

every muscle was twitching now and the remedy seemed almost worse than the disease. He began to wish he'd never done a crossword in his life, so compulsive was this need to keep inventing clues, to slot words across, fit others down.... he had a chequer board pattern in front of his eyes. (155-56)

His last defense gone, Stanley's decline is complete. Rendell's informing irony is operating again, and the fruits of Stanley's tainted attempts at independence are bitter indeed. A failure at the sustaining relationships of ordinary life, Stanley is also a failure outside the law, and justice (if not legality) is, as always in a Rendell novel, truly served.

Rendell depicts Stanley Manning in the same unsparing, unsentimental way she has depicted the more appealing Graham Lanceton and Susan Townsend. Unlike Graham and Susan, Stanley is not a sympathetic character. Yet, in describing his disintegration, Rendell arouses pity for him if not empathy. Stanley pays the full price for remaining outside the human family, and his creator allows him the compassion of the reader, thus multiplying the impact of an excellent suspense story.

Stanley crumples because he has little imagination, he has no empathy; for him, other human beings are merely tools to be manipulated to suit his own needs. His concept of the good life is the acquisition of wealth and comfort, the achievement of power over others. In sharp contrast is Alan Groombridge of *Make Death Love Me*. Alan's concept of the larger life includes expansion of the mind and spirit. As Stanley's narrow vision leads him to crime and disintegration, Alan's broad vision leads him to crime and the realization of his own true, fuller nature. The irony that informs Alan's story arises from his generosity of heart; unlike Stanley, he cannot shrug off his responsibility toward others.

Trapped in a dreary marriage, a dull suburb, a hack job as token manager of a tiny branch bank, Alan seeks escape in two ways. Gluttonously, he reads, moving from escape fiction to serious literature which has a profound effect upon him:

his wits were sharpened, his powers of perception heightened, and he became discontented with his lot.... Unless all those authors were liars, there was an inner life and an outer experience, an infinite number of things to be seen and done, and there was passion. He had come late in life to the heady intoxication of literature and it had poisoned him for what he had. (25)

Among the many good things he reads about is love, love as he has never known it in life. "It was adolescent to want to be in love, but he wanted to be. He wanted to live on his own too, and go and look at things and explore and discover and understand" (25).

Alan's second escape is less savory but equally dangerous. Every working day, he fondles three thousand pounds of the bank's money. The act is so ritualized, so personal, that the reader is uneasy observing it:

With the kind of breathless excitement many people find about sex ... he looked at the money and turned it over and handled it. Gently he handled it, and then roughly as if it belonged to him and he had lots more. He put two wads into each of his trouser pockets and walked up and down the little office. He got out his wallet with his own two pounds in it, and put in forty and folded it again and appreciated its new thickness. After that he counted out thirty-five pounds into an imaginary hand and mouthed thirty-three, thirty-four, thirty-five, into an imaginary face, and he knew he had gone too far in fantasy.... As he felt himself blush (1).

Alan's life is so confined that to him three thousand pounds is a *great* deal of money; it comes to represent utter freedom, the chance to shrug off a sterile life and to explore the larger world which is so vivid to him in his books and his imagination. Alan fears his preoccupation with the bank's money and he understands that it is unhealthy. Yet he cannot abandon his ritual, for, like his reading, it is the only portion of his life that is not controlled by others. So involved with the money and with his dreams has Alan become that, when the chance arises, he makes off with the money.

Twin ironies inform Alan's new freedom. Because he has slipped off with the funds during a robbery, he is considered victim rather than thief; he is assumed to have been kidnapped. His assistant really has been kidnapped and chance exposes one of the abductors to him. To Alan Groombridge, onetime prisoner of shallow wife, exploitative father-in-law, thankless children, comes the opportunity to be a story book hero. To be that hero, however, he must risk a great deal.

Certainly he risks exposure and the punishment that will follow. But even more importantly, he risks losing independence, peace—and love. For Alan has fallen in love, not with a fairy princess, but with Una Engstrand, a gentle, abused woman who returns his affection and who cares for him as deeply and as subtly as he loves her. To rescue his assistant is to chance destroying Una who has validated his dreams, "It was years since he had felt happy. Had he ever?. . . A great joy possessed him. Energy seemed to flow though his body and out at his fingertips" (136).

Alan has escaped from a kind of static horror into joy and vigor. What he has read is true; there is a way of life which enriches, ennobles, and prompts human beings into positive actions. Yet to take the action his reading has taught him is correct, is, indeed, mandatory, is to risk the very factor which gives him strength to act.

Alan Groombridge is a fine study of free will. Trapped by an unlucky accident into the constraints of his early adulthood, trapped by his obsession with the money into thievery, he has at last achieved the freedom to make choices. His awareness of that freedom is the factor which keeps Alan a sympathetic character. It would have been easy for Rendell to depict Alan merely as a pitiable character; instead she uses his self-awareness, his ability to examine his intentions and his acts as a means of enlarging her protagonist and of arousing reader empathy. In this way, she produces a novel of genuine depth, commanding the reader's attention, engaging his intellect, and arousing his full enjoyment.

Like Susan Townsend, Alan is greatly influenced by those about him; like Graham Lanceton, he is not only capable of folly but also bound by a strict ethical code. Like Stanley Manning, Alan is tempted into crime, but he remains aware of his human condition, aware that the fully realized life is a life of choice and decision-making.

Because of her control over the development of her central figures and her remarkable ability to dramatize character analysis so vividly as to make it serve as a subplot in her non series novels, Rendell has come to undertake fiction of increasing complexity. The crime around which each story evolves is never merely the stroke of blind fate; instead, the character and personality of each protagonist naturally, inexorably involves him in that crime. No sympathetic protagonist is ever idealized, and no unsympathetic central character is ever exploited. Rather, each personality is examined with cool insight and honest compassion. Just as her non series minor characters are well realized portraits which serve the plot, so are her protagonists clearly drawn as generators of and respondents to the action.

III

    One of the strengths of Rendell's series of novels is, of course, her focal character, Inspector Reg Wexford. A big man, the Inspector is tall and "thick-set without being fat, fifty-two years old, the very prototype of an actor playing a top-brass policeman" (*Doon*, 30). A life long resident of his manor, Kingsmarkham, in Sussex, he knows both the area and the residents very, very well; they trust and respect him and are drawn to him:

Wexford was an ugly man, but his was the face that arrested the eye, compelled even the eyes of women, because it had in it so much lively intelligence and zest for life, so much vigour, and in spite of his seniority, so much ... of youth. (*Sleeping*, 8)

    The Inspector's intelligence manifests itself in several ways. An avid reader, he has (like his creator) a very good memory and salts his comments with apt quotations. Perhaps more importantly, that intelligence is the seat of his compassion. Unwilling to bend the law, he is nevertheless both intuitive and imaginative, qualities revealed in his "expression that was not so much easy-going as tolerant of everything but intolerance" (*Lie*, 2). He is also introspective:

it occurred to him how she, the dead, she whose death was the cause of this enquiry, had for some days past seemed to fade from its screen. It was as if she, as a real person, a personality, had lost her importance.... And he saw her—vividly but briefly—as a pawn, a used creature, her life blundering across other, brighter lives, falling through folly and vanity into death (*Lie*, 150-51).

Wexford is responsive to nature as well as to literature and to people; his work is never far from his mind, and he constantly strives to keep it in perspective. It must be central to but not dominating of his world view:

    Today all man-made noise was drowned by the chatter of the swollen river.... It spoke of timeless forces, pure and untameable, which in a world of ugliness and violence resisted man's indifferent soiling of the earth. Listening to it, sitting in silence, Wexford thought of that ugliness, the scheme of things in which a girl could be beaten to death, thrown into a bower.... Like garbage. He shivered. He could never quite get used to it, the appalling things that happened, the waste, the pointlessness (*Lie*, 102-03).

    The Inspector has his human foibles, and one of them is his pride. The strong alliance between his pride and his respect for justice reenforces his fear that killers will go free, and once his investigation becomes almost obsessive, causing him to further antagonize his already unsympathetic superior, Charles Griswold, who shares the initials and some of the attitudes of Charles De Gaulle (*Shake*).

Generally, however, Wexford maintains his sane, humane balance, and an important factor in that balance is the key member of his professional family, Mike Burden. Burden is less imaginative than Wexford, but a very good officer, capable of working on his own, and their "often acrimonious but always fruitful discussions" (*Wedding*, 165) have led the men into warm personal as well as professional alliances.

Because readers have become caught up in Burden's biography, his presence lends continuity, giving Rendell the means to dramatize Wexford's thought processes, and also yielding a useful source of development and subplot. Burden is a passionate man, devoted to his first wife, Jean. Her death has very nearly destroyed him, and his sufferings are the deeply satisfying subplot of *No More Dying Then*. Wexford supports Mike through that difficult period and through his extended widowerhood, sometimes mitigating Mike's tendency to moralize. When Burden marries Jenny Ireland, Wexford rejoices:

Dear Mike, thought Wexford with a flash of sentimentality that came to him perhaps once every ten years, you'll be OK now. No more carnal lusts conflicting with a puritan conscience, no more loneliness, no more worrying about those selfish kids of yours, no more temptation-of-St.-Anthony stuff (*Wedding*, 148).

Wexford's personal family is as interesting as his professional crew. His younger daughter, Sheila, is a stunningly beautiful successful actress. The Inspector indulges her, though sometimes ruefully as when she foists upon her parents the care of a friend's unprepossessing dog (*Best*). Sylvia is married and herself the mother of two small sons; a major crisis between Sylvia and her husband serves as subplot and a contrast to the life of the victim in one novel, and it provokes a tart comment that reveals as much about Dora Wexford's personality as it does about her elder daughter's:

'What's got into Sylvia?'
'Women's Lib.... If Neil wants to bring a client home he ought to cook the meal. He ought to come home in the afternoon and clean the house and lay the table. She's taken the children home for the sole purpose of getting him to put them to bed. And she's taking care to stir them up on the way to make sure he has a hard time of it' (*Sleeping*, 2).

Like her husband, Dora Wexford sees people for what they are, and while she loves her daughters dearly, she does not flinch from their faults. Perhaps her comment about Sylvia's new views is colored by the fact that Dora's job is and always has been to make their home a refuge for her husband. She does it well, and he knows it:

> although he had only parted from her four hours before,he ... kissed her warmly....
> Contented with his lot as he was, it sometimes took external disaster to bring home to
> him his good fortune and how much he valued his wife. (*Shake*, 20).

He not only values her, he also loves her. But though their relationship is surely stable, the Inspector is not above sexual temptation. It comes in the shape of Nancy Lake, one of Rendell's most richly realized characters, and the axis for the subplot in *Shake Hands Forever*.

She singles Wexford out for attention; he is flattered and stirred. Clearly, Nancy symbolizes the potential richness of the autumn of Wexford's days, attractive in herself and for what she represents:

> When a pretty woman ages, a man's reaction is usually to reflect on how lovely
> she must once have been. This was not Nancy Lake's effect. There was something
> very much of the here and now about her. When with her you thought no more of her
> youth and her coming old age than you think of spring or Christmas when you are
> enjoying late summer. She was ... a harvest-time woman, who brought to mind
> grape festivals and ripened fruit and long warm nights (33).

The Nancy Lake situation reveals one of the great sources of the reader's interest in Wexford—he is a man of depth and complexity who is never wholly revealed. This quality makes him serve the novels well. He and his richly drawn phalanx of companions are much more than symbols of normality and wholesomeness against which the grim stories of murder are contrasted. They are interesting characters in their own right who keep the novels contemporary, who keep them part of the recognizable world, and who tantalize readers with the hope of learning more about their lives.

Once the importance of Wexford's professional and personal families has been recognized, it's not surprising to discover that one of the most profitable ways of considering the series novels is to view them as examinations of comparable and contrasting families. Just as the Wexford group represents the saneness and balance of the majority of the human family, other characters and their relationships represent the wildness and imbalance of others in that larger circle. In the familial relationships of the characters are revealed the motivations for the behavior of both victim and victimizer. The clarity of these motivations is a driving force of these books, and the family patterns are among their most enriching qualities.

The family motif (a unifying force in the series) focuses on two major sets of relationships—those between parents and children and those between husbands and wives. In both instances, Rendell often uses descriptions of the homes her characters occupy as a means of swiftly established characterization or foreshadowing.

Linda Grover is a major character in *Wolf to the Slaughter*. A very beautiful girl, Linda attracts Mark Drayton, one of Wexford's staff, and their love story is a subplot, a device fairly common to detective fiction. Here, however, Rendell, as she generally does, adapts rather than adopts, and when hidden features of Linda's personality are revealed, the reader sees that an early description of her parents' shop validates the revelation:

> In the shop window the displayed wares looked as if they had been arranged there some years before and since left utterly untended. Easter was not long past and the Easter cards were topical. But their topicality must be an accident in the same way as a stopped clock must be correct twice a day, for there were Christmas cards there as well, some fallen on their sides and filmed with dust.
>
> Dying houseplants stood among the cards. Perhaps they were for sale or perhaps misguidedly intended for decoration. The earth around their roots had shrunk through dehydration, leaving an empty space between soil and pot. A box containing a game of snakes and ladders had come open, so that the coloured board hung from a shelf. The counters lay on the floor amng rusty nails, spilt confetti and shed leaves (42).

Exploitative Linda is the true product of her environment, for she has been as neglected and uncared for as the stock.

From Doon with Death compares and contrasts married couples; the marriages appear stable on the surface, and Rendell establishes their outward appearance through descriptions of their homes, revealing social class, financial status, and some motivation for at least one of the partners of each marriage. Helen Missal is a thwarted actress whose home is a stage which symbolizes the artificiality of her life:

> Wexford and Burden found themselves in a large drawing room whose bow windows faced the street. The carpet was green, the chairs and a huge sofa covered in green linen patterned with pink and white rhododendrons. Real rhododendrons, saucer sized heads of blossoms on long stems, were massed in two white vases. Burden had the feeling that when rhododendrons went out of season Mrs. Missal would fill the vases with delphiniums and change the covers accordingly. (61)

The house of victim Margaret Parsons so reflects the mundaneness of her daily life that it underlines the shock of her death, just as the drudgery of that life explains why she was lured into victimization:

> He tried to stop staring round the little hole of a kitchen, at the stone copper in the

corner, the old gas stove on legs, the table with green American cloth tacked to its top. There was no washing machine, no refrigerator. Because of the peeling paint, the creeping red rust, it looked dirty. It was only by peering closely . . . that Burden could see it was in fact fanatically, pathetically, clean (28).

Often the key to relationships between husbands and wives lies in the selfish behavior of one partner. Ivor Swan, for instance, has ruined another man's marriage to acquire the woman he loves, and his obsession with her is based wholly upon the comfort she offers him:

'I want to be in the country with Roz, just the two of us, in peace. She's the only person I've ever known who wants me for what I am. She hasn't made an image of me that's got to be lived up to, she doesn't want to jolly me along and encourage me. She loves *me*, and she really knows me and I'm first with her, the centre of her universe ' (*Dying*, 159).

Swan's obsession with his comforts and desires makes him a chief suspect in the investigation of the murder of his stepdaughter and affords a useful complication.

Similarly, Elizabeth Nightingale is utterly preoccupied with her own beauty and fashionableness; she loves the clothes, unguents, and beautiful furnishings her husband's money brings her, and she ignores his misery. Even her lover is coldly realistic in summing up her character: " 'Her aim was to have me . . . and at the same time to keep her position, her money and her reputation. She wanted the best of both worlds and she got them' " (*Guilty,* 183). But selfishness does not go unpunished in a Rendell novel; Elizabeth is the victim, and her heedless cruelty generates enough motivation for a goodly range of suspects.

Other obsessions are the keys to Rendell's analyses of other marriages. In *The Best Man to Die,* victim Charlie Hatton is obsessed with possessions. For Charlie, buying things for people serves two purposes: it demonstrates his manhood, but more importantly it demonstrates his love, never mind that his money comes illegally. Rendell constrasts the Hattons with the Fanshawes. Dorothy Fanshawe is strangely unmoved when her husband is killed; "someone had told her that Jerome was dead and had waited for her to cry. Mrs. Fanshawe had twisted her rings— they were a great comfort to her, those rings—and said: Then it's all mine now. . . ." (42). The explanation for her behavior is simple and awful; her rich husband, a tireless philanderer, bribes her to stay with him for appearances' sake. Her love of possessions makes her accept them as payment for services rendered. Both couples center their lives on acquisitions; for the Hattons they represent love; for the Fanshawes, they represent love's absence. The Hatton-

Fanshawe motif deepens the novel and lends an element of social criticism to a good murder mystery.

Just as her explorations of marital relationships are valuable to Rendell's novels, so are her examinations of the relationships between parents and children. These portraits are varied, but several patterns can be noted.

Some of the portraits depict sunny and nurturing bonds. The brief glimpses allowed into the lives of Brian and Stella Parker and Brian's grandmother show cooperation and love at every turn. Old Mrs. Parker, ninety-two, has outlived six of her eleven offspring and now makes her home with her grandchildren. She contributes to the family in very meaningful ways; for instance, her savings helped to buy the house. Brian says, "She's a wonder, my gran," and Mrs. Parker is as enthusiastic about the young couple, "Brian and Stell have been wonderful to me. They're a wonder, they are, the pair of them" (*Sleeping*, 10, 26). The Parkers' slang places them firmly in the working class and reveals their esteem for one another. Both factors are important elements in the novel which contrasts the Parkers with neighbors, the Comfreys, who have no concept of how to love or value one another.

Realist that she is, Rendell can also see joyously indulgent parental love as a potential danger. Stephen Dearborn is totally absorbed in his baby daughter:

I'd like to get the moon and stars for my daughter but, as this is impossible, she shall have all the good things of this world instead.... I didn't know what real happiness was till I got Alexandra. If I lost her I'd—I'd kill myself (*Once*, 79).

Dearborn's extreme preoccupation with fatherhood is the reason for his being suspected of murder.

Another father who takes parenthood seriously achieves amazing success through his largeness of heart and generosity of spirit. Tess Kershaw is her father's adopted daughter, child of her mother's first marriage to a man executed for murder. That early background could well have ruined Tess' life, but because of Tom Kershaw's loving-kindness and determination, Tess has instead become a poised, happy young woman.

'She says that it was his love that helped her to bear ... the stigma of her father's crime when she learnet about it at the age of twelve. He followed her progress at school, encouraged her in every way, and fostered her wish to get a County Major Scholarship' (*Lease*, 49-50).

Kershaw's acceptance of Tess for what she is in herself is contrasted with the doubts of her prospective husband's parents, this tension motivates the informal reopening of one of Wexford's earliest cases.

But not all the parent-child relationships in the series novels are nurturing; others are negative and damaging. Some of the children of these families suffer extremely. Louise Sampson, the child of Melanie Sampson Dearborn's first marriage, is an example. Louise comes to know Stephen Dearborn through a friend, and she falls in love with him. Dearborn appears to be either ignorant of or insensitive to Louise's feelings, and when he meets, falls in love with, and then marries Louise's mother, the strain of keeping her sense of betrayal secret shadows Louise's entire life. The family becomes estranged; Louise abandons her sucessful studenthood and drifts for a long time. Her feeling of abandonment is contrasted with the adulation that surrounds her stepsister, Alexandra, and her loneliness is compared to that of the victim, another estranged daughter.

That victim is Rachel Vickers, who has "been brought up in a strict morality, but a morality which leaves out what ordinary human beings call ethics" (*Once*, 194). Rachel and her parents belong to a repressive religious sect, the Children of the Revelation, who substitute legalistic doctrine for an honorable code. When Rachel becomes pregnant by her church's preacher, she gets neither understanding nor comfort from her parents. Her father turns her out, and she faces a world for which she is totally unprepared. Completely unworldly and naively unaware of the working ethics upon which bargains are based, Rachel is bound to fail. As she has been cheated by her family and gulled by her minister, she is killed by the last of a series of exploiters. The barrenness of Rachel's family life lends poignancy to her death and is clearly identified as its root cause.

Similarly, Rhoda Comfrey is the victim of an exploitative, unloving family long before she falls prey to her killer. When middle-aged Rhoda is murdered in Kingsmarkham, Wexford discovers some amazing facts:

'This is unbelievable. She doesn't give her address to her aunt or the hospital where her father is or to her father's doctor or his neighbours. It's not written down anywhere in the house, he hasn't got it with him in the hospital ' (*Sleeping*, 24-25).

Rhoda has, in fact, cut her adult life entirely off from the life of her family.

At first this behavior does seem unbelievable, but as Wexford develops the case, he discovers that Rhoda has been taught to be cold and unloving. As a child, the girl is surrounded with unfeeling, jeering relatives. Rhoda is not conventionally pretty or desirable, and her family takes care that she knows it. She is, however, intelligent, but her father's insistence that she drop out of school

cuts off that avenue of development. Eventually, in order to realize
her potential, she leaves Kingsmarkham and creates a new identity
for her new life. Unfortunately, she continues to reflect some of her
family's behavior, so wounding a member of her new circle that
murder results. In *A Sleeping Life,* Wexford pursues three inquiries:
he seeks Rhoda Comfrey's murderer; he uncovers her secret London
life; and he unravels the mysteries of her grim youth. Thus Rendell
draws multiple strands of complication from one well conceived,
strongly motivated character, one of her cleverest unifications of
plot and characterization. *A Sleeping Life* is one of Rendell's colder
novels; readers do not like Rhoda Comfrey much, but her situation is
so clearly drawn that they do understand and pity her.

These same responses are aroused by Elizabeth Crilling, like
Rhoda, first victim then victimizer, though Elizabeth remains tied
to the scene of her exploited childhood. Josephine Crilling,
Elizabeth's mother, is an unbalanced sycophant who uses five-year-
old Elizabeth as a means of ingratiating herself with a wealthy old
woman. When the old lady is killed, it is little Elizabeth who
discovers the body. Because of her mother's shallowness and lack of
understanding, the child is never allowed to come to terms with her
terror:

'I was five. Five, my Christ! They put me to bed and I was ill. I was ill for weeks. Of
course they'd arrested ...[the murderer], but I didn't know that. You don't tell
children that sort of thing. I didn't know what had happened at all, only that Granny
Rose had burst open and he had made it happen and if I said I'd seen him he'd do the
same to me.... You wanted to tell *her*, but she wouldn't listen to you. 'Don't think
about it, Baby, put it out of your mind,' and you did put it out of your mind. But it
wouldn't go out....' (*Lease,* 189)

Seeking vengeance against her mother, the teenaged Elizabeth
steals Mrs. Crillings' boy friend; seeking peace, she turns to drugs;
as a result of both, she becomes a killer. The Crilling women retreat
from reality, but they seem unable to retreat from one another. "An
invisible thread held mother and daughter together but whether it
was composed of love or hatred" (*Lease,* 75), no one, not even they,
can tell. In the Crilling's case, it is misguided concern and ambition
that cause the mother to ruin her daughter and their story contrasts
with that of Tess Kershaw to deepen the novel and to strengthen the
family motif which dominates it. This is another fine example of the
unification of characterization and plot.

IV

Close examination of Ruth Rendell's fiction, then, reveals that
her concern with character and its development is perhaps the

greatest of her many strengths as a writer. Each personality is clearly drawn; each is believable because each is honestly motivated. From this careful development, plot sources and complications arise; subplots employing comparable or contrasting characters and situations unfold, often generating irony or humor.

The process seems entirely natural because it is so thoroughly thought out and so carefully rendered, and thus the crimes at the center of each plot become the logical, though horrible, results of the interactions of the people involved. Rendell's mastery of her craft and command of her chief interest fuse entertainment and thoughtful examination of the human personality. She succeeds in this study of the human condition by refusing to compromise the integrity of the characterizations she depicts, and that integrity holds for the long term in the steadily developing portraits of Wexford and his circle as well as in the memorable single appearances of other characters.

Just as sound characterization is the unifying quality between Rendell's series and non series works, it is also the factor which combines with careful plotting, fair clue-planting, and sensitive use of irony and humor to produce serious, thoughtful works which help to narrow the gap between crime/suspense writing and "mainstream" fiction. This is indeed a major achievement, enriching to the genre and gratifying to the reader. It places Rendell well forward among current practitioners of the art of fiction.

Notes

[1]The chronological list of Rendell's books follows. All further references are indicated in the text by a key word from the title and by a page number.

1964   *From Doon with Death*, Garden City, NY: Doubleday, 1965 (*Doon)*
1965   *To Fear a Painted Devil*, London: John Long, 1965 (*Painted*)
1966   *In Sickness and in Health*, Garden City, NY: Doubleday, 1966 (*Vanity Dies Hard*) (*Sickness*)
1967   *A New Lease of Death*, Garden City, NY: Doubleday, 1967 (*Sins of the Fathers*) (*Lease*)
1967   *Wolf to the Slaughter*, Garden City, NY: Doubleday, 1968 (*Wolf*)
1968   *The Secret House of Death,* Garden City, NY: Doubleday, 1969 (*Secret*)
1969   *The Best Man to Die*, Garden City, NY: Doubleday, 1970 (*Best*)
1970   *A Guilty Thing Surprised*, Garden City, NY: Doubleday, 1970 (*Guilty*)
1971   *No More Dying Then*, Garden City, NY: Doubleday, 1972 (*Dying*)
1971   *One Across, Two Down*, Garden City, NY: Doubleday, 1971 (*Across*)
1972   *Murder Being Once Done*, Garden City, NY: Doubleday, 1972 (*Once*)
1973   *Some Lie and Some Die*, Garden City, NY: Doubleday, 1973 (*Lie*)
1974   *The Face of Trespass*, Garden City, NY: Doubleday, 1974 (*Face*)
1975   *Shake Hands Forever*, London: Hutchinson, 1975 (*Shake*)
1976   *The Fallen Curtain*, Garden City, NY: Doubleday, 1976 (*Curtain*)
            The Fallen Curtain (Fallen)
            People Don't Do Such Things (People)

A Bad Heart (Heart)
You Can't Be too Careful (Careful)
The Double (Double)
Venus' Fly-Trap (Trap)
His Worst Enemy (Enemy)
The Vinegar Mother (Vinegar)
The Fall of a Coin (Coin)
Almost Human (Human)
Divided We Stand (Stand)

1976   *A Demon in My View,* Garden City, NY: Doubleday, 1977 (*Demon*)
1970   *The Lake of Darkness,* London: Hutchinson, 1980 (*Lake)*
1977   *A Judgement in Stone,* London: Hutchinson, 1977 (*Stone*)
1978   *A Sleeping Life,* Garden City, NY: Doubleday, 1978 (*Sleeping*)
1979   *Make Death Love Me,* Garden City, NY: Doubleday, 1979 (*Make*)
1979   *Means of Evil,* London: Hutchinson, 1979 (*Means*)
        Means of Evil (Evil)
        Old Wives' Tales (Tales)
        Ginger and the Kingsmarkham Chalk Circle (Circle)
        Achilles Heel (Heel)
        When the Wedding Was Over (Wedding)

[2]Dorothy B. Hughes, rev. of *From Doon with Death,* by Ruth Rendell, *Book Week,* 24 January 1965, p. 13.

[3]Newgate Callendar, rev.of *One Across, Two Down,* by Ruth Rendell, New York *Times Book Review,* 7 November 1971, p. 26.

[4]Haskell Frankel, rev. of *A Guilty Thing Surprised,* by Ruth Rendell, *Saturday Review,* 30 January 1971, p. 29.

[5]Charles J. Keffer, rev. of *A Demon in My View,* by Ruth Rendell, *Best Sellers,* 37 (April 1977), 8.

[6]Newgate Callendar, rev. of *No More Dying Then,* by Ruth Rendell, New York *Times Book Review,* 2 July 1972, p. 15.

[7]Rev. of *No More Dying Then,* by Ruth Rendell, *Times Literary Supplement,* 31 December 1971, p. 1638.

[8]Jane S. Bakerman, "Rendell Territory," *The Mystery Nook,* No. 10 (1977), A3.

[9]Don Miller, "A Look at the Novels of Ruth Rendell," *The Mystery Nook,* No. 10 (1977), A8.

Anna Katharine Green

Anna Katharine Green

1846   Born, November 11, in Brooklyn, New York, the third
daughter and fourth child of James Wilson Green, a well-
known criminal lawyer, and his wife, Katharine Ann
(Whitney) Green

1850   Mother dies; father subsequently marries a woman from
Buffalo, New York

1857   Family moves to Buffalo

1866   Graduates B.A. from Ripley Female College, Poultney,
Vermont; while there, she meets and corresponds with
Ralph Waldo Emerson, and sends him samples of her
verses; his reply is sympathetic but delphic

c. 1870   Family moves back to New York City

1878   *The Leavenworth Case,* her first novel

1884   *Hand and Ring,* her own favorite of her novels

1884   Marries, November 25, Charles Rohlfs, an actor who had
appeared with Edwin Booth. (After their marriage, he
becomes a famous furniture designer whose work is
purchased for Buckingham Palace; he eventually
becomes a FRSA.) They settle in Buffalo. The Rohlfs
have three children, Rosamond, Sterling, and Roland,
of whom only the third survives the mother. Both sons are
well-known aviators; Roland is an associate of the
Wright brothers

1892   *The Leavenworth Case,* dramatised by its author,
appears on the stage, featuring Charles Rohlfs

1900   *The Circular Study*

1915   *The Golden Slipper*

1923   *The Step on the Stair,* her last novel.

1935   Dies, April 11, in Buffalo (Charles Rohlfs dies June 29,
1936)

by Barrie Hayne

"It is admirable," said Poirot. "One savours its period atmosphere, its studied and deliberate melodrama. Those rich and lavish descriptions of the golden beauty of Eleanor, the moonlight beauty of Mary!"

"I must read it again," I said. "I'd forgotten the parts about the beautiful girls."
"And there is the maidservant Hannah, so true to type, and the murderer, an excellent psychological study."
I perceived that I had let myself in for a lecture. I composed myself to listen.

Thus Hercule Poirot, in *The Clocks* (1964), expresses his admiration for one of the detective novel landmarks of nearly a hundred years before. And thus a later Queen of Crime salutes the Queen of Crime of the Gilded Age. Three years ago the centenary of *The Leavenworth Case* seems to have passed unnoticed, except for a display in the Buffalo and Erie County Public Library[1]; and despite Agatha Christie's homage, Anna Katharine Green is, in 1981, a writer hailed perfunctorily, if at all, and scarcely read. Though widely acclaimed as the grandmother, mother, even godmother, of the genre, she dwells in the house of detective fiction as a Victorian cabinet portrait towards the rear of the mantelpiece; the center rear indeed, but rarely taken down and dusted anymore. Howard Haycraft, whose judgments have been copied over into so many subsequent histories, summed her up a generation ago with that very mixture of general acknowledgement and particular depreciation: "Her style is unbelievably stilted and melodramatic by modern standards, her characterizations forced and artificial [*pace Poirot*]. But her plots are models of careful construction that can still hold their own against today's competition. For this quality, and by virtue of precedence and sustained popularity, she occupies an undisputed and honorable place in the development of the American detective story." There are those who would take away that place. Thirty years after Haycraft, Julian Symons gave her a paragraph, dismissing *The Leavenworth Case* as "a drearily sentimental story" "with passages of pious moralizing which are pulled through only with the most dogged persistence." Most recently, in their *Encyclopedia of Mystery and Detection,* Chris Steinbrunner and Otto Penzler, usually scrupulous in describing rather than judging, praise her for her plot construction, but note, with implicit distaste, her "substantial love-story qualities and melodramatic flourishes." In the year before her death, the *New York Times* had headed a story on her "Kept World Awake Half a Century"; forty-five years later, when the Buffalo *Courier-Express* wrote her up on the centenary of her most famous book, the sub-editor had to find a more catchy (and local) headline for a writer "now generally forgotten"—"Pioneer Whodunit Author Deduced Them in Buffalo."[2]

Yet *The Leavenworth Case* had sold 150,000 copies down to her death (fifty-seven years after its publication) and, according to her obituary in the *New York Times,* was still much in demand. Eight years before *The Mystery of a Hansom Cab,* and nine years before Sherlock Holmes made his *first* bow, *The Leavenworth Case* was a best-seller, "one of the all-time best-sellers in the literature," as Haycraft noted. As late as 1926, Norman Hapgood could mention Green with Poe, Doyle, Gaboriau: "we might as well close the list." In 1927, Willard Huntington Wright argued that the very success of *The Leavenworth Case,* rather than any innovations it made in the detective genre, was its importance, for it brought the detective story to a wider reading public. Even Wright, it may be noted, saw Green's novels as "over-documented and as too intimately concerned with strictly romantic material and humanistic considerations," but Wright was speaking for his age, as he admitted, the Golden Age of the detectival cryptogram, and of "the complex, economical and highly rarified technic of detective fiction."[3] Still, *The Leavenworth Case* was in print for most of its first sixty years. G.P. Putnam's Sons, which published it, renewed its copyright in 1906, when the novelist was still writing, with great popularity, in the genre, and the reprint of that year reads "105th thousand" on its titlepage. I myself have seen later, undated reprints with presumed contemporary inscriptions dated 1911 and 1923, as well as a paperback edition of 1937, itself a reprint of a 1934 edition, with introduction by Wright, evidently not ashamed to put the name and imprimatur of S.S. Van Dine, then at the height of his own popularity, on the old novel. *The Leavenworth Case* was dramatized, enjoyed a long run on the stage, and was also twice filmed: as a silent feature in 1923, which seems to follow the novel fairly closely, though dropping Gryce to leave the lawyer-narrator as the only detective; and in a sound version in 1936 which appears to bear little relation to the original. In the last forty years, however, *The Leavenworth Case* seems to have dropped largely from sight, though a facsimile edition was produced by the Gregg Press in 1970, when a bullish publishing market brought three other titles of

Green's back into print.[4]

Attempts have even been made, however, to explain away the great popularity of *The Leavenworth Case*. Julian Symons sees three reasons for that popularity, of which two can be quickly disposed of: that it was written by a woman, aside from the patronizing quality of the statement, is invalidated in any case by the enormous number of popular women writers contemporary with Green—Susan Warner, Elizabeth Wetherell, Miss Braddon and Mrs. Henry Wood (both detective story writers, by the way), not to mention Mrs. Stowe and George Eliot. Symons also attributes the popularity of the novel to the fact that so few detective stories were being written; the refutation of that lies in its evident continuing popularity—and more generally hers—through the Golden Age of detective fiction. Symons' other reason for its popularity, her realistic presentation of legal detail (her father was a famous trial lawyer, Symons is compelled to remind us) is a more cogent reason, though to it might be added her grasp of police procedures generally. Indeed, this takes us to the heart of Anna Katharine Green's continuing claim on our attention—her essential realism.[5]

If Anna Katharine Green is to be reinstated as a figure commanding the attention—the reading attention—of the critic of detective fiction, it must be on two grounds: her consolidation of the detective novel as a *realistic* art form, and her contribution to the development of the detective hero. On the first count, she takes her place as a representative American of her time, a writer writing in the post-Civil War period when the "real" began to replace the "romantic" as the dominant element in American fiction. On the second count, going beyond the partnerships of Dupin and his chronicler, of Sergeant Cuff and Franklin Blake, of even Lecoq and Old Tabaret, she established on firm basis the convention of professional and amateur detective, each supplementing the work of the other to solve the crime. And she claims our attention, too, for presenting the first really credible woman detective.

It will first be as well, then, to place her historically, for what longevity she had! Born while Poe was still writing, she died after Hammett had published his last novel. Her own first novel appeared before Old Sleuth, but when her last appeared, *Black Mask* was already publishing. Her principal predecessors, of course, are Poe, Wilkie Collins, and Gaboriau. A mystifier, who wrote three of the most influential of detective stories for the sake of the puzzle, a sensation novelist whose formula was "make 'em laugh, make 'em cry, make 'em wait," and a hack who spun his *romans policiers* partly from factual narratives, partly from the lurid yellow books of his time. These are the detectival components to which Anna Katharine Green is heir. In representing the dominant realistic strain in post-Civil War fiction, she is also the synthesizer of two sub-genres of fiction: the detective novel, for which she established the rules, consolidating the work of Poe, Gaboriau, and the Collins of *The Moonstone;* and the sensation novel, as written by Collins in much of the rest of his *oeuvre,* by Mrs. Henry Wood, by Miss Braddon, and by countless others more obscure. The synthesis she made of these two sub-genres is more realistic than the sensation novel, while maintaining the verisimilitude essential to the detective story.

It is perhaps not excessively reductive to assume that in the late nineteenth century the sensation novel is the principal repository of what Henry James would later call the "romantic," while the detective novel of the same period embodies what he designates the "real." This assumption carries, of course, a *caveat:* as James's own work amply demonstrates, the real and the romantic are never absolutely to be separated. With that qualification, however, the detective novel is at base realistic, the sensation novel at base romantic, in James's terms: "The real represents to my perception the things we cannot possibly *not* know, sooner or later, in one way or another; it being but one of the accidents of our hampered state, and one of the incidents of their quantity and number, that particular instances have not yet come our way. The romantic stands, on the other hand, for the things that, with all the facilities in the world...we never *can* directly know; the things that reach us only through the beautiful circuit and subterfuge of our thought and our desire."[6]

Kathleen Tillotson reminds us that both sensation novel and detective novel spring from the same root: at the centre of each lies a *secret.*[7] But what distinguishes the two sub-genres is the way that secret is treated. Where it is merely sprung upon the reader for the *frisson,* or where the reader is privy to it, his thrill deriving from the ignorance of the other characters and his own consequent superiority, then we are fairly in the realm of the sensation novel. Where the emphasis lies upon a character in the novel unraveling that secret by the exercise of his intellect, with the reader's participation, we have a detective story.

To put the matter in another way, using two terms given currency by Northrop Frye[8] the *eiron,* or self-deprecating, but knowledgeable, character, is represented in detective fiction by the detective and his partner the reader. Such a character is missing in sensational fiction, where all the characters are either in ignorance of the secret, or like the reader himself, in possession of it, but also with an interest in concealing it. They are all, readers and characters of the sensation novel, *alazons:* dupes or impostors.

Where all the characters are *alazons*, there must be a notable absence of ultimate moral order unless it be imposed from outside. But moral order is the very goal of the detective novel; it is what is reinstated at the end as a direct result of the detective's ratiocinations.

Because the sensation novel, moreover, is at a further remove from reality, it becomes more than the detective novel a catalyst for the reader's fantasies, allowing him to live for the time being an existence which could never be his in real life; "the things...we never *can* directly know" are its staple. The sensation novel is more the product of a class sytem; its middle class readers eavesdrop on the ways of the upper classes who are invariably its dramatic personae (The less marked lines of division between the classes in American society did not make Collins and Wood, Braddon and Ouida, any less popular in America, though the sensation novel *set* in America is a rarity, no doubt because of the absence there of the castled towers and ivied ruins which are so much a part of the genre).

The classic detective novel aims at maintaining a difficult synthesis between formula and reality: the clues must be given to the reader, the broken key, the complicated time scheme, the disposition of the characters at any given time; and all this must be related to familiar and recognizable fact. The hound of the Baskervilles cannot remain, in a detective novel, a specter of supernatural legend; the phosphorous on his snout must eventually return us to reality. Generally speaking, the things we probably never shall directly know—for murder, even in a violent age, is still outside the personal experience of most of us—must be brought into conjunction with the kind of reality we do know. "Wild, and yet domestic"[9]—so Dickens characterized *The Moonstone,* and Henry James commended Collins for "those most mysterious of mysteries, the mysteries which are at our own doors."[10] This is the essence of the classic detective novel. The nineteenth-century sensation novel, on the other hand, deals with a world either necessarily outside the experience of its readers (the supernatural), or practically so (the upper class of life). The detective story is therefore less escapist; it invites the reader's step-by-step participation, with the detective, in the solution of the mystery, and that solution is the final ratification of reality and social and moral order. The end of the sensation novel is more typically the ratification of a middle class ethic, coupled with an ambivalent rejection of aristocratic values. In a sensation novel, moreover, the supernatural may be allowed to stand, as the Ghost's Walk is left unexplained in that magnificent hybrid of detective novel, sensation novel, and so much else, *Bleak House*—I allude to it here only to point to the perils encountered by the formulator of "rules ":

In the sensation novel, finally, Fate has a much greater role to play. For Mrs. Henry Wood, or Miss Braddon, character is emphatically not destiny; Fate, usually malign, at best capricious, moves their characters like so many puppets. With Fate, goes her more lowly handmaiden, coincidence. Plot spins the passions. Green, however, partly because of her essentially American concern with the inner lives of her characters, partly because of her adoption of Poe's ratiocinative method, avoids the concept of an outside destiny, and centers her interest in the detective's intellectual pursuit of the criminal. Wilkie Collins, the master of Wood, Braddon, and countless others, is primarily a novelist of "character," though still as guilty of forcing character to conform to plot as his sensational disciples are, even in the best of his sensation novels, such as *The Woman in White* and *Armadale.* It is striking, therefore, that he found "the one weak side" of *The Leavenworth Case,* which he read in a sitting, to be "the want of truth to Nature in some of the characters."[11] But in urging Green to subject plot to character, he was not only welcoming her to his profession of detective story writer, but also giving her advice she did not really need.

To illustrate these generalizations, we may compare Mrs. Henry Wood's *East Lynne* (1861), sensation novel, with *The Leavenworth Case* (1878), detective novel. Both were first novels, both runaway best sellers, both, dramatized, highly popular plays. In *East Lynne,* Lady Isabel is left penniless on the death of her spendthrift father, and shortly afterwards marries the highly respectable and rich lawyer, Archibald Carlyle, who has bought East Lynne, her father's estate. They have three children, before Isabel is seduced by *Captain,* later *Sir,* Francis Levison, who eventually abandons her. She returns, disguised, but also greatly disfigured by her privations, to East Lynne, where Carlyle has married again, and where she becomes governess to her own children. One of them dies in her arms, and shortly afterwards she also dies, still in the house of her former husband, still unrecognized until she herself discloses her identity on her deathbed.

A subplot doubles the chance of coincidence: one of the factors causing Isabel to flee with Levison has been her jealous fears of losing her husband's love to Barbara Hare, a youthful neighbor, whose own love for Carlyle is evident to all save Carlyle himself. In fact their relationship is a professional one—he is advising her and her brother, who is a fugitive from a murder charge seeking the real murderer, whom he knows by sight. Much later, that murderer turns out to be Levison.

Of the three secrets of *East Lynne*—that Carlyle and Barbara's relationship is quite innocent, that the governess Madame Vine is

actually Lady Isabel, that Levison is a murderer—only one, the last,
is a secret from the reader. But all the characters in the novel, sooner
or later, are the dupes of one or other of the secrets—Lady Isabel does
not know that her husband does not love Barbara Hare, Carlyle does
not know his former wife is now his children's governess. All
alazons, no eirons. There is *one* eiron, though of the all-knowing
rather than the self-deprecating kind, and that is the narrative
presence itself of *East Lynne,* from whom the view that the
aristocracy are more prone to vice than the middle class, from whom
the constant recitation of a series of moral maxims which are
punitively ratified in Isabel's intolerably long penance and
miserable death. And the same narrative presence manipulates
Isabel's malign destiny so as to bring her by coincidence, just as she
fears losing her husband's love, into the hands of the supremely
attractive Levison.

    The Leavenworth Case begins in Leavenworth's lawyer's office
as the secretary of the rich retired merchant appears to announce
his employer's murder. The senior partner is absent, so the junior,
Raymond, returns with the secretary to the Leavenworth house,
where a coronial inquiry is about to begin. Leavenworth has two
nieces living with him, Mary, to whom he has left the bulk of his
fortune, and Eleanore. Mutual suspicion seems to create dissension
between the two women, and also has the effect of moving readers'
suspicions to and fro between the two. Also suspect is the mysterious
figure of Henry Clavering, who has been seen in the Leavenworth
mansion both before and after the murder. What finally emerges is
that Clavering, an Englishman, is secretly married to Mary—the
secrecy has caused the rift between the two women—and has
written to Leavenworth, who detests everything English,
complaining of her behavior in refusing to see him. Leavenworth is
therefore about to disinherit his niece, when he is murdered by his
secretary, who loves Mary and, not knowing her married, wishes to
marry her himself. The set of secrets, all plausibly connected, is
painstakingly uncovered by Gryce's reasoning.

    East Lynne, undoubtedly, will live longer than *The
Leavenworth Case:* it touches more universal feelings, touching
them in a highly sentimental way—mother love, and the sympathy
for, yet the reprobation of, the erring woman. It even contains a
murder mystery, with Francis Levison, in high retribution, finally
unmasked as the murderer. In its kaleidoscope of thrilling incidents,
it far overmatches *The Leavenworth Case.* But in that very
overmatch is the superior realism of Anna Katharine Green. *The
Leavenworth Case* does not strain our credulity as *East Lynne* does.
Green adds a second murder, but it follows logically from the first:
the secretary has lured away with a promise of marriage a

maidservant who has seen him leaving the room of the murder, and then has poisoned her. There is none of Wood's reliance upon fate and coincidence.

Most important of all, whereas *East Lynne* imposes through narrative omniscience a moral unanimity which brooks no contradiction, in *The Leavenworth Case,* through the narration of lawyer Raymond, naive and in love with Eleanore, yet following every step of the reasoning of the great detective Gryce, we get a nice balance of partiality and reasonableness which commands our trust. Raymond, unlike the omniscient persona of Mrs. Henry Wood, is of the same class as the Leavenworths, not peeping up from below stairs, and his initial interest in the Leavenworth mansion is not prurient, but harmlessly voyeuristic—he wants the thrill of seeing the dead body. Even the love interest in *The Leavenworth Case,* which in one of Green's disciples, Mary Roberts Rinehart, becomes a gratuitous convention, is part of its realism, and essential to the tenor of Raymond's narration. There is no moralizing voice in *The Leavenworth Case;* even with Raymond's partiality the approach to the solution of the crime is ratiocinative, and the emotional manipulations of Mrs. Henry Wood's moral attitudes are missing.

Given Mrs. Wood's rather prurient distaste for the aristocracy, one has the sense that she is pulling back the curtain on the elegance and serenity of aristocratic life to reveal the presence—the inevitability, we almost believe—of scandal and crime behind. Green has no such titillatory purpose; though she almost invariably sets her crime not far from a great house, or involves it with the reputation of a great family, the opulence is there to provide a believable contrast with the more pedestrian activities of the police. and it *is* more believable, for two reasons: it is more fully realized and described than Wood managed to make her presentment of upper class life, and, unlike British upper class life, the American *haut monde* was not hidden behind so many closed doors, but was more familiar, less the subject of prurient interest, to an American public. Both novelists described the upper classes, but the detective novelist described them in truer terms.

If the kind of novel that Green was writing can be distinguished, then by its higher realism, from the sensation novels of Mrs. Henry Wood and her school, Green's novels are still not quite of a piece with those of her predecessors in the detective novel. The realism of Poe's detective stories comes not from minute descriptions of the Rue Morgue or the hotel of the Minister D—, for these locales are scarcely even glimpsed, but from the ratiocinative movement, the pure logic, of Dupin's mind. The realism of *The Moonstone,* which has on analysis a plot quite as sensational as Collins's non-detective novels, comes from the plausibility of the narrators who give us that plot. The realism of Gaboriau comes from his faithful presentation of the streets and alleys of the metropolitan underworld which most of his characters inhabit. Green clearly owes something to Poe's logic, something to Collins's plausible narrators, though she never uses his multiple narrative method, but she owes much more to Gaboriau's descriptive realism—save that her subject is the salon rather than the street. The upper classes, who are always at the centre of Green's mysteries, are offstage in Gaboriau's.

Green herself, suggestively, preferred the term "criminal romance" for her fiction. Interviewed by a journalist in 1902, she said: "Please do not call my books 'detective stories'...I abhor the word detective. It is too often applied to atrocities. I choose crime as a basic subject because from it arise the most dramatic situations, situations which could be produced by nothing else."[12] Even if we forget here to trust the tale rather than the artist, Green's habit of collecting newspaper accounts of actual crimes as the germs for her novels, as well as the fact that a contemporary critic called her "the foremost representative in America to-day of police-court literature "[13] (and that she was asked at least once for her solution to a local Buffalo crime), lay the emphasis upon the "criminal" rather than the "romance." Indeed, her plots never strain the credulity at their most ingenious, and are most often scientifically ballasted: *The Leavenworth Case* itself turns partly on scientific evidence, and one of her last novels, *Initials Only,* has the victim killed with an ice pellet, which when it melts leaves the investigators with a seemingly supernatural, but actually quite plausible, cause of death. (To take "romance" in a different sense, while her "love" interest has been condemned by modern commentators, it is worth noting that she herself regarded her last novel, in 1923, as "my first love story."[14])

It is in this understanding of the fundamental realism of her fiction—what Barzun and Taylor see as her presentation of "the tempo and the mores of New York and Washington society in the period 1875-1900"[15]—that it is time to introduce her principal detective, Ebenezer (in some novels spelt "Ebenezar") Gryce. The introduction is made in the first chapter of *The Leavenworth Case:*

And here let me say that Mr. Gryce, the detective, was not the thin, wiry individual with the piercing eye you are doubtless expecting to see. On the contrary, Mr. Gryce was a portly, comfortable personage with an eye that never pierced, that did not even rest on *you.* If it rested anywhere, it was always on some insignificant object in the vicinity, some vase, inkstand, book or button. These things he would seem to take into his confidence, make the repositories of his conclusions; but as for you—you might as well be the steeple on Trinity Church, for all connection you appeared to have with him or his thoughts. At present, then, Mr. Gryce was, as I have already suggested, on intimate terms with the door-knob (6-7).[16]

So Gryce on his first appearance before the reading public, but actually in mid-career as a detective. The Dickensian touches, not necessarily via Collins, are clear, as is the sense that Green is alluding to, but departing from, a literary stereotype. Noting, in 1903, the vast difference between Old Sleuth and Sherlock Holmes on the one hand, and the real detective on the other, Green observed that all the detectives she had met were "tame and uninteresting."[17] In making Gryce a fairly pedestrian figure, she was determinedly, therefore, moving away from romance to realism.

It will be as well to place beside this passage one from the short story which describes Gryce's earliest case, "The Staircase at the Heart's Delight," set in "the spring of 1840" (late versions say 18—), but published in 1894:

Fortunately for me, I was in the building at the time, and was able to respond when a man was called up to investigate this matter. Thinking that I saw a connection between it and the various mysterious deaths of which I have previously spoken, I entered into the affair with much spirit...Accordingly, I appeared there [in a certain pawnshop], one dull November afternoon, in the garb of a certain Western sporting man, who, for a consideration, allowed me the temporary use of his name and credentials.

Entering beneath the three golden balls, with the swagger and general air of ownership I thought most likely to impose upon the self-satisfied female who presided over the desk, I asked to see her boss (185-86).

Between them, these two passages strike several of the keynotes of Gryce's character: the diffidence in the presence of his social superiors unless he is actually masquerading as one of them; a certain hostility towards women, contained within his patronization of them; his professional ambition which becomes a proper professional vanity as he grows old, older, oldest; his abstraction, sometimes assumed, sometimes despondent at failure, which can spring in a moment to alertness when a new lead is discovered.

Gryce is a member of the official police force of New York, and it is mainly in the metropolis, or its suburbs, where Green grew up, that the novels take place, though there are trips into the countryside, one to Vermont, where Green had her schooling. *Hand and Ring,* her own favorite of her novels, is set in upstate New York, as well as in Buffalo, where she lived for part of her childhood and all of her fifty years of married life. Her detectives do not stray far from those scenes she knew and could realistically describe.

Gryce's career runs through eleven novels and two short stories published between 1878 and 1917, and, within a certain latitude, he ages correspondingly. His career, as it is written, runs in the novels from the Centennial year of Hayes-Tilden to the year of Woodrow Wilson's inauguration, with the two retrospective short stories taking it back to more than a decade before the Civil War. Though not all these events are mentioned, some of them are, and there is a greater sense of the specific kind of larger world that exists beyond Gryce's smaller world than in most detective novels. Above all, there is the sense of Gryce's gradual aging, and the incidental references to telephones, automobiles, and even airships can only enhance that sense, anchoring it in reality. In "The Staircase at the Heart's Delight," looking back, he describes himself as "a young man in those days, and full of ambition" (182). In "The Doctor, His Wife, and the Clock," set in 1851, published in 1895, he is "a young man of thirty" (110). In *The Leavenworth Case* his age is not specified, though the middle fifties seems about right, and he is laid up through most of the novel with a serious attack of the rheumatism which afflicts him constantly in the still later novels. In two novels in which he plays only a small part, *A Strange Disappearance* (1880) and *Hand and Ring* (1884), his appearance is largely taken for granted, but by the time of *Behind Closed Doors* (1888) his rheumatism has become "proverbial" (42), though he still has a "fine figure," and "when hurry is demanded" the infirmity does not stand in his way. He is by now in his mid-sixties, we presume, and his figure is still "portly" (75).

In *A Matter of Millions* (1890), "he is an old man now, verging on seventy, and both from age and infirmity in no condition to engage in the active exercise of that detective work which has employed his energies for so many years" (79-80). With age, of course, has come increasing fame: on the first page of *A Strange Disappearance,* the narrator-detective is referred to as "the most astute man...in the bureau, always and of course excepting Mr. Gryce." At the beginning of *Hand and Ring,* one of his subordinates calls him "one of New York's ablest detectives" (5). Though in *Behind Closed Doors* he has "passed his prime," he is "the great Gryce yet" (479). And in *A Matter of Millions,* as the authorial voice says, his "record, after all, is chiefly one of triumphs" (114).

In his first collaboration with Amelia Butterworth, *That Affair Next Door* (1897), he looks to her on their first meeting (in 1895) "seventy-five if he was a day" (21); he later himself says, "I'm seventy-seven, but I'm not too old to learn" (317). In this novel he remains "portly and easy-going in appearance" (14). While her sensitivity about her own "uncertain" age makes her call him "old," she translates "old" in a different way in their second collaboration in *Lost Man's Lane* (1898): " 'You mean old enough to pull the wool over other people's eyes' " (225); and when he carries a young and attractive woman over an obstacle, she acidly remarks, "Where was his rheumatism now?" (374). In *The Circular Study* (1900), Gryce, the "old reader of human nature," is an "octogenarian" (9), thinking of retiring to his little farm in Westchester (age and fame have their tangible rewards, too), but still drawn to the life of action over mere thought. This case, the authorial voice notes with an authority it may have regretted, was "one of the last to engage the powers of this sagacious old man" (48). Indeed, a year later, in *One of My Sons* (1901), Gryce is now "sagacious but sickly" (137), but he is still "a large, elderly man, with a world of experience in his time-worn but kindly visage" (56-57). At the end of *That Affair Next Door,* in the wake of failure, he had contemplated retirement, and in *One of My Sons* he relies more heavily upon his assistant Sweetwater, a reliance that becomes more marked still in *Initials Only* (1911), where he has in fact retired; his is the "directing mind," and Sweetwater's the active work. He seems to be losing flesh, even despite the apparent remission of years between 1901 and 1911, for he is now "a tall, angular gentleman" (11), and, though "an old and rheumatic invalid" (35), still "kind-faced, bright-eyed" (30). Though temporary failure brings its sense of uselessness—" 'I've meddled with the old business for the last time, Sweetwater. You'll have to go it alone from now on' " (112)—when the old hound scents the trail he has "an antidote against old age" (128). In this novel, though, he needs a taxicab where before the train had served; the subway is for the young. "I can no longer manage the stairs" (132).

In his last novel, *The Mystery of the Hasty Arrow* (1917), he who had his origins in the world of gas-jets and hansoms makes his appearance in an automobile, from which he has to be helped, and at which he looks rather askance. This novel is set in 1913, presumably to keep its events clear of the war, even in distant Europe (though the principal woman becomes, at the end, a nurse close to the trenches), and presumably also to make more plausible Gryce's continuing longevity; if he was thirty in 1851, he must be beyond ninety by now. So at one moment of despondency in the novel, "the lines came out in Mr. Gryce's face till he looked his eighty-five years and more" (the last two words are conveniently ambiguous—did he have those extra years, or merely look them?). He seems, indeed, "at first blush...past the age where experience makes for efficiency" (13), yet "this physically weak but extremely wise old man" dominates the scene with his "mental power" (14). None of his vanity has gone— " 'I have been said to be able to spot a witness with my eyes shut. Let's see what I can do with my eyes open' " (17). Neither has his legendary complaint gone—"An extra twinge or two of rheumatism warned him that he was approaching the point of disablement" (255). As always failure, or in later years the sense that he must arrest a good or likeable man, brings despondency (" If

my death here and now...would avail to wipe out the evidence I
have so laboriously collected against this man, I should welcome it
with gratitude"—309), but with the game afoot, the spirit
rekindles—"the almost extinguished spark of early genius had
suddenly flared again into full blaze" (36). These words, in fact, are a
fair description of Anna Katharine Green's own powers, in this
next-to-last of her novels, one of her very best. After it, Gryce goes
into the silence. And, after one more novel, so does Anna Katharine
Green.

Gryce's principal two social limitations I mentioned in
introducing him. He feels his inferior social status, even though his
position gives him power; and he has an eye, if at times it is a cold
eye, for the ladies. On the first point, he twice notes in *The
Leavenworth Case* that he is not a gentleman, and cannot act the
part:

'Have you any idea of the disadvantages under which a detective labors? For
instance, now, you imagine I can insinuate myself into all sorts of society, perhaps,
but you are mistaken...I can enter a house, bow to the mistress of it, let her be as
elegant as she will, so long as I have a writ of arrest in my hand, or some such
professional matter upon my mind; but when it comes to visiting in kid gloves,
raising a glass of champagne in response to a toast—and such like, I am absolutely
good for nothing' (130).

Though Gryce is "dejected" by, responds "broodingly" to, this
deficiency of his, it is later noted that whereas Raymond, the
narrator of the novel, is prevented by gentlemanly scruples from
intercepting a letter, Gryce the non-gentleman is not so hampered.
Raymond, a young lawyer of the same class as the Leavenworth
girls whose uncle has been murdered, is eager to solve the crime, for
he has fallen in love with one of those girls, who is suspected of the
murder. Gryce thus "employs" the younger man to garner
information from those rarified social circles while he pursues his
own investigation at a lower level of society. The relationship
between Gryce and Raymond is thus one of division of labor
between the mole and the hound. As Raymond puts it—" 'any
hearkening at doors, surprises, unworthy feints or ungentlemanly
subterfuges, I herewith disclaim as outside of my province; my task
being to find out what I can in an open way, and yours to search into
the nooks and corners of this wretched business.' " " 'Just so, I know
what belongs to a gentleman,' " Gryce replies (148).

It has been argued that Gryce's deference to his social superiors
is Anna Katharine Green's main breach of realism, taken over from
the relationships that exist between Lecoq and his more truly
seignurial betters, especially in *M. Lecoq* and its sequel *The Honour
of the Name,* where the detective is powerless to bring the ducal

criminal to justice in the first part, and in the second part, while he tricks him into a confession, allows him to go free. Earlier, in *The Widow Lerouge,* a woman is murdered for what she knows of an exchange of babies in the cradle; the murderer, the low-born child, is brought to justice, and one has the distinct impression that were he the aristocrat he would go free. But in democratic America such contemporary documents as Pinkerton's memoirs showed the professional detective as standing at no such disadvantage. It is worth remembering that not only Lecoq, but two more of Gryce's ancestors, Inspector Bucket of *Bleak House* and Sergeant Cuff of *The Moonstone,* are socially the inferiors of those they are investigating: Sir Leicester treats Bucket with aristocratic disdain as he probes for the truth of Lady Dedlock's past; and Lady Verinder summarily dismisses Cuff from the case when his suspicions settle upon Rachel as the thief. But it is unthinkable, as Gryce's own words make clear, that an American Lady Verinder could turn the American Cuff away from her door. The arrest will be made, though it be a social gaffe, and realism is not sacrificed thereby. As the policeman-narrator of *A Strange Disappearance* says: "I felt a certain degree of awe at the thought of invading with police investigation, this house of ancient Knickerbocker respectability. But once in the room of the missing girl, every consideration fled save that of professional pride and curiosity" (17-18). So Gryce faces down, in his second novel, a man who has been a congressman, and, in his last, unmasks a man who is bidding fair to be a U.S. Senator.

Moreover, Green augments Gaboriau's realism in other ways. His maps of open terrain become in her novels detailed room or house plans, which remind us of their different settings, his the mean streets Maigret would tread fifty and seventy-five years later, hers the parlors of the detective novel's Golden Age (S.S. Van Dine is also a great draughtsman of interiors). Truly, Anna Katharine Green, after Gaboriau, took crime out of the streets, but in doing so she did not make its perpetrators inaccessible to those who still patrolled those streets. Her house plans, too, pin the reader to a greater specificity of detail. And there is a wealth of realistic observation in her frequent use of trial procedures to provide exposition: the knowledge she had from her father *does* give her the authority to use the frame of a trial or inquest to put the reader in convincing possession of the facts of the case.

The way in which Green deals with the inferior status of the policeman, therefore, omnipotent with a writ of arrest in his hand, but hampered in investigating aristocratic guilt as yet unproven, finally brings together realism with significant generic innovation: when the policeman cannot enter freely the great house, he finds an accomplice who can. While the unofficial partnership of Cuff and

Franklin Blake is a single earlier example of such an alliance between the street and the salon, the relationship of Gryce and Raymond, between policeman and social habitue, recurs again and again in Green's novels, and adds her own touch to the relationship she may have found in Poe between the thinking detective and his sometimes more active, usually less intelligent, and almost always more narrative, partner—one scarcely needs reminders of those who come after! Much too elementary.

Such a relationship (though the intelligence is more equally balanced) is the stuff of three of Green's best novels, those which describe the partnership between Gryce and a feisty "woman of inborn principle and strict Presbyterian training," with "no faith in premonitions, but once seized by a conviction...never...mistaken as to its import," with "very few old maid's way or notions," and "none of [her] sex's instinctive reliance upon others which leads it so often to neglect its own resources"—all these are self-descriptions of Amelia Butterworth. One may say that to Ebenezer Gryce this wealthy, fiftyish spinster is always *the* woman (he actually calls her "a woman in a thousand"—Affair, 317). She is not of course his adversary, and yet she is, in the way that she elicits the other social limitation I mentioned, his hostility, his attraction, to women, and his patronization of them. For the relationship between Gryce and Miss Butterworth is truly a battle of the sexes, in which the antagonists sound less like Mirabell and Millamant, or even John Tanner and Ann Whitefield, and much more like an older, less uxorious, more acerbic Nick and Nora Charles.

She refers often to her father, "a shrewd man of the old New England type," whose "hauteur" she frequently cultivates (Affair, 23). At a triumphant moment in the same novel, she rhapsodizes: "I began to feel my importance in a way that was truly gratifying, and cast my eyes up at the portrait of my father with a secret longing that its original stood by to witness the verification of his prophecy" (278). She doesn't like young men in general (100), and when she first sees Gryce he strikes her as "paternal-looking" (20). When he acknowledges her detective abilities, "I felt as if my father's daughter had received her first recognition" (56). In Gryce, clearly, she finds a reminder of her father, and their relationship, so established from the beginning, develops as a wrangling, affectionate one, in which each seeks from the other the grudging praise in which neither professes openly to be interested. "Though I have had no adventures," she says at the outset, "I feel capable of them, and as for any peculair acumen he may have shown in his long and eventful career, why that is a quality which others may share with him" (22). And in the second novel, she describes occasional meetings with him of a merely social kind—Gryce is rising in the social scale—"in which he gained much without acknowledging it, and I gave much without appearing conscious of the fact" (Lane, 2).

Beyond their relationship, certainly, since there is a quarter of a century between their ages, and since Green herself so often sees Gryce as fatherly, it is not fanciful to see the author projecting her own father into her male detective and herself into her female detective. The creative energy so released makes, in my opinion, these three novels the best in all her more than forty; better than *The Leavenworth Case,* where the coadjutor is so pale in character, a mere juvenile lead, and challenged only by *Hand and Ring* and *The Mystery of the Hasty Arrow,* the best two of her many novels that show a figure of high fame and flourishing prosperity stalked by a nemesis from the distant past, more than once an abandoned wife.[18] If, as they do, so many of Green's novels deal with marital tragedy— another mark of her realism, by the way—misalliances which are often corrected by murder, then the Gryce-Butterworth alliance gives the comic obverse of that theme. It is noteworthy that Gryce seems to have no family life, until in *The Mystery of the Hasty Arrow* he has a much loved granddaughter who, newly married, has just left him, he complains, "for a man many years my junior" (233). In Miss Butterworth he has a female partner who in her frequent rivalry of his "peculiar acumen" is his comic nemesis, a resurgence of the real family members he has so rigidly excluded from his public life that they do not emerge until the third generation, and then only over his protest.

Moreover, as befits a self-projection, Amelia Butterworth, even more than Gryce, is Green's most human character. Gryce has few sins to soften him; Miss Butterworth has a myriad humanizing touches. She is capable of personal as well as professional vanity, and a certain cattiness: "I am not handsome myself, though there have been persons who have called me so, but neither am I ugly, and in contrast to this woman—well, I will say nothing. I only know that, after seeing her, I felt profoundly grateful to a kind Providence" (Affair, 92). She is also capable of a disarming brand of self-aware rationalization: "The door to the closet was, as I expected, slightly ajar, a fact for which I was profoundly grateful, for, set it down to breeding or a natural recognition of other people's rights, I would have found it most difficult to turn the knob of a closet door, inspection of which had not been offered me. But finding it open, I gave it just a little pull...." (Lane, 164).

Whereas Gryce has only his habit of not looking his interlocutor in the eye,[19] his rheumatism, and the portliness which eventually gives way to lanky emaciation, Miss Butterworth has her irrational fear of dogs ("my one weakness"—Lane, 35), and her habit of carrying with her extra candles and her own tea, without which she cannot get to sleep. With her own carriage and a house in Gramercy Park, she is a woman of wealth, whose dress is "rather rich than fashionable" (Lane, 109); fashion "counts for nothing against convenience" (Lane, 167). However, in the same novel she explores an old house, full of beetles and spiders, in a "three-dollar-a-yard silk dress" (160). For all her wealth, too, she has an eye for a bargain; at recess during an inquest she "improved the opportunity by going into a restaurant near by where one can get very good buns and coffee at a reasonable price. But I could have done without them" (Affair, 90). She is rather a snob: when a police official tells a servant, "and this other woman, too," to "stay around" for a coroner's inquest, she remarks, "By other woman he meant *me*, Miss Butterworth, of Colonial ancestry and no inconsiderable importance in the social world." But then her common sense resumes: "But though I did not relish this careless association of myself with this poor scrub-woman, I was careful to show no displeasure, for I reasoned that as witnesses we were equal before the law, and that it was solely in this light he regarded us" (Affair, 19-20).

As to her femininity, she uses "no perfumes" (Lane, 168), but towards one character who eventually proposes marriage and to whom she gives a "reluctant no" (Lane, 349), she shows a certain flirtatiousness. She is, however, as we have seen, thoroughly down-to-earth, and her response to another suitor is rather more characteristic: " 'I am not easy to suit, so I advise you to turn your attention to some one much more anxious to be married than I am' " (Lane, 343). She is as free as she professes to be of feminine foible. She is a thoroughly independent woman, perhaps unliberated only in her deference to Gryce, but of certain kinds of feminine independence her old-fashioned qualities do not allow her to approve. When, not entirely without irony, she curtseys to a group of men, she comments: "It was a proper expression of respect when I was young, and I see no reason why it should not be a proper expression of respect now, except that we have lost our manners in gaining our independence, something which is to be regretted perhaps" (There may be a second thought in the last word—Affair, 312). In truth, Amelia Butterworth, christened Araminta, which is what her father has always called her, *is* a dependent woman only in her daughterly "Araminta" role, and overwhelmingly the independent woman denoted by the name she chooses to use; she is scarcely at all "the piece of antiquated sentimentality suggested by the former cognomen" (Affair, 23). At one of her moments of self-doubt, with a sense of being led astray by that sentimentality (which she sees as a feminine trait), she looks in a mirror and remarks that she ought to be called Araminta after all. The "stern image" which looks back at her sets her again on the accustomed path (Affair, 168).

The particular help Amelia Butterworth is to Gryce, aside from her ease of entre into a society whose doors are closed to him, lies in the insight into feminine behavior of which he is also ignorant. (In *Behind Close Doors* (286), it is said of him that he "knew men—he never boasted that he knew women.") In *The Leavenworth Case,* without her aid, he makes a deduction, much ridiculed in recent years, that the murderer was not a woman, for a woman may fire a gun, but would not clean it afterwards. In *That Affair Next Door,* she deduces from the dead woman's bare hands that she has been indoors at least long enough to remove her gloves, for "so well-dressed a woman would not enter a house like this, without gloves" (29; O tempora! O mores!). She also deduces that a woman's hat has been worn only once from the single puncture made in it by the hat pin.

In their three collaborations, or rather encounters, Miss Butterworth gets closer to the solution than Gryce in the first, is bested, partly through her feminine vanity, in the second, while the third may be said to be a friendly draw. Their final parting, at the end of *The Circular Study,* as Gryce bows "lower even than his wont," foreshadows a further collaboration: "Was he wondering if a case of similar interest would ever bring them together again in consultation?" But Gryce by the turn of the century was a gentleman himself, with his farm in Westchester, and the need for upper-class coadjutors was behind him. What he still had need for, as from the beginning, was the subordinate alter ego, the man who could do what he, through age, lack of agility, concern for dignity, or even his high degree of recognizability, could not do for himself. So Holmes used his Baker Street Irregulars when he could not take advantage of his penchant for disguise. So Gryce uses a number of auxiliaries, in particular his principal protege, Sweetwater. If Amelia Butterworth looks to him as a daughter, these young men are much more plainly his bequests to the future, his trainees, his surrogate sons.

The earlier avatars of this type, the assistant called "Q," and the detective Horace Byrd, are preliminary sketches of, or searches for, the much more developed Sweetwater. Q makes his appearance in *The Leavenworth Case,* "an agent of mine who is a living interrogation point" (135). Disguised as a woman, crawling across roofs to peep in windows, and with his card inscribed with a single "?", he is a comic character, however serious his function, and he fades out of the story once Gryce is in possession of the information he has acquired. In *A Strange Disappearance,* now a regular member of the police force, he is, after two introductory paragraphs describing him as "the rising young detective," the narrator of the story, still performing the same tasks—he disguises himself as a seedy French artist, and to enter a house climbs a tree with rural expertise ("thanks to fortune I was not brought up in New York"— 95). While the first-person narration works against a primarily comic characterization, the return to the third person in *Behind Closed Doors* again makes Q—"Q the curious", as he calls himself, 417—a figure of fun, a lounger whose main task is to shadow Gryce's suspect. He is not a comic contemptible, however, and one takes seriously enough his statement: "And to be a good detective is meat and drink to me, and more. I have ambition to take Mr. Gryce's place when he is laid up. There are those who say I will" (417).

Before *Behind Closed Doors,* another of Gryce's juniors had appeared, Horace Byrd. That this minor detective is listed in Hagen's *Who Done It?,* while Q is not, is no doubt due to Byrd's presence in *Hand and Ring,* which is one of Green's most popular novels, still in print in the 1920s. Byrd does however have a kind of primacy that Q never attains, and is in fact the principal detective in the novel until his failure causes him to call Gryce from the metropolis to upstate New York. Before that, at least part of the story's interest lies in the duel between Byrd and yet another detective, a private one. But Byrd is a colorless figure, more a functionary than a character. In *A Matter of Millions,* when Byrd is again Gryce's bulldog, it becomes clearer that his principal cachet is his "attractive features, good expression and cultivated manners. He is a detective, too, but neither in speech, look nor action does he show it; hence his usefulness and growing favor with the chief" (80). Byrd is, in fact, a transitional figure between Raymond, persona grata in society, and Q and Sweetwater, who are more like Gryce himself. And the relationship between him and Gryce is not filial: he is more Raymond than Sweetwater.

Sweetwater, Gryce's last and most attractive male auxiliary, appears first in *Agatha Webb* (1899), where he is not a detective, but a musician ("'a fiddler, a nobody'", as one character calls him—113) living in the rural New England town of Sutherlandtown; and much of this novel's interest exists in the conflict between the professional detective, suggestively named Knapp, from the big city (Boston), and this young amateur, like Q a country boy. Sweetwater is early described, self-described, as "not prepossessing to look at" (114), but there his comic potential stops; his confidence, even in the presence of the supercilious Bostonian, is supreme, and carries him through in his "self-imposed role of detective" (196). He is a more authoritative figure than Q. His scruples may be subordinated to his ambition at this stage of his career (he is "not so much high-minded as large-hearted"—209). But even this early his character is penetratingly possessed by Green, for his ugliness is shown to be the moving principle behind his will to success and fame. At the denouement Knapp is outfoxed, and "Sweetwater was a made man" (359).

In the next novel, *The Circular Study,* is a plethora of riches— not only Gryce and Miss Butterworth, but again Sweetwater, now for six months a member of the New York police force, under Gryce, still supremely confident: his cheer penetrates a mystery as yet impenetrable to the old detective ("But then he was not twenty-three, with only triumphant memories behind him"—47). Already he demonstrates a greater detectival skill than Q or Byrd, and already Gryce's attitude is explicitly paternal for a " 'young man I propose to adopt into my home and heart.... Not much to look at, madam, but promising, very promising' " (78). While Miss Butterworth butters up Gryce by comparing his "genius" with the new pupil's mere "skilfulness," the understudy's role is clearly now taken up with more authority, and approval, than ever before. In *The Circular Study* his primacy yields to the Gryce-Butterworth alliance, but this is the last of Miss Butterworth, and only the next-to-first of him.

In *One of My Sons,* indeed, the balance of interest shifts from Gryce to Sweetwater. The narrative is a first-person one, told by a young gentleman who is summoned from the street to witness the dying moments of a wealthy patriarch. Sweetwater, while professing to wish for Gryce's help at a crucial juncture, solves the case with a shrewd deduction from a typewritten message from the victim (Shades of Ellery Queen!). Between the narrator and Sweetwater there is something of a reprise of the Raymond-Gryce arrangement of twenty years before; but Sweetwater's pertinacity (one of his emphasized qualities) carries him so much farther, in a less rigid age, that the roles of the two partners are virtually reversed:

Meantime, Sweetwater, with an air of perfect nonchalance admirably assumed, had stepped past Hewson into the house. Evidently he was accustomed to go in and out of the place at will, and though the old servant did not fail to show his indignation at this palpable infringement upon the family dignity, he did not abate a jot of his usual politeness.... But his complaisance did not extend to me (337-338).

The next appearance of Sweetwater, after a lapse of five years in which Green was writing a more romantic kind of fiction, though still within our genre, including two serials for Edward Bok's *Ladies' Home Journal,* is a continuation of such regression. *The*

Woman in the Alcove (1906) is again a first-person narrative, this time by a society woman, and the romantic element is dominant. Though in *One of My Sons* attention was drawn as usual to Sweetwater's physical grotesqueness—"his lank frame and inharmonious features" (135)—in *The Woman in the Alcove* he is described as "of a commonplace type" (272), and his task of merely shadowing a suspect puts him back into Q's role. The only chapter in which he has any prominence, indeed, is actually entitled "Sweetwater in a New Role."

But four years later, in *The House of the Whispering Pines* (1910), which Haycraft recommends over *The Leavenworth Case* ("connoisseurs prefer...."), Sweetwater, without Gryce, again has pride of place. He calls himself at the denouement "a pupil of Mr. Gryce" (413), however, and the trap that he lays to elicit a sign of guilt from the villain recalls many of Gryce's similar stratagems, from *The Leavenworth Case* on. Sweetwater, who would by now be in his early thirties, has grown in both ugliness and authority. To the male narrator, as usual of the gentlemanly class, he is "no beauty,...plain-featured to the point of ugliness" (98), yet "there was a magnetic quality in his voice and manner that affected even one so fastidious as myself" (384). In a court appearance, his "receding chin and far too projecting nose," though matched with "his cheerful, modest, winsome disposition" (98), call forth the suspicion of the presiding coroner, who is mollified only by a letter of recommendation from Gryce, whose fame by now, of course, opens all doors. This letter commends Sweetwater in the same terms that have been so often used for Gryce himself—"'a man of sagacity and becoming reserve'": the understudy is moving, with approval, towards the central role.

In *Initials Only,* as we saw, Gryce's age enforces now an even greater reliance on his assistant, and the principal interest in the novel is in the mutual relationship between the two detectives. Sweetwater again carries the case to a successful conclusion, ingeniously identifying an apparent stabbing in which the weapon is missing as in fact a shooting with a bullet of ice, which has melted by the time of the medical examination. As we also saw, the collaboration between Gryce and Sweetwater comes to a suspended end in *The Mystery of the Hasty Arrow.* Here there is a return to the earlier pattern of Gryce as the mental and Sweetwater as the active part. And Sweetwater is again distinctly secondary. When he makes his first appearance at the museum where the murder has just been committed, and notes "the Curator's evident chagrin at his meagre and unsatisfactory appearance" (13), he humorously points out that he is not the principal, that Mr. Gryce will be there presently. Throughout the novel he is Gryce's "recognized factotum" (146).

Gryce "was the absolute master of everything, even of Sweetwater, he sometimes thought. For the young fellow loved him—had reason to." Though Gryce's manner to his assistant is more *de haut en bas* than in the previous novel, there is still a strong sense of cooperation, and they spend more time actually conferring. The chapter entitled " 'Write Me His Name' ", in which the two exchange theories and then, on paper, suspects, is a good example of their relation—and it is Gryce who is correct in his choice of culprit.

So Sweetwater remains to the end secondary, never taking over the role of what Carolyn Wells calls "the Transcendent Detective."[20] Though most of Gryce's subordinates, and on two occasions Gryce himself (in *Hand and Ring* and *Lost Man's Lane*, not counting his very first case), carry out the essentially menial side of detective work by disguising themselves, none does this more than Sweetwater. The relationship between a detective writer and his detective—especially if it has lasted long, and both have grown old together (Holmes, Poirot, Miss Marple spring to mind)—is obviously a complex and intimate one. Anna Katharine Green evidently did not wish to see Gryce die, and one of the great successes of *The Mystery of the Hasty Arrow* is its climactic delineation of the coming dissolution of the paternal figure. A weak novel, *The Step on the Stair,* without Gryce, followed tardily six years later, and for the last twelve years of a very long life Anna Katharine Green published no more.

But two years before *The Mystery of the Hasty Arrow,* Anna Katharine Green had created her last important detective and a current favorite, Violet Strange, who made her appearance, or series of appearances, in *The Golden Slipper* (1915). The book, with the first of nine "problems for Violet Strange," opens with an exchange between the head of a detective agency and a prospective client, at the theatre: " 'Do you mean to say...that yon silly little chit, whose father I know, whose future I know, and who is called one of the season's belles is an agent of yours.' " At the end of Green's procession of detectives comes one who is *both* professional and amateur, *both* detective agent and socialite. This "small, slight woman," "vivacity incarnate,...and a woman's lofty soul [shining] through her odd, bewildering features" (5), and "of the size of a child of eleven" (371) truly leads a double life, kept secret from her financier father. She is working as a detective for money to train her older sister as an opera singer, the sister her father has disowned for marrying a singing-master, and he would disown Violet too, if he knew. Amid a round of parties, balls and musicales she continues her detective work: "Violet Strange in society was a very different person from Violet Strange under the tension of her secret and peculiar work" (56).

Amelia Butterworth of Gramercy Park at the turn of the century had her carriage; Violet Strange of Seventy-Second Street in 1915 has her limousine. But her habits are much less plain than Miss Butterworth's: she draws her limousine up outside the house of crime on Seventeenth Street ("her entrance was a *coup du theatre*"— 77). The girl is much more stereotypically "feminine" than the older woman, and despite her frequent displays of courage much less truly liberated: *The Golden Slipper* is, in such unity as it has, her love story, as the young Boston aristocrat whose wife's murder is her fourth "problem" returns as an accessory figure in her eighth, and is poised to marry her in her ninth and last. It is difficult to agree with Haycraft's view—"Her feminine detective, VIOLET STRANGE, is best forgotten"—but it is clearly wrong, at the other end of the spectrum, to see Violet as engaged in a "positive act of resisting patriarchal domination,"[21] for she is very much and always concerned lest her father find out about her secret profession. Somewhat disagreeably she uses her feminine wiles and weaknesses: to gain entrance into the house of crime she plays the flibbertigibbet; it is no excuse to say that "back of this display of mingled childishness and audacity there lay hidden purpose, intellect, and a keen knowledge of human nature" (82). She seems to accept her lover's belief that her mind "has an intuitive faculty more to be relied upon than the reasoning of men" (124); and when at the end she explains to him her reasons for undertaking detective work, it is an explanation of "why, with all the advantages I possess, I should meddle with matters so repugnant to a woman's natural instincts" (401). Though she with great nerve crawls, as her size allows, into a sealed room which contains—literally—two family skeletons, the room is in the mansion of one of her own class. One cannot see her soiling her three-dollar-a-yard dress (both price and hem would be up by 1915 in any case) in places alien to that class. In fact, Violet tells her employer that she "not be asked to touch the sordid or the bloody"—" 'I have no fancy for handling befouled spider webs" (68). As we saw, Amelia Butterworth had no such scruples.

This then, is the progression over forty years from Ebenezer Gryce to Violet Strange. Conveniently, we can close with one of Green's most famous stories, "The Doctor, His Wife, and the Clock," for this story, written for Gyce in the 1890s, was retailored as Violet Strange's Problem 7 twenty years later. The story, briefly, concerns a midnight shooting in fashionable New York City, in his bed, of a man without enemies; the neighborhood is alerted by a woman's shriek. The inquiry leads to the blind Doctor Zabriskie and his wife, living in a nearby house. The doctor insists he has committed the crime, but the police ignore his confession, because of the accuracy of the killer's aim and the alacrity of his escape. The doctor insists on a test: a clock is to be placed at a distance from him as a target when it strikes the hour. At the last moment his wife, holding another clock, moves into the line of fire and is killed. He shortly thereafter kills himself.

In Gryce's first-person narration the tale is straight-forward, a policeman's account, with some interpolated statements. Gryce is early convinced that the doctor committed the crime (though by mistake), and expects him to be able to shatter an audible target. In *The Golden Slipper* the story is enclosed within the author's omniscience: Violet's employer at the detective agency brings her the narrative, largely unaltered from the Gryce version, but now attributed to "an everyday police detective" (252). With its ending, obviously, not yet disclosed, for that is Violet's task, the narrative is given to her at a time when she is "already in a state of secret despondency" (296), either over her sister's plight or her growing love for her young Bostonian (it is not clear which). The narrative is also given to her in two parts, and between the first and the second she wavers as to whether she will undertake the case, being won to do so only "for pity's sake" for "a lovely member of [her] sex." A friendship grows between herself and the doctor's wife, whose "hungry heart opened to the sympathetic little being who clung to her in such evident admiration" (297).

Mrs. Zabriskie is extremely beautiful, and in the earlier version the young Gryce was "much under the dominion of woman's beauty" (110), but not so as to be blinded to the husband's guilt. Violet is convinced of his innocence, and it is she who proposes the test of the blind man's skill with the pistol, for she is sure the test will fail. she is thus, in the result, "overcome by this tragic end to all her hopes" (329). As she says in her next investigation: " 'I have never got over the Zabriskie tragedy. It haunts me continually.... I feel guilty. I was responsible—' " (336-337).

What is most striking in the rewriting of this famous story (invariably anthologized, as far as I know, in its earlier version) is first of all the perceived difference between the male and female detectives. What makes an early triumph for Ebenezer Gryce become a scarifying failure for Violet Strange is that though his susceptibilities could have been involved, his rationality has consistently the upper hand; her emotions and intuition hold sway throughout. In all his stories, Gryce is a thinker, albeit a plodding one, and certainly not an armchair one; Q, Byrd and Sweetwater are primarily doers, and Violet Strange is primarily a feeler. It is one of Amelia Butterworth's most interesting features that she is all three. To go back to an early distinction in this essay, *The Golden Slipper* approaches the novel of sensation; all Gryce's novels are predominantly novels of detection, and Amelia Butterworth's good commonsense keeps her two narratives solidly in that category (There is none but the most superficial resemblance between *That Affair Next Door* and *Lost Man's Lane* on the one hand, and the "Had I But Known" sensation novels of the daughters of Mary Roberts Rinehart on the other). The first version of "The Doctor, His Wife, and the Clock" is a short fiction Poe might not have been ashamed to have written; the second version is as though recast by Mrs. Henry Wood.

Notes

[1] I am especially indebted to Mr. William Loos, curator of the Rare Book Room, for the use in the library of two scrapbooks of clippings and press photographs concerning Anna Katharine Green, hereafter cited as *Scrapbooks*.

[2] The terms grandmother, mother, godmother may have been first used by Howard Haycraft (*Murder for Pleasure*), New York, 1941, p. 84) and from there broadcast to the four corners. In the *Mystery and Suspense Engagement Calendar* for 1978, however—the very year of her centenary—there is a portrait with the caption: "Anna Katharine Green, who was until recently considered the mother of the mystery novel."

See also Tage la Cour and Harald Mogenson, *The Murder Book* (New York, 1971), p. 73; Eric Quayle, *The Collector's Book of Detective Fiction* (London, 1972), pp. 90-91; Nancy Y. Hoffman, "Mistresses of Malfeasance," in *Dimensions of Detective Fiction* (Bowling Green, 1976), p. 97. A. E. Murch (*The Development of the Detective Novel*, London, 1958, pp. 158-64) gives Green her best due, though Haycraft does list *The Leavenworth Case* as one of his "detective story cornerstones," and Ellery Queen retains it there. EQ, however, suggests that the novel need not be read, if one waives "historical value in favor of readability"; see Dilys Winn, *ed. Murder Ink* (New York, 1977), p. 18, and *Murderess Ink* (New York, 1979), pp. 43-44; Symons, *Bloody Murder* (London, 1972), pp. 62-63; *New York Times,* August 13, 1933; *Courier-Express,* December 17, 1978.

[3] See Alice Payne Hackett, *70 Years of Best Sellers, 1895-1965* (New York, 1967), p. 62; Hapgood, letter of November 11, 1926 (*Scrapbooks); The World's Great Detective Stories, ed.* Wright (New York, 1927), p. 15. Worth mentioning here is the admiration of several famous statesmen for Green, including Mr. Gladstone, James G. Blaine, Woodrow Wilson, Theodore Roosevelt, and Stanley Baldwin, whose praise Symons characteristically cites as proof of the subliterary taste of politicans! John Dickson Carr (*The Three Coffins,* New York, 1935) has Gideon Fell deliver a brief lecture on Green's pioneering role.

[4] Four works are currently in print, in addition to *The Leavenworth Case: The Circular Study* (Garland); *A Difficult Problem* (Mss Info); *The Filigree Ball* (Arno); *The Old Stone House* (Arno).

[5] See Carolyn Wells, *The Technique of the Mystery Story* (Springfield, 1913), pp. 313-315: "Women as Writers of Detective Stories." Green is the writer most cited in this pioneering "Poetics" of the genre.

[6] Preface to *The American,* in *The Art of the Novel,* ed. R.P. Blackmur (New York, 1934), pp. 31-32.

[7] Introduction, *The Woman in White* (Boston: Houghton Mifflin, 1969), xv-xviii.

[8] *Anatomy of Criticism* (Princeton, 1957), especially pp. 39-40, 172-174.

[9] *The Letters of Charles Dickens,* ed. Walter Dexter (London, 1938), III, 534.

[10] "Miss Braddon," *Notes and Reviews,* Cambridge, Massachusetts, 1921, p. 110.

[11]Letter to George Haven Putnam, December 6, 1883, in the Humanities Research Center, University of Texas at Austin.

[12]Buffalo *Courier,* May 25, 1902 *(Scrapbooks).*

[13]See E.F. Harkins, *Famous Authors (Women)* (Boston, 1901), p. 105.

[14]Clipping, February 25, 1923 *(Scrapbooks).*

[15]*A Catalogue of Crime* (New York, 1971), p. 215.

[16]Here follows a list of the detective and mystery novels and short stories of Anna Katharine Green, with the editions used. All are the first editions, with the following exceptions: *The Leavenworth Case;* "The Doctor, his Wife, and the Clock," which is cited from *The World's Great Detective Stories* and *The Golden Slipper;* and "The Staircase at the Heart's Delight," from *Masterpieces of Mystery.* This last story first appeared in 1894, and was first collected in *A Difficult Problem.* In the version used here, there are minor verbal differences, most notably in the title: "The Staircase at Heart's Delight."

The Leavenworth Case. New York: G.P. Putnam's Sons, 1906 (Leavenworth)

A Strange Disappearance. New York: G.P. Putnam's Sons, 1880.

The Sword of Damocles. New York: G.P. Putnam's Sons, 1881

X.Y.Z. New York: G.P. Putnam's Sons, 1883.

Hand and Ring. New York: G.P. Putnam's Sons, 1883.

The Mill Mystery. New York: G.P. Putnam's Sons, 1886.

7 to 12: A Detective Story. New York: G.P. Putnam's Sons, 1887.

Behind Closed Doors. New York: G.P. Putnam's Sons, 1888.

The Forsaken Inn. New York: R. Bonner's Sons (1890).

A Matter of Millions. New York: R. Bonner's Sons, 1890.

The Old Stone House. New York: G.P. Putnam's Sons, 1891.

   "The Old Stone House"

   "A Memorable Night"

   "The Black Cross"

   "A Mysterious Case"

   "Shall He Wed Her?"

Cynthia Wakeham's Money. New York: G.P. Putnam's Sons, 1892.

Marked "Personal". New York: G.P. Putnam's Sons, 1893.

Miss Hurd: An Enigma. New York: G.P. Putnam's Sons, 1894.

The Doctor, His Wife, and the Clock. New York: G.P. Putnam's Sons, 1895.

Dr. Izard. New York: G.P. Putnam's Sons, 1895.

That Affair Next Door. New York: G.P. Putnam's Sons, 1897 (Affair)

Lost Man's Lane. New York: G.P. Putnam's Sons, 1898. (Lane)

Agatha Webb. New York: G.P. Putnam's Sons, 1899.

The Circular Study. New York: McClure, Phillips, 1900. (Study)

A Difficult Problem. New York: Lupton, 1900.

   "A Difficult Problem"

   "The Gray Madam"

   "The Bronze Hand"

   Midnight in Beauchamp Road"

   "The Staircase at the Heart's Delight"

   "The Hermit of—Street"

One of My Sons. New York: G.P. Putnam's Sons, 1901.

Three Women and a Mystery. New York: G. Putnam's Sons (1902).

The Filigree Ball. Indianapolis: Bobbs-Merrill (1903).

The Millionaire Baby. Indianapolis: Bobbs-Merrill (1905).

The Amethyst Box. Indianapolis: Bobbs-Merrill (1905).

The House in the Mist. Indianapolis: Bobbs-Merrill (1905)

The Woman in the Alcove. Indianapolis: Bobbs-Merrill (1906).

The Chief Legatee. New York: Dodd, Mead, 1906.

The Mayor's Wife. Indianapolis: Bobbs-Merrill (1907).

The House of the Whispering Pines. New York: G.P. Putnam's Sons, 1910.
Three Thousand Dollars. Boston: R.G. Badger, 1910.
Initials Only. New York: Dodd, Mead, 1911.
Masterpieces of Mystery. New York: Dodd, Mead, 1913.
  "Midnight in Beauchamp Row"
  "Room No. 3"
  "The Ruby and the Caldron"
  "The Little Steel Coils"
  "The Staircase at Heart's Delight"
  "The Amethyst Box"
  "The Grey Lady"
  "The Thief"
  "The House in the Mist"
Dark Hollow. New York: Dodd, Mead, 1914.
The Golden Slipper. New York: G.P. Putnam's Sons, 1915.
  "The Golden Slipper"
  "The Second Ballet"
  "The Intangible Clew"
  "The Grotto Spectre"
  "The Dreaming Lady"
  "The House of Clocks"
  "The Doctor, his Wife, and the Clock"
  "Missing: Page Thirteen"
  "Violet's Own"
To the Minute and *Scarlet and Black.* New York: Dodd, Mead, 1916.
The Mystery of the Hasty Arrow. New York: Dodd, Mead, 1917.
The Step on the Stair. New York: Dodd, Mead, 1923.

[17]Buffalo *Express,* March 14, 1903 *(Scrapbooks).*

[18]Régis Messac (*Le 'Detective Novel' et L'Influence de la Pensee Scientifique,* Paris, 1929) has some fun with the undoubted prevalence of this theme in detective fiction. *Hand and Ring,* though scarcely as grim, has something of the flavor of Ross Macdonald's *The Chill* (1964).

[19]"Whether this is a mere habit caught in the long exercise of a calling demanding secrecy of intention, or whether it is the result of a deliberate determination on this man's part to seem to know less and see less than he really does, has never been decided.... (*A Matter of Millions,* p. 79). Whatever the reason, it is Gryce's most emphasized trait.

[20]*The Technique of the Mystery Story,* pp. 74-75.

[21]Audrey Roberts and John Cornillon, "Early Self-Images in Women's Mystery Fiction," a paper delivered at the Popular Culture Association Conference, Indianapolis, April, 1973

As a general footnote on Violet Strange, I should like to dispose of the *canard* that she owes her success to a bloodhound variously described as "sagacious" (A.E. Murch), "sagacious and suspicious" (Eric Quayle), and "acutely clue-sensitive" (Dilys Winn). Those who actually read *The Golden Slipper* will find no bloodhound at all: it seems to have been whelped from a metaphor of Ellery Queen's ("Anna Katharine Green, whose *Violet Strange* made bloodhound history...," *The Female of the Species,* Boston, 1943, vii).

Here is a dog which not only did nothing in the night time, but does not even exist, except through the big fleas and little fleas of detectival criticism! Let's send it back, once and for all, to the doghouse.

Mary Roberts Rinehart
Photo by Hal Phyfe

Mary Roberts Rinehart

1876 Born August 12, Allegheny, Pennsylvania

1893 Graduates from Allegheny High School. Enters nurse's training at Homeopathic Hospital, Pittsburgh

1895 Suicide of Rinehart's father, Thomas Roberts, November 14

1896 Marries Dr. Stanley Marshall Rinehart, April 21

1897 Stanley Marshall Rinehart, born, August 18

1900 Alan Gillespie Rinehart born, November 18

1902 Frederick Roberts Rinehart born, September 14

1904 First short story, "His Other Self," published in December in *Munsey's.*

1906 First Mystery, *The Man in Lower 10,* serialized in All-Story (January—April)

1907 *The Circular Staircase* serialized in *All-Story* (November 1907-May 1908)

1908 *The Man in Lower 10,* first mystery novel to make annual best-seller list. Hit play, *Seven Days* (with Avery Hopwood), runs 397 performances

1910 First "Tish" story, "That Awful Night," published in *Saturday Evening Post* (January)

1915 January-March, in Allied front lines, Belgium and France; subsequent articles published in *Saturday Evening Post.* With Howard Eaton travels through newly-opened Glacier Park

1918 Returns to France for War Department, November 1918-January, 1919

1919 Works in Hollywood as one of Samuel Goldwyn's Eminent Authors

1920 *The Bat* (with Avery Hopwood), smash hit mystery play, opens August 23; runs 878 performances in New York

1922 Moves to Washington D.C., January

1923 Honorary Doctor of Letters, George Washington University

1929 Rinehart sons, with John Farrar, form Farrar and Rinehart publishing company

1931 Autobiography, *My Story,* published after serialization in *Good Housekeeping*

1932 Dr. Rinehart dies, October 28; buried at Arlington National Cemetary

1935 Moves to Park Avenue, New York

1936 *The Doctor* sold to *Ladies' Home Journal* for $75,000; the last of Rinehart's 11 novels on annual best-seller lists

1937 Buys "Far View" in Bar Harbor, Maine. Attends

coronation of George VI. Last "Tish" story published in *Saturday Evening Post*

1941-44 War work: writing for several boards and agencies; air-raid warden

1947 Homicidal attack on Rinehart by Reyes, her chef, Bar Harbor fire destroys "Far View"

1948 *A Light in the Window,* last non-mystery novel, published

1952 *The Swimming Pool,* last full-length Rinehart mystery published (serialized in *Saturday Evening Post)*

1954 "The Splinter," last mystery story published, in *Ellery Queen's Mystery Magazine* (May). Special award, Mystery Writers of America

1958 Dies, September 22; buried at Arlington National Cemetary

by Jan Cohn

"The Detective Story"

A murder is committed, and that page is full of gore,
Of smashed and broken furniture, and bloodstains on the floor.
A livid, ghastly corpse is quite essential to the tale,
And people standing round with trembling hands and faces pale.

***

Envoy

Oh, thanks to British Conan Doyle, to French Gaboriau,
And also many thanks to our own Edgar Allan Poe.
To them we own a debt of gratitude that's hard to pay,
For teaching us to frustrate crime in such an easy way.

Above are the opening and closing stanzas of a burlesque on mystery fiction that appeared in *Munsey's Magazine* in 1904; ironically, it was the first work of Mary Roberts Rinehart to appear in a national magazine.[1] In between the first and last stanzas a detective of the inductive school solves crimes by subtle clues: a cuticle, a single hair, a cigar ash, a footprint. Apparently, young Mrs. Rinehart read detective fiction, but what she wrote at the time were poems and short stories. Crude and derivative, these stories sold for thirty or forty dollars, and between 1904 and 1905 she published several dozen. Then, in the summer of 1905, encouraged by *Munsey's* editor Robert Davis, Rinehart tried a full-length mystery novel. In three or four weeks she completed *The Man in Lower 10.*[2]

What Robert Davis had suggested to Rinehart was a combination of mystery and romance, and it would be the combination that sustained Rinehart's mystery novels for the next fifty years. But at the moment, impressed by the money ($400 for serialization), if somewhat embarrassed by the genre (her husband and friends did not read cheap thrillers), she turned out another mystery the next summer. That was *The Circular Staircase* and it was worth $500. A third thriller, *The Mystery of 1122,* was written for serialization before any of Rinehart's work appeared in book form.

In her autobiographical writing, Rinehart attributed book publication to her Uncle John Roberts' enthusiasm for her mystery serials. Encouraged by him, she sent the manuscript of *The Circular Staircase* to Bobbs-Merrill and delighted editor Hewitt Howland took a train to Pittsburgh to discuss publication and to see if there were any more manuscripts at home like that one. Howland bought all three of Rinehart's serialized murder stories, publishing them in 1908, 1909, and 1910. Because it was clearly the best of the three, he brought out *The Circular Staircase* first, and his judgment has been justified by the great and continuing success of this mystery, now a classic in the genre.

Given Rinehart's previous short stories, her three early mysteries are an astonishing achievement. Each written in a matter of weeks and scarcely revised, they are fully developed and richly plotted fictions, blending not only mystery and romance but humor as well. For the mysterious, Rinehart combined intellectually puzzling clues and events with eerie and chilling occurrences—"the creeps." Her murderers leave their share of footprints and bloodstains but much more fascinating to Rinehart, and her readers, were less conventional clues: a stolen basket of crockery, altered numbers on railway berths, slips of paper with the message "1122." The puzzles provoke interest; the creeps provide thrills, and from the earliest of her mysteries on Rinehart's characters encounter terrors. Her heroes and more especially her heroines wander around in the dark, despite the mounting number of local murders, and more likely than not the least they can anticipate is a clammy hand reaching out of the darkness to grab them.

From the beginning, too, Rinehart knew how to develop a richly complex plot. Often, as in *The Man in Lower 10,* there are two separate, but eventually related plots, two lines of evil-doing. The romantic story adds further complexity and, since at least one of the romantic pair in each early novel is victim or suspect (or both), the elements of mystery and romance support one another in mutual suspension until the denouement.

Despite similarities in the structures of these early works, they are different enough to indicate how far Rinehart yet was from developing any kind of pattern or formula for her mysteries. The three have different settings and social environments, present widely varying motivations for crime, and demonstrate considerable uncertainty about the source of evil except perhaps to suggest that it lies in greed. Theft is a much more important element in early Rinehart than it would become in her mature works.

The Man in Lower 10 (1906)

Lawrence Blakely, hero and narrator, travels from Washington to Pittsburgh to take a deposition from steel-magnate West about a forgery case. Returning to Washington on the train, his papers are stolen and, the numbers on the berths in the sleeping car having been altered during the night, his assigned berth is discovered to contain a dead body. A train wreck follows and Blakely finds himself sitting on an embankment, sooty and shaken, with Alison West, the steel man's granddaughter and his own partner's fiancée.

Although the mystery opens with the problem of forgery compounded with the theft of some bonds from Blakely's briefcase, a second criminal conspiracy soon appears. Alison West is the prize in this network of villainy: a particularly wicked woman forces her weak-willed brother Sullivan to woo Alison. Although Alison is already engaged (and Sullivan married!), he manages to press his suit to the point where he compromises her—unfairly of course— and, her reputation apparently ruined, she elopes with him.

Blakely confronts a mass of difficulties. He must recover the bonds, prosecute the forger, release Alison from her false (bigamous) marriage, and persuade her to break her engagement to his partner. These tasks are undertaken in an atmosphere of considerable creepiness: a hand appears mysteriously out of a trap door; a carriage ride to a deserted country mansion brings Blakely into the darkness of an old and unfamiliar house to be terrorized by enemies both human and feline.

Sometimes Rinehart develops comedy in *The Man in Lower 10* by deliberately deflating the horror of the creeps, as she does with the black cat who terrorizes Blakely in that dark mansion. But there is another source of humor as well and it probably had its origin in Rinehart's self-consciousness about writing thrillers. Just as she had burlesqued the mystery genre in her early poem, "The Detective Story," so she parodies the detective himself in the character of Wilson Budd Hotchkiss. Hotchkiss is an altogether disinterested person; he involves himself in the murder in Lower 10 for intellectual reasons alone. As he tells Blakely, "I use the inductive method originated by Poe and followed since with such success by Conan Doyle" (31). Armed with enthusiasm and a small notebook, he collects clues and tails suspects, finally announcing his discovery of the murderer. Unfortunately, he sends the police off to arrest Blakely's own confidential clerk, the most innocuous of men.

The Circular Staircase (1907)

This is the story of how a middle-aged spinster lost her mind, deserted her domestic gods in the city, took a furnished house for the summer out of town, and found herself involved in one of those mysterious crimes that keep our newspapers and detective agencies happy and prosperous (1).

So *The Circular Staircase* opens, and so readers for over seventy years have first met Rachel Innes, the adventurous, curious, and undaunted spinster who happens onto a summer of crime and has the best vacation of her life. It is Rachel Innes' voice that more than any other element has made *The Circular Staircase* a perennial delight—and a classic. A perfect lady, a responsible guardian to her orphaned niece and nephew, she finds in the course of her adventures altogether new aspects to her character: "somehow, somewhere, from perhaps a half-civilized ancestor who wore a sheepskin garment and tailed his food or his prey, I have in me the instincts of the chase" (4). She becomes certain that she would enjoy a life of trapping criminals and regrets that her sex closes this career to her: "with the handicap of my sex, my first acquaintance with crime will probably be my last" (6). The reviewers of *The Circular Staircase* did not want to believe this; they hoped for another Rachel Innes mystery. That never happened. Instead, Rinehart's comic spinster was transformed into Tish Carberry whose zany adventures appeared in *The Saturday Evening Post* for twenty-five years.

The Circular Staircase is a considerable advance over *The Man in Lower 10* not only in the creation of Rachel Innes but in Rinehart's discovery of the closed-world setting. Because Gertrude and Halsey, Rachel's niece and nephew, are now at the courting age, Rachel decides to rent a country house for the summer and Sunnyside becomes the first of many summer houses in Rinehart's fiction. Spacious and rambling, with promising cellars and attics, they are effective settings for mystery. Moreover, such houses exist as part of small summer colonies, microcosms to be rent by violence and, finally, restored to their former calm. The community in *The Circular Staircase* extends beyond Rachel's household to include, somewhat untidily, the family of Sunnyside's owner, some local people, and the friends and lovers of Gertrude and Halsey, who provide the romantic interest.

Rinehart's characteristic blend of the puzzling and the chilling marks *The Circular Staircase*. Terror comes largely from eerie shadows and sounds, usually enhanced by midnight darkness through which her characters show a remarkable penchant for wandering. Similarly, her villains suffer an insatiable need to break into houses and Sunnyside is often as busy after midnight as a good-sized bus terminal. Puzzles, meanwhile, develop with curious clues and bizarre events. As the plot of *The Circular Staircase* unravels at the close, it turns out that a good number of the oddest clues and events are by no means to be laid to the criminal. For all kinds of reasons from self-protection to selfless loyalty, the characters defend themselves and one another by withholding information, destroying evidence, and planting false clues. The police must work their way through this welter of red herrings, for Rinehart's characters are not intimidated by the law. If they don't want to talk, they announce, with no little sense of social superiority, that they will not talk. And if they don't want to tell the truth, then they lie—even the best of them.

The principal characters not only conceal things from the police, they also conceal things from one another, and this adds further complexity to the plotting and further befuddlement for the narrator and the reader. Both Gertrude and Halsey are engaged, and both decline to tell their Aunt Rachel. Unknown to Halsey, his fiancée arrives mysteriously from the west coast and takes refuge in the lodge at Sunnyside. Gertrude's fiancé is accused of absconding with one and a quarter million dollars worth of securities, but Gertrude believes in his innocence and, without informing Rachel, helps him to hide out at Sunnyside disguised as a gardener. Rachel herself finds Halsey's revolver in the tulip bed and that remains her secret—from Halsey and from the police.

With all the major characters pursuing their own ends secretly, the number of puzzles mounts and it early became one of Rinehart's conventions to set down periodically a list of unanswered questions. Here is Rachel trying to assess the situation to date:

If I knew now why Rosie had taken the basket of dishes, I did not know who had spoken to her and followed her along the drive. If I knew that Louise was in the lodge, I did not know why she was there. If I knew that Arnold Armstrong had spent some time in the lodge the night before he was murdered, I was no nearer the solution of the crime. Who was the midnight intruder who had so alarmed Liddy and myself? Who had fallen down the clothes chute? Was Gertrude's lover a villain or a victim? Time was to answer all these things (89-90).

To these puzzles are added more conventional clues—a golf stick, half a cufflink, a partly obliterated note, and the hole in the trunk room wall—to make up the texture of *The Circular Staircase* and of Rinehart's mysteries to come.

One of the finest elements in the plotting of *The Circular Staircase* is the rush of events that makes up the climax. Since all of these involve Rachel Innes, there is not only terror and excitement but also the comic delight of watching her cope with them. She joins in a midnight excursion to the cemetary to dig up a grave and she really has quite a lovely time, grateful to be part of things: "I felt that they were doing me honor in making me one of the party..." (216). She takes time *en route* to admire the night sky and even after she has unluckily stepped over her ankles into ditch water, wonders "if I had ever tasted life until that summer" (217).

Soon after, Rachel's sleuthing leads her to the roof of the house.

Though she has some fear of heights, "I climbed out on to the Sunnyside roof without a second's hesitation. Like a dog on the scent...to me now there was the lust of the chase, the frenzy of pursuit, the dust of battle" (233-34). And finally, she finds the device that opens the secret room—and ends up locked inside. Worse, a figure joins her in the darkness and at the consummately creepy moment, Rachel feels his hand, "cold, clammy, death-like" (239). Rescue and resolution follow rapidly and Rachel's adventure, to her great discontent, is over.

When *The Circular Staircase* was published by Bobbs-Merrill in the spring of 1908, Mary Roberts Rinehart had no notion of what she had created. In fact, embarrassment at publishing a thriller and anxiety over the reviews combined to send her into hiding out of town, where she rented rooms at a farmer's house for herself and her three sons. Almost fifty years later, she told Mary Margaret McBride in a radio interview that, without in the least knowing what she was doing, she found that she had altogether altered the form of the mystery novel by adding flesh and muscle to the skeleton of plot.[3]

The Window at the White Cat (orig: *The Mystery of 1122)* (1908)

Rinehart clearly did not recognize what she had accomplished in *The Circular Staircase,* for in the next and last of her early mysteries she dropped both the female narrator and the closed setting of that book. Like *The Man in Lower 10, The Window at the White Cat* presents a young male narrator and a wide canvas of political graft and corruption.

The Window at the White Cat traces the effects of malfeasance in state government as it is manipulated by the burly, but always shadowy figure of State Senator Schwartz. The book opens as State Treasurer Fleming's disappearance is reported by his nineteen-year-old daughter Margery to lawyer Jack Knox. Knox falls in love with Margery and blunders through a series of mysteries and mishaps with the intention of clearing suspicion from her fiance Wardrop so that he can fight fair for her hand.

The novel's most violent action centers around the White Cat, a seedy political club where Fleming is found murdered. Political power controlling the police and all but one newspaper, the murder is called suicide; therefore, Knox, a very amateur sleuth, is aided only by a reporter who brashly maintains his and his paper's independence. This surprising foreshadowing of the corrupt world of Hammett and Chandler is maintained to the end, for Schwartz buys up the lone independent paper and remains untouched by crime or scandal.

More mysterious if less violent events occur in the homes of the central characters. There are the usual number of midnight break-ins, particularly frequent in the vulnerable home of the elderly Maitland sisters, the book's most engaging characters. The mystery of Miss Jane Maitland's disappearance adds to the complications, but in its solution proves disappointingly independent of the other material in the novel. Still, these and the other comic, romantic, and domestic elements are far better realized than the political ones.

In *The Window at the White Cat* is an early example of Rinehart's interest in new-fangled ideas and technologies, among them psychoanalysis, used here to help solve the mystery. Knox brings Wardrop to a nerve-specialist who has agreed to employ the psychoanalytic technique of word-association to discover what Wardrop is concealing. A long passage follows as Wardrop responds to stimulus words with the first thing that comes to mind. The doctor measures the response-time on his "chronoscope" and, after dismissing Wardrop, studies the associations and their times with Knox. They find what they are after as the doctor observes, "Psychology is as exact a science as mathematics; it gets information from the source, and a man cannot lie in four-fifths of a second" (243).

* * *

Although *The Window at the White Cat,* like *The Man in Lower 10,* was a best-seller, Rinehart gave up mystery writing for the next five years. During that time she was developing her skills in other ways, creating the first "Tish" stories, collaborating with playwright Avery Hopwood on *Seven Days,* and writing her first two serious novels, *Street of Seven Stars* and *"K."* All these ventures succeeded and it looked very much as if Rinehart would build her career in directions other than the mystery novel.

In fact, almost all the writing Rinehart did in these five years had some element of mystery or crime. Tish frequently blunders on crime and always manages to get her man. *Seven Days,* a farce, features missing jewels and suspected robbery. And *"K"* is constructed on the mystery of identity, as we shall see, a crucial problem for Rinehart. The early mysteries succeeded in fusing romance and comedy with crime. Now Rinehart's comedies, farces, and romances had plots developed at least in part out of mystery and crime.

When Rinehart returned to the mystery novel in 1913, she did so with a considerable gain in narrative skill and with more carefully developed ideas about crime, the criminal, and the nature and source of evil. As a result, there are more interesting problems raised and more complex characters drawn in the mysteries written between 1913 and 1925. On the other hand, Rinehart continued to see her crime fiction as secondary, to believe her important work lay in serious fiction and the theater. That attitude, compounded no doubt by the pressure of time—these were extraordinarily busy years in Rinehart's life—led to serious imperfections in a number of these novels.

However imperfect, the mysteries of this period do show Rinehart moving toward the structural and thematic materials that would inform her mature work. Rinehart came to recognize that the basic structural element of her best mysteries was what she called the "buried story." As she explained it in a *Ladies' Home Journal* editorial in 1931,[4] the buried story was a sequence of events in the past leading to the explosion of violence and murder in the present. The novel related the story of the present time, the chronology of murders and sleuthing. Rinehart alone knew the entire narrative of the buried story, and she allowed it to appear only as clues, hints— what she called "outcroppings"—in the course of the surface story. It was Rinehart's belief that after her first three mystery novels she came upon the device of the buried story and used it from that point on. In fact, the technique developed a good deal more slowly than Rinehart realized, not appearing in its fully realized form until *The Album* in 1933.

It is true, however, that Rinehart became increasingly conscious of buried motives, repressed emotions, of lives that appeared conventional and staid on the surface but were in fact marked by some hidden passion or drama, and much of this she worked out first in her romances, notably *"K."* Then when she turned back to mysteries, the idea, if not its full structural possibilities, was one she exploited consistently. For example, in *Sight Unseen,* a 1916 mystery novella, she has a character observe:

You and I... live our ordered lives. We eat, and sleep, and talk, and even labor. We think we are living. But for the last day or two I have been seeing visions—you and I and the rest of us, living on the surface, and underneath, carefully kept down so it will not make us uncomfortable, a world of passion and crime and violence and suffering (101-02).

In *Sight Unseen* the character who elicits this remark does have a secret, but he does not have a history of long-hidden and long-suppressed passion or deception driving him to crime in the present. The idea is there, but not the plotting to sustain it.

Similarly, Rinehart was coming closer in this period to full exploitation of the problem of identity in relation to crime and violence. From the beginning of her career, identity had fascinated and troubled her. Her very first short story, "The Double Life" (1904), involved an amnesia victim of some twenty years who suddenly and traumatically rediscovers his true identity. In *"K"* the central character deliberately assumes a false identity to hide something he cannot face in his past. Again in *The Breaking Point* (1923) amnesia accounts for the confusion of identity and in this case, although *The Breaking Point* is not a mystery novel, the protagonist's search for his past uncovers a murder that occurred many years before. As we shall see, the problem of identity and the structural possibilities of the buried story would eventually come together for Rinehart in the mysteries of her mature period, but for the present each is explored rather tentatively and in isolation.

Finally, the mysteries written between 1912 and 1925 are remarkably varied in subject and setting. In nearly every case they represent not so much an experiment in technique as an opportunity to use whatever interested Rinehart at the moment. Since her interests ranged from real-life murders to spirit-return, the mystery novels from these years are a pretty varied lot.

The Case of Jennie Brice (1912)

The Case of Jennie Brice, like *"K"* written at about the same time, provided Rinehart an opportunity to recreate the world of her childhood. The narrator, Mrs. Pitman, runs a boarding house in Allegheny, across the river from Pittsburgh, where Rinehart grew up and where her mother, too, took in roomers after Rinehart's father failed in business and, eventually, committed suicide. If Mrs. Pitman is like Rinehart's mother in being widowed and poor, she is altogether different in her background. She has, indeed, a buried story, but she shares it with the reader from the outset. Originally from a wealthy and aristocratic family, she was permanently disavowed by them when she ran off to make a marriage even she now calls "the sordid tragedy of my life" (114). After some time she meets and befriends her sister's daughter, but she maintains her changed identity as landlady, never claiming her relationship. Of course, her breeding is apparent to the really refined, and her niece's fiance asks, "Who are you, anyhow?... You who turn to the world the frozen mask of a Union Street boarding-house landlady, who are a gentlewoman by every instinct and training, and a girl at heart? Who are you?" (154).

This rich material is the most interesting part of the novel, but it has nothing whatever to do with the mystery, the murder, or its solution. The mystery story itself is disappointing; clearly it held little interest for Rinehart. The problem is too simple: first the disappearance of an actress and second the identification of her body. While there are numerous clues, there is never more than a single suspect; the plotting is far less intricate than in the earlier mysteries; and the atmosphere is nearly free of suspense and terror. *Jennie Brice* does have some fine details of local color, recreating the Johnstown flood as it hit Pittsburgh. And here, as occasionally in other mysteries, Rinehart surprises us with technological newfangledness. One character, intent on some spying, constructs a periscope, "modeled," as Mrs. Pitman explains, "after something or other that is used on a submarine..." (88).

The After House (1913)

Rinehart based *The After House* on a real murder case she learned about from a lawyer friend. Nearly twenty years earlier, a series of axe murders had been committed aboard the *Herbert Fuller,* a lumber schooner. The Mate, Bram, was tried, convicted, and sentenced to life imprisonment. The story intrigued Rinehart and her reading of the court records convinced her that Bram was innocent. The eye-witness testimony crucial to his conviction looked phony, for it appeared that the position of the after house on the deck of the schooner must have made a clear view of the crime impossible. Rinehart checked this out with the Kearsage Association of Naval Veterans and they confirmed her idea. Moreover, there was now another suspect, one of the crew had subsequently attacked a nurse with a knife and had been incarcerated as a homicidal maniac.

With an eye to her audience, Rinehart carefully altered the original story of the *Herbert Fuller* murders. The lumber schooner became a private yacht leased out to a group of upper middle-class characters off on a pleasure cruise. On board as well is a young doctor, recently graduated from medical school and eager to find summer work. The doctor serves as narrator and amateur sleuth and, since he falls in love with one of the passengers, provides the love interest as well. Animosities and suspicion among the passengers fester, growing more virulent after the grisly murders when all are more or less imprisoned on the closed world of the yacht.

The After House is a pretty good mystery tale but the real life story is even better. When the novel was serialized in *McClure's,* it roused interest in the case of Mate Bram and as a result, he received a parole and eventually a pardon. Writing to Rinehart in 1914, Bram thanked her for her part in his release and swore his innocence of the axe-murders. That story was interesting enough for television to exploit in 1957 when the Bell Telephone Hour presented a play about Rinehart and *The After House* with Claudette Colbert in the lead.

"The Buckled Bag" and "Locked Doors" (1914)

"Miss Pinkerton," the only character of Mary Roberts Rinehart to appear in a series of mysteries, made her debut in a pair of double-installment stories in *The Saturday Evening Post.* "The Buckled Bag" and "Locked Doors" (January 10 & 17, 1914; August 22 & 29, 1914). At first, the nurse-detective was known simply as Hilda Adams. As "The Buckled Bag" introduces her, she is twenty-nine and about to leave hospital work to take private cases, a future she regards without enthusiasm. Mr. Patton, a wounded police detective, is one of the last of Hilda's hospital patients and her resistance to his bullying so impresses him with her firmness of character that he offers her the opportunity for undercover police work. Hilda is not sure: the nursing profession is one of service, and police work could make her a spy in her patients' homes. Patton, however, assures her that against the ethics of nursing stands the moral responsibility to defend society from criminals. Hilda, fascinated by "the chance to pit my wits against other wits and perhaps win out," agrees (*Post,* January 10, 1914).

Hilda writes, she tells us, under an assumed name in order to protect her profession: "So far I have been able to keep my double calling a profound secret," and adds ominously, "I may have been in your house" (*Post,* August 22, 1914). By "Locked Doors" Hilda is fully outfitted as a detective, with skeleton keys, a small revolver, handcuffs, a pocket flashlight, and a badge from the chief of police. She can as well boast of a considerable record in law-enforcement. This case, she tells us, is the sixth in the "record of my crusade against crime and the criminal" (*Post,* August 22, 1914). But there are no criminals in these two stories. In fact, Rinehart seems to have designed the first Hilda Adams stories as a compromise with murder mysteries, for no one is killed in either "The Buckled Bag" or "Locked Doors." The stories are really puzzles with bizarre clues and even more bizarre solutions. In "The Buckled Bag" the problem is a family's missing daughter; the solution: she has been curing herself, cold turkey, of cocaine addiction! In "Locked Doors," a young scientist has emptied out the first floor of his house, burned the carpets, locked his family up on the second floor, and now prowls the neighborhood cellars by night; why? to capture his escaped laboratory rats, for he suspects they are carrying bubonic plague! Later Miss Pinkerton stories will maintain the bizarre elements of the early pieces, but by 1930 Hilda will deal with murderers very efficiently.

Sight Unseen (1916)

Rinehart contrived *Sight Unseen* around her growing interest in spiritualism, and seances, mediums, and spirit-return altogether dominate the novella to the detriment of the mystery plot. The mystery centers on an apparent suicide, in fact a murder, and while some amateur sleuthing takes place, the problem is solved when the victim's wife appears, for the first and the last time in the story, to explain the means, explicate the motivation, and name the murderer. Rinehart was surely not unaware of the weak fabric she had woven, and her narrator frequently explains that the solution of the crime was secondary to the verification of certain psychic phenomena.

These phenomena occur first at a seance when the medium through her control witnesses a murder in progress. When those present at the seance investigate, they discover that a murder did occur at that time and they gradually unearth evidence to support each detail in the medium's vision. The evidence proves the apparent suicide to be a murder but, much more important, it proves the medium to be genuine.

The murder solved, Rinehart is left with the difficult problem of accounting for a considerable amount of supernaturalism in the story, including of course the medium's knowledge of the murder. Her answer is a compromise. Some phenomena are explained away: ghostly sounds are the effect of a carpet stealthily pulled aside. Some are attributed to relatively less mysterious causes: unwittingly, the medium was mind-reading as she witnessed the murder. And others are left entirely unexplained: perhaps the result of powers which are "the survival of some long-lost development by which at one time we knew how to liberate a forgotten form of energy" (151). Such material, quasi-mystical and pseudo-scientific, ill-suits the rational mode of mystery novels.

The Confession (1917)

The story of *The Confession* came to Rinehart through the local district attorney who wanted her professional judgment about a real-life mystery. A workman repairing a telephone box had discovered in it a scrap of folded paper bearing the confession to a murder some years earlier in a brothel on Pittsburgh's Second Avenue. The D.A. showed Rinehart the confession because, having failed to find records of a body deceased around that date, he questioned its authenticity. Rinehart had no doubts. The note not only struck her as genuine but it supplied her with a fine plot device. Of course, neither her editors nor her public would tolerate a brothel, so she transported the confession and the telephone box to a more respectable setting.

The Confession, abandoning the psychical murkiness of *Sight*

Unseen, opens with the level-headed statement of its rational narrator: "I am not a susceptible woman" (175). This is the voice of another of Rinehart's spinsters, Agnes Blakeston who, like Rachel Innes, rents a house for the summer and finds herself deep in mystery and violence. But the crime that Agnes confronts is no longer, like that of *The Circular Staircase*, motivated by simple greed. With this novella Rinehart moves decisively into domestic violence, neighborhood intrigue, and a world where motivations are psychological rather than economic. Appropriately, there is some suggestion—genteel, to be sure—of repressed sexuality. The dainty, aged maiden lady about whom the mystery develops is "as childlike and innocent as she was at ten," but that innocence belies "a deep and strong nature underneath. She should have married and had children," says the village doctor (302). In the popular Freudianism of the period, powerful sexual energy dammed up erupts in equally powerful violence.

With this kind of material to work with, Rinehart drew closer to the full development of the buried story. In *The Confession* the crime is itself a part of the buried past, revealed only by the discovery of the written confession. As one of the characters puts it reading the scrap of paper found in the telephone box, "There's a queer story back of all this" (272). Until that queer story is unburied, the world of *The Confession* is a world atrophied, out of time. The house Agnes rents is furnished in the style of the nineteenth century, its surface of quiet antiqueness covering repressed emotions, blocked sexuality, homicidal rage. Nor does the fact that the crime took place long ago make it less appalling; as we discover the facts of the murder they take on a particularly gruesome unwholesomeness.

With *The Confession* Rinehart began to find her material and the novella shows the most significant gains in Rinehart's work since *The Circular Staircase*. Nevertheless, the resolution provided difficulties Rinehart could not yet overcome. In the end, the solution is given rather than discovered; secondary characters privy to the old story simply tell it. The telling is graceful, but remains basically unsatisfying—as if there was nothing really to be discovered or solved, only a story waiting to be recounted.

The Bat (1920)

Until Agatha Christie's *The Mousetrap*, Rinehart's *The Bat*, written in collaboration with Avery Hopwood, was probably the most successful mystery play ever mounted. Rinehart conceived of the idea for the play in the early years of World War I and asked producer Edgar Selwyn about the prospects for a mystery play in which the identity of the criminal would be withheld until just before the fall of the curtain. He said, in what proved to be an understatement, that it would be worth a million dollars. Estimates are that *The Bat* earned nine million. Intermittent work on the play was halted in 1918 when Rinehart went to France for the U.S. War Department. She turned the partially completed manuscript over to Hopwood, expecting that he would finish it. As it turned out, she and Hopwood worked and reworked the play up through the spring of 1920.

A good deal of the material for *The Bat* comes from *The Circular Staircase*. Rachel Innes—with a name-change—rents a summer house and the fine familiar mix of humor and horror proceeds. Rinehart and Hopwood did, however, add a new character, and a new twist, in the figure of the criminal, "the bat." That new material, the criminal and his late unmasking, makes for a good deal of the theatricality in *The Bat* and goes a long way toward explaining its great success. But some of that success must also be attributed to the unusual blend of comedy and mystery and, of course, to the central character—Rachel, under any other name.

The Red Lamp (1925)

In *The Red Lamp,* her first mystery in eight years and her first full-length mystery novel since *The After House* in 1913, Rinehart returned to the subject of spiritualism, this time successfully. *The Red Lamp,* a first-class work, fully develops the elements of mystery and crime along with materials of psychic phenomena, centering about a "queer" house that the narrator has inherited from his Uncle Horace. The narrator's quiet and sensible wife, somewhat to her embarrassment, is sensitive to supernatural stimuli and she resists a summer vacation in that house. As a compromise, the family decides to live in the lodge on the property and to find a tenant for the main house. A number of inexplicable events occurs and some of them remain unexplained at the end of the novel: spectral bluish lights, the herbal odor of (deceased) Uncle Horace's special cigarettes and some physical manifestations at the two seances held at the main house. But unlike *Sight Unseen, The Red Lamp* finds a satisfactory resolution in the solution to a series of crimes; the irrational does not outweigh the rational.

Rinehart recalled that *The Red Lamp* held a special interest "in that it is related by a man. Otherwise, I seem to have stuck very firmly to my own sex as narrators..." *(Mary Roberts Rinehart's Crime Book,* v.). Her memory was, to be sure, inaccurate, but the lapse may be understood in that Professor "William A. Porter, A.B., M.A., Ph.D., Litt. D., etc." (5) is certainly her most memorable male narrator. Porter has his own voice, dry, precise, professorial. He narrates the mystery in his daily journal, providing something close to present time for the reader, but since we are to understand that Porter has gone over the journal and revised it, there is also some sense of retrospect, exploited very nicely for foreshadowing.

The novel is rich in murderous and mysterious elements that, unlike the supernatural materials, call for rational solution and considerable sleuthing. The professional police figure in the book primarily as incompetent and mildly threatening since they suspect the professor. The real sleuthing is done by Halliday, a young law student in love with Porter's niece. With the romantic material Rinehart had found the shape for one important aspect of her mature mysteries: young lovers kept from marrying (often for reasons of class or economic differences) become central to the crime story—as victims, as suspects, as sleuths. Porter's niece Edith, too, takes on certain of the characteristics of the later Rinehart heroine. Although Edith still has some of the frivolousness of the stereotyped young woman of the 20s, she does attempt to provide money for her hoped-for marriage by selling articles to magazines.

The Red Lamp appeared at a difficult time in Rinehart's personal and professional life; she suffered periods of severe psychological stress and depression, and her serious fiction was attracting unfavorable, even hostile, reviews. But with *The Red Lamp* Rinehart won the favorable critical response that would continue to elude her as a serious novelist.

***

In the decade of the 30s Mary Roberts Rinehart wrote her finest and most fully developed mystery novels. In these mature mysteries the structure of the buried story and the theme of identity came together to create a complex texture and a dense sense of evil. Added to these was a constant concern, almost an obsession, with cross-class marriage, past liaisons between attractive, ruthless young women and aristocratic men from which erupt present violence. The closed-world setting for these mysteries adds tension as well as density in the complicated relations among the characters.

The crucial element in Rinehart's fully developed mysteries is the construction of a plot adequate to the idea of the buried story. Although she had earlier conceived of the idea of a hidden past, Rinehart did not develop the requisite plotting until the 1930s. Even in *The Confession,* where some information about the past comes out during the narrative, the solution is finally given rather than revealed. What Rinehart learned to do was to peel away layers of the past, one concealed story giving way to another yet more deeply buried. While there is a good amount of conventional detective work, the real focus turns to the discovery of the past and often to the psychological investigation of passions and frustrations.

As Rinehart learned to make the richest use of the buried story at this time, so she found in her long-time fascination with identity the second crucial element for these mysteries. Once the structure for the buried story had been worked out, the formal problem became the linking of the surface and buried stories, the discovery of a way to carry some passionate past action into the present, to create one or more characters who so disguised their passionate past as to fit into a tranquil world. The solution lay in lost, mistaken, and especially assumed identity. When a character could pretend to be (or even believe himself to be) other than what he really was, he could fit into a world he did not really belong to. Then, when the disclosure came or was threatened, violence was triggered.

Mysteries, of course, have long been vehicles for disguise, and Rinehart's earlier mystery novels presented characters in disguise of one kind or another from the beginning. It is important, however, to distinguish between a disguise and an assumed identity here. A disguise is put on; it is a mask that conceals the real person while he or she must pretend to be someone else. In her mature mysteries Rinehart occasionally has a character in the surface story put on such a disguise, often to aid in solving the crime. But for Rinehart assumed identity was something much deeper: a character *becomes* someone else. Assumed identity always stems from the buried past and is always reserved for evil or tragic personalities. A character usually assumes a new identity because he wishes to remake himself, to be recreated, but sometimes a character actually loses his old identity through amnesia and the recreation is innocent, though dangerous. More often though, the assumption of identity is malevolent and typically involves the adoption of a false set of class and family credentials.

With a young woman of low social origins who assumes the identity of an upper class woman, Rinehart discovered both the connection she needed between the surface and buried stories and the conception of evil that would control the mysteries of this period. Evil lay in the problem of sexuality. Whether Rinehart ever recognized the thematic burden of her buried stories is unclear; she certainly never mentioned it in writing about her work. But what these stories warn of is the evil effects of romantic misalliance, of affairs or marriages across class lines and under false pretenses. Most typically, a young man of good family is sexually drawn to a beautiful, vulgar, unprincipled woman acting in a false character, an assumed identity. For example, she may come from a small midwestern town and then, moving east, change her name and the facts of her past. Afterwards, having married into society, she lives under the assumed identity of an aristocrat, for decked out in borrowed feathers, she does not belong. Rinehart locates the source of evil quite specifically in the intrusion of such a woman into a refined and ethical and aristocratic world.

In some Rinehart mysteries these women are central figures; in others they may not even appear, but their effects on others, in terms of multiple liaisons, are devastating. In the closed-world setting of these stories, moreover, serial affairs or marriages, along with family secrets and changed names, create the potential for liaisons between characters who are, unknown to themselves, related. Although Rinehart never directly refers to the fact, relationships occur that are clearly incestuous. In *The Great Mistake* one man courts his half-sister and another has an affair with his daughter-in-law.

The corrective to the buried story and its vicious cross-class marriages lies in the surface story. Here the romantic interest typically centers on a young woman of good family and a man who at least appears to be from "the people," clearly reversing the class affiliations of the buried story. With the Depression Rinehart's best families are often in economic straits, at least relatively so, and her young women must assume responsibility for something more than their clothing and party invitations. In some cases, they must work. Usually these women are older than the girls in Rinehart's early stories. The eighteen year olds of that period were pretty, innocent, sometimes endangered, and usually engaged to the wrong man. In the 30s the hero no longer needs to fight his way over a rival for the girl's affection. What keeps the lovers apart is real or apparent class differences along with the complications arising from the mystery which they both work at solving. As a result of these changes in her young women, Rinehart created heroines with considerably more character and a far more interesting "voice" than in her earlier work, and in them she found particularly suitable narrators for several of the mysteries of her mature period.

The Door (1930)

The first of Rinehart's novels to be published by her sons' new firm, Farrar and Rinehart, *The Door* is a rich and complicated mystery with a large and varied cast of characters. Diverse in age, class, and personality, they are all interconnected, members or dependents of the family of Rinehart's last spinster narrator, Elizabeth Jane Bell. Elizabeth's is a large family, whose spouses and children and servants create a world adequate to encompass the very considerable number of crimes and clues in *The Door*. There are four murders, three assaults, numerous break-ins, assumed identities, a questionable will, and almost as many would-be detectives as there are suspected murderers.

The Door offers some fine examples of Rinehart's techniques for spinning out the puzzling elements of her mysteries and creating suspense. She has long been regarded as a major proponent of the "Had I But Known" school of mystery fiction but, while she does resort to that kind of foreshadowing, other techniques are at once more interesting and more important. Foreshadowing itself may be accomplished by the device of startling the reader with the banal tone used to present shocking material. Here, for example, is how the reader first hears the name of Florence Gunther: "I do know...that Sara was murdered on a Monday, the eighteenth of April, and that the death of Florence Gunther did not take place until the first of May." Suspense follows on shock as the narrator imagines the last days of Florence's life. "We know that she was terrified, that at night she must have locked herself in her room and listened for stealthy footsteps on the stairs..." (48-49).

The combination of the ordinary and the shocking works as well to create the creeps. A bland domestic scene closes the novel's early exposition. Elizabeth and her niece Judy finish a quiet dinner together; Judy lights a cigarette.

> Then I happened to raise my eyes, and they fell on the mirror.
> There was a man on the staircase (17).

In The Door as in earlier mysteries Rinehart's characters turn a fairly difficult police investigation into a quagmire of confusion by withholding information, thereby creating a good half of the mysterious events and clues that develop texture. Many apparent clues turn out to be red herrings, but if these false trails confuse the main issue, they do eventually illuminate the motivations of many of the characters.

One technical problem that would continue to baffle Rinehart was the matter of the resolution. As she noted more than once, the necessity to solve the surface crime, to unravel the buried story, and (she might have added) to resolve the romantic tangle made endings very complex indeed. In The Door Rinehart succeeded in what she commonly found so difficult, and the solution here comes in the next to last line of the novel. After that, there is only Elizabeth Jane's last word: "And with that I believe that I fainted" (288).

Miss Pinkerton (1932)

Nearly two decades after the Nurse Adams stories were published in the Post. Hilda reappeared in Miss Pinkerton, but she is disappointingly no longer quite the same youthful, independent, strong-minded character she once was. She is said to be young, but her manner and her voice are middle-aged. In many ways she does show independence, even spunk, but the paraphernalia Rinehart associates with her are confusing. Gone are the handcuffs and badge; in their place in her boarding-house room is a canary— named "Dicky." Strong-minded she is, but much of the zesty, unrestrained quality has seeped away.

The novel itself is uneven. Rinehart happily abandoned the weird problems and weirder solutions of the early Hilda Adams stories, but in *Miss Pinkerton* the murders and mysteries are erected on an elaborate and wobbly scaffold of means and motive. The motive hangs on a complicated insurance scheme, hard to recapitulate and harder to believe. The means are muddied by the attempt to mask murder as suicide. That attempt depends upon a shot fired at close range but without tell-tale powder burns, the powder absorbed by a newspaper folded so that the bullet passes between the inner sheets of the paper but not through the folded-back outer ones. The tell-tale paper, therefore, appears to be intact. It is not simply that the scheme is improbable; what is preposterous is that almost all the characters in the novel have heard of such an idea—including the octogenarian invalid, Miss Juliet Mitchell.

The novel is set in Miss Juliet's somewhat down-at-the-heels mansion, where Hilda is sent to look after the invalid whose condition has worsened from the shock of learning of the suicide of her ne'er-do-well nephew. In and around the household are the characters and suspects, a very conventional crew including the young lovers, the butler and maid, the doctor and lawyer. Not only is the cast stereotyped, it is simply too small, with an insufficient number of characters around which to develop suspicion.

Not that *Miss Pinkerton* is without some fine touches. Probably the best episode in the book comes when Miss Pinkerton herself administers a hypodermic of nitroglycerin to a heart patient. When tenseness and twitching ensue, she gives a second dose. Convulsions follow and then death. Hilda's medicine had been tampered with, strychnine substituted for nitroglycerine, and as a result, the unwitting Miss Pinkerton has herself committed murder.

Miss Pinkerton's continuing relationship with Inspector Patton falls into an established pattern. Their romance is an accepted but unobtrusive fact: Patton will continue to propose and Hilda will continue to return to her boarding house and her canary. More important is their conflict over crime. Patton follows the official police line, Hilda follows her instincts and she, of course, is right. Typically Hilda must act to save a character from Patton and his perfect case, her alliance with the inspector notwithstanding. When

Patton arrests a character Hilda intuitively knows to be innocent, she sets to work: "I had to do my thinking then, if ever; I knew that something terrible was going to happen if I did not" (158). Disappointingly, though, the thinking that Hilda Adams does leads her into precious little discovery, and in *Miss Pinkerton* she ends up helping the police most by being nearly strangled, locked in a closet, and left for dead.

The Album (1933)

The Album is a fine mystery novel and one that so well represents Rinehart's mature style that it is worth analyzing in some detail. Rinehart constructs a closed world in the novel, a secluded private street called the Crescent, where five old and aristocratic families live in a world apparently decorous, placid, and—over the past forty years—unchanged. The brutal axe-murder of bedridden old Mrs. Lancaster shatters that decorum, leads to further murders and assaults and disappearances, and finally unlocks the deep story, the twenty-year-old history that has brought about the present eruption of terror.

All five families in the Crescent have eccentricities. The Talbot family consists of Hester, deserted some quarter of a century ago by her husband John, her spinster sister-in-law Lydia, and her son George. Hester lives in mortal—or neurotic—terror of something, for the house is entirely locked up, even the inside rooms bolted off from one another. The Lancasters are an old couple, she bedridden and he aging. Mrs. Lancaster was widowed by John Talbot's brother before marrying Mr. Lancaster, and with them live her two middle-aged spinster daughters, Margaret and Emily Talbot, their lives devoted to nursing their mother. At the center of the Crescent live Mrs. Hall, herself a widow of some twenty years, and her daughter Louisa (Lou), the narrator. Lou is twenty-eight, repressed, doomed to spinsterhood herself until rescued by romance in the shape of Herbert Dean, criminologist. The Daltons, Bryan and Laura, are middle-aged; their pecularity is that they have not spoken to one another in twenty years—not one word. The Wellingtons, finally, are a young couple, stormily married and frequently separated. Jim is an orphan, his mother a Talbot, and he and Helen live in the house he inherited.

Servants, too, play important roles, in some cases echoing the actions and destinies of the householders. They may intermarry, just like the Crescent families, though secretly. Thus, the Halls' chauffeur turns out to be married to the Lancasters' maid. Or they, too, may be victims of the buried past. Thus, the Talbots' maid Lizzie, who knows too much about the secret past, is murdered. And even the street-cleaner turns out to be a pivotal figure in the story of the past and the crimes of the present.

The surface story relates the narrative of the murders that suddenly assault the Crescent and of the detecting that goes on to solve them during the two weeks of present time the story consumes. Central to this story is the trunk of hoarded gold kept under Mrs. Lancaster's bed. We follow the history of this gold carefully. How lead weights have been substituted for it in small canvas bags in the locked trunk. How the keys have been secreted in a bird cage. How small amounts of the gold have been smuggled away in a book, its pages carved away to construct an innocent-looking box. How it has been stored in a trunk in a boarding house room rented under an assumed name. How the trunk has been illegally removed, the gold taken out and buried, and a headless corpse placed inside it. The gold, then, would seem to provide the motive for murder, but that is not the case. In the face of the buried story the gold becomes trivial; "The money in a way was incidental," says criminologist Dean (295).

While the police are carefully pursuing the gold, Dean is reconstructing the buried story, fully developed in *The Album*. "...it's my belief that somewhere buried in this Crescent is a story. I'm leaving the rest to the police and going after that story," says Dean (151). A bit later on, Lou comes to realize that

Now every house on the Crescent had been shown to have its story.... Under those carefully tended roofs, behind the polished windows with their clean draped curtains, through all the fastidious ordering of our days, there had been unhappiness and revolt. We had gone our polite and rather ceremonious way while almost certainly somewhere among us there had been both hatred and murderous fury (205).

The deep story begins to emerge in the final third of the novel. It is known in part to the older members of the Crescent and it is one of Rinehart's clever strokes that, Lou Hall being treated like an ingenue by her family and friends, she does not know about it. The reader, then, learns with Lou as she overhears parts of conversations or discovers, with Dean, pieces of evidence about "the unfortunate story," about "a crime of passion:" the long-missing John Talbot had not only run off with another woman but had subsequently murdered her. He was arrested and tried in another state under another name; the Crescent maintained its silence.

Not until the very end of the novel do we learn that the buried story itself covers a still deeper story, that not John but another had murdered that woman. And with that revelation comes the discovery of the murderer and the motive, as well as the real history of the sordid past. The deepest layer uncovered, finally, is a story of sexual passion and the havoc it reaps when uncontrolled. And at its deepest level this story turns on the theme of incest.

The integration of the surface and buried stories in *The Album* depends on the assumption of false identity. John Talbot had first assumed a new identity when, decades before, he ran off with a woman. Arrested and tried under that assumed name, he was sent to an insane asylum from which he later escaped. Then, in order to return to the Crescent, he assumed a third identity, and that role is no simple disguise, for he fully lives his new life. Finally, Talbot succumbs to amnesia; the result of unendurable stress is the loss of all identity. Not until the murders are solved is Talbot restored to his original self.

Much of the material in the buried story is locked in Talbot's mind and apparently lost with the onset of amnesia. Herbert Dean, however, is prepared to experiment and Rinehart has another opportunity to play with some new-fangled psychological ideas. In *The Window at the White Cat* she had introduced her readers to free association as a way to unravel mysteries; now she gives us truth serum. Under the guidance of a "professor of neuropsychiatry," Dean has the doctors administer sodium amytal to Talbot, and with that, we learn, Dean "very possibly...added a new arm to crime detection." Lou explains that "Talbot roused, not fully but to a certain level of consciousness; enough to answer all their questions, but not enough to allow the brain censors, whatever they may be [Lou is not scientific enough to understand all she repeats here] to close down and alter the facts" (291-92).

Psychoanalytic theory, too, plays a part. Lou is in danger, less from the murderer loose in their midst than from the repressive society of the Crescent to which she has remained in bondage. Once briefly engaged to Jim Wellington, she has been forced back into the role of dutiful daughter, like Emily and Margaret Talbot devoted to the care of her mother. She is about to be the next victim of the Crescent, "a strange and perhaps not very healthy human garden" (1). She is saved by Dean but she must help to save herself, if only by small rebellions against her mother's will. The fact that the narrator is in the grip of a conflict of her own and the fact that the conflict is tied closely to the problematic social atmosphere of the Crescent itself make *The Album* a tighter work than the earlier mysteries in which the romance was pleasant but gratuitous.

In *The Album* Rinehart faced again the practically insoluble problem of unraveling both the surface and the buried stories at once, and she now went a long way toward alleviating the difficulties she faced by explaining a number of the mechanical elements of the mystery and the less significant clues along the way, leaving only the largest questions for the end. Lou simply tells the reader that a particular incident or clue was later worked out by the inspector: "Inspector Briggs summed it up later," she says and resolves that problem (p. 144). This succeeds not only because there is more than enough material to explain (and still a great deal to handle at the close of the story) but because the really important material is being uncovered by Dean. Dean does not discount the police, nor does he consider himself one of them: "...I'd be helpless without the police, while they need me only now and then.... What I have is a line of specialized knowledge, odds and ends. Actually, I look after the little things, while they do the big ones" (98). Despite that disclaimer, Dean solves it all—the big clues and the little ones, apprehends the murderer, and uncovers the buried story. He may not belong to the rarified aristrocracy of the Crescent, but he is a gentleman—with a college education—and in the end he wins the girl.

The Wall (1938)

In *The Wall* Rinehart portrays the first of her fully developed young women on the make. Juliette Ransom is beautiful, unprincipled, vicious, and extraordinarily attractive to men. In the closed-world setting of Rock Island, an aristocratic summer colony modeled on Bar Harbor and Seal Island, Juliette has been purely trouble. Her sudden reappearance in that world leads almost immediately to her murder and, since she has had affairs with every one of the young or youngish men in the summer colony, all those men—and their womenfolk—become suspects. Everyone has a motive for wanting her dead.

Juliette's affairs, at least the fairly recent ones, do not make up the buried story. The uncovering of the deep story in *The Wall* means the complete uncovering of Juliette's past with the consequent discovery of assumed identity. Juliette was born Julia Bates, a no one (in Rinehart's lexicon) from a small midwestern town (a Rinehart equivalent for nowhere). She escaped by running off with a sporting goods salesman, whom she discarded upon arriving in the east. There, she renamed, in fact recreated, herself and in her new identity used her charms to lure aristocratic young men, finally marrying (and subsequently divorcing) Arthur Lloyd.

Lloyd's sister Marcia narrates the novel. She is orphaned and single, responsible for maintaining Sunset House, built by her grandfather in the 1890s and for supporting her faithful old servants. Her responsibilities extend even to handling her brother's ex-wife, for the novel commences with Juliette's unexpected and unwelcome visit to Sunset House. Marcia is, as well, the romantic center of the novel. She meets and falls in love with Allen Pell, a painter living nearby in a trailer. Pell, too, is constructing a new identity; under his real name of Page he has just been released from jail after serving time for manslaughter.

The buried story of Juliette's past is woven intricately with the story of Allen Page, and as a result the romantic thread of the surface story is deeply entangled with the murder plot, for Page must clear himself before he and Marcia can marry. He and Marcia, then, slowly unearth the deepest layers of the buried story, learning more and more of Juliette's vicious and violence-provoking past.

Like all of Rinehart's better mystery stories, *The Wall* derives a good part of its interest from its social setting. The aristocracy of Rock Island is portrayed as a vanishing American phenomenon, half to be lamented and half to be satirized. Old women of forthright and unaffected character, like salty, outspoken Mrs. Pendexter, typify the best of the vanishing breed. Others, with too much new money, live absurdly, and Rinehart satirizes them in scenes such as a picnic with footmen formally in attendance. Such satire underscores the theme, for there is a basic weakness in the society of this novel as is demonstrated by the swathe that Juliette Ransom cuts. If no man resists her, then none is really man enough.

The Great Mistake (1940)

The great complexity of both surface and buried stories in Rinehart's mature mysteries sometimes created narrative problems that could not be solved within the unwritten rules that customarily legislate the relationship between writer and reader. *The Great Mistake* is the best example of both that complexity and the consequent necessity for Rinehart to pull a couple of pretty fast ones on her audience.

When the novel opens, Pat Abbott, the narrator, has just been hired by Maud Wainwright, mistress of The Cloisters, as her social secretary. We meet the characters who make up both the Hill (the millionaires' part of town) and the Valley (the older settlement), and life is pleasant enough until two characters—strayed out of their marriages—return to complicate and upset matters. The first is Bessie Wainwright, wife of Maud's son Tony, who was once infatuated with this fast and hard young woman and has lived to regret it. She is back to make money and trouble. Soon after, Don Morgan returns, ostensibly ill, and convinces his former wife Lydia to take him in and care for him. Before long, the expected series of murders and assaults begins.

The murders in the surface story result, as is to be expected, from events in the buried story. To put it another way, Rinehart creates a set of characters who appear to fall into a pattern of relationships in

Relationships of the Major Characters in *The Great Mistake* as Defined in the Surface Story

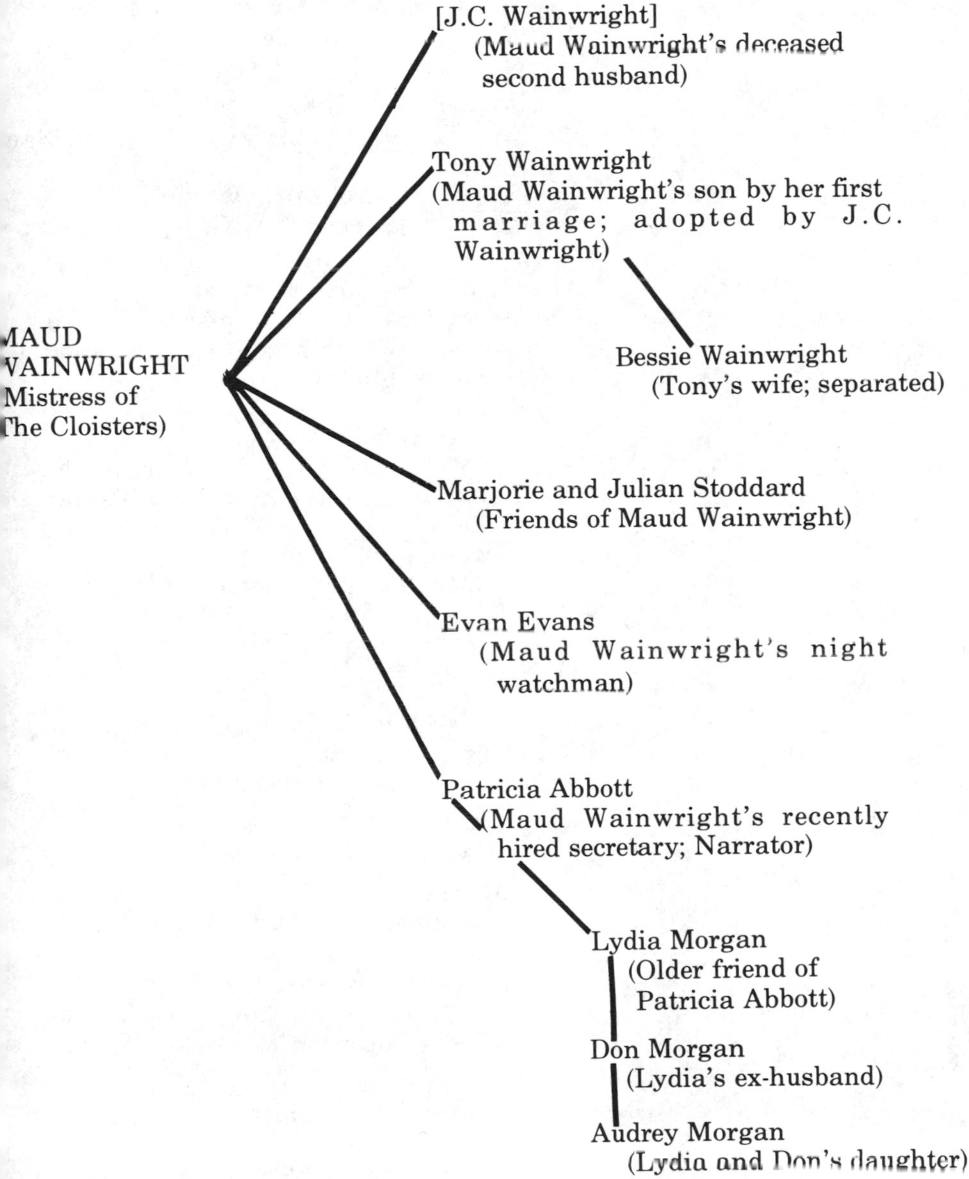

[J.C. Wainwright]
    (Maud Wainwright's deceased
    second husband)

Tony Wainwright
(Maud Wainwright's son by her first
    marriage; adopted by J.C.
    Wainwright)

MAUD
WAINWRIGHT
(Mistress of
The Cloisters)

Bessie Wainwright
    (Tony's wife; separated)

Marjorie and Julian Stoddard
    (Friends of Maud Wainwright)

Evan Evans
    (Maud Wainwright's night
    watchman)

Patricia Abbott
    (Maud Wainwright's recently
    hired secretary; Narrator)

Lydia Morgan
    (Older friend of
    Patricia Abbott)

Don Morgan
    (Lydia's ex-husband)

Audrey Morgan
    (Lydia and Don's daughter)

Fig. 1

Relationships of the Major Characters in *The Great Mistake* As Defined in the Buried Story

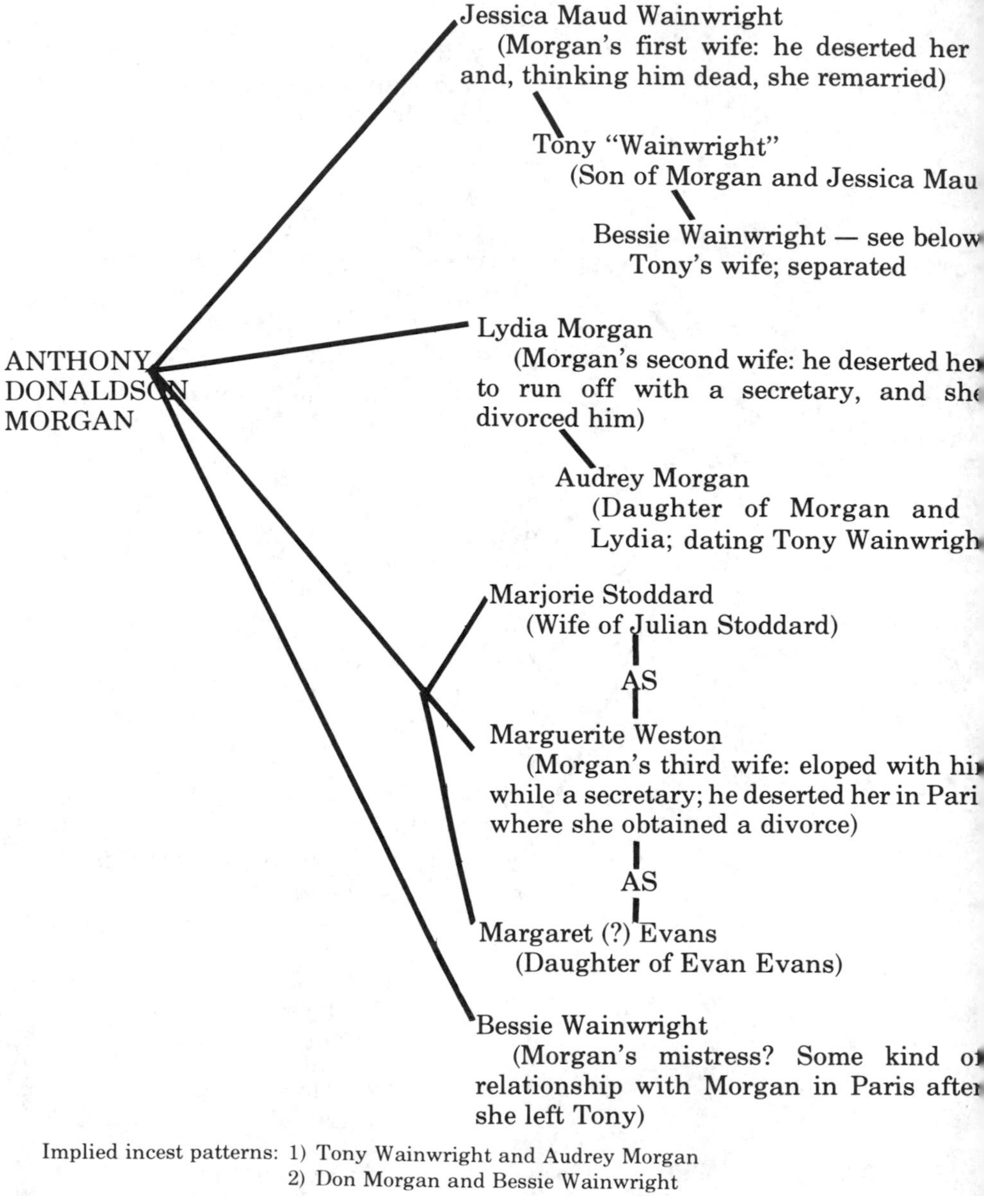

ANTHONY
DONALDSON
MORGAN

Jessica Maud Wainwright
(Morgan's first wife: he deserted her and, thinking him dead, she remarried)

Tony "Wainwright"
(Son of Morgan and Jessica Mau[d])

Bessie Wainwright — see below
Tony's wife; separated

Lydia Morgan
(Morgan's second wife: he deserted her to run off with a secretary, and she divorced him)

Audrey Morgan
(Daughter of Morgan and Lydia; dating Tony Wainwrigh[t])

Marjorie Stoddard
(Wife of Julian Stoddard)

AS

Marguerite Weston
(Morgan's third wife: eloped with hi[m] while a secretary; he deserted her in Pari[s] where she obtained a divorce)

AS

Margaret (?) Evans
(Daughter of Evan Evans)

Bessie Wainwright
(Morgan's mistress? Some kind o[f] relationship with Morgan in Paris afte[r] she left Tony)

Implied incest patterns: 1) Tony Wainwright and Audrey Morgan
2) Don Morgan and Bessie Wainwright

Fig. 2

the present, but whose real relationships when uncovered, form an entirely different pattern. The uncovering of the buried story depends on the discovery of assumed identities and the reconstruction of the original pattern of relationships. In *The Great Mistake* that reconstruction doubles back on the present. Although Rinehart makes no overt reference to the fact, the reconstructed past shows relationships in the present to be incestuous.

The Great Mistake provides a fairly dramatic instance of patterns of relationship. The surface story centers about Maud Wainwright (see Figure 1); all the major characters have either a direct or a close second-hand relationship with her. And it is essentially a story of women and their relations with their children and the men they love.

The buried story disposes the same characters altogether differently. That story centers around (Anthony) Donald(son) Morgan (see Figure 2). It is again a story of women, but only insofar as each has had an intimate relationship with Morgan (excepting of course the narrator), three as his wife and the fourth, at least implied, as his mistress. Since all these women live in the same town, the coincidences—and the fact that all are unaware of these coincidences—strain credulity. It is in handling this problem that Rinehart plays fast and loose with her reader; only by manipulating the names of several characters can she manage to carry it off. Therefore, Maud can continue to believe that her first husband, Anthony Donaldson Morgan, died in the war even though she knows that Lydia was deserted by a Donald Morgan. And therefore, no one can suspect that the old tattoo on Morgan's chest carried Maud's name, for the scar from its removal indicates that the first name began with a "J"—for Jessica Maud. Mystery novel readers consider such sleight-of-hand unfair, and rightly so.

The buried story as it has been laid out here diagrammatically would seem to focus all evil in the person of the much-married Don Morgan. It is one of the most curious aspects of the novel that Morgan is not really seen as evil: he just has a weakness for women, otherwise a perfectly decent fellow. To quote the local police chief: "Now you knew Morgan. Outside of women he wasn't a bad sort" (275).

Evil in *The Great Mistake* lies quite specifically in the character of Bessie and stems, just as specifically, from cross-class marriage, which occurs in multiples here. Morgan, married into a respectable family, eloped with a secretary, the daughter of a night watchman. That woman subsequently married an aristocrat, in fact the master of the local hunt, and although her character remains remarkably untainted, her marriages are the source of a good deal of the novel's murderous violence. Far worse, though, is Tony's brief passion for

Bessie, for in marrying her, he admitted into his and his mother's world the Rinehart monster full blown, the ruthless, hardened, promiscuous girl from nowhere.

At first we are led to believe that Bessie has a marginal—very marginal—claim on respectability. Although she is "nothing....Just nothing. Tony met her in a bar somewhere in New York," she seems to have had some upbringing.

She had been a New York girl, one of that band of young women who hangs on the fringes of society. She had gone to a good school, however, and somehow she had managed to get into the Junior League. Her people were quiet and respectable enough... (52-53).

As Pat Abbott grows more and more suspicious of Bessie, she reconsiders those quiet and respectable parents: "a clever girl could have managed that, have borrowed parents for the occasion and invented the rest" (148). Improbable as those borrowed parents sound, that is all Bessie ever produced for Tony and Maud's scrutiny. Private investigators in New York have brought Tony the truth: " 'When you married me you had no people. God knows where you got the ones I saw, or what your life had been before I met you' " (253). Bessie is like Juliette Ransom in being "nothing...just nothing," but even worse in the final analysis, for she is never identified with any family or any hometown at all; she has no real self.

*   *   *

With World War II Rinehart's mysteries underwent change, losing some of their fine plot complexity and psychological edge. At times she seemed to have lost interest in working out full-length murder stories and some fiction shows odd lapses, sometimes in tone, occasionally in details of fact. At the same time she began writing mystery short stories with greater frequency than earlier. In all her career to date she had published only six such short stories (excluding some very early "storiettes"), including the two Hilda Adams stories in 1914. Between 1941 and 1953 she published eleven, seven during the war. The mystery short story was never Rinehart's forte, for the form was too brief to allow her to work with the buried story and assumed identity, forcing her instead into tricky plots and trickier solutions.

Deeply troubled by the war and sorely frustrated that a worsening heart condition prevented her from visiting the war zone as a correspondent, as she had in the First World War, Rinehart often viewed fiction writing as a futile activity—at least for the duration. And the world of war-time America failed to provide a comfortable fit with the world of Rinehart's mysteries. Rich and aristocratic old families were not popular subjects. Moreover, with all able-bodied and right-minded young men in the service, how could she construct her romantic plots? Rinehart worked it out by sending her heroes home to recuperate from war-wounds and by having her heroines rebel against the privileged society they had been born into. It worked fairly well, but the mysteries from these years are mostly flawed.

Hilda Adams: *The Secret* [1941?] and *Haunted Lady* (1942)

Miss Pinkerton is in a pretty foul mood throughout *The Secret*. As the story opens, she is being turned down for overseas service; like Rinehart she has trouble with her heart. When Inspector Fuller (Was "Patton" now an unacceptable name?), relieved but sympathetic, is misguided enough to send flowers to cheer her up, Miss Pinkerton nearly jettisons not only their romantic but even their professional relationship.

Hilda returns to police work nonetheless, goaded by her curiosity when Fuller tells her about a girl who appears to be trying to murder her mother. The case is puzzling and the clues even more so. As the Inspector sums it up:

Here you had a locked door to start with, a bandage on Nina Rowland's arm, a volume of the *Encyclopaedia Britannica*, a bump on your head, a stolen watch returned, a lady named Hayes who registered horror, and a letter from Honolulu (254-55).

That, of course, is enough for Miss Pinkerton, who knows intuitively and at once that Tony Rowland is not a would-be matricide. She single-handedly learns the secret, solves the mystery, and with a message sent to the murderer permits suicide as an escape from the electric chair.

The clues are bizarre again in *Haunted Lady*. Old Eliza Fairbanks goes to the police with the information that bats, rats, and even a sparrow have been introduced into her locked bedroom. Bats and rats turn out to be less dangerous, as Hilda discovers, than Eliza's family, her children, their spouses and ex-spouses, and the servants. Their relationships are complicated by jealousy and greed, but they extend only over the surface of the narrative. Without a buried story, the work here seems thin.

There is an overall uncertainty to both these novels. Miss Pinkerton is no longer a clear character. Her hair is turning gray, but the Inspector talks about her youthful innocence; "she looks as though she still thought the stork brought babies" (5). She is tough

and clever, tactful enough to hold off the Inspector when he wants to
propose and sentimental enough to warn the murderer (again) so
that suicide prevents arrest. And, very oddly, she is now feminine
enough to faint—"for the first time in her life" (219). Strangely,
Rinehart turned to third person narration for these two Miss
Pinkerton stories. It was not a successful experiment, for she lost the
advantage of Hilda's voice and at the same time distanced the
reader from the action of the story.

Episode of the Wandering Knife (1943)

Episode of the Wandering Knife is almost pure comedy. There
are murders, assaults, midnight terrors, and a buried story, but none
of the these grim features seriously discountenances the narrator or
dilutes for long the comic tone. As if Rinehart could not direct her
full imaginative force toward stories of crime and detection, she
turned that energy toward the portrayal of a new character type for
her mystery fiction—the overrich, somewhat vulgar, and slightly
eccentric widow. And curiously, for Rinehart frequently excoriated
excessively wealthy women in her romances, she treated her with
comic affection.

Mrs. Shepard, overweight, with dyed red hair and a diamond
choker thick enough and tight enough to hold up her sagging chins,
appears at the opening of the novel giving a dinner party for two
hundred in her monstrous house. When the guests leave, her son
walks to his own house on the estate to find the murdered body of his
wife. In a state of near shock he returns to tell his mother and his
sister Judy (the narrator), who then race back to his house. At that
point Mrs. Shepard takes over. Seeing her son's hunting knife on the
stairs near the body, she simply sits on it, and she refuses to move,
insisting on providing companionship for the corpse while the
police conduct their investigation.

The knife goes into Mrs. Shepard's stocking and from there into
her toilet tank. Mrs. Shepard takes to her bed, "whitewashes" her
face to convince her doctor she is too ill to leave her room, and
watches that toilet tank. Nevertheless, the knife begins it
wandering, and its appearances and disappearances along with the
reactions of Mrs. Shepard are nothing but comic.

The narration, too, is bright and witty, and although the
narrator reports her distress and even her terror, it is difficult to take
them seriously, perhaps because of the intense focus on Mrs.
Shepard and the tone her daughter takes in discussing her:

Mother had taken off her chin strap and was looking fairly cheerful. She said she
had decided to see our senator instead of the Governor, and of course they couldn't

hold Larry under the circumstances. After all we had always contributed to the Republican Party, and had I any black stockings for the funeral that day (72).

Similarly, the romantic interest is light-hearted. Judy Shepard meets Tony Armstrong, a photographer working with the police. As it turns out, he is a convalescent war hero, and, rather like Cinderella, does not appear in his full beauty till the end of the novel when he turns up in the splendor of his army officer's uniform. Having learned that the Shepards are turning their house into an army convalescent hospital—for Judy must prove her own worth by disowning the more egregious trappings of wealth—Tony proposes, or as he puts it to Mrs. Shepard, "Judy, here, has just made me an offer of marriage. At first I was inclined to refuse, but on thinking it over—"(113).

Episode of the Wandering Knife, despite or because of its wit and comedy, finally fails as a mystery novel. For one thing, there are too many deaths to accord with the tone. For another, the solution is not developed gradually through clues the reader can attempt to unravel; it is pretty much delivered in a piece by the police chief and Tony Armstrong. These are serious drawbacks; still, as comedy, *Wandering Knife* is a delight.

The Yellow Room (1945)

With *The Yellow Room* Rinehart returned to real mystery writing. Like her other mysteries from this period, *The Yellow Room* presents the closed world of the very rich, a convalescent war hero, and a love story between him and the rich girl who repents of her social station, but here these elements are embedded in a dense and complex mystery.

Carol Spencer travels to Maine to open the family's summer estate, preparing for her war-hero brother's visit home. A body in the linen closet is the first in a chain of mysteries and murders in the summer colony. Major Jerry Dane, recuperating from a leg wound, does the principal sleuthing, sometimes aiding but more often independent of the local police. We slowly discover that he is "Intelligence," and eventually learn that he has been an FBI agent, hardly an occupation for one of Rinehart's gentlemen heroes; however, we are given parenthetically, some assurance about Dane: his father was a Senator. Dane, though, need make no accommodations to Carol; on the contrary, she must demonstrate that, unlike the rest of her family, she is not poisoned by great wealth. Even her innate good taste and modest behavior are not enough to assure the reader or Major Dane that she is worthy of him and Rinehart signals clearly that the experiences of the novel have wrought a deep change in her: "Carol Spencer was not the same girl.... That sheltered, carefully set-up young woman had vanished" (152).

The buried story in *The Yellow Room* is immensely complicated, involving several favorite Rinehart themes; cross-class marriage, amnesia, and the suggestion of incest. Both surface and buried mysteries are so complex that their unraveling demands even more than the usual secret and devious acts, half-truths, and evasions on the part of some half-a-dozen characters. The resolution indicts half the cast for one or another of the various bizarre and terrifying events. In other words, not one but many characters are, unknown to one another, guilty of something.

The Yellow Room is a good mystery novel, flawed only by its over-complicated denouement. One oversight, however, brought Rinehart a good deal of mail. The body found in the linen closet had been carried there on the small elevator installed behind the stairs of the Spencer home. Unfortunately, the electric power in the house had not yet been turned on for the summer and Rinehart makes a good deal of the lack of electric light. How, asked her readers, did the elevator run in an electricity-less house? That remains the unsolved mystery of *The Yellow Room*.

The Swimming Pool (1952)

As she reached her seventies, even Rinehart's astonishing energy flagged somewhat, and after publishing a long, serious novel and a new edition of her autobiography in 1948, she wrote only two or three short stories a year until *The Swimming Pool,* her last full-length novel. *The Swimming Pool* is a first-rate work of Rinehart mystery fiction, displaying all her technical skills in the buried story and extending her "democratization" of the surface romance.

Narrator Lois Maynard lives with her bachelor brother Phil at The Birches, the over-large and somewhat rundown old summer place where the family moved after losing its money in the Crash of '29. Mr. Maynard committed suicide early in 1930 and his wife lived only a few years longer, long enough, however, to assure the marriage of her beautiful daughter Judith to wealthy Ridgely Chandler. Only Judith "succeeded" as her mother had wished. The other daughter, Anne, lives modestly on the income of her not-too-successful architect husband. Lois, still single, copes with comparative poverty and writes mystery novels.

Lois's quiet life at The Birches ends when Judith, a fast-living socialite, becomes terrified of something, decides to divorce and, after a trip to Reno, moves in with her brother and sister. The murders that follow depend, as we might expect, on events of the past, events manipulated by Mrs. Maynard, desperate for her daughter Judith's wealthy marraige. Just as the past controls the present, so Mrs. Maynard, in the large portrait painting of her that dominates The Birches, continues to exercise her influence on the world of her children. The portrait is a nice symbol for the interconnection of past and present, and that portrait, carefully described, is an exact copy of a painting artist John Lavalle did of Mary Roberts Rinehart.

In the course of the novel the events of the past and the motivations of the characters acting in the past come in for thorough reinvestigation and reinterpretation. This difficult unraveling becomes the responsibility of Lieutenant O'Brien, on leave from the police force, who rents the lodge at The Birches and falls in love with Lois, making him the most democratic of the romantic heroes in Rinehart's mysteries. At the same time, the cross-class marriage is inverted in the buried story, where the girl now comes from a monied family and the young man from "the people." As a result of this inversion, the surface story constitutes a reconsideration of a parallel relationship, in this instance to be resolved—despite Lois's sisters' horror at her romance with a cop. " 'I think Mother would turn in her grave if she thought you were serious about [O'Brien],' " says Anne. " 'A policeman, and an Irish one at that! Good Lord, Lois, have you lost your mind?' " Lois defends him, arguing that " 'he's a college man' " (285). Eventually, the sisters capitulate, even agreeing that the cop is a "gent." And the problem of money, always so difficult for Rinehart's romantic heroines, is easily solved: the Maynards lost theirs in the Crash; O'Brien has inherited a tidy legacy.

The Swimming Pool was the first of Rinehart's novels in over four decades not to be serialized before publication. Magazine editors, perhaps fearing that Rinehart was losing her audience, were not interested. It had been, after all, forty-four years since the publication of *The Circular Staircase* and much had changed in the mystery genre in that time. Nevertheless, *The Swimming Pool* did very well, becoming one of the mystery best-sellers of the year.

The Frightened Wife (1953)

In *The Frightened Wife* Rinehart seems to have set out deliberately to write something "modern." Wade Forsythe II, a young lawyer, is grappling with his clients' income tax returns when we meet him. He becomes involved in murder when a beautiful young woman bolts into his office, locks the door, and nearly passes out from terror—and the reader wonders if he has wandered into the world of Perry Mason. The young woman, Anne Collier, is married to a brute and she suspects that he has discovered how much money she has earned—secretly writing scripts for a radio soap opera—and hidden from him, planning to save it for her son.

Forsythe is retained to write Anne's will but soon finds himself deep in violence. Anne falls down the stairs, tripped by a hidden wire, and it looks as though her husband no longer plans to wait for her money. And then the husband is found dead, Anne is arrested, and their son kidnapped. Forsythe handles it all, practically single-handed, for the police, too, have been "modernized" and are bent on arresting the wrong person. Thus, like the heroes in much detective fiction contemporary with *The Frightened Wife,* Forsythe must fight the police as well as the criminal. But in the last analysis Rinehart cannot quite maintain the tough guy mode and, accepting the congratulations from the commissioner for having solved the case, the police lieutenant shares the credit with Forsythe—who solves the murder, finds the kidnapped child, and wins the now conveniently widowed girl.

The Frightened Wife was Rinehart's final mystery novella and, except for three short stories, the last of her published writing. It was serialized in *The Saturday Evening Post* early in 1953, forty-three years after her first story appeared in that magazine. The *Post* paid well, $30,000—exactly $29,900 more than they had paid her back in 1910.

* * *

Curious changes have been rung on Rinehart's reputation. Until about 1940 she was thought of as a novelist and short story writer, not a mystery writer primarily. Her enormous public apparently preferred her serious and romantic novels, for they were generally the ones that made the annual best-seller lists between 1910 and 1936. Reviewers, however, began as early as 1920 to see significant flaws in the romances and equally significant successes in her mysteries. That judgment has been echoed since Rinehart's death in 1958 and her name has been altogether associated with the mystery novel, her romances nearly forgotten.

Most recently, in the Dell paperback reprints of her work, Rinehart is being promoted as a writer of Gothics. Dell apparently made a change in marketing strategies for Rinehart novels about 1968. During most of the 1960s, Dell Rinehart covers promoted mystery and crime, with pictures of bodies, weapons, and clues. Subsequently, reissues turned to Gothic images with dark-haired maidens fleeing sinister houses.[5] No doubt the decision to place Rinehart among the Gothics on supermarket shelves was part of an effort to capitalize on a hot market, based on what might seem a reasonable argument that recurrent elements in Rinehart mystery fiction are the elements of Gothic novels: the mansion as setting, the supernatural as a source of mystery, the young woman as narrator and hence *apparently* as central figure.

In fact, these elements are not handled in the Gothic mode. Rinehart mansions are not castles, merely excessive expressions of bourgeois over-reaching. There are, after *The Circular Staircase,* no hidden rooms, secret stairs, or locked chambers. Midnight intruders gain entry not through hidden passageways but by means of unlocked window screens. Similarly, the supernatural is treated in ways that are distinctly anti-Gothic. Seances and spirit-return were part of popular, and sometimes even intellectual, science in the early part of the century, and so they were for Rinehart.

Most important is the role of the female narrator. For one thing, she is central only to the surface romance. Both the surface mystery and the buried story have other characters for their focus. It is also significant that the female narrator is only marginally endangered; she is not the object of murderous violence. Nor is she the object of sexual violence, real or threatened, for this young woman is pursued only by the romantic hero, a man of the purest intentions.

The Gothic label may be hard to detach, however, and not only for reasons of marketing. Rinehart's mysteries do not fit tidily into either of the two schools of detective fiction that dominated mystery writing in her lifetime. She clearly does not belong to the American school of tough guy detectives. And just as surely she is not part of the British school of intellectual puzzles and country-house murders, and for two important reasons. First, her use of the past, while not in itself unique, is so in its complexity and its intensity. Second, despite the comic elements in her mysteries, Rinehart lacks the wit of British mystery fiction, the tone that brings it close, murders notwithstanding, to comedy of manners.

Rinehart started her career ashamed of her mystery thrillers and for a very long time, perhaps for her whole life, she viewed her crime novels as less significant than her serious fiction. Still, as she reviewed her work in the 1948 edition of her autobiography, she paid tribute to the skill that her mysteries demanded, a skill far beyond that her other fiction required: she assured her readers that "ponderous tomes" are relatively easy to write; in fact, "the more easily anything reads, the harder it has been to write," for "almost anyone with sufficient determination can make a roast beef. But it takes a light hand to make pastry."[6]

Notes

[1]Mary Roberts Rinehart, "The Detective Story," *Munsey's Magazine* (May,

1904).

Following is a bibliography of the mystery stories, novels, and collections of Mary Roberts Rinehart. Since a complete bibliography of her work runs twenty printed pages and is beyond the scope of this essay, I have limited this list to her crime fiction. However, a number of novels and, particularly, short stories do not fit neatly into one category or another; I have therefore excluded fiction in which elements of crime merely enhance the plot of a romance or add complexity to a comedy or a farce. I have, on the other hand, included some short stories where murderous violence is accomplished or contemplated, whether or not there is mystery involved, and some in which only accidental good fortune prevents the protagonist from committing a well-planned murder.

This bibliography lists first magazine serialization followed by first book publication (where both occur) for Rinehart's novels. Stories are listed by first magazine publication and first collection. Where page numbers for material quoted in the text refer to a subsequent edition, that edition is also listed. In all cases, the publication to which parenthetical page numbers in the text refer is marked with an asterisk (*). Finally, collections of Rinehart mystery stories and novels are listed together at the end of the bibliography.

Crime Fiction by Mary Roberts Rinehart

"The Housekeeper's Story: Tale of an Ancient House." *Short Stories* (1906?).
[Some material from *The Circular Staircase* appears here.]
The Man in Lower 10. All-Story (January-April, 1906). Indianapolis: Bobbs-Merrill, 1909. *New York: Dell, 1971.
The Circular Staircase. All-Story (November, 1907-March, 1908). Indianapolis: Bobbs-Merrill, 1908. *San Diego: University Extension, University of California, 1977.
The Mystery of 1122. Live Wire (February, 1908-?). As *The Window at the White Cat.* *Indianapolis: Bobbs-Merrill, 1910.
The Case of Jennie Brice. Everybody's (October, 1912-January, 1913). Indianapolis: Bobbs-Merrill, 1913. *New York: Dell, 1960.
The After House. McClure's (June-October, 1913). Boston: Houghton Mifflin, 1913.
"The Buckled Bag." *The Saturday Evening Post* (January 10 & 17, 1914). In *Miss Pinkerton* (See below).
"The Papered Door." *Collier's* (March 21, 1914). In Mary Roberts Rinehart. *The Romantics.* New York: Farrar and Rinehart, 1929.
"Locked Doors." *The Saturday Evening Post* (August 22 & 29, 1914). In *Miss Pinkerton.* (see below).
The Curve of the Catenary. Pictorial Review (June-August, 1916). In *The Mystery Book* [by various hands]. New York: Farrar and Rinehart, 1939.
Sight Unseen. Everybody's (June-August, 1916). In *Sight Unseen and The Confession.* New York: Doran, 1921.
The Confession. Good Housekeeping (May-August, 1917). In *Sight Unseen and The Confession.* New York: Doran, 1921.
The Bat [play], with Avery Hopwood. Opened August 23, 1920. Fictionalized version, anonymous [Stephen Vincent Benet]. New York: Doran, 1926.
The Red Lamp. Cosmopolitan (January 7, 1925). New York: Doran, 1925. *New York: Dell, 1961.
"If Only It Were Yesterday." *The Ladies' Home Journal* (August, 1929). In Mary Roberts Rinehart. *The Romantics.* New York: Farrar and Rinehart, 1929.
"The Old Man Cleans His Revolver." *Cosmopolitan* (August, 1929). In Mary Roberts Rinehart. *The Romantics.* New York: Farrar and Rinehart, 1929.
The Door. The Saturday Evening Post (February 1-March 22, 1930). New York:

Farrar and Rinehart, 1930. *New York: Dell, 1968).

Miss Pinkerton. The Saturday Evening Post (January 2—February 13, 1932). *New York: Farrar and Rinehart, 1932.

The Album. The Saturday Evening Post (April 8-Mary 27, 1933). New York: Farrar and Rinehart, 1933. *New York: Dell, 1971.

"The Man Who Killed His Wife." *Cosmopolitan* (August, 1935). In Mary Roberts Rinehart. *Married People.* New York: Farrar and Rinehart, 1937.

The Wall. The Saturday Evening Post (May 14-July 9, 1938). New York: Farrar and Rinehart, 1938.

The Great Mistake. The Saturday Evening Post (September 7-November 2, 1940). New York: Farrar and Rinehart, 1940. *New York: Dell, 1970.

"The Dog in the Orchard." *Cosmopolitan* (September, 1940). In Mary Roberts Rinehart. *Familiar Faces.* New York: Farrar and Rinehart, 1941.

"The Door That Would Not Stay Closed." *Good Housekeeping* (June, 1941). In Mary Roberts Rinehart. *Familiar Faces.* New York: Farrar and Rinehart, 1941.

"The Secret" [written 1941?] In *Episode of the Wandering Knife* (see below). Perhaps compare Mary Roberts Rinehart. *The Nurse's Secret.* Warner Brothers Film, 1941.

Haunted Lady. Cosmopolitan (March-May, 1942). New York: Farrar and Rinehart, 1942. *New York: Dell, 1971.

"The Lipstick." *Cosmopolitan* July, 1942). In *Alibi for Isabel and Other Stories* (see below).

Episode of the Wandering Knife. Good Housekeeping (June & July, 1943). In *Episode of the Wandering Knife* (see below).

"The Clue in the Closet." *Cosmopolitan* (March, 1944). In *Alibi for Isabel and Other Stories* (see below).

"The Portrait." *Cosmopolitan* (June, 1944). In *Alibi for Isabel and Other stories.* (see below).

"Murder and the South Wind." *Good Housekeeping* (August, 1944). In *The Frightened Wife and Other Murder Stories* (see below).

The Yellow Room. The Saturday Evening Post (September 8—October 27, 1945). *New York: Farrar and Rinehart, 1945.

"Four A.M." *Cosmopolitan* (September, 1948).

"The Unbreakable Alibi." *The Saturday Evening Post* (April 9, 1949). As "The Man Who Hid His Breakfast" in *Episode of the Wandering Knife* (see below).

"The Scandal." *The Saturday Evening Post* (July 15, 1950). In *The Frightened Wife and Other Murder Stories* (see below).

"The Case is Closed." *This Week* (March 10-24, 1951).

The Swimming Pool. New York: Rinehart, 1952. *New York: Dell, 1970.

The Frightened Wife. The Saturday Evening Post (February 14-March 7, 1953). In *The Frightened Wife and Other Murder Stories* (see below).

"The Splinter." *Ellery Queen's Mystery Magazine* (May, 1954).

Mystery Collections

Mary Robert Rinehart's Mystery Book. New York: Farrar and Rinehart, 1930. Contents: *The Circular Staircase, The Man in Lower 10, The Case of Jennie Brice, The Confession.*

The Crime Book. New York: Farrar and Rinehart, 1933. Contents: *The After House,* "The Buckled Bag," "Locked Doors," *The Red Lamp, The Window at the White Cat.*

Alibi for Isabel and Other Stories; New York: Farrar and Rinehart, 1944. Contents [including only mysteries]: "The Clue in the Closet," "The Portrait," "Alibi for Isabel," "The Lipstick."

Episode of the Wandering Knife. New York: Rinehart and Company, 1950. Contents:

Episode of the Wandering Knife, "The Man Who Hid His Breakfast," "The Secret."
The Frightened Wife and Other Murder Stories. New York: Rinehart and Company,
   1953. Contents: *The Frightened Wife,* "If Only It Were Yesterday," "The Scandal,"
   "Murder and the South Wind," "The Burned Chair."
The Mary Roberts Rinehart Crime Book. New York: Rinehart and Company, 1957.
   Contents: *The Door, The Confession, The Red Lamp.*
Miss Pinkerton. New York: Rinehart and Company, 1959. Contents: "The Buckled
   Bag," "Locked Doors," *Miss Pinkerton, Haunted Lady.*

   [2]Biographical information in this essay comes from Mary Roberts Rinehart, *My
Story: A New Edition and Seventeen New Years* (New York: Rinehart and Company,
1948); and Jan Cohn, *Improbable Fiction: The Life of Mary Roberts Rinehart*
(Pittsburgh: University of Pittsburgh Press, 1980).

   [3]Tape of Mary Margaret McBride interview with Mary Roberts Rinehart,
February 4, 1952.

   [4]Mary Roberts Rinehart, "Thoughts," *The Ladies' Home Journal* (May, 1931).

   [5]For example, early Dell reprints of *The Door* (1964) and *The Red Lamp* (no date)
picture a door and a bloodstained swordstick, and a lamp and a dead body,
respectively. In my own limited collection of Dell reprints, long-haired girls are
shown in flight on *Alibi for Isabel* (1967), *The Door* (1968), *The Wall* (1968), *The Man
in Lower 10* (1969), *The Bat* (1969), and *The Swimming Pool* (1970) [an earlier,
undated, edition shows a dead body in a swimming pool]). In no case does the newer
Gothic cover reflect the story.

   [6]*My Story,* p. 521.

Margaret Millar

1915   Margaret Ellis Sturm born 5 February in Kitchener, Ontario

1929-1933 Educated at Kitchener Collegiate Institute, Ontario

1933-1936 Studied classics at University of Toronto; became interested in psychiatry

1938   Married Kenneth Millar, i.e. Ross Macdonald

1941   *The Invisible Worm,* first novel published

1942-1944 Lived in Ann Arbor, Michigan

1945-1946 Screen writer for Warner Bros., Hollywood, California

1947   *Experiment in Springtime,* first non-criminous novel published

1956   Edgar award of Mystery Writers of America for *Beast in View*

1957-1958 President, Mystery Writers of America

1958   Moved to Santa Barbara house in a wooded canyon

1965   Named Woman of the Year by *Los Angeles Times*

1979   *The Murder of Miranda,* her twenty-third book published

by John M. Reilly

Margaret Millar has never lacked approval for her mastery of popular narrative.[1] Will Cuppy, presiding as mystery reviewer of *Books* for the *New York Herald-Tribune* when she introduced her first detective, the consulting psychiatrist Dr. Paul Prye, heartily welcomed the appearance of *The Invisible Worm* in the summer of 1941.[2] In the winter of 1942 Cuppy was convinced by *The Weak-Eyed Bat* that Millar was a "humdinger" of an author, "right up in the top rank of bafflers, including the British."[3] Just six months later, in August 1942, the third Prye novel, *The Devil Loves Me*, rang the bell again. Cuppy placed Millar among the best. The Canadian author, he said, "is certainly a triple threat to some of our own high-ranking bafflers."[4]

Later reviewers continued the praise. James Sandoe, succeeding Cuppy at the *Herald-Tribune*, especially liked the "zany vein" of writing that permitted Millar to be funny about "grue" in *Rose's Last Summer*.[5] Meanwhile, Leonore G. Offord consistently remarked in the reviews she wrote for the *San Francisco Chronicle* how her professional eye appreciated the concealed craft of Millar's work. *An Air That Kills*, appearing in 1957, Offord found to be characterized by "underdone brilliance,"[6] while *The Listening Walls*, from 1959, achieved a style in which "smooth convolutions of plot and deception are scarcely visible."[7]

Such skill of craft displayed in one of Millar's finest works, *A Beast in View*, the Edgar winner of 1956, led Anthony Boucher to cite the novel as the best the mystery genre can accomplish. It is, he wrote,

a pure terror-suspense-mystery story, complete with murder, detective and surprise twist. But it is also so detailedly convincing a study in abnormal psychology, so admirably written with such complete realization of every character, that the most bitter antagonist of mystery fiction may be forced to acknowledge it as a work of art.[8]

Even though her publication has become less frequent since the mid-1960s, Millar continues to impress reviewers and readers alike, enough so that Avon Books planned in 1973 to reissue ten of her novels that lend themselves to marketing with cover art that suggests a modern gothic tale. With the help of Avon Millar possibly added an entirely new readership to the audience that admires her as a baffler, a stylist and a psychological novelist.

Despite her varied audience and approving reviewers, though, Millar has failed to gain extended critical attention. So far as I know, the only critical commentary on her writing, apart from reviews, appears in the brief essays written by myself for *Contemporary Novelists* and by Edward D. Hoch for *Twentieth Century Crime and Mystery Writers.*[9] For craft Millar may rank among the best in the mystery genre, but she has not been treated as a major presence. Nor has such virtuosity as Boucher noted earned her consideration as one of the handful of mystery writers who are said to be also "serious novelists."

There are familiar explanations for the fortunes of a popular writer's reputation. Prolific writers who accept the burden of repetitive convention may become dominant because they persist in satisfying our evident taste for the familiar. For other authors the rules by which they create a leading character may constitute the formula of a culture hero, or their plots may caricature a plausible world so successfully that their books are popularly believed to epitomize the times. Then, too, there are even more familiar, extra-literary causes of critical success. Reputation once attained reinforces itself, so that a popular writer who is described as worthy by credible authority in publications more conspicuous than mystery book columns is likely to become, by the power of that suggestion, worthy of serious critical attention. And, finally, there is to explain literary reputation a version of a law of supply and demand. Of all the skilled writers only a few will be selected for the top spots, regardless of the criteria or mechanisms of selection. Otherwise, attribution of greatness loses significance. How many masters and mistresses of mystery can there be?

Some, or all, of these reasons can explain Millar's modest reputation. She is neither prolific nor the creator of a sustained formula meant to embody her times. But, of course, consideration of the causes of popular reputation or its lack is secondary in the task of critical apprehension of a writer's achievement. We want a literary estimate of the workings of texts. At best the social milieu signified by reputation offers indirect access to the ways the books work.

There is that, though. An indirect access to the writer's project. Noticing the reviewers' approval of Millar's novels, their marketing promise for a mass paperback publisher, and the paucity of subsequent critical consideration of those novels, we are led to a genuine critical issue manifest in those gothicized covers Avon chose to bind her books. Each shows in montage the head of a woman, eyes closed or looking past the observer into her own thoughts. She is placed against a background emphasizing her isolation (perhaps a darkened house), a charged atmosphere (leafless trees) and a motif of the story (iron gates, a graveyard, the figure of a child). The whole picture is washed in soft pastels. The iconography of these Avon covers accurately symbolizes the novels to the extent of predicting that we will find a rising terror in the stories. Beyond that, however, there is difficulty in classifying the books as gothic because they lack a relationship between heroine and hero consistent with Kay J. Mussell's definition of the gothic as a form in which women are "cast as victims in a man's world, but through the demonstration of feminine virtues ... prove worthy of the love of the hero, who becomes her deliverer from the terrors that beset her."[10]

To be sure, some less crucial gothic requirements are met in many of Millar's tales. Nearly always women are at the center of the plot, their domestic affections and arrangements troubled, and often there is a man who becomes a partial agent of resolution. Other times, however, the central female figure is a villain, or the troubles more deeply structured into character than problems of love or atmospheric terror usually are; and the resolution often as not is ironic. As gothics Millar novels are only partially representative, because they are something in addition. Rather than conforming to gothic typology, they try to "improve upon" the conventions,[11] causing the dilemma evident in Elsa J. Radcliffe's bibliography, *Gothic Novels of the Twentieth Century,* which provides an entry for Margaret Millar and then explains that her works "are more correctly labeled mystery, suspense, and detective."[12]

Similarly, the appellation "detective story" is imprecise in Millar's novels. Will Cuppy's admiration for the stories about Dr. Paul Prye was soundly based, for those first three novels appeared to be the start of a series in which the psychiatrist would be the modern version of consulting scientists such as Sherlock Holmes or Dr. John Thorndyke, and the narrative as mannered as Trent's or Wimsey's. Then Millar was apparently bent upon observing the conventions of the classic detective novel: creating complex puzzles to be solved by an eccentric and attractive amateur sleuth whose tale could be comically related. In her next novel, however, she abandoned the amateur Prye for the professional Inspector Sands of the Toronto Police and substituted an atmosphere of terror for the earlier comedy. Eventually she would create at least a half dozen other detectives, several of them attorneys like Eric Meecham of *Vanish in an Instant,* Paul Blackshear of *Beast in View,* or Tom Aragon who appears in her most recent books *Ask for Me Tomorrow* and *The Murder of Miranda.* Still others are private eyes such as Joe Quinn the ex-Reno security man of *How Like An Angel* and Steve

Pinata of *Stranger in My Grave*. And besides Inspector Sands there is Lieutenant Easter of *Do Evil in Return*, as well as other police officers playing lesser roles in other novels.

It is evident from this list of detectives that Millar has little interest in capitalizing on the repeated appearances of a series figure who would become a "great detective" around whom she could construct a cycle of stories. What's more, the characterization of Millar's detectives is decidedly underplayed. She gives some of them individualizing backgrounds and intrinsically attractive traits, but none receives enough emphasis to be converted into the idealization of a splendid reasoner who presides over the classic detective story or the extraordinary moral figure common to the hard-boiled version of the genre. Millar's detectives are almost entirely defined by their function as technical necessities. They are agents of exposition providing a means to move along a plot that derives its significance from sources quite apart from the detective's presence.

Furthermore, the puzzles these agents must explain are also markedly different from those associated with the well-known types of detective story. Cuppy was correct in speaking of Millar's capacity as a "baffler," just as Julian Symons was correct when he wrote more recently that "she has few peers, and no superiors in the art of bamboozlement."[13] Yet it must be added that the baffling and bamboozling are not due to ingenious crimes or cunningly imaginative means of detection. The surprise and reversal in her plots always come from causes deeply seated in the non-rational interior lives of characters. With or without conscious design on the part of a protagonist, and absent or present a detective to help explain them, the sequence of plot would play itself out. The plots issue in crime, but their puzzling dimensions exist prior to, and independently of, the crime.

Thus, Millar fits no more neatly into the generic category of detective fiction novelist than she does into that of gothic romancer. Except perhaps for the term "suspense," which is also featured on the Avon covers in a quotation from *Library Journal* ("One of the most skillful writers of the suspense genre."), none of the labels we use for convenient tagging of a popular writer are exact enough to denominate Millar's fiction, because she has restlessly reworked the mystery narrative, resisting the imperative demands of its conventions in order to discover narrational means for themes she knows cannot be fully accommodated in established ways. Critically one can appreciate the evident skill of craft displayed in Millar's search, as her reviewers have done, but fuller discussion has been limited, since on the one hand she does not fulfill generic expectations, and on the other hand she never completely departs from their familiar patterns. Millar can hardly be classified either as a "Mistress" of detective or gothic fiction, or yet as a serious writer who owes little to the popular genres. And anomalous popular art rarely gets critical attention.

This, then, is our access to Millar's project. The inexactness of common categories of description reveal the tension between the institutionalized form of the mystery and detective genre and her individual art. While such tension exists in the writing of all but the most derivative authors, there are significant degrees of difference. At one end of the spectrum appear the books which nearly perfectly fulfill the norms of detective character and plot development. At the other end lie the books that innovate so extensively upon narrative conventions they become the model for a new literary type. The fiction of Dashiell Hammett in which dramatically new suppositions about reality are artistically combined with the techniques of pulp magazine writing illustrates the creation of a new model. S.S. Van Dine whose considerable talent is devoted to burnishing the paraphernalia of the Golden Age detection story provides novels to represent the fulfillment of the norms. I am less sure about candidates to represent innovation and fulfillment in the vein of romantic suspense, but perhaps Daphne du Maurier will serve to illustrate the first achievement, Phyllis Whitney the second.

Millar is neither a Hammett nor a du Maurier, but the dialectic between established form and artistic purpose in her fiction reveals her to be, at the very least, a fundamental revisionist attempting to re-imagine the premises of the mystery story. Millar's sort of revision should not be confused with purely technical variation. For example, when Agatha Christie violates the rule of detective fiction that proscribes the use of a narrator as the murderer, or wittily applies the axiom governing probability (eliminate the impossible, and whatever remains, however improbable, must be the truth) to reveal that since no single person is the murderer, everybody on the Orient Express sleeper must be, she is approaching the minor conventions of the detection puzzles as technical materials for bafflement. She transgresses the rules to place her signature upon the form, but the effect of surprise depends upon the rules remaining valid except in one case. Contrasting with pure technical variation of this sort is Millar's reversal of detective function in *Ask For Me Tomorrow*. In that novel the attorney Tom Aragon is hired by Gilda Lockwood Decker to locate her first husband in Mexico. Key informants meet with accident, and worse, before Aragon can interview them; still, he pieces together evidence to formulate a satisfactory hypothesis about Lockwood's disappearance. The final pages of the novel, however, completely redefine Aragon's role. Lockwood, the victim of a stroke, is living with Gilda as a second husband under the name of Decker. He had truly gone to Mexico, been imprisoned and otherwise abused, then remarried Gilda. She had vowed to avenge her husband and accomplished the vendetta by employing Aragon to seek out the people who had been instrumental in Lockwood's Mexican period. She had then sent his male nurse to execute them. Unknowingly the detective has become a fingerman; the distressed client is the criminal; and the missing man has never been lost. Such comprehensive reversal must be described in terms of variations upon features of the narrative that our experience with detective stories has led us to expect, but in their significance they go well beyond technical bafflement to suggest a fictional environment very different from the one where we first developed our now disappointed expectations.

Millar's revisions in generic patterns must also be distinguished from the practice of enriching a story by the addition of secondary themes. Her provision, for example, of a Chicano background for the detectives Steve Pinata and Tom Aragon, and her relation of ethnic prejudice to events are not patently didactic as is, say, the information about Judaism offered by Harry Kemelman in the Rabbi Small stories. Nor is Millar's revision of the same sort as Dorothy L. Sayer' integration of the interestingly adult relationship of Harriet Vane and Lord Peter Wimsey into the detective story. Sayers gives detective stories a greater range and modifies their characteristically male outlook, but she leaves the essential patterns of the classic story intact, since they can well accommodate her innovations. In contrast to Sayers, Millar finds that her innovations are necessary in the first place, because her basic suppositions will not readily accommodate to the available patterns.

Millar's generic revisionism is on-going, because it seems that form follows conception. The possibility for recasting the mystery narrative, however, was already evident in her earliest novels— those classically derived Prye novels. For instance in one, *The Weak-Eyed Bat*, the consulting psychiatrist is shown vacationing in Mushaka, a summer colony in northern Ontario. His fellow residents are introduced and described as though they will provide the stuff of manners comedy. In one cottage there lives Professor Henry Frost and his daughters Joan and Susan, the first a thieving coquette, the second a jealous and false young woman. The professor dislikes them both, and except for recording their doings in a diary leaves them alone while keeping the company he prefers, classical scholarship. The oldest resident of the colony both in terms of longevity and permanence in the resort is Miss Emily Bonner, who observes life from her wheelchair with the aid of binoculars. Her nephew Ralph who is engaged to Joan Frost lives with her, along with a Miss Alfonse, a nursing companion, whom Prye realizes he has seen before as the defendant in a murder trial. Close by live Tom and Mary Little whose marriage is shaky for reasons in addition to the fact that Tom is having an affair with Joan Frost. Nora Shane, with whom Prye becomes romantically involved, lives in a fifth cottage, and the sixth is the summer home of Mr. Smith, a suspicious chap because no one seems to be able to learn much about him. The narrative voice of the novel relates information about these characters in a tone suggesting observation of the socially ridiculous. The impulses and feelings lying beneath the surface of social life seem, however, to threaten more than decorum, and they do so in ways that throw doubt on the idea that crime may be a simple aberration briefly disturbing an essentially harmonious community.

After knocking her father down in an attempt to seize his diary record of her thefts and school expulsions, Joan Frost disappears, and the same night Prye is attacked and hit on the head. Next day, Joan's body is found in the lake. This is effective for plotting the novel, since nearly everyone has a motive for wishing Joan dead. Prye goes about his investigation as a comic sleuth. With a yellow scarf on his head to conceal his bandages, he seems dressed to excite opinions about his eccentricity. The eccentric doctor also provides comedy in his running exchange with the local constable on the differences between his own urgent wish to pursue the case and the local's penchant for prolonging the excitement. When Tom Little's body is found in the lake, Prye, as the expository voice in the novel provides Miss Emily a definitely uncomic framework for hypothesis about the killings. "The insane and the sane kill for the same motives," he says, "to make life easier for themselves. If the insane person appears to kill without reason, it is because we don't know enough of his history" (178-9). The difference between the two lies in their attitude toward the consequences. The sane go to pains to avoid them, the insane do not, because they think they're doing right.

In the light of such an explanation Miss Alfonse, once tried for a despicable crime, seems the likely suspect. Except she is drowned, apparently accidentally, while trying to escape across the lake with $1,000 concealed on her person. To conclude the investigation, in its traditional fashion, Prye assembles all the remaining characters at a meeting. It is there that Mary Little condemns herself. "They," the forces of justice, told her to kill her husband and the woman who tempted him. Miss Alfonse's death has its own justice to it, since she was partly an accessory in the murder of Tom.

As the summary indicates, *The Weak-Eyed Bat* is one of Millar's most traditional novels. Tone, characters and plot are exactly what we expect from the work of the first-rate "baffler" who has studied her predecessors in the art of mystery writing. There is even a ritual dinner party at the end of the story so that new romances may bloom and the sleuth can fill in the details to complete the solution of the puzzle. At the same time, though, there is a less than neat fit of content to form. For one thing the extensive criminal motive in the summer colony nearly undermines comedy. Besides Mary Little's derangement, which seems to belong to another world, there is Joan Frost's kleptomania and nymphomania, as well as the unrevealed sources of Miss Alfonse's crime before the story opens. Even Miss Emily, the observer of life in the summer place, has traits suggesting abnormality. It is she who is referred to by the book's title—a weak-eyed bat whom the sun never tempts to leave the close walls of her habitat. As Prye's remarks on insanity indicate, criminality may be structured into character. Appropriately he adds to that categorization of criminal behavior the observation that the middlemen between the sane and the insane are the most dangerous. Though they may be a bit odd, they will pass as normal to most people, until a shock acts as a detonator, setting them off on a crime to which conscience and social controls offer no obstacle (p. 179). According to this explanation any one of the assorted characters in the novel might be a middleman, even Prye himself.

Regardless of the gap between form and suggestion of content in *The Weak-Eyed Bat* the classic detection story still maintains the dominance of reason. The criminal acts occur beyond the narrative focus so that they can be reported in a controlled way, just as the description of madness is related in the voice of a detective trained in clinical observation. Moreover, the comic tone depending upon recognition of the incongruity between expected roles and actual behavior sustains, in this case, the notion that the world is amenable to rationality. That implication was soon to disappear from Millar's fiction.

After completing the three novels featuring Prye, Millar proceeded to loosen the detection story form to permit first-hand accounting of the irrational sources of crime. *The Iron Gates*, published in 1945, illustrates this development in a case of Inspector Sands'. The novel first gives attention to Lucille Morrow, the second wife of Andrew Morrow. Andrew's first wife, Mildred, died a murder victim in a Toronto park sixteen years before. Lucille experiences a horrifying dream of Mildred's death. The terror of the dream reinforces Lucille's feeling that she is an outsider in the Morrow house. The children of the first marriage are cool to her, especially Polly who eagerly anticipates her own marriage as a way of leaving the uncomfortably forced relationship with her step-mother. Andrew's son Martin already on his own, so to speak, as the successful literary editor of the *Toronto Review* is less competitive, but hardly warm. Andrew's sister Edith also lives in the home, often acting as a peace maker to sustain her imprecise position.

Lucille's unease continues an entire day while the rest of the family, except for Edith, are off to meet Polly's fiance. A train wreck at which they help recover the injured delays their return, and when they do arrive at the Morrow home Lucille is beside herself with anxiety. The following day she disappears. She has received a package, contents unknown, and shortly afterwards fled into the snow, taking no belongings, not even a coat. The mysterious departure so defies explanation that Andrew tells Edith the motives must be unconscious:

People aren't always capable of making sense.... There are forces—forces in the mind.... Look, Edith. See, it's like a jungle, the mind, dark and thick, with a million little paths that the light never reaches. You never know the paths are there until something pops out of one of them. Then, Edith, you might try to trace it back looking for its spoor and tracks, and you go so far, but the path is too twisted, too lightless, soundless, timeless.... (50).

Given such circumstances the search for Lucille and the cause of her disappearance seems to require the professional conduct of Inspector Sands of the Toronto Police. The case is a fortuitous assignment for Sands, since he worked on Mildred's murder and had been unable to allay his sense of frustration with facts that had pointed to her death as the result of a chance encounter with a person or persons unknown. As he conducts his search for Lucille, Sands revives the details of the earlier case, and the Morrow family further reveals the uneasy life they have also been living for the past sixteen years.

Lucille is found quickly, deranged but alive in a downtown hotel. She is placed in a hospital, while Sands continues his investigation to determine what provoked her flight. Before he can enter the jungle undergrowths of motive he establishes an external cause: someone has been methodically trying to drive Lucille over the brink of sanity. The package delivered to her on the day of flight contained a human finger; the man who delivered it has been murdered. At this point in the narrative Millar introduces a rapid shifting among perspectives on Lucille's condition. Her subjective mind is presented in response to a nurse, in scenes of interrogation with Sands, and in receipt of Edith's thoughts on her situation contained in a letter. Meanwhile, the objective events of the story present the findings of police investigation. Thus, there is effective coverage of all the puzzling features as they can be seen by police routine and by movement along the twisted paths of the mental jungle.

Soon the plot to destroy Lucille succeeds. She is driven to try to escape from the hospital and dies in the attempt. To Sands it is evident murder. Continuing his investigation he begins to merge police empiricism and imaginative consideration of the minds of the Morrows, finding the spoor and tracks leading him back sixteen years into the suppressed events surrounding Mildred Morrow's death. Evidence, both material and testimonial, attests to a love affair between Andrew and Lucille beginning long before Mildred's death. The material evidence is a diary whose entries indicate that Lucille had cultivated a friendship with the wife of the man she coveted and patiently waited for the chance to use the friendship in order to lure Mildred to her death. The plan devised at the command of Lucille's unconscious indeed led along timeless, concealed paths. Andrew has found the diary, which Lucille must have periodically reread at the insistence of her haunted mind, and contrived out of rage and some shared sense of guilt the anguishing punishment of a mental breakdown. To conceal the workings of his "justice" Andrew also killed Edith, along with the man who delivered the ominous package containing a finger Andrew had collected at the train wreck. He caused also the death of a patient in the mental hospital who became the accidental victim of his campaign of terror. Andrew's vengeance is complexly motivated. Besides his guilty love and rage at its consequences, he harbors in his mind an embittered idealism derived from excessive introspection about the inadequacy of his medical talent to preserve life, and a misogynous resentment of the women he believes have managed his life. He certainly spoke well when he described the motives that defy the common sense of daily reality.

To represent a world driven by such hidden forces Millar ironically varies the gothic formula—love conquers all—to show the irrational drives associated with sexuality directing ingenuity and reason to destroy the hated obstacles to emotional gratification. Focusing directly upon the characters possessed by irrational needs she makes their minds the primary reality of the novel. The detective figure is no longer permitted the privilege of comic dominance in the story, while his rituals of exposition and summation are reduced to instrumentalities in scenes that allow characters to portray themselves.

Millar's progressive effort to revise generic convention to permit an accounting of the psychological sources of criminal evil is further illustrated by a book that appears to have been especially the result of her consideration of the possibilities of gothic formulation. *Do Evil in Return* opens with the representation of a constellation of lives subjectively interacting. Dr Charlotte Keating, a competent physician, tries to organize her life through detachment in professional work and acceptance of a categorical separation of personal feelings that is necessary for her to continue a love affair with a married man. Charlotte's receptionist, Miss Schiller, has decided views on proper behavior that the world is always disappointing. She is given to self-righteousness and back pains. Lewis Ballard, Charlotte's lover, expresses old-fashioned ideas about women, despite his affair. To some degree, then, each character is controlled by the artificial values of society, and each experiences the control as constraint. This extends also to Violet O'Gorman who comes to Charlotte and explains that she is pregnant because she rebelled against a stultifying life with one night of desperate romance.

Violet intrigues Charlotte, the more so when she dies an apparent suicide. She visits Violet's step-uncle Voss, with whom Violet was staying, and becomes associated with Lieutenant Easter, acting as the unofficial co-investigator of Violet's death. Soon investigation becomes more than an act of generalized sympathy. Charlotte is threatened with blackmail and assault by Voss and a friend, and she finds her lover Lewis behaving curiously about her interest in Violet. Predictably the frank and open relationship Charlotte has with Easter begins to supplant the feelings she had for Lewis, especially since she must continue to pay professional visits on Gwen, Ballard's wife.

Within *Do Evil in Return* there are interesting examples of criminality directly related to engender a sense of involvement on the reader's part. The first appear in presentations of Voss, Violet's step-uncle, and Eddie O'Gorman, her husband. They visit Charlotte and try to blackmail her with such crudeness that they seem to embody elemental greed. They claim Violet's visit to the doctor helped send her to her death, and that Charlotte's "friend" will surely help her pay to prevent the police from hearing about it. The scheme of blackmail is so unreasonable that it is frightening. In an attempt to act positively against it Charlotte visits the shoddy Voss house where she finds Mrs. Voss beaten and evidence that in a fight with Voss and Eddie another man has died. Charlotte maintains her professional manner, reminding herself that she owes the unlucky residents of the street some tolerance and understanding. But they deserve no more than that. They are sleazy, small-minded crooks. Their weaknesses are infuriating, not pitiable, because their behavior cannot really be explained as the result of environment or any other external circumstance. Without redeeming traits, Voss and Eddie O'Gorman are incarnations of evil on a small scale.

On the larger scale is Gwen Ballard. It is she who reveals herself to be the murderer of Violet, since Violet was pregnant with the child Lewis conceived with her on an out-of-town trip about which he had lied to both Gwen and Charlotte. After Violet's death, Gwen also killed Eddie and Voss and hid their bodies in Charlotte's garage to implicate her in their death as punishment for the affair Gwen had long known about. Gwen reveals also that with the logic of madness she had chosen Charlotte as her physician in order to foster uneasiness and guilt. The ingenious schemes are all to keep Gwen's home intact as the place where she reigns emotionally over her man as she had done when a youthful belle.

Gwen Ballard's actions are no more amenable to easy explanation than are Voss and Eddie O'Gorman's, or for that matter Lewis Ballard's. In the conclusion of the novel he shows himself submissive to Gwen, trapped by his guilt and by social convention. It becomes clear he could never have left Gwen and lived with Charlotte in a way that would permit them to integrate their lives. Categories such as love and hate can be offered as labels for motive in *Do Evil in Return*, but only if they are applied in the complexity of neurosis. The constellation of the characters' interconnected lives is predacious, Charlotte Keating's present world dysfunctional. It can never become harmonious or provide objects appropriate to her subjective feelings. The only satisfactory action for her to take is to leave that world behind, as the relationship she is developing with Lieutenant Easter promises to make possible.

Yet, one has nagging doubts. The evil is too extensively diffused through everyday life to allow the belief that the love of a good man might free Charlotte Keating. That love could conquer all is precisely the problem, as the symbiosis of the Ballards illustrates, and the damaged characters from all social strata suggest the idea that anywhere along the mental paths concealed by the surface of ordinary life lies a potentiality for pathology.

Acknowledging pervasive irrationality as her subject Margaret Millar had to produce a narrative informed by that irrationality. First, she began to alter the narrative patterns of the detection story. Then, she began to work with the possibilities of the gothic, which offers a set of developed means to convey the anxiety in personal relationships. However, the modern gothic has its own severe limitations: a burden of simplistic ideology about feminine salvation through masculine protection. Millar obviously found that unpalatable as well as inadequate for serious presentation of her conception of the complex fate inherent in human psychology. So she had no choice but to apply her imagination to rethinking the premises of the mystery narrative.

In her rethinking Millar was not led to abandon the received forms entirely, because latent within them is an insight she believes to be profoundly true: the family generates criminal psychology.

Centering so consistently as they do on crime in domestic settings both the detection and the gothic story contain an incipient portrayal of the bourgeois family's system of repression and guilt. Traditional conventions of narrative, however, reduce the conflict of feelings generated within the family to the material of a puzzle drained of the anxiety and ambivalence of love-hate feelings. Thus neutralized, domestic criminality becomes, through stress on a detective's clever unraveling of a web of externalized events (the means and opportunity for murder), and by addition of wit and characterization suitable to comedy, entertainment hardly any longer suggesting its psychological sources. While gothics lack the comic dimension of classic detection stories and envelop the puzzle in an atmosphere with emotional significance, the gothic psychology is also neutralized. Motive simplified as greed or closely channeled hatred in detection and gothic stories appears to be entirely individual, rather than an impulse possibly shared by others living in the family system. Crime arising in socially shared settings, thus, becomes the aberrational acts of single maladjusted persons. Discovery of their attacks on victims, and the exposure of their personal guilt reestablishes the community's presumed state of harmony and in the process confirms the value of the social system that creates the cultural complex of the family.

Within such confirmative novels lies another story that is perhaps available to readers' fantasies but is never allowed to surface, except as it may provide clues to the detective. Jan Cohn reports that no less a writer than Mary Roberts Rinehart was well aware of the workings of parallel stories. In her biography of Rinehart, *Improbable Fiction,* Cohn explains that after writing her first novels Rinehart became aware that her formula consisted of a surface narrative and a "buried story," often concerning unsatisfactory marriage, that is presented through the implications of explanatory clues and suggestive references. The underlying story fleshes out Rinehart's fiction by giving characters greater dimension, their feelings and actions increased intensity, but the emotionally charged secondary stories are never laid open to readers.[14] Rinehart must have sensed that the "buried story" threatened her primary narrative. Once brought to the center of the novel for examination it would seize attention and transform a tale of suspense into an exploration of the psychology of domestic combat.

Rinehart's formula provides a convenient way to interpret the major accomplishment of Millar's canon, for the "buried story" of tensions within the institutional forms of domestic intimacy has surfaced. Inverting generic priorities Millar reduces the criminal puzzle's importance. In the categorical trinity necessary to the explanation of crime detectives usually concentrate on the objective realities—means and opportunity. In Millar's revision motive becomes primary, and as both occasion and subject of the novel it requires techniques that will probe the subjective consciousness of characters. Consequently Millar's narratives represent sexual enmity, the competition for love, and the forms of violence these drives produce. The fictional world where they are dynamic forces cannot confirm order. Where the tales of detection conclude with ritual affirmation of the control of reality by reason, and gothics close with the assurance of love's transformation of distress, Millar's book *The Iron Gates* ends with Inspector Sands leaving the Morrow house to enter a world where knowledge and feeling provide little consolation:

He stood on the veranda for a moment and looked across the park where the phallic points of the pines were thrust toward the sun. He felt outside time, naked and frail and percipient. Evergreens and men were growing toward decay. Time was a mole moving under the roads of the city and imperceptibly buckling the asphalt. Time passed over his head in a thin gray rack of scudding clouds, as if the sky had fled away and its last remaining rags were blowing over the edge of the world (191).

The imagery describes an environment where the constructions of culture—the plantings of the park, its roads—give apparent shape to nature but cannot suppress or contain its force: sexuality, represented in the trees, pursues its own end like the burrowing mole. Sands' epiphany confirms powerlessness. In the realm of human psychology, the ultimate referent of the imagery, primal drives issue in refractory behavior violating the norms of culture, and the source of the behavior is organic nature. An overlay of inventions such as family contend with nature for control of a person. The locale of their contest is the mind. There is where the schemes are devised to permit the eruption of forbidden feelings, where primal needs are invested with a shape to give them social acceptability. There, too, is where the frustration of desire and distress at the loss of its object creates the necessity to transform the experience of reality.

Appropriation of the role of an agent of justice, as in the cases of Mary Little, Andrew Morrow and Gwen Ballard is one psychic invention frequently available to Millar's characters. The grandest accomplishments of mental dissembling occur, though, in the minds of Birdie Loftus of *Vanish in an Instant* and Helen Clarvoe, protagonist of *Beast in View*. The narrative of the first of these novels is largely presented through the investigative steps followed by Eric Meecham, an attorney who has been retained to represent Virginia Barkley, accused of the murder of a lover. Virginia's mother, the possessive Mrs. Hamilton, seems at first to dominate the story as she has her daughter's life. We enter the story when Mrs. Hamilton sets about to use her will to free Virginia. The shocking means she employs is payment to the terminally ill Earl Loftus for a confession to the murder. Since the motive Earl alleges in his confession is so slight—he thought he would rid the world of a third-rate crook—Meecham burrows into Earl's past, discovering the tragedy of his alcoholic mother, a failed marriage, and an unusually personal relationship between Earl and his landlady, Mrs. Hearst. Unraveling the strands Meecham establishes that Earl's estranged wife, Birdie, was the mistress of the murdered man, and because of jealousy his killer. Moreover, in another role she is also the oddly maternal Mrs. Hearst who nurses and cares for Earl to the extent of providing him details for his false confession.

The presentation of Birdie's multiple identities achieves effect in two ways. First by the shift in narrative concentration from the account of dominance and rebellion in the relationship of Mrs. Hamilton and her daughter Virginia to factual revelations of Birdie as vamp, young wife and surrogate mother. Secondly, effect is enhanced because while the truth about Birdie emerges through the agency of detective investigation, it surprises less as the solution to a criminal puzzle than as a manifestation of the incredible capacity of the human mind to devise multiple versions of the self.

Millar's fascination with the ways people become alternate selves has its consummate expression in the splendid story of Helen Clarvoe, *Beast in View*. Thirty years of age, generally considered to be odd, Helen has confirmed general opinion by leaving the home of her mother and brother Douglas after the death of her father to live reclusively in a resident hotel. As her story begins, Helen has been receiving annoying phone calls from Evelyn Merrick, a childhood acquaintance. The narrative concentrates closely upon Helen as she enlists the help of Paul Blackshear, her attorney, in getting to the bottom of Evelyn's plot against her. Seeking to learn more of Evelyn, Paul visits a charm school and several artists' studios where Evelyn has been seen. Gradually he constructs a portrait of her as a gratuitously evil meddler who harasses many people besides Helen with her viciously insinuating phone calls. As Evelyn extends her campaign of vilification to Helen's mother, we get a picture of the Clarvoe family. The weak Mrs. Clarvoe refuses reality, including the fact that Douglas' brief marriage to Evelyn Merrick was annulled because he is homosexual.

At this point the narrative opens out beyond Blackshear's perspective to plumb the Clarvoe family relationships. The late Mr. Clarvoe, it appears, was incapable of understanding Helen's shy personality. During a humiliating evening at a dance she had hidden in the lavatory but told her father she had been a success dancing with the boys. When he discovered that she lied, he collected his anger and contempt at her failure into a devastating declaration: "Your punishment, Helen, is being you, and having to live with yourself" (97). For her part, Mrs. Clarvoe had expressed her feeling about Helen by remarking what a pity it was she had not had a daughter like Evelyn Merrick. For Helen these sentences embody the pain she feels in the family circle; even as an adult the very words are fresh in her mind.

While Helen relives her agony, her mother creates new misery in an exchange with Douglas. She reports to him the call from Evelyn, vainly planning a "cure" for his sexual preference with the aid of all the ignorant cliches. Douglas attempts suicide, fails and then accidentally kills himself in a fall. For a brief while the story assumes gothic form. Paul's concern for Helen's plight verges on love to which she shows signs of response. Thus invested with emotion, Paul's task as detective seems a champion's race to rescue the distressed woman. The suspense of imminent conflict between champion and nemesis heightens in two chapters closely related to Evelyn Merrick. In one the narrative for the first time provides direct portrayal of Evelyn Merick by entering her consciousness during an evening's trouble-making which includes a telephone call to Mrs. Clarvoe informing her that Helen works as a call girl. The second chapter directly focused on Evelyn objectively presents Paul interviewing her. Evelyn is so oblivious to criminal events, so unguarded and direct, that Paul concludes the split in her personality is complete.

In a grand reversal the rising tempo of a race to rescue Helen Clarvoe collapses with the dramatic revelation that it is Helen herself who suffers schizophrenia. The narrative that had carefully sustained the autonomy of the two parts of Helen finally merges in representation of her speaking with both of her voices in a bitter dispute that concludes in the murder/suicide of Helen Clarvoe at the hand of "Evelyn Merrick."

In conjunction with Margaret Millar's other stories of the mind's reaction to stress in affectional relationships, *Beast in View* demonstrates that she has accepted the idea that the great detective of modern times is Sigmund Freud. Millar is not a Freudian in the sense that she adopts Freudian theory as the armature of her fiction. She does share, however, the psychoanalyst's dedication to exploration of the secrets concealed within the mind and the conviction that fate originates in the conflicts between an individual's needs or desires and the repressive control exercised upon these instinctual expressions within the family setting. Thus, Helen Clarvoe, frustrated in her need for love has recreated herself as the preferred Evelyn Merrick, and, with the psychic logic that provides for the astonishing turn of the plot, she has undertaken a vendetta against those who denied Helen love.

Devotion to narrating the mind's secrets offers an author various possibilities for development of the mystery, including the creation of detective as analyst preferred by Millar's husband, Ross Macdonald. Millar's own choice, however, is to direct attention upon the neurotic or psychotic personality, leaving the detective figures in the shadows as instruments of plot. Before the readers' eyes characters act out their fantasies of dominance and submission, while incidents of plot serve to strip away rationalizations by offering new perspectives upon the mad players so that details will combine, as in a diagnosis, to link behavior with its source. This is not to say that Millar's fiction is constituted from psychiatric anecdote or case study, though it has the same fascination. The verisimilitude of the texts enacts rather than reports the obtrusion of irrational inner life into external circumstances. In contrast to the effect of such rationalistic forms of prose as the case study, or the classic detective story, Millar novels give an unsettled feeling. True, the plot will be resolved by the final reversal or revelation, and readers can experience the familiar pleasure of literary closure. Perhaps also they will be gratified by a sense of knowledge acquired, for in their position of observation they are due the pleasure other tales will reserve for the detective. But there is a bothersome sense of identification and involvement that is not easily quelled. In European-American culture we are so well-acquainted with the paradigm of psychology derived from Freud that it has become one of nearly everybody's assumptions about reality. With such reinforcement Millar's stories inevitably excite recognition. Like Inspector Sands we know the motives of crime are not strictly individual, that lodged in our minds are secrets that differ from the criminal's only in the degree of influence they have over our destiny.

Were Millar less engaged by the mysteries of character her craft would be devoted to the construction of plots that would interest exclusively for their own sake, and her ability to represent the sinister in ordinary circumstances would offer the controlled pleasure of a diversion. In short, the artifice of fiction would be an end in itself. But since Millar's work, taken as a whole, resonates with our cultural assumptions and stimulates identification, the reader tends to get preoccupied with meaning. Of course no author could be displeased by the tendency of her audience to find news about life in her novels. Nevertheless every professional author knows it is good writing, not life, that makes good stories. From conception to execution a novel is the result of a series of interdependent decisions about technical matters. These decisions must be recovered by criticism, because they are the ultimate vehicle of meaning.

Within Millar's texts the localized technical feature that first impresses is the author's compelling detail. Consider *How Like An Angel*. This story of the private eye Joe Quinn's search for the whereabouts of Patrick O'Gorman opens with Quinn coming upon the religious cult of True Believers numbering among its adherents Brother Tongue of the Prophets, Sister Blessing of the Salvation, Brother Behold the Vision, Brother Crown of Thorns, Brother Light of the Infinite, Brother of the Steady Heart, Sister Karma, Brother Faith of the Angels, Sister Contrition, the inevitable Master, and Mother Pureza who came out of the fleshly world with sufficient wealth to sponsor the group's patient wait for ascension to Heaven. There is an element of the absurd in figures who take on such ponderous names when they convert, as well as in the weaknesses they display—Sister Blessing entertains a wish for the comforts of fluffy slippers and bath towels. In that regard the True Believers could be ridiculed as California cultists so often are by the rest of us. But Millar refuses the stereotype.[15] In her presentation of the cult characters speak and act as people struggling to express the sublime aspirations for which ordinary speech, even in a community of true believers, will never be adequate, and because they speak without interference from some superior narrative voice their sincerity is unquestioned. Indeed, the sympathy Millar creates by the fullness of presentation makes the symbolically named sisters and brothers as available to understanding as the counterparts we know bearing such names as Sister Mary Joseph or Brother Francis Paul.

As it turns out in the story the descriptions of the True Believers also provide a functional contrast with the secular world. When Quinn investigates the disappearance of O'Gorman he finds the family and acquaintances reluctant to help. Motivated by the wish for respectability some hope to evade knowledge, others to conceal murder and fraud. In flight from his own complicity in the tawdry shams Patrick O'Gorman, on the model of other Millar characters, has withdrawn into an alternate, ever-silent, self who came to live among the True Believers under the ironic name of Tongue of the Prophets. In Millar's tale the cult that in other hands might have been only material for sarcasm becomes a suggestive source of themes to enrich the story of a private eye's sounding the depths of concealed crime.

Discussion of Millar's careful rendering of plausible details must not fail to consider also the use she makes of reference to ethnic conflict in her California novels. For instance, investigation of the causes of a young woman's nightmare in which she foresees her own death (*Stranger in My Grave*) is conducted by Steve Pinata, an orphan of Mexican parentage. Pinata eventually helps to explain the young woman's state of terror as the consequence of a complex scheme of false representations following upon her mother's shame over conceiving her child with a Mexican lover. Anglo hostility toward Mexicans is equally prominent in *Beyond This Point are Monsters*, a novel in which ethnic prejudice at first appears to be part of a straight-forward explanation for the disappearance and presumed death of Robert Osborn, only to be displaced by an accounting of Robert's fate that shows generalized ethnic antagonism served to divert attention from the secret guilt of a family crime. Thus, the prejudice is all the more disturbing; bigotry is so familiar that it constantly threatens the possibility of genuine knowledge.

A Stranger in My Grave and *Beyond This Point are Monsters* use detail of California race relations first of all to satisfy the requirement that the text should seem to refer to some reality other than itself. For that matter the appearance of conformity to extra-literary actuality is a basic explanation for the presence of all sorts of information about setting, the appearance of characters, and their behavior, not only in Millar's works but in all fiction within the broad boundaries of realism. On this level the aim is to create sufficient density to make the story seem plausible. The elemental appeal of believable detail makes it possible for some writers to lay into their texts well-researched data about the sights of distant localities and exotic behaviors, while other writers encourage imaginative participation in their tales by reporting the precise layout of the streets that typify the settings we ourselves live in. Somewhere in between lies Millar's creation of San Felice. At the beginning of her publishing career she specified her native Ontario, and the city of Toronto where she attended university, as the sites of her stories. These were adequate enough to provide the stories some place to happen without requiring Millar to give setting more than minimal attention. San Felice, however, represents an attempt to create a fictional setting for her more recent novels that will suggest relationship to other places of its type. San Felice seems to be located in the same part of California as Millar's home city of Santa Barbara, and the choice of its name that recalls the Spanish mission background of the state without specifying an actual city allows Millar to add a nearly symbolic dimension to her stories.

Readers can find the religious community in *How Like an Angel* or the evidence of California culture in other works intrinsically satisfying in the same way as Raymond Chandler's representation of the incongruous associations of sleaze and opulence in Los Angeles of the 1940s, or Ross Macdonald's revelation of meretricious contemporary Southern California. Still, social reference does not complete the function of Millar's detail, any more than it does Chandler's or Macdonald's. At their best the particulars of Millar's descriptions assume the function of units in a coded message from the characters' inner being. For example, Lucille Morrow's estrangement from husband and family in *The Iron Gates* first becomes manifest through the description of a morning's routine in the household. Her husband's habitual inability to locate a scarf seems to reassure her of the household's normality. Gradually, though, the guilt symbolized in Lucille's dream of the night before arises in barely controlled anxiety when Andrew leaves the house without saying goodbye. She looks down at the memo pad she meant to use for planning menus and sees that she has drawn caricatures of Andrew's first wife. Absentmindedly she burns holes in the eyes with her cigarette. In this opening chapter the book's whole is adumbrated through concentration on details of mundane life that overlay the life beneath its surface like the ice on a Canadian lake. Similar illustrations can be found in each of Millar's novels; each shows the mark of her craft in providing the elemental appeal of a plausible reality at the same time as the characters, their manners, and their habitats unobtrusively reinforce the dynamics of plot.

The impressive integration of localized details in Millar's fiction is matched on a structural level by the merger of two constituent parts of the texts, one concerning the investigation into criminal events, the other revealing subjective psychology.

The investigation, undertaken in the novel's present time, begins in the world we assume is natural. Its events occur chronologically in the context of an historical and material reality the significance of which can be apprehended by inferential reasoning and communicated in familiar language. This is the reader's native region. The laws governing it we assume will apply everywhere. The second part of the fictional structure defies natural time; in it the past remains vividly present to force reality into patterns of privatized meaning that emerge as bits within the initially dominant story of investigation. The bits are evidence from a submerged reality implying the existence of a mode of experience that cannot be naturalized. As these bits become intelligible as clues the narrative dramatically begins to represent the "alien" experience by acquiring the properties of its abnormal subject. Time becomes plastic so that causes may be revealed after their effects, and the plot twists and reverses in agreement with the movement characteristic of the mind's subconscious efforts to govern facts. As the novel concludes in presentation of solution to a criminal problem, the structural relationship of the narrative completes an inversion. The emergent plot of subjective psychology prevails over the story of criminal investigation, its revelations reaching backward to enforce reconsideration of the entire narrative.

The masterful unity of Millar's art can be observed in the fact that this description of the structural dynamics of texts has a counterpart in the psychological model we have already seen to be present in her fiction. The antecedent convictions Millar has about the mechanisms of human psychology have asserted themselves as the premises for key technical choices she makes in construction of narrative.

Typically we experience the reciprocity of premises and techniques in Millar's writing as tension between the expectations we have for the text and its impending revelations. Because of our residence in that natural world where investigation begins, and because of our literary experience, too, we are not particularly likely to anticipate Helen Clarvoe's being the beast in view. Nor when we are provided the circumstances of a court hearing on the subject of Robert Osborne's disappearance as the framework of *Beyond This Point Are Monsters* do we expect the eventual explanation to depend on a family environment that drove Robert as a young boy to patricide. Once we know that Helen is the beast, Robert the patricide the text assumes a fresh appearance.

Millar's technique of creating the pull of subjective plot against the predictable form of the convention story depends on her use of narrative perspective. The novels rarely open with the focus upon the character whose motives will be revealed as the cause of the central problem. Instead narration seems to circle around, relating scenes that involve or report each of the characters responding to the others, without settling upon a normative perspective. The most familiar narrative contract between author and audience distinguishes between readers and characters within the novel, granting the former the most comprehensive view of truth in the book. Even in the classic detection story the readers are at least companions, if not equivalents in reasoning power, of the sleuth and, therefore, considerably more privileged than characters in the tale whose access to the elements of the puzzle and its solution is restricted by limited wit, as in the case of the comic sidekick, or their lack of familiarity with the evidence. In Millar novels the absence of a controlling narrative voice leaves the reading audience with no better basis for determining what is real, before the plot takes its last turns, than any of the observers within the book. In this way we are encouraged to reflect with Inspector Sands on the possibility that the world, as well as a text, is based upon elemental forces ever-present in the mind.

The goal of creating narrational means for the exposure of subjective plot gives us the technical reason that Millar abandoned the preeminent figure of a detective after the novels about Paul Prye.

It explains, too, why the issues of identity and transformation of roles arise so regularly in her subsequent books.

To date Margaret Millar has published eighteen novels that can be classified as crime and mystery fiction, three non-criminous psychological novels,[16] an amusing idyll about a precocious young girl entitled *It's All in the Family,*[17] and a personal account of her experiences and pleasures bird watching in her wooded canyon near Santa Barbara.[18] Among the writers of popular fiction in her generation Millar's production is respectably average.

What is not average is the concern she has shown throughout her forty year career to devise techniques for the craft of mystery writing that will embody an epistemology relevant to events energized by the interplay of pre-rational psychology and the circumstances of ordinary experience. Selectively adapting the imperatives of the puzzle-centered detective story and the atmospheric gothic she has created a marvelously reflexive art in which a conception of the secretive human mind uses narrative techniques that are the most effective possible proof of their own premises.

Anyone concerned with the continued vigor of popular narrative must find Millar very impressive. A genre as heavily burdened with convention and repetition as popular crime and mystery fiction requires frequent innovation if it is to survive redundancy. Millar has done us the favor of taking the genre seriously enough to make its revision the project of her imagination and her art. There is no greater justification for critical approval.

Notes

[1]Editions used for this essay are included in the chronological list of Millar's crime and mystery writing below. Citations appear in the text.

1941 *The Invisible Worm,* New York: Doubleday, 1941.
1942 *The Weak-Eyed Bat,* New York: Doubleday, 1942.
1942 *The Devil Loves Me,* New York: Doubleday, 1942.
1943 *Wall of Eyes,* New York: Random House, 1943.
1944 *Fire Will Freeze,* New York: Random House, 1944.
1945 *The Iron Gates,* New York: Avon, 1974.
1950 *Do Evil in Return,* New York: Avon, 1974.
1952 *Rose's Last Summer,* New York: Random House, 1952.
1952 *Vanish in an Instant,* New York: Avon, 1974.
1955 *Beast in View,* New York: Avon, 1974.
1957 *An Air That Kills,* New York: Random House, 1957.
1959 *The Listening Walls,* New York: Random House, 1959.
1960 *A Stranger in My Grave,* New York: Avon, 1973.
1962 *How Like an Angel,* New York: Random House, 1962.
1964 *The Fiend,* New York: Random House, 1964.
1970 *Beyond This Point Are Monsters,* New York: Random House, 1970.
1976 *Ask For Me Tomorrow,* New York: Random House, 1976
1979 *The Murder of Miranda,* New York: Random House, 1979.

[2]*Books of the Herald-Tribune*, 20 July 1941, p. 9.

[3]*Books of the Herald-Tribune*, 22 February 1942, p. 18.

[4]*Books of the Herald-Tribune*, 9 August 1942, p. 13.

[5]*New York Herald-Tribune Book Review*, 16 November 1952, p. 24.

[6]*San Francisco Chronicle*, 28 July 1957, p. 22.

[7]*San Francisco Chronicle,* 14 June 1959, p. 30.

[8]*New York Times* 26 June 1955, p. 21.

[9]James Vinson, ed., *Contemporary Novelists*, 2nd ed. (New York: St. Martin's Press, 1976), pp. 952-54; John M. Reilly, ed., *Twentieth Century Crime and Mystery Writers* (New York: St. Martin's Press, 1980), pp. 1078-79. There is also a brief note on Millar in Chris Steinbrunner and Otto Penzler, eds., *Encyclopedia of Mystery and Detection* (New York: McGraw-Hill, 1976), pp. 287-88.

[10]"Gothic Novels," in *Handbook of American Popular Culture*, ed. M. Thomas Inge, vol. 2 (Westport, Conn.: Greenwood Pub. Co., 1978), p. 151.

[11]The idea of "improving upon" a popular genre is discussed in Tzvetan Todorov, "The Typology of Detective Fiction," *The Poetics of Prose* (Ithaca, N.Y.: Cornell University Press, 1977), pp. 42-52.

[12]Elsa J. Radcliffe, *Gothic Novels of the Twentieth Century: An Annotated Bibliography* (Metuchen, N.J.: Scarecrow Press, 1979), p. 1952.

[13]Julian Symons, *Mortal Consequences: A History from the Detective Story to the Crime Novel* (New York: Schocken, 1973), pp. 190-92.

[14]Jan Cohn, *Improbable Fiction: The Life of Mary Roberts Rinehart* (Pittsburgh: Univ. of Pittsburgh Press, 1980), pp. 219-221, 233.

[15]For a contrast between Millar's handling of the cult and the style of other writers see Symons, p. 191.

[16]*Experiment in Springtime*, New York: Random House, 1947.

The Cannibal Heart, New York: Random House, 1949.

Wives and Lovers, New York: Random House, 1954.

[17]*It's All in the Family*, New York: Random House, 1948.

[18]*The Birds and Beasts Were There*, New York: Random House, 1968.

Emma Lathen

"Emma Lathen" is the pseudonym of two women: Mary Jane Latsis and Martha Henissart. They also write as "R.B. Dominic." As they prefer that information about their lives not be revealed, no chronology can be given.

by Jeanne F. Bedell

When you have been in the banking business for as long as I have, you will learn that money has a very strange and powerful effect on human behavior.
John Putnam Thatcher in *Banking on Death*[1]

Modern psychology may give short shrift to the idea that love of money is the root of evil, but readers of Emma Lathen's detective stories know that it is invariably the motive for murder. In creating their detective, John Putnam Thatcher, senior vice-president and head of the trust department at the Sloan Guaranty Trust, economist Mary Jane Latsis and attorney Martha Henissart, who write as Emma Lathen,[2] have constructed a perfect focus for investigating both sophisticated financial chicanery and plain old-fashioned greed.

From her first novel, *Banking on Death* (1961) to her most recent, *Double, Double, Oil and Trouble* (1978), Lathen has followed a consistent and consistently successful pattern which introduces her audience to such diverse aspects of modern business as trust administration and oilfield construction. The novels, many with chapter titles using the terminology of the particular business being emphasized, open with brief descriptions of the power and activities of Wall Street. *A Stitch in Time* (1968) is typical of both techniques: set in a suburban hospital where a group of physicians have set up an illegal drug company to overcharge their patients for necessary medications, the novel begins with a chapter called "Medical History" and includes, among others, "Malignancy," "Deficiency," and "Graft." As "Graft" indicates, the titles are not arbitrarily chosen but reflect a significant aspect of plot development. Similarly, the comments on Wall Street serve to establish an atmosphere of money and power which is important for an understanding of both milieu and motivation:

Wall Street is the money market of the world and its outward trappings are plainly visible. Proud bastions rise from high priced curbs with glass walls, contemporary decor and pampered foliage to bespeak financial might. From Brooklyn to the Bronx whole armies of men and women are drafted to service Wall Street by carrying papers, typing letters and answering telephones....
In an era which puts a premium on visual communication, the face of Wall Street, is entirely satisfying (1).

But outward appearances, especially in detective fiction, are often deceptive, as Thatcher's musings remind the reader: "This cosmetic effect was misleading. Wall Street's power is not embodied in its profligate real estate, in its streams of myrmidons or even in its throbbing pulse of activity.... No, the real power on Wall Street lurked unseen behind this facade, in the hands of men who could make one telephone call and raise the price of steel."

The Sloan may be "too important to concern itself with, say, Christmas Savings Accounts" (*Banking*, 1), but Thatcher, who is a traditional, ratiocinative detective, recognizes the significance of detail. He solves his first case (although the word is never used in the novels) through a chance remark overheard at an airport and subsequent checking of airline schedule deviations during a blizzard. The same abilities which enable him to spot flaws in his subordinates' investment proposals—trained intelligence, board business experience and practical knowledge of human nature—underlie his skill in identifying murderers.

Thatcher's duties as a banker also provide the rationale for his involvement with crime: In *Banking on Death* he sets out to solve problems connected with disbursing a family trust; in *Sweet and Low*, as a member of the board of directors of the Dreyer Foundation, he is drawn into the activities of the Dreyer Chocolate Company, trading on the cocoa exchange, and two murders. His most unusual assignment, delivering $1.5 million in ransom money to an international terrorist organization, arises because of his presence in Zurich "reshuffling" European credits. The financial knowledgeability of both detective and criminals serves as the basis for complex plots with extensive political and social ramifications. But the financial is always paramount: Lathen is the only writer I know who uses revolution, nationalism and racism as red herrings!

Each novel deals with a specific and different business activity and each is similarly and traditionally structured with careful attention paid to the unobtrusive planting of clues and the development of a rational denouement. The opening description of Wall Street is immediately followed by introduction of a business crisis: rivalry between two Sloan divisions in *The Longer the Thread*; a lawsuit against a valued Sloan client in *Ashes to Ashes;* and the loss of $985,000 via a forged bill of lading in *Murder Against the Grain*. This technique effectively limits the circle of suspects without resort to geographical or social isolation. The action of *Double, Double* ranges from Zurich to Istanbul to Houston to London and a construction site on the North Sea, but the suspects are the principal participants or beneficiaries in negotiations for the construction of shore-based facilities for North Sea oil drilling.

Simultaneously investigating business problems and murder

and naturally concentrating on the financial activities of his suspects, Thatcher utilizes the expertise of his staff as well as that of outside experts. He cooperates closely with high ranking police officers who are always models of gentlemanly behavior and professional acumen. Occasionally, when sufficient evidence for arrest is unavailable, a trap is set for the criminal. These activities result in the apprehension of the murderer and restoration of fiscal sanity to the business involved. The last chapter is devoted to Thatcher's detailed explanation of crime and motivation.

And since money is the only motive for murder in Lathen's novels, Thatcher is uniquely qualified to expose it. In *Double, Double* he refuses to be distracted by kidnapping or terrorists and asks himself, "If you interpreted Macklin's drama in terms of standard operating procedure rather than poetic license, what did you have? An accounting record for the costs of crime" (195). In *The Longer the Thread* he discounts Puerto Rican nationalism and student revolutionaries to say that "the only change, after everything settled down, would be the sale of one garment factory at distress prices" (208). The original disruption of order in the novels is financial; therefore, restoration of order must include not only the capture of the murderer but the resolution of business problems and the continued operation of companies on sound fiscal bases.

Despite this lack of variety in structure and motivation, Lathen manages to sustain interest and create fresh situations to revitalize the formula. Careful meshing of background materials with plot development is important in preventing feelings of *deja vu*: intent on ice hockey or fast-food restaurants, the reader tends to forget obvious similarities in the novels.

II

Lathen's popularity[3] and her reputation as the finest living American author of classic detective fiction, however dependent they may be upon the skill with which she manipulates the traditional formula,[4] also reflect her genuine flair for comedy. Displaying, like her English predecessors Sayers and Christie, a talent for comedy of manners, Lathen possesses wit, a deft hand with verbal irony, and an ability to create comic characters. Mild social satire enlivened by wildly snowballing farcical scenes contributes to a comic atmosphere that is actually the distinguishing feature of her work

Unlike the traditional detective, Thatcher is not an eccentric; he is a distinguished, urbane executive in his early sixties.[5] Realistically, this is essential to Lathen's technique: Thatcher's position and the power he wields dictate his essential normality. Yet eccentric, exaggerated characters abound in Lathen's fiction, and especially important in establishing the comic atmosphere are Thatcher's own subordinates, whose individual foibles reinforce his superiority. Chief among these is Everett Gabler (Rails and Industrials), a melancholic, cantankerous conservative whose "wholehearted approbation" had been given to only two institutions: "The old Union Pacific (back in the days when a railroad was a railroad, by God) and Du Pont" (*Grain*, 49). Parsimonious to the point that his cables are nearly indecipherable ("One of his passions was testing the limits of the cable code"), Gabler is also a vegetarian with a weak stomach, an aspect of his character which provokes humorous incidents in several novels, most notably *When in Greece* where he is abducted by revolutionaries. Sure that a steady diet of Greek food will kill him, he poisons his captors with motion sickness pills and escapes. Perfect contrasts to Gabler are the sanguine Walter Bowman (Chief of Research), a man subject to "violent enthusiasms," and *bon vivant* Charlie Trinkham (Utilities), a bachelor with only two apparent interests: business and beautiful women. Thatcher's competent secretary, Rose Theresa Corsa, is "never excited about anything," maintains a calm, even phlegmatic, manner throughout every crisis and views his forays into crime as irritating disruptions of office routine. Solving murders is not, implies Miss Corsa, as important as completing the day's dictation. This admirable devotion to the Sloan's affairs, shared by all of Thatcher's subordinates, does not, however, extend to the bank's president, Bradford Withers. As president of a major financial institution Withers is unbelievable; as a comic creation he is superb. Withers' role is "largely ceremonial and, as such, ideally suited to a man whose outstanding characteristic was that he never saw what the trouble was " (*Overcome*, 5). Vast inherited wealth and extended absences from Wall Street—cruising on his yacht or enjoying some "fine shooting" in India—are his chief qualifications for his position. His interest in the bank centers on redecorating his office, arranging the staff Christmas party, and taking up John Thatcher's valuable time.

Each of these characters is so rigorously defined—one might almost say caricatured—by dominant personality traits that they resemble those in an Elizabethan comedy of humors. Melancholic Gabler, sanguine Bowman, and phlegmatic Corsa are obvious humors types, but numbers of others are characterized largely through specific peculiarities or obsessions: Withers is well-bred but stupid; Clarence Fortinbras in *Accounting for Murder* is "a *passionate* accountant"; and investment banker Tom Robichaus is memorable solely because of his frequent marriages and divorces. Such characters are clearly useful in the world of detective fiction where their predictability contributes to the development of a stable social order.

Just as Thatcher's civilized urbanity and intelligence set the standards by which other characters are judged, his views, along with Lathen's ironic commentary, define both social and business norms. Established norms are necessary in comedy and especially in comedy of manners which "ridicules the affectations of a particular society."[6] Lathen's obvious glee in describing social occasions from art shows to college reunions and her frequent commentary on American customs reveal her affection for the form. She writes, however, within a much less rigid social code than that of her English counterparts. Her world is basically upper class and affluent, and she values social *savoir faire*, but she is typically American in her emphasis upon the importance of hard work and making money. Competence, not birth, is the criterion by which she—and Thatcher—evaluate people. Lathen herself has commented on the "ultimate mystification" in Christie's novels: "What in the world do these people do, day in, day out?" The American reader, she suggests, cannot evaluate "normal English behavior" when he is confronted with a village like Chipping Cleghorn "where no single middle-class household seems to work for a living."[7]

A Place for Murder, the only one of Lathen's novels with an idyllic rural setting, illustrates her distinctly American attitudes:

Shaftesbury, Connecticut, is not suburban Connecticut. In Shaftesbury, there are not spirited struggles over four-acre zoning, no petitions for better commuter service, no interest at all in the local school system (which exists primarily to serve the needs of servants' children). Instead there is a sense of remote calm and plenty, a sense of spreading fields, and a sense of remote detachment from the business office... (15).

The isolated rural community so beloved by interwar English writers fails to attract Thatcher: "Unfortunately . . . a farm is a farm anywhere." Shaftesbury in autumn is described as "a riot of careful, tax-deductible delights" where Black Angus are valued as tax losses and gentleman farmers like Bradford Withers live in opulent ignorance. Withers' comment that few New Englanders know much about farming these days evokes Thatcher's amused reflection that "This would have surprised no financier except Bradford Withers... considering that New England farming has been unprofitable since 1870" (40).Viewing the Shaftesbury Grange with evident sarcasm, he thinks, "No doubt local cultivators, outfitted by Abercrombie and Fitch, gathered there frequently to discuss livestock" (p. 29). The inhabitants of this sheltered enclave of inherited wealth attract Thatcher no more than the place itself, attempting to arrange a property settlement for the imminent divorce of Withers's sister, whose husband has left her for the local dog handler, he must deal with quarrelling women, irate relatives, and, of course, Withers, whose infatuation with the owner of the local inn causes him to be a suspect in two murders. The solution to the murders is Lathen's final irony: because a potentially profitable business is being claimed as a tax loss and a farm manager is living above his income, Thatcher, who is *not* bored by discussions of "relative incomes in Shaftesbury" and *not* oblivious to the difficulties of a salaried man in an atmosphere of great wealth, identifies the murderer.

Thatcher has little respect for inherited wealth unless its possessor is an intelligent businessman. Withers' nephew, product of New England preparatory schools and Harvard, is depicted as nearly witless, a trait no doubt inherited from his uncle. In *The Longer the Thread*, Withers tells Thatcher, "Now John ... I've been reading this report about Puerto Rico and you'd be surprised at what's going on there. Why, they've kidnapped one of our customers! I don't think we should encourage that sort of thing" (144). This naivete is emphasized later when Withers offers his solution: "I would simply refuse to deal with these people," and Thatcher thinks, "Given the source, it was a reasonable attitude. Brad Withers, protected by money, position and privilege, often resorted to the stance he was advocating.... But reality on the beach of the Caribbean was a far cry from Brad Withers' dream world" (149).

Mocking the pretensions of rich adolescents who lack humility and humanity in *Come to Dust* and the extravagance of bored, wealthy women in *Accounting for Murder*, Lathen saves her praise for men like octogenarian Bartlett Sims who retains his business acumen and "come hell or high water or six inches of snow ... hauled himself into the office from Amagansett three days a week" (*Sweet and Low*, 10) and women like Lucy Lancer, wife of the Sloan's board chairman. With charm, intelligence and good sense added to great wealth, Lucy Lancer exercises her social skills to make the world pleasant and comfortable for all her associates. Thatcher's affection for Lucy makes her a natural criterion by which the reader evaluates other women and, especially, other wives: marriage, Lathen implies, is much like business and requires the same talents if it is to be successful.

Privilege without responsibility occasions some of Lathen's most biting irony. In *Murder to Go* Barton Ogilvie, scion of an old and influential Philadelphia family, poisons hundreds of customers of the fast-food chain Chicken Tonight in order to prevent a takeover of his poorly managed insurance firm and to retain his position as a "leading Philadelphia businessman." Ogilvie is presented to the reader in this way: "he thoroughly enjoyed the camaraderie of the

Jockey Club, where the owners mingled with members in an atmosphere of unobtrusive luxury and cushioned comfort, far from the run-of-the-mill two-dollar bettors. His place in this kind of world was as dear to Ogilvie as Southeastern Insurance; in many ways, they were one to him." Contemptuous of ordinary men and women, Ogilvie ignores the possible effects of mass poisoning and sets about to destroy the reputation and financial stability of Chicken Tonight. In a novel which devotes considerable attention to the difficulties faced by small businessmen and contains affectionate portraits of two of Chicken Tonight's franchisees, Ogilvie's megalomaniacal selfishness is evident. In this, he is a typical murderer. But he is also the representative of a particular class and attitude:

Upstairs, the Jockey Club was thronged. There were tanned, handsome men, mostly lean and fit from lives of sport, outdoor exercise and expensive living. Their women, all tastefully turned out, were also lean and fit.... Men and women alike ... had what Ogilvie felt was the unmistakeable hallmark of good breeding. He had been more affected by his wife's interest in stables than he knew. (63)

The last sentence is devastating. It is also extremely funny and serves effectively to distance both author and reader from Ogilvie's smug, enclosed world.

Lathen's frank admiration of money and power and her devotion to the capitalist economic system are essentially free of class bias. Although her approach and subject matter preclude inclusion of large numbers of characters from lower socio-economic brackets, she treats sympathetically those described. In *Ashes to Ashes*, set in Flensburg, a working-class district of Queens, her respect for the community's honest, hard-working citizens is evident: funeral director Francis Omara, truck driver Bob Horvath and A & P manager Sal Ianello are competent, experienced men, and Thatcher pays Ianello his ultimate compliment when he wonders if "Ianello has ever considered working for a bank" (85). In fact, Thatcher, who believes that "the upper echelon of the U.S. Government had lapsed into permanent insanity," takes comfort in competence wherever he finds it: he is impressed by the expertise of customs inspectors on the New York docks, the political commentary of a cab driver, and the undoubted talents of labor leader Annie Galiano.

Laconically commenting that "The Jockey Club at the Garden State Race Track embodied one form of togetherness. There are others," (*Murder Must Go*, 69), Lathen pinpoints one of her greatest triumphs. Despite the conservative political and economic views which inform her social commentary, her wide interests create a relatively open world and extend her sources of humor. She moves with ease from a church-sponsored Bingo party in Queens to a display of European gouaches at the Gary Museum of Modern Art and from a class reunion at an Ivy League college to the small, overcrowded apartment of secretary Tessie Marcus. Real estate speculators, hiking enthusiasts, and Turkish policemen share the stage with ambassadors, museum curators and Puerto Rican politicians. In her most amazing cultural cross-section in *Murder Against the Grain*, Thatcher works with Inspector Lyons of the New York Police Department and Mikhail Maseryan, a Russian troubleshooter one assumes to be a high-ranking official in the KGB.

In fact the Edgar-winning *Murder Against the Grain* shows Lathen at her best. Her wittiest and simultaneously her most compassionate book, the novel contains pungent social criticism, strong characterization, and several of Lathen's best set pieces of humor. The plot concerns U.S. grain trade with the USSR and the theft of $985,000 from the Sloan, which finds its attempts to recover the money frustrated by FBI investigations of the New Left, CIA consideration of a plot by the Russian government, and State Department insistence that *any* Sloan action will be bound to offend a foreign power. In one anarchic day Thatcher interviews farmer Homer Chuddely of Parched Creek, Iowa, who advocates sending farmers, not wheat, to Russia, and promoter Abe Baranoff, who is about to introduce to the U.S. public Plomsky's Otter Ensemble, a group that can "sing *The Volga Boatman*, dance a rousing mazurka, and assemble a three-stage rocket" (64). At the aquarium in the Brooklyn Botanical Gardens Thatcher's attempts to talk with Baranoff are interrupted by Plomsky's cries of "Smelt. Give me smelt" and "Here Mitya ... Bad Otter." He returns to the Sloan to be told that "The Cuban Navy is blockading the port of New York."

There is little wonder that Thatcher is delighted with the company of Maseryan, a "born worker." Ignoring the idiocies of their respective governments, the two men set out to discover who is responsible for the missing money. Lathen does not, however, resist the opportunities for humor such a relationship possesses. Thatcher takes Maseryan to lunch at the Bankers Club, "that Valhalla of capitalist hopes," and later, because of Masyeran's wish to view "al-i-en-ated youth," to a coffeehouse where the Russian is accused of having middle-class attitudes. Thatcher explains that the young man "only means that you're over thirty," but Maseryan smarts under the attack. The final, the funniest, interruption to their work comes when both men accompany a Russian trade delegation to Chipsies, Inc., an automated potato chip factory in Bridgeport, Connecticut. After an extensive tour of the factory, the guests are taken to the Chipsie Pub where they are offered such delights as "chippsburgers, chippslaw, chipps fu yung, tuna chip salad," steaks dipped in crushed chips and chocolate-chip cookies. The only appropriate comment comes from a member of the delegation: "after potato chip soup no one would want to defect" (135, 139).

Lathen also turns her satirical eye on the Russian Consulate, whose employees are terrified of Maseryan. Tongue-tied in his presence, they contribute only occasional platitudes to the conversation at a dinner party where he and Thatcher first meet: "Seeing a country that is not one's own is educational . . . . It teaches one to value one's own country," or, in a livelier vein, "The concerts in New York are excellent" (99-100). Maseryan confides to Thatcher that they are afraid he will report them for buying "high-fidelity sets on the installment plan" or listening to jazz music. He has, he says with disgust, been forced to drink Crimean brandy in Paris so that consular officials can prove their patriotism.

Witty as Lathen's social satire is, she further distinguishes *Murder Against the Grain* by the compassionate understanding shown the criminals—both before and after their identities are revealed. During their discussion of modern youth, Thatcher mentions to Maseryan that youth is "for love and communication"; he is distracted by the Russian's remarks about nihilism and forgets the subject. The author warns, "If he had been wiser, he would have pursued the subject of love and communication in a divided world" (115). Both the culprits are thieves and one of them is a murderer, but the victim is a blackmailer and the theft was planned to enable them to build a "new life," to escape from isolation and loneliness to love and companionship. Their apprehension costs the U.S. and Russian governments $18 million in "aid" to Mexico, and Thatcher, for one, wishes he had had no part in it.

Although Lathen's talent for farce is perhaps best displayed in *Murder Against the Grain,* it also forms the comic core of *Come to Dust, Ashes to Ashes* and *Death Shall Overcome.* What John Cawelti has called "comic chaos" and "comic anarchy"[8] are based upon a snowballing sequence of events which build from minor action to major reaction. In *Ashes to Ashes* the efforts of a small group of concerned parents to prevent the closing of St. Bernadette's Parochial School in Queens escalate into national importance when their leader is murdered and the proverbial outside agitators use the neighborhood as a base for demonstrations against the Church's stand on birth control. Media publicity attracts new groups to the once-quiet parish: the Metropolitan Council of Concerned Laymen arrives in a mini-bus to distribute literature, four "Bhagavad Catholics" clad in saris chant "Hare Krishna! Hare Rama! Get the Pill here!" while suburban housewives with placards picket the parish church. School lets out and dozens of children add their voices to the cacaphony of slogan-shouters. "Order," writes Lathen, "trembled in the balance. The New York City Independent subway system toppled it." Among the commuters emerging from the subway were

> several men simply plodding home after a long shift with pile drivers. All of them were fathers. One of them was the father of Jeanette Vertuno, a well-developed eighth grader. Jeanette was looking, with dawning interest, at the packet that the young man ... had thrust upon her. *Don't,* the leaflet urged Jeanette, *Don't Let Sex Hang You Up.*
>
> Dominic Vertuno was a man of few words. Around him priests, nuns, policemen, flower children, reformers, and Shorty Grimes were giving tongue.
>
> Mr. Vertuno swung (98).

In the ensuing melee, "all vignettes were engulfed by the maelstrom. There were placards and fists. There were nuns' habits and saris. And, from far away, there was the shrill scream of police sirens" (100).

Such farcical incidents demonstrate not only Lathen's talent for comic writing but also her understanding of the importance of order and social stability in detective fiction. Detached, controlled and unaffected by the emotional excesses of ordinary men and women, the detective is able to solve the crime whose commission unleased anarchic forces and to effect the restoration of social stability. Identification of a murderer is only a part of Thatcher's duties; as mentioned earlier, he must also oversee the restoration of economic prosperity. In Flensbuug he negotiates a settlement which will allow the building of a high-rise apartment building and substantially increase property values in the neighborhood and, at the same time, preserve the parochial school. Tradition *and* progress triumph through his efforts, and he thus not only restores but improves the social order.

Ending such anarchical disruptions obviously enhances Thatcher's stature. In *Death Shall Overcome* the proposed election of a black multi-millionaire to the New York Stock Exchange sets off a chain of events which threatens Wall Street itself: members of CASH (Colored Association of Share Holders) stage a singing kneel-in at the Sloan, plan a mass sale of Vita Cola shares to drive down its price and display their economic power, and mount a mass march on the Stock Exchange which leads to "pandemonium" on the floor. In *Come to Dust* a professional fund raiser disappears with, supposedly, a $50,000 bearer bond and the College Board scores of several hundred applicants to prestigious Brunswick College. The subsequent disruption in the lives of prospective students and their parents serves as the basis for the description of fast-spreading chaos and provides Lathen with one of her best opportunities for social satire:

the entire East Coast was up in arms.
    Embattled mothers paraded with placards: WHY MUST OUR CHILDREN PAY
FOR THE CRIMES OF ELLIOT PATTERSON? Irate fathers could not believe
Brunswick expected their sons to turn down perfectly good colleges in favor of
problematic acceptance by Brunswick. Particularly ... when the alternative to
college admission was the draft. A psychologist with a daily news column spoke
tellingly of the trauma caused by the effort to get into college. A sociologist ... said all
this would merely confirm youth's lack of faith in the older generation. Preserving
that faith was a parent's most sacred duty. To that end the parent must be unfailingly
reasonable, totally unbiased, open to cultural innovation and undismayed by
personal hostility. The sociologist did not explain how this was supposed to prepare
the young for a world that could be relied upon to display none of these characteristics
(80).

Differences between the generations form one of Lathen's
favorite subjects for satire: youth, she implies, is usually curable.[9] A
recent college graduate finds that "the facile judgments of the Delta
Kappa house at Brunswick seemed almost irrelevant when brought
to bear on the older generation" (*Dust*, 23). Her view of the
maturation process is traditional:

Sukey as a campus radical had appalled her father, dismayed her faculty adviser,
and terrorized her roommate. Sukey's mother, however, had ... remained
preternaturally placid. She had made one visit to SDS headquarters and noted the
large number of attractive young men. Without doubting Sukey's sincerity for a
moment, she had decided that nature, as usual, had found the shortest distance
between two points. The path was tiresome, of course. But a great deal less tiresome
than young couples throbbing sympathetically to Maeterlinck's *Blue Bird*, which
had been the path obligatory for nineteenth-century romantics (*Sticks*, 111).

In fact, revolutionaries among the young cause Lathen scant
distress; Puerto Rican student leader Prudencio Nadal, haranguing
workers at a garment factory, finds himself laughed off the premises
after he has tangled with experienced labor organizer Annie
Galiano.
    Marriage is a no doubt useful institution, but sex is overrated:
"Very few lost loves cast an enchantment as enduring as Polaroid"
(*Sweet and Low*, 11). "Sex," says Lathen, "is not the only outlet for
deep-rooted, life-shaping forces. There are also buying and selling."
Such contemporary concerns as identity and communication come
in for their share of mockery. And communication itself, whether
interpersonal or international, often draws barbed remarks: the
wife of a businessman who has disappeared is at a loss to explain
her husband's action: "I knew Elliot. I knew his every mood, his
every thought...." (*Dust*, 98). Thatcher refers to mass
communication media as "the tragedy of our time. The illusion of

refuge is gone. No comfortable sensations of security rise at the thought of Tahiti, the Himalayas, or Arabia Deserta" (*Overcome*, 115). Advertising comes in for its share of attention as Lathen cleverly juxtaposes television product advertising with a news broadcast detailing murder in the company being advertised. Public relations men, a species Thatcher detests, are uniformly inept, but Lathen is sensitive to the power of advertising: despite the well-publicized murder of two of its employees, the Dreyer Chocolate Company finds its new candy bar, Old Glory, a resounding success. American eating habits are gently mocked: Chicken Tonight offers for sale "cranberry wriggle and brandied onion rings," while one of its customers says, "how can you feed seventy-five youngsters without creamed chicken on toast?"

The pretentious and affected receive little sympathy: radical *cinema verite* producer Craig Phipps, whose films include such gems as *Incest*,"fifteen installments about life in parts of West Virginia that Jay Rockefeller would never see," and "*Foetus*, the frank-investigation-in depth of the eighth pregnancy of an unwed mother," is planning a new film, to be called *Greed*. At a cocktail party at the Metropolitan Museum of Art where an Etruscan vase insured for over a million dollars is on display, Phipps approaches Thatcher and his companion Dr. Umberto Mercado. He wishes to contrast Thatcher's "indifferent hands" with Mercado's reverent, humble handling of the vase. His comeuppance is quick: "I'm not an artist. I'm a capitalist," explains Mercado, adding that he is a doctor of electrical engineering from Rensselaer Polytech and makes cathode ray tubes for television sets. Thatcher is peeved to have been singled out to represent Greed, but Lathen's point is well made: the radical view of capitalists is no less mythical than its preconceptions about Italian sensitivity.

Politicians, whether American or foreign, come off little better than radicals, and while working women are treated with admiration, those who have abandoned responsibility in search of "identity" receive little respect. The breadth of Lathen's social satire extends from minor mockery of national insularities ("My God," says a Greek policeman discussing the name Owen Gifilian, "how do they keep from laughing out loud?" "Get on with the story, Triantaphillocopous," replies his superior) to extensive comment on American manners and mores.

With one exception the satire is light in tone. The picture of U.S. medicine given in *A Stitch in Time,* is, however, acidulous, both thematically and linguistically. Testimony during *Freebody v. Atlantic Mutual* reveals that during emergency surgery at Southport Memorial Hospital *seven* hemostatic clips were left in the body of aged millionaire Pemberton Freebody. The surgeon, pompous, arrogant and dictatorial Wendell Martin, sees no reason why *anyone* should be allowed to question his actions. Martin, who has a "positive genius for alienating people" and who has "never been guilty of considering any well-being but his own" (14), is understandably murdered. Thatcher's investigations reveal extensive incompetence, large numbers of unnecessary operations and possible criminal abortions at the hospital, in addition to the illegal drug company a group of physicians and a local pharmacist have formed to extract still more money from their patients. Even when confronted with criminal charges, one of the doctors is "still laboring under the delusion that ... the jury would realize that he had only been exercising his God-given right to benefit from the American system" (122). Lathen's indictment of the physicians is particularly damning because she introduces a young couple, Nancy and Gene Perkins, who are swamped with medical and drug bills. Positively portrayed, the Perkinses work continuously to meet their obligations: although Nancy's surgery is recent, she babysits at home, and Gene has a regular job, specific Saturday and Sunday jobs, and a nighttime job. Outside intervention cleans up the hospital situation, and the Perkinses' financial burden is relieved when Thatcher finds Gene a new and better paying position. But the picture of Southport remains, and it is not a pretty one.

But a discussion of Lathen's humor should not end on a sour note. And it should not end without mention of the puns to which she is addicted, especially in her chapter titles. These range from the concluding chapter of *A Stitch in Time* ("Witch Doctor")—dreadful—to that of *Pick Up Sticks* ("His Last Bough")—wonderful. The final chapter of *Death Shall Overcome*, which uses lines from hymns as titles, is "There Is a Line, By Us Unseen"; *Murder to Go* opens with "Prepare for Cooking" and closes with the delightful "Take a Disjointed Tale."

III

In addition to the sixteen novels published under the name Emma Lathen, Latsis and Henissart have also written five as R.B. Dominic. Featuring Congressman Benton Safford (D., Ohio), they are structurally and thematically similar to the Lathen books. Safford, a veteran member of Congress who is "unmistakably on the balding side of the generation gap," is a practical politician who routinely deals with the problems of his constituents in Newburg as well as national issues. Rumpled and friendly, he lacks Thatcher's aloof dignity but shares his understanding and appreciation of the uses of power. Ideologues and reformers may capture public attention momentarily; Safford keeps his home fences mended and has been re-elected often enough to be a "fixture" in the House. His involvement in crime arises directly from his Congressional duties—helping a constituent who has been kicked out of the Central American country of Nuevador with the aid of a faked photograph in *Murder in High Place* or serving as the chairman of a sub-committee investigating bribery charges in *Epitaph for a Lobbyist*—and he continues work on a day-to-day basis while solving crimes. Safford's frequent journeys to Newburg provide Dominic with opportunity to offer entertaining vignettes of everyday life and social change in a small midwestern city where the urban and the rural mingle in uneasy proximity.

Any reader familiar with Lathen would immediately recognize her hand in the Dominic novels. Each begins with a brief description of Washington, D.C., and each contains a continuing cast of characters drawn from Safford's close associates. Eugene Vallingham Oakes (R., S.D.) is a consummate politician and a "notable charmer, causing temperance ladies and whole Baptist congregations to champion his reprobate cause" (*Place,* 165). Anthony Martinelli (D., R.I.) is a streetwise liberal and convinced urbanite who nevertheless routinely supports farm-price legislation in return for Safford's favorable vote on bills that affect his constituency in Providence. The conscience of the small group is Elsie Hellenbach (R., Cal.), who represents affluent Marin county. Impeccably groomed and staunchly conservative, she has no toleration for dishonesty or the Army Corps of Engineers. Safford is also supported by his sister, Janet, a sister-under-the-skin to Miss Corsa, and her husband, Fred, owner of Lundgren's Ford Agency, the largest in southern Ohio. An indefatigable committeewoman and charity worker, Janet knows everything that goes on in Newburg and is, according to Val Oakes, "the real political talent in the family." Safford is grateful for his sister's help but does wish "that she did not have this passion for putting him on platforms whenever four or more voters gathered for any reason whatsoever" (*Justice*, 28). Although these characters have definite, established personality traits which are regularly mentioned, none is so rigidly limited—nor so amusing—as those in the Lathen series.

Structurally, the Dominic novels follow a regular pattern. Each deals with a specific event or agency which is introduced in an expository first chapter which also presents Safford and his colleagues. Sample subjects include Senate confirmation of a Supreme Court nominee in *There is No Justice,* the proposed building of a nuclear power plant in Murren, Ohio, in *Murder Out of Commission*, and Medicaid abuse in *The Attending Physician.* There are usually two murders per book, and Safford, like Thatcher, cooperates with a competent police official who aids in setting the trap with which each murderer is cornered. A set piece explanation occurs in the final chapter. The plotting is less secure than in the Lathen novels—in *Murder in High Place* the vital clue is repeated so often that the reader grasps it long before Safford does—and the predictable reliance on the trap device a definite weakness. The motive for murder, as one would expect, is invariably money.

The tone of the novels is sophisticated and urbane; in *Epitaph for a Lobbyist*, in which several Congressmen are under suspicion of having accepted a $50,000 bribe to defeat air pollution legislation for private power companies, Safford dismisses two of the suspects immediately because they "had been voting against every conceivable form of federal regulation for over twenty years. Bribing them would have been a waste of money" (13). Dominic understands how institutions work, and if Congress is portrayed as a less efficient version of the Sloan, that is only to be expected. She realizes the impact of television upon Congress but treats with disdain those members who plead their causes in the media instead of hammering out compromises in sub-committees. Political disagreement, she shows repeatedly, is no barrier to close friendship. The game has its rules, and those who follow them succeed: when Safford accepts the chairmanship of a sub-committee investigating bribery charges against fellow House members, a highly undesirable task, he does so because he knows the Speaker will return the favor and that Newburg's urban renewal program is "as good as funded." Although the novels reflect contemporary political and social issues—nuclear power, for example—Dominic does not intend, nor, with one exception, offer serious consideration of issues. *Murder in High Place*, published in 1971, includes an SDS leader whose sole interest lies in gaining personal publicity: "You know the kind of thing—he's always occupying buildings and burning files" (67). This curt dismissal, although in keeping with the light, conservative tone of Dominic's satire, presents an inaccurate and misleading account of the importance of the SDS during the period.

In fact, an acquaintance with American society gained solely from the Lathen-Dominic novels would lead readers to believe that America's only serious problem is its medical community. Like *A Stitch in Time*, *The Attending Physician* presents a damning indictment of American medicine and an implicit brief for national health insurance. Much the best book in the Dominic series, *The Attending Physician* is a devastating satire which reveals flagrant abuses of Medicaid and characterizes physicians as arrogant thieves: "Every single one of them is convinced he's got a God-given right to anything he wants and nobody should even ask questions" (53).

This description applies specifically only to a group of physicians known as the Newburg Seven who have collectively and fraudulently billed Medicaid for more than $1 million, but since Dominic's medical cast is limited to those whose sole professional concern is the making of money ("As long as he could keep his license to steal, he did not insist on public acclaim") the statement has extensive implications. Individual instances of Medicaid fraud may be humorous—a vasectomy billing for a female patient or four separate charges for three complete hysterectomies followed by an abortion on the same woman—but their consequences are not:

Picture how it's going to look to a jury. There's Tommy Soczewinsky in a wheel-chair, trying to defend his wife with his last ounce of strength. There's Wanda Soczewinski looking young and frail and embarrassed. And there's Isham describing how she's working herself to death taking care of a husband who's been incapable of fathering a child for over two years when along comes White to tell the world—entirely for his own fraudulent purposes—that she has to have an abortion (108).

While the Newburg Seven continue to insist that "laymen" have no right to interfere in any way with their conduct, attorneys file suits against them, their insurance company threatens to withdraw malpractice coverage, and Safford's committee hears an impassioned plea for dismantling the entire medical establishment and making physicians salaried employees of the U.S. Government. For once in the Lathen-Dominic *oeuvre* the all's-well-that-ends-well feeling common to traditional detective fiction is missing. Thatcher sets businesses to rights with ease, but even a U.S. Congressman cannot reform the corrupt practices of American physicians.

IV

Satirical though Lathen's view of American society may be, it is essentially a positive one. Senators may be shot while jogging in Rock Creek Park and aged Armenian ladies poisoned at family reunions, but business continues as usual. And, given Lathen's basic premise, the validity and superiority of the capitalist economic system and her concentration upon the business world, the continued and prosperous functioning of that world—despite government lunacy, foreign threats, or an occasional murder— serves to create the stability which is the necessary framework for her comic approach to detective fiction. The system may have its flaws, but it works.

Lathen has praised Christie as a chronicler of social change because of her "quick and unerring eye for the homely detail,"[10] a quality she shares with Christie. Lathen's emphasis is different, of course, but her novels offer readers a fairly thorough, if lightweight, record of changes in American life and business during the last twenty years. No female reader of Lathen's description of Chipses, Inc. can fail to appreciate her knowledge of the food industry, which turns out new recipes faster than it turns out new products and, in fact, creates recipes solely to stimulate product sales. Her attention to fast-food franchising highlights an economic and cultural phenomenon of great significance, just as her mildly ironic picture of small-town banking reveals our nostalgia for the past. In Gridleigh, New Hampshire, Thatcher visits the local bank:

It was a long time since he had seen a bank like this. There was dark oak wainscoting halfway up the walls, the single plate-glass window bore the bank's title in gold script, and behind the elaborately carved grilles, an ancient and gigantic safe stood in the tellers' quarters (*Sticks*, 74).

An enthusiastic young banker tells Thatcher of his plans for modernization and for installation of new data processing equipment but says he has no intention of modernizing the premises because new customers "think they're really getting away from it all. Back to small-town America and old-time virtues." (75).

The Sloan keeps up with the times in a different way when it exchanges the television sponsorship of symphony concerts for ice hockey games. *Murder Without Icing* gives Lathen her chance to document American sports madness, and *Pick Up Sticks* to analyze the markets for second homes in recreational complexes. "Eminent architects" offer plans for housing developments to be built on pilings over the Pacific Ocean, and real-estate developers compile lists of prospective customers drawn from Porsche owners or patrons of S.S. Pierce. The hard sell is often successful, but businessmen recognize the appeal of romance: "*all* Oriental rugs are woven by nomads pitching their tents under starry skies as they follow the seasons and the tinkling of camel bells" (*Crook*, 61). With characteristic irony, Lathen adds, "Very little is heard of state-supported factories and capital investments by big-city promoters."

Life is good in Lathen's America. People reveal quirks and oddities, and sometimes whole groups demonstrate peculiar behavior, but serious social problems go unmentioned. From a detached, conservative stance, Lathen mocks our personal and social foibles. Sympathizing with a client whose son has refused to join the family business, Thatcher thinks that he had listened to "fathers whose sons had joined communes, embraced Zen Buddhism, gone to the clink in Turkey, or were still seeking the perfect wave" (*Sweet and Low*, 57). Told that the son in question wishes to become a veterinarian, Thatcher senses a new trend: "The day of the guru was over. Was he now destined to hear a trail of fathers complain that their sons were settling down into pedestrian occupations, bringing home pay checks and supporting their families?"

Hippies are fair game, but Ivy Leaguers do not escape: discussing paternity with a Harvard Business School student, one of Thatcher's subordinates wonders "if the entire student body felt it necessary to procreate before achieving the Master of Business Administration" (*Place*, 121). And Thatcher too wonders about changes in patterns of procreation.

He remembered the waiting room of thirty-five years ago.... It had always contained a motley assortment of men—trim, taut executives, big, sweating blue-collar workers; tidy, worried little clerks—but all of them, indisputably, *adults*. And what did he find here, for Christ's sake? Schoolboys? There were two of them, with book bags at their feet, actually doing homework! (*Greece*, 85)

As Lathen chronicles changing American mores, she develops a society, which, despite lunacy in the higher echelons of the government and corruption in the medical profession, is fundamentally sound. Men of good sense with a rational understanding of human behavior and a healthy respect for money counterbalance the forces of disorder, and, inevitably, anarchy and confusion yield to order and stability. Lathen's comic detatchment and ironic, civilized commentary aid in creating the illusion of a safe and secure world. Her novels, refreshingly contemporary in subject matter and rigorously traditional in structure, demonstrate that classic detective fiction, that supposedly moribund form, is as alive now as during the Golden Age.

Notes

[1]The editions of the Lathen-Dominic novels used in this essay are listed below in chronological order of publication. All quotations will be cited in the text, using, where necessary, the abbreviations given after each entry.
Emma Lathen
Banking on Death, New York: Macmillan, 1961 (*Banking*)
A Place for Murder, New York: Macmillan, 1963 (*Place*)
Accounting for Murder, New York: Macmillan, 1964 (*Accounting*)
Death Shall Overcome, New York: Macmillan, 1966 (*Overcome*)
Murder Makes the Wheels Go 'Round, New York: Macmillan, 1966
Murder Against the Grain, New York: Macmillan, 1966 (*Grain)*
A Stitch in Time, New York: Macmillan, 1968 (*Stitch*)
Come to Dust, New York: Simon & Schuster, 1968 (*Dust*)
When in Greece, New York: Simon & Schuster, 1969 (*Greece*)
Murder to Go, New York: Pocket Books, 1972. Originally published in 1969.
Pick Up Sticks, New York: Simon & Schuster, 1970 (*Sticks*)

Ashes to Ashes, New York: Simon & Schuster, 1971 (*Ashes*)
The Longer the Thread, New York: Simon & Schuster, 1971 (*Thread*)
Murder Without Icing, New York: Simon & Schuster, 1972
Sweet and Low, New York: Simon & Schuster, 1974
By Hook or by Crook, New York: Simon & Schuster, 1975 (*Crook*)
Double, Double, Oil and Trouble, New York: Simon & Schuster, 1978 (*Double*)

R.B. Dominic
Murder in High Places, New York: Doubleday, 1970
There Is No Justice, New York: Doubleday, 1971 (*Justice*)
Epitaph for a Lobbyist, New York: Doubleday, 1974
Murder out of Commission, New York: Doubleday, 1976
The Attending Physician, New York: Harper & Row, 1980

[2]"Masters of White Collar Homicide," *Forbes*, 1 Dec. 1977, p. 89.

[3]According to "Masters," p. 89, a typical hardback sale is 10,000 copies. Many public libraries stock multiple copies of Lathen's books; I counted six of one title in the Richmond, Virginia public library.

[4]See John Cawelti, "Emma Lathen: Murder and Sophistication," *New Republic*, July 1976, pp. 25-26 for a discussion of Lathen and the classic formula.

[5]Thatcher's age, like that of many series detectives, is problematical. He once says he entered banking in 1925, and the authors refer to his having been in the AEF and having fought in the Battle of the Marne, an impossibility since the Marne was fought in 1914 and the U.S. did not enter the war until 1917.

[6]Frederick B. Shroyer and Louis D. Cardeman, *Types of Drama* (Glenview, IL: Scott, Fresman, 1970), p. 25.

[7]"Cornwallis's Revenge," in *Agatha Christie: First Lady of Cirme*, ed. H.R.F. Keating (New York: Holt, Rinehart and Winston, 1979), p. 88.

[8]Cawelti, p. 27.

[9]See Jane S. Bakerman, "A View from Wall Street: Social Criticism in the Mystery Novels of Emma Lathen," *Armchair Detective*, 9 (1976), 213-17, for intelligent discussion of satire.

[10]"Cornwallis's Revenge," p. 90.

Amanda Cross

1926	Born in East Orange, New Jersey, on 13 January
1945	Married James Heilbrun
1947	Received B. A. from Wellesley College (Phi Beta Kappa)
1951	Received M.A. from Columbia University
1959	Received Ph. D. from Columbia University
1959-60	Instructor at Brooklyn College
1960-62	Instructor at Columbia University
1961	Published *The Garnett Family* as Carolyn Heilbrun
1962-67	Assistant Professor at Columbia University
1964	Published *In the Last Analysis* as Amanda Cross; received a scroll from the Mystery Writers of America
1968-70	Visiting lecturer at Union Theological Seminary
1970	Visiting lecturer at Swarthmore College; published *Christopher Isherwood* as Carolyn Heilbrun
1972	Became full professor at Columbia University
1973	Published *Toward a Recognition of Androgyny* as Carolyn Heilbrun
1974	Visiting lecturer at Yale University
1976	Edited *Lady Ottoline's Album* as Carolyn Heilbrun
1979	Visiting Professor at the University of California at Santa Cruz; published *Reinventing Womanhood* as Carolyn Heilbrun
1980	Published *Death in a Tenured Position* as Amanda Cross; became a member of the Board of Supervisors of the English Institute and also the Book Critics Circle

Note: In addition she has received Guggenheim, Rockefeller and Radcliffe Institute fellowships; served on the Executive Council of the MLA, and published numerous articles and reviews.

by Steven R. Carter

Although Carolyn G. Heilbrun's pseudonym, Amanda Cross, is reminiscent (surely intentionally) of Agatha Christie, her true literary ancestor is Dorothy Sayers, who, like herself, was a noted scholar and feminist. Heilburn has discerned in Sayers a delight in the comedy of manners, erudition and formal English that she finds missing in contemporary mysteries and wishes to revive. She has also been pleased by the intellectual challenge of Sayer's puzzles, though, like Sayers herself, she has come to find the emphasis in classic detective fiction on an elaborate, multi-clued puzzle both confining and destructive to other literary values. As Sayers did in *The Nine Tailors, Gaudy Night* and *Busman's Honeymoon*, she has learned to subordinate her puzzles to the full portrayal of a social environment and the presentation of a personal vision. Because she too possesses immense talent, she has been able to create detective novels with a wit, style and breadth of knowledge that should more than satisfy the admirers of Sayers.[1]

What is distinctive—and at least as fascinating—in the Amanda Cross canon is her irony, her ability to construct a mystery around the ideas of a single literary or intellectual figure, her application of her research on androgyny and a feminist history, the increasing complexity and appeal of her detective, Kate Fansler, and her responsiveness to the crises of her time, such as the student rebellions of the Sixties and the Vietnam War. Even more intriguing is her evolution as a writer. Eventually becoming a strong advocate of social change, she has, appropriately, undergone changes in some of her attitudes and in her approach to the mystery. Shifting away from a defense of institutions and a mild contempt for homosexuals and the opinions of the young, she has more recently displayed a forthrightness and a desire for social justice that are matched by few other mystery writers, classic or hard-boiled. And the further she has moved from traditional stances, the further she has moved from the traditional forms. Her last two novels, *The Question of Max* and *Death in a Tenured Position*, make numerous innovations that enable her to express the full complexity and irony of her social vision.

Her first novel, *In the Last Analysis*, is the most conventional, remaining firmly within the Sayers tradition at its most puzzle-

270

bound, as in *The Five Red Herrings*. As in the majority of classical detective novels, the only fully-developed character is the detective, though some minor characters are lively and interesting. Wit abounds, as always in the series, and there are some perceptive observations on Freudian psychoanalysis and departmental politics at bureaucratically-run universities. However, the major source of interest is unquestionably the puzzle. This puzzle is probably the most intriguing and best developed in the series, but it is an end in itself; the solution to it makes only the conventional point that order—personal, social, moral—can be restored through reason. The novel, though engrossing and entertaining, is therefore minor; it succeeds in its aims, but its aims are limited.

In her first appearance, Kate Fansler seems like a combination of Lord Peter Wimsey and Harriet Vane. Like Lord Peter, Kate is a rich amateur detective who undertakes cases out of friendship for the falsely accused and curiosity. Also, as Heilbrun wrote of Lord Peter, Kate, "true to the tradition of the Comedy of Manners, brings (as Auden has said) more energy to [her] conversation than the situation requires. And more erudition."[2] Like Harriet Vane, she is a professional intellectual (Harriet was a writer; Kate is an English professor) with an unconventional attitude toward sex and an uncommon integrity. She has too great a love for independence and for her work to desire marriage.

At the same time, Kate is also an individual with a personal history. *In the Last Analaysis* presents some important facts about her that are not repeated in subsequent mysteries: 1. she was a member of a "reform political club" during "the short period of political activity in Kate's life" and it was there she met Assistant District Attorney Reed Amhearst for whom politics had been a "more continuous affair" (36); 2. she "rescued" Reed from some unspecified trouble he had gotten into through "a series of impulses and bad judgments" (36); and 3. she met Emanuel Bauer, the psychiatrist falsely accused of murder, "at that identical point in their lives when each was committed to a career, but had not yet admitted the commitment" (46) and the two of them became lovers and afterwards remained friends. The relationship between Kate and Emanuel illustrates a point which Heilbrun, writing under her own name in *Toward a Recognition of Androgyny*, made about George Bernard Shaw: "The friendship of a man and woman is one of the most unexplored of all human experiences, only Shaw, for example, recognizing that when a man and woman have ceased to be lovers, a friendship, a love, awaits them that is as ardent as an account of it is rare."[3]

Like Emanuel's wife, Nicola, Kate makes a distinction between morality and convention and is willing to abandon "surface rectitude" in favor of "honesty" (48-49). However, she makes only a few important decisions in *In the Last Analysis*. The first and most important is to try to save Emanuel by finding the real murderer. Her friendship provides only part of her motivation; she also wishes to help him because he embodies some of her most firmly held values, especially those relating to work and selfhood. She tells Reed that "Emanuel, and others like him, love their work; and if you want my recipe for integrity, find the man who loves his work and loves the cause he serves by doing it." (63). Later, while preparing a lesson on George Eliot's views concerning the "persistent self," an activity in which she displays her own love of work, Kate decides that "the persistent self lived...in that work where one's attention was wholly caught" and "it occurred to Kate that few people possessed 'persistent selves,' and that Emanuel, as one of them, had to be saved" (68). The murderer, significantly, turns out to be someone who had appropriated another person's work and who wanted that work only for the money it could bring him. Kate also points out to Reed that "it would be a hell of a blow to psychiatry if they arrested Emanuel" (147), and she specifically sets out to defend the institution of psychiatry as well.

Kate's other moral decisions concern whether to ask Reed Amhearst and her niece's fiance, Jerry, to assist in her investigation. She is reluctant to go to Reed for help in getting information about the police's case against Emanuel because she would seem to be asking him to repay her in this way for having gotten him out of trouble. She asks him finally because he is the only one who can do this for her, and she curses her mind for being "too finely tuned to moral dilemmas which more sensible people ignored" (37). Her reluctance to seek Jerry's aid comes from her realization that she would be encouraging an adventurous, somewhat irresponsible side of Jerry's character and that this might lead to problems between him and her emphatically nonadventurous niece. She also hesititates to use him because she believes that "youngsters cannot judge" and she is "not willing to risk all on the opinion of a twenty-one-year-old who made up in brashness what he lacked in wisdom" (120). After she breaks down her initial resistance, however, she finds him an able investigator, but her distrust of youth continues up to *The Theban Mysteries*. The seriousness of these decisions becomes clear when Kate defies Reed's appeal to let Jerry go. She reflects then that Reed would "have a fit" when he learned that she had given Jerry an increased role in the investigation "but the preservation of people's feelings was one of the goods which had vanished with the new state of affairs....She remembered wryly with what difficulty, in the beginning, she had brought herself to use Reed at all. But each ruthless act makes the next one not only possible but inevitable. Perhaps this was how one ended in committing murder" (122).

She faces no moral dilemma concerning what to do about the murderer once she identifies him since he has been totally ruthless and is totally unsympathetic. Her only concern becomes getting the evidence to convict him, thereby restoring Emanuel's reputation and the stability of her world.

Reed Amhearst faces even fewer moral dilemmas than Kate. He is willing to gain unauthorized information from the police for Kate and he sets up an unorthodox trap for the man Kate believes is the killer, but apart from this he is wholly conventional in his morality. He has no qualms about prosecuting a pornography case and is disgusted when he loses. He becomes angry at the idea that he might be willing to help Kate if she were guilty of murder as an anonymous letter had charged: "Do you think I would help someone, even someone for whom I felt gratitude and affection, to cover up a murder?" (109). Later, he will, to some extent, aid in cover-ups in *Poetic Justice, The Theban Mysteries* and *The Question of Max* for the sake of people who matter far less to him than Kate, but here he is less individualized and humanized.

The James Joyce Murder, though somewhat less conventional than *In the Last Analysis*, is, in several ways, a derivative work and a minor one. In spite of considerable ingenuity and technical dexterity, such as the often ironic use of short story titles from Joyce's *Dubliners* as chapter titles, the form owes a little too much to writers like Sayers, Marsh and Stout (all of whom are mentioned in the text) and the major theme, the life-denying quality of conventional sexual morality, is taken from Joyce. It is clearly an early novel, less innovative, less provocative, and less complex than subsequent ones, though not lacking the distinctive "Amanda Cross" voice and intellectual ambiance. Symptomatically, it is quick and easy to read, a little too quick and too easy since it leaves the impression of being lighter in content than it actually is. Even Kate, who never fails to be interesting, is less fully drawn than usual and is nearly, though not quite upstaged by Reed. It does, however, skillfully manipulate its conventional mystery form to support the unconventional thesis, and it provides a delightful, myth-deflating view of country life.

The puzzle is thoroughly conventional, depending on circumstance rather than psychology. The situation is an artificial one, typical of Sayers, Queen, Christie and Carr; every morning Kate's nephew, under the supervision of his tutor, William Lenehan, fires an unloaded rifle at the head of an obnoxious women who is driving cows to the barn, and on the only morning the tutor fires the rifle, he finds, belatedly, that someone has placed a bullet in it. The solution to the riddle of who did the loading hinges on the point that it would have been foolish for the murderer to place a bullet in a gun to be used by someone else since he could not control that person's actions; he could only be sure of killing the right person by keeping the rifle in his own hands. The murderer is therefore William Lenehan.

The obvious solution to the crime is obscured by the traditional means of red herrings. The biggest of these is Padraic Mulligan whose desire to conceal his authorship of a series of books about a James Bond-like hero is so great that he is even willing to sabotage Kate's car and steal her driver's license to give him time to reach his publisher and swear him to silence. These actions whose motivation is not explained until later distract attention for a substantial portion of the book. Mulligan's motive is based on his awareness of the prejudice among academics of his time against mysteries and his desire to remain respected as a professor. He particularly wants to conceal how he had pressured the publisher of his Frank Held thrillers into printing his unimaginative academic books as well so that he could receive rapid promotion to full professor. His actions and fears stress the publish-or-perish pressures that also drive William Lenehan. Lenehan's attempt to hide a previously unknown manuscript by James Joyce, his hope for academic advancement, in the barn of Mary Bradford, the obnoxious woman, makes him subject to her blackmail and thus provides one of his motives for murdering her. In this way, "Cross" accomplishes the neat trick of simultaneously obscuring the identity of the murderer and highlighting one of his motives. In addition, this motive exemplifies a minor theme, the dangers of the publish-or-perish system.

Another theme-related red herring is the romance between the seemingly pure William Lenehan and Eveline Chisana and the threat offered to it by the unseemly seducer, Padraic Mulligan. This provides a distraction because of the reader's expectations that true love will triumph over lust, as it has in countless conventional mysteries. Cross's point, however, is that William's chastity is life-denying and narcissistic and that it leads to a destructive self-righteousness. It makes him a suitable partner not for the sensuous Lina Chisana but the vicious Mary Bradford, whose self-righteous condemnation of everyone else's sexual impurity shades into prurient interest and self-worship. It is ironically fitting that William's fear that Mary might tell others about the hidden manuscript forces him to let her seduce him, possibly on the bale of hay concealing the manuscript. Naturally, his resentment of the way she has spoiled his purity makes him self-righteously wish to destroy her afterwards. The breaking of convention about romance in classical detective fiction thereby reinforces Cross's unconventional, Joycean attitude toward sex.

In contrast to *In the Last Analysis* wherein Kate had controlled the investigation from beginning to end, reaching the solution through her skills in literary and psychological analysis, Reed here unsurps the role of detective and performs in the traditional manner, solving the case through logic applied to circumstance and devising a ruse to trick the murderer into betraying himself. As before, once the murderer is identified, Reed immediately turns him over to the law. However, he and Kate decide to ask their lawyer friend, John Cunningham, to continue to defend William after they know he is guilty. Neither of them wish to see him executed, and Reed offers Kate the consolations that, although he will probably spend from eight to thirty years in prison, at least William will receive much needed psychiatric help and innocent people, such as Mary Bradford's husband, will now be cleared of all suspicion. In keeping with the conventional form (even though it has permitted some unconventional ideas), the question of the nature and degree of William's guilt and its appropriate punishment—the question of the justice of the law's refusal at that time to consider such a crime insane—is only lightly touched on and then dismissed. The law is simply taken for granted and no one suggests that any other course might be possible.

Even though Kate is denied the role of detective, she retains much of her independence and resourcefulness. A Professor of Victorian Literature, she is fully capable of dealing with material outside her specialty, offering a sound interpretation of Joyce's "Ivy Day in the Committee Room" and editing the letters of a man who published Joyce, Lawrence and other major twentieth-century writers. She unhesistantly refuses Reed's proposal of marriage because she prefers to hold onto her "world"—her job, her involvement in a variety of activities, her self-determined life. However, she is quite willing to flout convention by continuing to make love with Reed and openly acknowledging her noncelibacy. She also admits to being nonmotherly and lacking the conventionally feminine fondness for small boys, though she proves capable of coping with one when her nephew Leo runs away from home to her.

Unfortunately, Kate's attitude toward homosexuality is far more conventional than her attitudes toward sex and children, though it will becor more tolerant and humane in *Death in a Tenured Position*. William Lenehan tells Emmet Crawford, Kate's assistant in editing the letters, that Kate was concerned about having him near Leo since he had affected "effete mannerisms, positively inviting everyone within earshot or reach of gossip to consider you limp of wrist" (*Joyce*, 45). Later, when Emmet tells

Kate that "Americans might do well to wake up to the fact that homosexual men who deeply resent women are not absolutely always those who go about prancing like little fawns" but may be bluff, hearty men who direct boys' activities, like Leo's camp counselor, Kate responds, "Emmet, are you suggesting that I have not only exposed my nephew to a murderer, but have placed him in a camp filled with queers?" (*Joyce, 105*).

One type of comic technique used extensively in *In the Last Analysis* and *The James Joyce Murder* seems especially suited to detective fiction since it follows the basic pattern of the mystery itself, of initial confusion followed by a logical explanation. In *The James Joyce Murder*, for example, Reed, upon arriving at the house where Kate is editing Samuel Lingerwell's papers, knows nothing about the set-up and is totally confused about the people living with Kate. When Leo tells Kate that William is "arguing with Emmet about some guy called James Joyce," Reed fails to identify Joyce as "the Irish author of several indecipherable books" since "given the extraordinary aspects of this establishment, he might be the gardener" (4-5). Shortly afterwards, Emmet tells Reed that Lingerwell also "did the *Portrait* and the *Rainbow*" and Reed, failing to recognize these as book titles, asks if Lingerwell "was a painter" (6). Explanations follow in both cases, clearing up the temporary mysteries.

Comedy abounds in *Poetic Justice*. A delight throughout, it is, paradoxically, at once the most loosely structured of the series and the most traditional in many respects. The doctoral examination of Mr. Cornfield's dissertation on Auden by Professors Chang, Kruger and Pollinger has no connection with the mystery or the struggle for the preservation of University College, yet it adds much to the tone and the humor and few readers would wish it had been left out. Also, Professor Peter Packer Pollinger is irrelevant in almost every way, but the book would be poorer without him.

And there is a point to the examination scene and the presence of Prof. Pollinger. This book is intent on showing that the university, in spite of its defects and frequent irrelevancy, is worth preserving. If a student radical had written about the examination, he would have treated it as ample cause for the destruction of the university. However, Cross treats the scene with gentle humor, making the reader sympathetic toward these men at the same time that she points out their flaws. Their questions about Auden are splendidly irrelevant and narrow-minded, reflecting their total involvement with their specialties. Nevertheless, their good intentions are never in doubt and the combination of their extreme seriousness about their subject and their sense of fun is pleasing. To think about dismissing such men is to show oneself to be even more narrow-minded than they and humorless as well, something which they are not.

Peter Packer Pollinger is a special case. His obsession with William Sharp, the turn-of-the-century Irish author who wrote under the pseudonym Fiona Macleod and who became so attached to his female alter ego that he insisted she be invited to parties along with him, makes Pollinger at once a buffoon and a representative of androgynous wisdom. His attempt near the end of the novel to prove that Vachel Lindsay and Sara Teasdale were two halves of the same person is ludicrous if taken literally yet wise if taken figuratively since the manly man and the womanly woman together form an androgynous whole. Significantly, it is he who points out that the hostility of certain members of the College (the undergraduate school) toward University College (the school for returning drop-outs and older students) is the "same as the English toward the Irish; pure snobbism" and that Prof. Jeremiah Cudlipp's contempt for University College is based on the fact that he went there "when it was still just a group of extension courses, after they threw him out of the College and before they took him back" (80). As an affirmation of the importance of the seemingly irrelevant, one of the last things the reader learns about him is that he "brought out a book on Fiona Macleod with such insight into the odd dual nature of William Sharp that Professor Pollinger's colleagues looked at him with new attention" (164). A figure as minor as the poet/poetess he studied so assiduously, he probably holds a major place in the memory of most readers.

Apart from the question of the university's worthiness to survive, what holds the many facets of the book together is the life and ideas of the great twentieth-century poet, W. H. Auden. The applicability of Auden's poetry to everything from limestone landscapes to history to beds to personal and professional conflicts is illustrated throughout, but the character of Auden is of even greater significance since he seems the antidote to the destructive earnestness of the radical students and Jeremiah Cudlipp. Auden remarks at a reading that "the life of a poet is a balancing act between frivolity and earnestness," and Kate reflects that this "is Auden's greatness; he is the best balancer of all" (*Justice, 156*). *Poetic Justice* aims at the same kind of balance—and achieves it. The vision of the novel accords perfectly with the lines quoted from one of Auden's poems:

the funniest mortals and the kindest are those who are most aware of the baffle of being, don't kid themselves our care is consolable, but believe a laugh is less heartless than tears. (53)

The balance Kate seeks in *Poetic Justice* favors institutions and order, while acknowledging the necessity for change. Symbolically, she opens herself to change at the end by marrying Reed Amhearst, thereby accepting the institution of matrimony. At the beginning, she angrily notices that "the students, damn them, were trampling thoughtlessly across the new grass heedless of all the cautionary signs and fences erected by the University's tireless gardeners" (11), a view that could be taken as her reaction toward the student rebellion. When Vivian Frogmore, the Dean of University College, tells her that he is seeking her help because she was known to be sympathetic toward students before the rebellion, she responds that her sympathy has been "exaggerated" and that she doesn't like teaching undergraduates because "they are arrogant, spoiled, discourteous, incapable of compromise, and unaware of the price of everything they want to destroy" (39). She later tells Hankster, a radical colleague, that she always dislikes "people who are destroyers in principle" (104). Noting that they have both come from wealthy backgrounds, she observes to herself that "there are those who cling to the finger bowls, those who dismiss them with a shrug but not without nostalgia, and those like Hankster whose life was devoted to smashing the finger bowls against privy walls" (103). Kate, who belongs to the middle category, can admit that the type of privilege and snobbery represented by the fingerbowls with roses that she knew in her childhood should be eliminated and can recognize that the indifference and inflexibility of the administrators and faculty played a major role in provoking the student rebellion; however, she still feels that "there was little to be said for revolutions" (16). The fight to keep the University from mandating University College out of existence appeals to her so strongly because it enables her simultaneously to oppose snobbery and defend an insitition. One of the points in favor of University College, moreover, is that its student body was the only one who remained loyal to the University during the student troubles. Kate, at this time, values such loyalty because it matches her own for a beleagured institution, the University itself, whose existence has been profoundly called into question. Also, she approves of University College because it offers a second chance to older, more mature students who are strongly interested in their courses. She is especially pleased that it offers a chance for older women to escape from dreary housework and perpetual babysitting to work that will exercise their minds.

In line with this sympathetic attitude toward the institution, Cross emphasizes the damaging effects of the tensions of the rebellion on the faculty. Kate herself admits to Reed that she would like to live with him now because she feels insecure and weakened to the point that she would like to have a man nearby. She remains independent enough to refuse his initial proposal because she does not wish to marry out of weakness, but she is clearly less at ease than usual. A worse case is that of Jeremiah Cudlipp, whose holy war against University College is partly the product of his having cracked under the combined strains of the student rebellion and his wife's desertion. Frederick Clemance's motive for giving him the aspirin that, intended only to disable, leads to his death is to give him time to relax and recover from these tensions. Presumably Clemance is led to the risky—and accidentally fatal—aspirin gambit because the strain on him has hindered his normally large capacity for thought and moral sensitivity.

Appropriately, for a book emphasizing the value of tradition, the puzzle and its solution are also traditional. The chief mystery is how two aspirin pills could have been substituted for the special pills Cudlipp normally took for headaches because of his aspirin allergy. Reed's initial misleading assumption is that the aspirin must have been placed in the bottle while Cudlipp's attention was distracted, but the alert reader, who has probably encountered this situation in many previous mysteries, should be aware that the "murderer" would then have been unable to determine when Cudlipp would take the pills. The solution, like that to so many classical mysteries, comes through a slip of the tongue, Clemance's remark to Reed that "there are moments when, quite apart from wanting Cudlipp back again, I wish that someone had handed me a poison, instead of him" (140), thus indicating the real method Clemance used to give Cudlipp the aspirin.

Another tradition followed by this book is that, as in *The James Joyce Murder*, a male, Reed, solves the case. However, a nontraditional balance is supplied by Reed's and Kate's decision about what they should do with the knowledge that Clemance gave Cudlipp the aspirin. Noting Auden's distinction between the primary world we live in and the secondary world of art (or, in Kate's extension, of the revolutionary's dreams), Reed remarks that his decision not to turn Clemance over to the law for punishment is "the nearest I shall ever come to creating a secondary world" (161). With Clemance's concurrence, he agrees to enter a surreptitious account in the official file of how Clemance handed the aspirin to Cudlipp, though he intends to label this an accident, which in a sense it was. Thus, Reed, with Kate's approval, chooses not to apply the abstract, rigid principles of the law to this case but to rely instead on a more charitable personal judgment.

As the title *Poetic Justice* implies, there are ironies in Cudlipp's death. The most obvious is that Cudlipp helped to arrange his own death since he initiated the elevator sabotage that prevented Reed and the others from getting him to the hospital in time to save him.

Moreover, his death brings about the very thing the was trying to prevent, the preservation of University College, since his fellow conspirator, Dean Robert O'Toole, decides not to continue the fight after he realizes that his former teacher, Clemance, was responsible for Cudlipp's demise. Clemance himself, who had also opposed University College, is forced to accept its continuance as part of the fruits of his action. Thus, the laws of this secondary poetic world appear to be the same as those of the ancient Greeks, that harmful actions bring their own retribution, regardless of what society knows or chooses to do about them.

The most painful ironies concern Clemance's behavior. It is highly ironic that Cudlipp was killed not by someone who hated him for his opposition to University College but by a friend who was attempting to save him from himself. In addition, the man who caused Cudlipp's death is a believer in elitist education who is forced to face his own inadequacies and to accept the development of nonelitist education. Clemance acknowledges further that "we cannot guess the outcome of our actions—how often I have said that in discussions with students" (158), and this point comes home to him through his realization that the result of his action was the opposite of what he intended. He says that the unexpectedness of life "is why our actions must always be acceptable in themselves, and not as strategies" (158); his wasn't.

The irony that Hankster, whom Kate considers a destroyer in principle, was trying to stop some misguided radical students from sabotaging the elevators when Reed and Prof. Cartier caught him and assumed he was guilty implies the danger of pigeon-holing people. Kate recognizes this danger when she tries to threaten her colleague, Cartier, with sitting on his lap and finds that he is delighted by the offer; she notes then that "pigeon-holing people, thinking that you always know what they will say" is "the ultimate sin" (138). She had realized only a few pages earlier that she had made a mistake in thinking Cudlipp a villain without any redeeming traits when a student teacher told her how Cudlipp had permitted him to experiment in his classes and had given him encouragement. She had also learned that she was mistaken in assuming that Cudlipp's position toward University College was totally unjustifiable and had laughed at herself for "getting so cocksure as to forget there are two sides to every question" (134). She later observes that "it is probably one of the happier effects of the turmoil that people no longer sorted themselves out so neatly" (148).

Much frivolity occurs to balance the seriousness of the themes and of the campus situation. Reed's attempt to catch the elevator saboteurs, for example, is sheer slapstick. While he overlooks the elevator control panel from aloft on the water pipes, first Cartier

enters with his paint spray can and camera and then Hankster, both
of them remaining in the dark, literally and figuratively. Then the
real saboteur enters, a scramble begins and Cartier mistakenly
sprays Hankster instead. The comedy is compounded by the fact
that the radical Hankster is wearing an expensive suit.

There are also considerable dashes of wit. Kate's colleague
Mark Everglade tells her that English teachers are "not only
magnificently irrelevant, but are prevented, mysteriously, from
enjoying the fruits of irrelevance, which are frivolity and leisure"
(22). Another colleague, Emilia Airhart, tells Dean Robert O'Toole
that she is unable to understand "whether you think arrogant bad
manners encourage the illusion of manliness, or whether you think
that evident unmanliness is somehow obscured by arrogant bad
manners" (90). Best of all, Peter Packer Pollinger wishes Kate
"many happy weddings" and explains that his gift of *The Mountain
Lovers* (by Fiona Macleod naturally) "wasn't an easy choice...for
your first wedding. *The Immoral Hour, The Divine Adventure,* or
even, though I hope not, *The Dominion,* might have done equally
well" (90).

All in all, Cross achieves a balance between high seriousness
and fun that would surely have been pleasing to Auden, and *Poetic
Justice* is a worthy tribute to him.

Unfortunately, the blend of earnestness and humor is not
nearly as satisfactory in *The Theban Mysteries.* The opening scene,
for example, tries too hard to maintain a light tone in the midst of an
obviously distressing situation, the conflict between Kate's nephew,
Jack, and his father over the Vietnam War and his decision to run
away from home in protest. In addition, the literary source for this
novel, Sophocles' *Antigone,* is far less tractable and tolerant of
frivolity than Auden, and Cross's attempt to play it off against
Kaufman and Hart seems inevitably and justly doomed. Moreover,
the slick, happy, nearly painless ending at least partly violates the
spirit of the *Antigone,* which was, after all, a tragedy.

Nevertheless, the novel is highly ambitious and has a number of
strengths that raise it well above the level of *In the Last Analysis*
and *The James Joyce Murder.* Among its triumphs are the portraits
of Miss Tyringham and the Theban, Kate's seminar on *Antigone,*
her dialogues with Cedric Jablon, the character of Betsy Stark and
her comments on androgyny and the comedy of manners, Kate's
confrontations with Patrick and Angelica Jablon, and the concept
of a modern version of Antigone against the background of the
Vietnam War.

The puzzle in *The Theban Mysteries* is both a strength and a
weakness. On the one hand, it is one of the most intriguing types of
puzzle, the John Dickson Carr type that asks not only whodunit but

howdunit, the crime that couldn't possibly have happened but did. On the other hand, it undercuts some of the greatest virtues of this novel. While the puzzle is being presented, characterization and thematic development are often left hanging. Particularly damaging is Cross's failure to develop the characters of Patrick and Angelica Jablon in the early part of the novel, presumably to keep the reader from guessing that their mother's death from a heart attack was brought on by her accidental eavesdropping on Angelica's denunciation of her at an encounter session that Patrick had brought her to without telling anyone. However, the thinness of their characters prevents the reader from feeling much sympathy for them and their potential, largely unrealized tragedy. In place of a fuller treatment of their psychological and moral problems, about forty to fifty pages are devoted exclusively to details like the movement of guard dogs, the location of elevators, the identification of a tie label and the medical history of the deceased. This type of detail, which is the main source of interest in numerous classical mysteries, acts as an obstruction here to the more interesting analysis of generational conflict and the effects of the Vietnam War. The two kinds of material, puzzle and theme, are at odds with each other, though the solution partially blends them together.

At first glance, the solution seems only marginally attached to the story of Antigone and the major themes of the novel. Esther Jablon's conflicts with her children, Angelica and Patrick, appear to have nothing to do with the Vietnam War, apart from being heightened by her fear that their conflicts over the war with their grandfather, Cedric, may result in all three of them being kicked out of his house, an act that would end her life of luxury. They also have nothing to do with matters of principle, as do the conflicts between Patrick and Cedric or between Antigone and Creon. The conflicts occur because Esther Jablon is a hysterical, hypochondriacal, overbearing, self-centered harridan who is jealous of her own daughter and who is at least partly responsible for her husband's suicide. On the other hand, she has become the way she is partly because of the position of American women. Kate argues that the usual practice of making women "dependent on one man for everything" is highly damaging to their characters and to their relationships with men and that a major reason for war is that it gives men "an excuse to get away from their wives" whose total dependency fills them with "guilt" and irritation (134-135). Thus, there is a significant link between the solution and two important themes.

Even though the puzzle is conventional, Cross' handling of the detection is unusual and provocative. The detection is divided between Kate and Reed, suggesting the equality in their marriage and the value of cooperation. Reed solves the problem of why the guarddogs failed to stop in the presence of Esther Jablon, because she was dead when they entered the school gymnasium, and he passes the torch to Kate. Freed from the idea that Mrs. Jablon died in the gymnasium, Kate puts together her pieces of information about the Jablon family conflicts and the encounter sessions involving Angelica. However, it is only when she confronts Angelica and Patrick at their house that she realizes that the fatal encounter session could not have taken place there but probably occurred at the home of Angelica's fellow student, Irene Rexton, which has no inconvenient guards or servants to observe the movement of a corpse. Later, when Patrick lies about carrying the body to the school in a car that he had stolen, Kate guesses that he must be protecting someone and that this person is probably Mrs. Banister, the teacher who had initiated the encounter sessions. Even then, she fails to guess that Irene Rexton helped Mrs. Banister move the corpse from her home to the school. Kate only learns about Irene because Mrs. Banister tells her. Thus, although the reasoning powers of both Reed and Kate lead toward the solution, the whole truth only appears through dialogue, through Kate's willingness to listen and think carefully about what is said to her. This partially reinforces some of the major points of the book about the need to be flexible, open to other persons and ideas and willing to learn from the young.

As in *Poetic Justice*, ethical decisions are made on the basis of individual judgment rather than an easy adherence to a legal or religious code. Knowing that Esther Jablon was largely responsible for her own death since she expired in a frenzy brought on by her daughter's supposed ingratitude toward her, Kate, instead of seeking justice for the victim, wishes to offer "some sort of comfort" to those who are only indirectly responsible for her death (169). She feels that confronting the truth head-on is the only way to avoid being overwhelmed by it, and by forcing Angelica and Patrick to face it with her, she enables them to come to terms with their guilt and transcend it.

A more difficult decision for Kate is whether to tell Miss Tyringham, the Head of the Theban School, about Mrs. Banister's attempt to cover up for Angelica and Patrick since this may result in her dismissal. Kate therefore sounds her out, and, finding Miss Tyringham prepared to tolerate a great deal provided she could still consider a teacher "able to do her work properly" (151), Kate decides to tell her everything. She does so out of loyalty to the Theban because Mrs. Banister had endangered it by placing Mrs. Jablon's corpse in the gymnasium where the school's watchdogs could be blamed for causing the heart attack. However, Kate has no desire to punish Mrs. Banister and will say nothing to the police about her.

Kate's most intriguing moral decision occurs in the middle of her confrontation with Angelica and Patrick. When she feels she is failing in her attempt to reach them, she decides to leave and turn the story over to Miss Tyringham in the hope that she may be able to handle the situation better. She then admits, "I have been suffering from hubris" (172). This proves to be the turning point after which the two young people begin to trust her and beg her to remain and help. So many of the conflicts in the novel, such as those between Patrick and Cedric Jablon, Jack Fansler and his father, and Antigone and Creon, are based not only on a clash of principles but also on excessive pride in all the participants. Kate, in contrast, succeeds in healing the wounds of such conflicts because she can acknowledge her failings and self-doubts.

Kate also demonstrates her flexibility and abandonment of hubris in her seminar on Antigone, displaying notably more sympathy and respect toward the young than in *Poetic Justice*. She responds to a student challenge written anonymously on the blackboard that "we'll discuss what we agree on" (34) by doing just that, allowing the students to have a voice in determining the topics of discussion for the seminar. In conversation with a friend about how she should set up the seminar, she expresses her concern with striking a balance between "a bull session" and "a structural study" in her course (42). Kate agrees to limit her comments in class so that her students will have ample opportunity to express their ideas. In doing so, she is following Miss Tyringham's advice that learning should be a mutual experience, that the old can learn something from the young and not just the young from the old.

Like Kate, Miss Tyringham achieves balance, though it should be stressed here that balance is a dynamic concept. In his book on Matthew Arnold, Lionel Trilling points out the distinction between balance, which Arnold sought in his youth, and fixity, which he sought in his later years. Balance is a shifting concept, depending on the forces currently at work in society; it allows for growth and progress. Fixity is the opposite of growth; it attempts to freeze these forces in a set position from which there can be no alteration. Miss Tyringham "confirmed, in her downright, cheerful way, that change was possible" (20). Many of the changes she instituted at the Theban in the Fifties became those demanded by students at other schools in the Sixties: "She added contemporary literature and history to the curriculum long before that became fashionable, introduced Spanish as an alternative language to French in a city now heavily Puerto Rican, recruited for the school numbers of black girls, and bullied the trustees into providing scholarships for them." (20-21). However, she did all this without lowering academic standards. It is stated emphatically that the Theban "taught its students so thoroughly that all of them, to a woman, found college an anticlimax of almost unmanageable proportions" (19).

In contrast to both Kate and Miss Tyringham, Cedric Jablon and his earlier incarnation, Creon, reek of hubris and long for fixity. At the same time, Cedric is an intriguingly complex figure who remains sympathetic while defending inhumane and untenable positions, such as the "necessity" of using napalm in Vietnam. The reader can appreciate how his background as a poor Jew who found the chance to become wealthy in America gave him a sense of gratitude toward this country that makes him unwilling to listen to his son's reasons for refusing to "defend" the United States in Vietnam. It is also easy to sympathize with the way he took in his daughter-in-law with his grandchildren after his son's death because he saw that was the only way he could protect Angelica and Patrick against their mother. Moreover, he, like his grandson, is a man of honor and principle, though Patrick has more right on his side, as did Antigone against Creon. His error, as Kate points out, is that "like many of his generation and his experience, he had lost the connection between his personal morality and the national morality of his beloved country, on whose behalf he was willing to defend offensive practices on the grounds of national necessity that he would never for a moment have endorsed as personal actions" (157). However, unlike Creon who learned his mistake through the death of his son and who then became flexible because of his pain, Cedric takes refuge in his rationalizations and refuses to face the truth head-on. When Kate leaves him, she notices, "with sorrow, the absence of tears or anger. He had found his defenses and taken his position securely behind them" (160).

Cross's treatment of androgyny in *The Theban Mysteries* points up the overlap between Amanda Cross, the mystery writer, and Carolyn Heilbrun, the scholar. During Kate's seminar, Betsy Stark, a student, provides the kind of definition of androgyny that Heilbrun developed at length in her thoughtful and carefully researched study, *Toward a Recognition of Androgyny:*

"Both men and women," Betsy said, "have aspects of both sexes, with one sex predominating if you're lucky, and one sex predominating too much if you're unlucky enough to end up with a sewing circle or the Elks. Shaw called *them* manly men and womanly women." (58).

The Theban, significantly, is an androgynous institution, embuing its female students, "despite their inevitable destiny of cotillions and debuts, with a tomboy, bluestocking attitude which was never entirely eschewed" (18). When Kate mistakenly assumed that Irene

Rexton is too fragile and too feminine to have helped move Esther Jablon's corpse, Mrs. Banister reminds her that "one must *never* characterize people" (187), which implies, in this context, that one should avoid stereotyping and anti-androgynous distinctions.

Cross's masterpiece, *The Question of Max,* achieves the harmonious blending of its disparate elements that is so unfortunately lacking in *The Theban Mysteries.* The qualities that stand out most in this work of great artistry are its wit (that, for once, is always related to the themes), its skillfully developed feminist/androgynist vision, its commentary on Watergate ethics, the by-play between Kate's polysyllabic utterances and her nephew Leo's pithy obscenities, and, above all, its complex manipulation and reshaping of classical and hard-boiled detective formulas to fit a personal vision that is often at odds with the social visions behind both of these formulas.

The innovativeness of *The Question of Max* can be seen immediately in the puzzle. First, it is clear from the title and the absence of other suspects that the conservative literary critic, Max Reston, will prove to be the murderer of the dangerously curious student, Gerry Marson. This places the emphasis on Max's motives and directs the reader's attention to Max's character and social views. Second, like Ross Macdonald and James Jones, Cross uses the traditional literary device of foreshadowing more than the classical detective fiction convention of planting clues. Kate, for example, approaches the solution when she tells Max that his attitude toward the papers of the early twentieth-century novelist Cecily Hutchins seems "inextricably connected" in her mind with Gerry Marston's death, though she can't say why (77). Thus, when the truth comes out that Max killed Gerry because she learned that Cecily Hutchins had changed her mind about letting Max be her literary executor, the reader is prepared to accept it, even though he hasn't had much of a chance to guess it as he would have had if this had been a more detailed clue. Third, Cross' stress on the role of chance runs counter to classical detective fiction's attempt to fit everything into a pattern both observed and controlled by reason. Kate solves this case not through reason alone, but through her chance encounter with a student who tells her that Gerry Marston was interested in Cecily Hutchins rather than her writer friend, Dorothy Whitmore, as Kate had mistakenly thought and as Max had confirmed in a forged letter bearing Gerry's signature. With this information, Kate then realizes that her earlier reconstruction of Gerry's death was mistaken and that Max has lied to her in many sinister ways, thus suggesting that Max's role in the death was more vicious than she had suspected. Fourth, Kate's comically ineffectual attempt to solve the crime and determine its motivation solely through reason implies that the detective's function is, to a large extent, comic. Her mistaken theory about Max being the illegitimate son of Dorothy Whitmore reveals the limits of reason, particularly the type of reason exalted in detective fiction. Moreover, too great a certitude can lead to self-righteousness, the chief flaw that is attacked in the cheating students, Finlay and Ricardo, and in Max, as it had been earlier in Mary Bradford and William Lenehan. Kate's own loss of awareness that "nothing in life" is ever "clear-cut and obvious" (165) is only temporary, though, and she soon regains her customary balance between pride and humility (total humility is not shown as the answer). Unless certainty and doubt are held in tension, unless a person always retains an awareness that he may be wrong or at least will never hold the whole truth exclusively in his hands, inflexibility and intolerance will set in. This is an anti-detective fiction philosophy, even though, as Cross demonstrates here, it may be neatly developed in a detective format; all the major traits of the classical detective from Sherlock Holmes to Hercule Poirot—arrogance, aloofness and total belief in the efficacy of reason—are roundly condemned. Fifth, the one puzzle that the reader is given a fair chance to solve, Max's authorship of the spurious letters by Dorothy Whitmore, emphasizes psychological and social problems, while retaining some of the effect of classical detective fiction. As in the works of Agatha Christie and many other classical detective novelists, it depends on the reader's ability to overcome his (or her) preconceptions. The preconceptions here, the indications by Max writing as Dorothy Whitmore that all women are filled with self-hatred and desire male children, have been carefully undermined by the portrait of Dorothy as a dynamic, life-loving, courageous and, above all, fulfilled woman who, although she died young, had experienced more than most women—or men—who lived twice as long. However, many readers may fall into the trap of accepting the false letters' viewpoint because of their social conditioning and will then, as in the best classical detective fiction, be surprised by a truth that they should have known all along. As in many of Ross Macdonald's novels, the solution to the crime thus supports one of the themes—the need to acknowledge women's equality.

The novel begins, appropriately, with another departure from convention. In *Adventure, Mystery and Romance*, John Cawelti discusses the convention of opening the story in the detective's retreat whose peace is broken by the intrusion of a personal disorder from outside in the form of a victim of a crime. This personal disorder, moreover, has nothing to do with the detective until the moment he is asked for help. This traditional opening of so many Sherlock Holmes stories ironically parallels and contrasts with that of *The Question of Max*. Kate too is in a retreat when someone comes to ask her help, but her retreat is more complex than that of her male counterparts since her position as an achieving woman in a patriarchal society is more complex than their relation to their societies. Her relation to the person seeking help is also more complex than that of detective and victim in the classical detective novel. Far from being a victim, he is a murderer who is planning to hoodwink her into unwittingly covering up a crime that is an expression of his hostility and sense of superiority toward women. Furthermore, in place of the peaceful return to the retreat at the end of most stories, Kate is attacked by Max at the retreat.

Cawelti notes, "This manner of introduction also emphasizes the detachment of the detective, his lack of moral or personal involvement in the crime he is called on to investigate."[4] This is untrue of Kate. Her intense, personal feeling toward the victim, who is one of Kate's students and an achieving woman like herself, is a far cry from Holmsian detachment and it implies a further, even more personal reaction in Kate, a reaction toward the patriarchal society that attempts, with varying success, to suppress the possibilities for work and love in women. Kate, to some extent, has reined in her awareness—and resentment—of patriarchal pressures, but her involvement with Gerry's death and with the histories of the three remarkable women who attended Oxford together—Cecily Hutchins, Dorothy Whitmore and Max's mother, Frederica Tupe—force her increasingly to confront them and to do something about them. When Max first comes to her retreat, she seems a bit timid and overly willing to defer to his male prejudices. For example, knowing his regard for elegance and "sartorial distinctions between the sexes," she is reluctant to let him see her in "mud-stained sneakers and ancient blue-jeans" (12). Later, however, she notes with displeasure the oddity that Max, as Hutchins' literary executor, has decided to sell the papers of "a woman writer whose work is certainly getting more attention because of the women's movement ... to a stuffy male club that admits women only on occasional evenings and by special invitation" (*Max*, 76). Eventually she discovers that in questioning Max's values, she must also question her own: "The fact is, she told herself... I envy Max. I would like to write the biography [of Cecily Hutchins]. My motives are impure to a degree. Drag the disgraceful fact out into the open and face it, Kate Fansler. However good Max may be, a woman ought to write that biography. A thoroughly sexist remark, she concluded" (124-25). This implies the idea of female bonding to cope with the male bonding in a patriarchal society, one of the key points in Carolyn Heilbrun's feminist study *Reinventing Womanhood*. It also implies the impropriety of Max doing the biography and thus hints at Max's motive for Gerry's murder, her discovery that Cecily Hutchins had altered her will to remove Max's name as her literary executor and biographer once she understood how little he comprehended her life and ideas. Someone like Gerry herself would have been a better choice. Finally, Kate realizes exactly how far Max will go to protect his male privileges when he prepares to murder her at her retreat; she learns then that she must prepare herself to act in self-defense against the forces of male chauvinism.

Kate's alterations in the course of the novel also run counter to most classical detective fiction. Detectives like Holmes, Philo Vance, Nero Wolfe and Dr. Gideon Fell carry the same personality traits from one mystery to the next, failing even to show any signs of aging. Kate is fallible, however, and capable of growth. Her early timidity gives way to the courage she displays in the face of death at the end. Although her possibilities for action are limited when Max points a gun at her, she does not give way to hysterics; neither does she passively accept her fate. At the moment Reed arrives to save her, she is fleeing with a definite plan in mind, to sneak around behind Max once she is out of his sight.

Like hard-boiled detectives from Sam Spade to Lew Archer, Kate must be judge as well as investigator, and, again like them, her actions as judge are morally ambiguous. Her attempt to blackmail Max by promising to keep quiet about his part in Gerry's death if he will return some missing letters by Dorothy Whitmore to the library's Hutchins collection is done with the best of motives; though the law can't touch him (or so Kate believes), restitution should be made to the spirit of Gerry Marston, and valuable letters from Whitmore should be preserved for posterity. However, the letters Kate is seeking to preserve don't exist—Max is then forced to write them—and the law can grab Max firmly once Kate learns his true motive. Thus, Kate, like her nephew, Leo, who tried to bring justice to two cheaters at school, accomplishes little at this time. Reflecting on the results of their efforts, Kate observes: "They were both very modern solutions, inconclusive and unsatisfactory, though in both her case and Leo's, to have done nothing would have been worse; satisfactory to the wrong people, and conclusive in effect" (195). Ironically, Kate's action, based as it is on false assumptions, prompts Max to admit that he did have a role in Gerry Marston's death, even though he still conceals the extent and viciousness of that role. It also prompts him to write the pseudo-Whitmore letters that help Kate arrive at the truth about his actions. The final solution to the question of Max, placing him in a mental institution, also seems a modern one, and a bit inconclusive. It belongs more to the world of Lew Archer than to Sherlock Holmes.

Significantly, the form of Max's social training was opposed to androgyny as well as to feminism. Max is rigidly bound by ideas of what a man and a woman should be, and he wishes to be wholly masculine. He refuses to see any "feminine" traits in himself and resents any "masculine" traits in women, such as Kate wearing blue-jeans or Cecily Hutchins preferring to concentrate on her own work rather than continuing to help her husband with his. One reason why the refined, over-civilized Max can consider murder so easily is that he perceives the objects standing in his way, namely Gerry Marston and Kate, as something totally different from himself, something not quite as human as he and other males.

Several other characters, however, do reflect the ideal of androgyny. The most obvious of these is Tate, the librarian to whom Max gives charge of the Hutchins papers. In discussing Hutchins, Tate comments: "I first read her when I was eleven. It was the novel about a family who go to spend the summer in France with friends. All girls, except for one eleven-year-old boy, who was, of course, me. But before I was through I was all of them" (103). A man who can admit to this type of literary identification with females is obviously at ease with the "feminine" components in his personality. His subsequent approval of "the new interest in women writers" on the grounds that "we could scarcely go on in America worshipping forever manly types on the hunt for animal flesh" confirms this. Another readily identifiable example is Kate's husband, Reed. Reed too is comfortable with the "feminine" traits in his personality and can casually admit that he is more emotionally dependent on Kate than she is on him (63), and that he despises—or at least has no enthusiasm for—"manly sports" (71). Also, his sensitivity to Kate's need for privacy and his warning to Kate against "female guilt" over leaving Leo at a time of crisis to take care of her own affairs (100) show that he has no wish to confine Kate to "appropriate" sexual behavior any more than he confines himself. Kate, of course, is thoroughly androgynous: independent, highly rational, a skilled professional, yet caring, emotional, responsive to others—within limits. Cecily Hutchins and Dorothy Whitmore were also androgynous, but Max's mother was not. After her time at school with the two of them, she "dwindled into wife" (152), and this may be the origin of Max's rigid, sexually-polarized character, though it cannot supply the whole answer since his brother, Herbert, developed quite differently.

Androgyny is also stressed in another way. One of the most striking passages in *Toward a Recognition of Androgyny* is Heilbrun's commentary on the dangers of separation and polarization of the sexes:

Because "masculine" traits are now and have for so many years been the dominant ones, we have ample evidence of the danger the free play of such traits brings in its wake. By developing in men the ideal "masculine" characteristics of competitiveness, aggressiveness, and defensiveness, and by placing in power those men who most embody these traits, we have, I believe, gravely endangered our own survival. Unless we can effectively check the power of manly men and the women who willingly support them, we will experience new Vietnams, My Lais, Kent States.[5]

This argument indicates the main connection between the subplot involving Chet Ricardo (the cheating grandson of Cecily Hutchins), the main plot involving Max and the numerous references to Nixon. Ricardo, Max and Nixon are all seen as the products of social backgrounds emphasizing "masculine" ideals and warning against "feminine" frailties. The "ambiance" of St. Anthony's, the all-male school that Leo and Chet Ricardo attend, is treated unambiguously; its gymnasium "would certainly have been one of the circles of hell had Dante been prescient enough to have thought of it" (51). Granted that this is a comic description, it is amply supported by what we learn about the attitudes instilled in many of the boys who go there. The school's competitive practices in baseball, for example, have some disturbing overtones: "St. Anthony's ... played with what seemed to Kate sinister competence. That one was supposed to slide into base with one's spikes aimed at the baseman Kate had already heard, to her horror. That one could jeer at the pitcher to upset him and run into players for no other reason than to do them injury, appalled her further" (81). Leo's approval of the Texas Rangers throwing beanballs at the Yankees shows that he too has been affected by the St. Anthony's ethic, though his later decision to oppose Ricardo's cheating indicates that he is not beyond salvation. The St. Anthony's competitiveness and the Texas Ranger beanballing are linked to Nixon in Kate's response to Leo's defense of them: "As Vince Lombardi said to Nixon or somebody, winning isn't important, it's just everything. The connection with Watergate shall go unremarked upon" (82). Ricardo's decision to let his friend Finlay take the SAT exam for him is also linked to Nixon and Watergate. When Leo expresses anger over Finlay lying to him about the exam, Kate remarks that "according to Jimmy Breslin, that's why the good guys won over Watergate. They minded being lied to" (96). Kate later links the theme of the subplot to that of the main one when she asks Reed, "Do you think it possible the Ricardo boy could be at all like Max? Or do I mean Finlay?" (123). The answer is that Max is indeed like both of them in his competitiveness, aggressiveness, lack of honor bred from lack of concern for others, condescension toward women and other inferiors, viciousness, self-righteousness and belief that "he could control anything" (121). Significantly, some of the areas Max argued about with Cecily Hutchins were "Vietnam, Watergate, integration, women's rights" (207), suggesting the whole complex of disasters stemming from the glorification of "masculine" ideals and the concurrent vilification of the androgynous ideal. (The term "disaster" here is meant to include the pain to minorities and women resulting from white male supremacy.)

The main plot and the subplot are also interwoven in other ways than thematically. Kate's first encounter with Ricardo reminds her of Max and starts her thinking about the case of her dead student again. Her discovery of Ricardo's dishonesty makes her question Max's. Max's intervention in Ricardo's favor puts him and Kate back in contact. Leo, of course, is a common denominator, as Kate's nephew and Ricardo's foe. Kate's visit to St. Anthony's gymnasium to see Leo play basketball leads to her meeting with Ricardo. Her failure to show up at Leo's last baseball game of the season leads to Reed's realization that she is in danger and to his successful rescue of her. Thus, *The Question of Max* has been skillfully developed in both plot and theme; anyone who calls it plotless, an accusation that has often been thoughtlessly lodged against Cross, has not read it carefully.

Cross' most recent work, *Death in a Tenured Position*, also reaches a high level of innovation and artistry. A little less tightly plotted and tightly written than *The Question of Max*, it represents her sharpest break with both literary and social conventions. She has skillfully remolded the classical mystery form into a near perfect vehicle for her strong feminist vision.

The puzzle in this novel is almost as elaborate as the one in *In the Last Analysis*, but this time the various clues, physical, psychological and literary, all point to a central social issue, the destructive consequences of the suppression of women. The solution to Janet Mandelbaum's apparent murder, namely that she killed herself because the pressure on her as the first woman full professor in the English department at Harvard became intolerable, is obviously an embodiment of this issue. Given the nature of Janet's problems, it is fitting that the most pointed and revealing clue is psychological. When Prof. Allen Clarkville recounts how somebody at a departmental meeting, speaking to his fellow males with Janet as the sole woman present, told her she had only been hired because of pressures brought by Women's Studies advocates and how she then broke down in uncontrollable tears, remaining seated and crying after everyone else left, her despair and her motive for suicide are readily apparent. It had been spelled out earlier that what she had wanted most was to be respected by her male colleagues for her professional abilities. Her realization that they had accepted her only because they were forced to was obviously the last straw, following a large number of previous humiliations.

Since this mystery has both an academic setting and academic detective, it is also appropriate that some clues come from books that Janet had been reading. As in several of Ellery Queen's mysteries, such as *The Origin of Evil,* the person who hasn't read some of these works is at a disadvantage, but there are enough other clues to keep this from being unfair. The two poems by George Herbert that Janet had been drawn to are the most significant literary clues, and are completely fair since they are reprinted in full in the text. Both require interpretation, of course, and Kate's ability to probe their meaning confirms her skill both as a scholar and a detective. This is a crucial point since one of the major themes is the patriarchal denial of women's professional abilities, particularly in reasoning. The most brilliant stroke, however, is the way Janet's other books, Yvonne Kapp's life of Eleanor Marx (the noted translator of *Madame Bovary*) and Simone Weil's philosophical writings, simultaneously reinforce both the solution to the puzzle and the theme of the inhumane pressures placed on achieving women. Kate ties together Janet Mandelbaum's decision to kill herself with the similar suicide by cyanide of Eleanor Marx, the suicide by arsenic of Madame Bovary and the possible suicide by starvation of Simone Weil. Thus, Janet's death is shown to be a truly representative one.

The point which Cross makes so effectively here is that Janet Mandelbaum's suicide can also justly be considered a murder, that the patriarchal pressures that destroyed her are at least as vicious as any assassin. These pressures began with her two hearty, macho younger brothers who refused to take her seriously and who considered her academic achievements as of little importance beside the facts that she did not stay married and that she had no children. That she internalized some of the values of her brothers is indicated by her rejection of her husband, Moon Mandelbaum, for not being masterly enough for her. Thus, she finds herself in an untenable position, at once rejecting and holding onto her brothers' traditional masculine values. At Harvard, of course, the pressures on her are greatly intensified. Kate's friend, Sylvia Farnum, later tells her that there should have been a woman on the search committee, if only to make sure that the woman selected as the first tenured full professor in English would be tough enough to survive, and this remark underlines Janet's vulnerability, serving as a clue to her suicide. The greatest pressure, however, comes not from the male full professors—though they are unkind enough—but from a graduate student, Howard Falkland. Falkland's "prank" of getting Janet drunk (by secretly adding vodka to her campari) and then increasing the scandal by calling a radical lesbian to come and get her out of the bathtub where she passed out was almost certainly done with the intention of currying the favor of his favorite full professor. That this professor, Allen Clarkville, later pronounces Falkland a "fool" does not negate the fact that he and other male professors had talked enough against women as professors—and against Janet—to give Falkland ample reason to think he was doing something clever and worthy of being rewarded.

It is ironic that Clarkville, a leading opponent of women as full professors, is a homosexual. Cross, however, carefully avoids attacking him for his sexual preference—Kate even comments that one of the best changes to come out of the Seventies is the greater public acceptance of homosexuality—and confines her attack to his reactionary attitudes, which include a belief that we should not have ended the Vietnam War and that Nixon was railroaded, as well as his stand against women. Thus, Clarkville fits comfortably into the same company as Max Reston and Cedric Jablon.

Cross' attack on a specific patriarchal institution, and, by extension, on patriarchy itself is the most forceful and direct she has made and underlines again her divergence from traditional detective fiction and traditional attitudes. The crime here is not the act of an individual driven by personal motives; it is the spiritual harm done by ingrained social attitudes that need to be changed. Once Kate identifies the source of guilt as these attitudes, she works against them, and, in the last chapter, Sylvia Farnum writes her that, as a result of Kate's revelation of Janet's suicide and its motives, there will now be two endowed chairs for tenured women professors and that Sylvia herself will be part of the search committee so that she can make sure that stronger, more feminist women will be chosen this time. That this will not provide a full solution to the problem is indicated by the final letter of the book, that of the Dean of Arts and Sciences, telling Kate that she has been appointed to yet another committee at her university and thus will return to her previous, nearly futile status as "Token Woman." Nevertheless, Kate has accomplished the most important part of ﾟ hat she set out to do, to take action in a place where her actions could have an effect and to move a tiny part of the world one step further in the direction of humaneness.

Once again, Kate represents balance and growth, but, in contrast to *Poetic Justice*, her balance has shifted against the Establishment. This time she stands between the "man-identified" woman, like Janet Mandelbaum, who works in men's institutions, looks for approbation from men, sleeps with them, etc., and the "woman-identified" woman, like Joan Theresa, who lives in a commune with other women, despises all of men's institutions, looks for approbation from other women, sleeps with other women, etc. Significantly Kate feels more sympathetic toward Joan Theresa, the woman separatist admittedly willing to "use" men and women like Kate, than toward Janet. Although Kate remains within the patriarchal institutions trying hard to retain some belief in the fairness of the police, proving herself as a scholar and a detective against masculine competition, living with a husband (however non-macho and non-patriarchal) and having an affair with another male (however non-aggressive and non-competitive), she is not confined by them. She longs to see the institutions shake with change, can admit the justice of Moon Mandelbaum's claims that the law favors the powerful, and is willing to leave her job in New York to travel to Harvard in the hope of bringing about an alteration in the treatment of women there. Above all, she can recognize that the power structure does suppress women, and she is willing to bond with other women against this suppression.

Startlingly, like Lew Archer in Ross Macdonald's *The Doomsters* and the protagonist in Macdonald's earlier work *The Three Roads* (which was modelled on *Oedipus Rex*), Kate uncovers her own guilt at the same time she uncovers the truth about Janet's death. Near the end of the novel, she confesses to the lawyer John Cunningham that she failed to offer Janet the only kind of assistance she would have accepted, praise for her personal heroism and the hope that eventually the men would see her true worth. Kate feels that she was too intent on treating Janet as a cause rather than as a suffering individual dangerously close to cracking. This self-judgment, which seems a bit harsh in the light of what Kate actually said to Janet, leavens her justifiable pride in her detective abilities and in the help she has given to individuals and to feminism with a touch of humility. Macdonald has consciously striven to keep his detective humane by making him a man of "self-questioning self-doubt,"[6] and Cross seems to have done the same with Kate. In addition, Kate's awareness of her failure with Janet makes her even more desirous of assisting other women in the future.

Through Kate Fansler, Amanda Cross/Carolyn Heilbrun has suggested thoughtful approaches to many of our most serious and disturbing problems and provided an example of humane, unself-righteous action. Just as Kate has developed from a female Wimsey into a complex being with a life and value system all her own, her creator has also progressed, gaining mastery in a variety of comic techniques, in the elaboration of irony, and in the use and alteration of both classical and hard-boiled detective conventions as vehicles for an increasingly broad and wise social vision. As a result of her development, Cross should now be acknowledged as one of the most brilliantly innovative and thought-provoking contemporary detective novelists.

Notes

[1]The editions of Cross' works used for this study are listed below, preceded by the original date of publication. All quotations will be cited in the text using the abbreviation given after each entry.

1964   *In the Last Analysis*, New York: Avon, 1966 (*Analysis*)
1967   *The James Joyce Murder*, New York: Macmillan, 1967 (*Joyce*)
1970   *Poetic Justice*, New York: Avon, 1979 (*Justice*)
1971   *The Theban Mysteries*, New York: Avon, 1979 (*Mysteries*)
1976   *The Question of Max*, New York: Avon, 1977 (Max)

My comments on *Death in a Tenured Position* are based on a manuscript version, kindly furnished by the author, since the published version will not appear until after this article has been set in print.

[2]Carolyn Heilbrun, "Sayers, Lord Peter and God," in Dorothy L. Sayers, *Lord Peter: A Collection of All the Lord Peter Wimsey Stories*, compiled by James Sandoe, New York: Harper & Row, 1972, pp. 456-457.

[3]Carolyn Heilbrun, *Toward a Recognition of Androgyny*, New York: Knopf, 1973, p. 100.

[4]John G. Cawelti, *Adventure, Mystery, and Romance,* Chicago: Univ. of Chicago Press, 1976, p. 83.

[5]Heilbrun, *Androgyny*, p. xvi.

[6]Ross Macdonald in a letter quoted in Steven R. Carter, "Ross Macdonald: The Complexity of the Modern Quest for Justice," in *Mystery and Detection Annual: 1973,* ed. Donald K. Adams, Beverly Hills, Ca: Donald K. Adams, 1974.

Index of Characters

Index of Titles